CRM AS A RAPID DEVELOPMENT PLATFORM

MICROSOFT DYNAMICS CRM 4.0

DAVID YACK

Leveraging Microsoft Dynamics CRM 4.0 as an application development platform to build real world business solutions that go beyond what you think of as "Just CRM"

CRM as a Rapid Development Platform – Microsoft Dynamics CRM 4.0

Published by

We Speak You Learn, LLC
2928 Straus Lane Ste 200
Colorado Springs, CO 80907

www.thecrmbook.com

ISBN-13: 978-0-9815118-1-8

ISBN-10: 0-9815118-1-3

To my wonderful wife, Julie, and my two great kids, Drew and Jacqueline, who probably thought I was joking when I said I was going to write another book!

\- David Yack

About the Author

David Yack is the CTO of Colorado Technology Consultants, a Microsoft Gold Certified Partner based in Colorado. He is a Microsoft Regional Director and a Microsoft MVP for ASP.NET. As a senior hands' on technology and business consultant with over 20 years of industry experience, David enjoys developing applications on the Microsoft platforms, specializing in large system architecture and design. David embraced .NET during the final beta days of version 1.0 and has been helping clients migrate and build new applications on the technology, as well as helping to mentor and train their staffs.

David has a special interest in **Microsoft Business Solutions** and their integration capabilities. David has been involved in all aspects of multiple **Microsoft Dynamics CRM** deployments using both the onsite and hosted model. David has been instrumental in the development of numerous projects using the Microsoft Dynamics CRM platform as vertical solutions from an ISV perspective. David has been a trainer for CRM 4.0 and has been traveling globally on behalf of Microsoft training their leading ISVs on the capabilities of the new version of the platform.

David is a frequent speaker at user group and industry events and was on the author team of two other .NET related books. He lives in Colorado Springs with his wife and two children. You can always track David down via his blog at http://blog.davidyack.com where he writes about his .NET adventures and http://crm.davidyack.com which is devoted to Microsoft Dynamics CRM.

Credits

Editor: Julie Yack

Technical Editor: Cathy Hardman

Book Designer: Julie Yack

Acknowledgments

A page at the front of a book seems so little to express my thanks to the countless people who helped and inspired me to get this far with the book. Without the encouragement, I probably would have been willing to just stop and put the book on the shelf to collect dust.

The fact that I decided to explore self-publishing required a lot of extra help that would typically be done by an outside publisher. For that, I thank Julie Yack my partner and wife that really stepped up and jumped in to take on many of the traditional publisher roles.

I owe a big thanks to Microsoft, the CRM product team, and the Developer Evangelist organization for their support during the book creation. From early access as part of their technology adoption programs to the late night replies to my e-mail by Philip Richardson made a big difference. Without their input, I would have struggled indefinitely to try to complete the book. Undoubtedly, I will forget someone from the list – but the following are some of the people from Microsoft that I greatly respect and appreciate their help during the writing of the book.

Philip Richardson, Diego Matute, Ben Riga, Praveen Upadhyay, Humberto Guadarrama, Amy Langlois, Jonathan Randall, Henning Petersen, Corey Hanson, Charlie Wood, Alex Tkatch, Michael Lu, Girish Raja, Jim Glass, Tom Archer, Andy Bybee, Noor Merchant, Andrei Smertin

Early on and as the book progressed I relied upon a number of people to offer feedback on the table of contents. Often those were just informal discussions other times actual review of the list of chapters. Sometimes discussions resulted in a "reorg" or insertion of scope that I can clearly blame on this not just being a small white paper!

Shan McArthur , Ben Hoelting, Cathy Hardman, David Milner, Rob Hope, Julie Yack, Jeffry van de Vuurst, Wayne Warthen

As the chapters started to come together, I relied on a number of people to provide input and point out where I lost my mind. To volunteer to review is easy, to complete the review and provide feedback takes more work, and for those who did I offer many thanks.

Ben Hoelting, Cathy Hardman, David Milner, Carl Brown, Julie Yack, Chris Sutton, Chris Auld

Cathy Hardman, one our developers, spent endless hours helping to package up some of the code samples and enduring my crazy requests like "How about we include a Silverlight 2 example". Her patience and attention to detail made a definite impact on the amount of samples included in the book.

My Son, Drew who took time away from his XNA game programming to help with some of the sample code and to kick the tires on some of the steps in the chapters was greatly appreciated. I still have yet to convince him however, that CRM could be a game development platform too!

Through publishing my blog, conducting training classes around the world and attending conferences were I got to meet a lot of people doing CRM development your thoughts and comments helped to shape each chapter. I could not possibly list each of you here, but to each I extend my thanks.

As the final content was completed it was time to conduct a final book review . I put out a call for help in doing the reviews to Microsoft and the CRM MVPs. The support offered amazed me and realized what a great group they were to help out. Within about 20 minutes I had a bunch of people offering to review and provide feedback on the book chapters. I would like to thank each of the following people for taking the time to help with the final push. The feedback and catching of my errors by each of you will clearly make a difference.

Ayaz Ahmad, Marco Amoedo, Nythya Balasubramanian , Jim Daly, , Aaron Elder, Humberto Lezama Guadarrama, Michael Hohne, uMar Khan ,Amy Langlois, Darren Liu, Ronald Lemmen , Larry Lentz, , David Jennaway,, Matt Parks, , Guy Riddle, Praveen Upadhyay, Jeffry van de Vuurst , Mahesh Vijayaraghavan, Matt Wittemann,

From the editor

Sure Dave, let's publish a book.

Yes, I actually said those words.

Why you ask? Many reasons I suppose. First, I have loads of background in publishing, more on the author/edit side, but still loads of experience. Anyone that knew me back in the day would have expected me to be editor in chief of some huge international magazine by now. Second, I helped Dave and his other author teams on prior books, so I knew what to expect, right? Third, I can keep people and projects on track fairly well and every book needs a clock-watcher. Finally, why not? I'm always up for a new challenge and I haven't really found one yet that I couldn't do if I tried.

I knew from day one I would be primarily responsible for regular old editing. Been there done that, do it all the time. Dave is one of the smartest guys I know, but he doesn't really care about finessing little details like grammar in his writing if he feels his point is still communicated. Even the most minor grammar issues tend to get on my nerves. Now add book and page designer to my credits. Add more tech editing experience. Put in some formatting. Wait add extreme formatting experience. Publisher? I have that one now too.

I was only partially joking when I have said that I now understand why authors get such little monetary return on their books and the publishers get more. The writing, though a rather important ingredient, is only a fraction of the work that goes into getting a book on the market. I'm not sure who put more time on the clock into this book, Dave or me.

This sounds like a laundry list of complaints. It is actually far from that.

It is the realization of all that we've accomplished to get this far.

Many people think Dave and I are crazy for being married and being in business together. But, our skills are so well matched to help each other succeed it really shouldn't be any other way. I wouldn't want it any other way.

--Julie

Where I worked on the book

It was not until I was on the top of Pikes Peak at 14,110 feet that I realized it might be interesting to keep track of where I did some writing for this book. Looking back, I have done some of my best writing or planning either in the air, on a train, or in some place with great scenery.

The first concept of this book was fleshed out while traveling on a train in Europe going from one CRM training class to another. At the time, I was doing some very rough writing about Workflow based on then CTP2 bits. A lot has changed since then, and at that time the book was much more focused on workflow only.

During the fall, I had the opportunity to do some writing while looking at the fall colors. We went to Crested Butte in Colorado late in September and it was the perfect time to view the fall leaves. In between snapping hundreds of photos of the trees, I managed to crank out a chapter or two in the evenings.

In early October, we had a summit for the Microsoft Regional Directors, so myself, and a bunch of other RDs gathered in Aspen, Colorado. Again, I managed in between meetings and taking in the sights, to get a little more writing done.

Trains, planes and scenic places seem to be the key to getting me to crank out some pages – my next chance for some writing was on the Cog Railway on the way to and from the top of Pikes Peak. It is not that I do not enjoy the view, we had guests visiting and I think this was probably my 15th trip to the top. If you have never been up there it is a view that is amazing and something you have to do if you are in Colorado. In fact, I am not the only one who found the top of Pikes Peak inspiring; America the Beautiful was written when Katharine Lee Bates visited the top of Pikes Peak in 1893[1].

You probably will not see my office at work as one of the places I write, I just do not seem to get the ideas flowing there for writing. My home office is a completely different story, anytime after 10pm at night you can almost guarantee I can think of some great things to write. I also exchanged countless e-mails back and forth with the product team who were so willing to help with my tons of questions trying to understand the new features of the product.

---

[1] http://en.wikipedia.org/wiki/America_the_Beautiful

Airplanes have to be some of the best places to do writing. This is true if you are writing a book or some code. Find some good headphones to drown out the sound of the engines and start writing. I certainly did my share of writing of this book on planes heading to either training events, speaking engagements or clients. I am not sure if airport writing counts though because it is just so hard to concentrate sitting near a gate. Besides, what is with not being able to find power anywhere?

Regardless of where I did the writing, I cannot forget the most important thing. It is those thoughts that just pop into your head either in the middle of the night or just at random during the day. The key is to capture the concept so you can do the writing later.

The final inspiration really is not a where; it is a what. My blog served as the dry run for much of the content for the book. If you do not have a blog, go get one! They are a great place to store your notes!

Timeline of events

April 2007 - Started first draft of TOC – then it was The CRM Consultants Black Book and was only going to focus on workflow.

May 2007 – July 2007 – traveled extensively in Europe doing ISV training on CTP2 of CRM 4.0. I did a lot of deep digging to understand the platform and started writing about workflow.

August 2007 – Complete revision of the TOC based on feedback, and expanded the book to cover full range of development.

August 2007 – Decision to self publish instead of going with main stream publisher . We did the first trial print of content with LULU.com to see how book would look!

September 2007 – Prepared for CTP3 training and started updating content with CTP3 content.

November 2007 – Broke the 150 page mark!

December 14th 2007, CRM 4.0 Shipped! I'm on a boat for the next week hoping to get as much writing done as possible. Sitting at about 225 pages now, want to push to get as much done as possible before end of year.

January 1, 2008 – New year hit about 260+ pages and tons of great stuff worked out now just need to find time to write about it!

February 29, 2008 – With well over 300 pages completed things slowed down as CRM 4.0 was released. Also some decisions to hold in order to include some key things like Silverlight 2.0. March will be the final push to complete all the content.

March 2008 – After returning from Convergence and many discussions we finally have a draft cover and a new working title – With just over 400 pages the end of the tunnel is near!

May 2008 - over 550 pages – so much I could keep writing about but that will have to wait for Version 2.0!

June 2008 - Final content completed - Call for Review by MVPs and Microsoft

July 2008 – Feedback from over 20 people including MVPs, Microsoft and others integrated back into the book.

Introduction

Years ago, the only way you could build an application was to start from scratch each time. The concept of re-use then became popular, where we had some components we could leverage and not have to re-invent the wheel each time. Today we are encouraged to use third-party vendor controls or components to do as much as we can to build solutions more quickly. The current business climate is such that they no longer have patience to wait for long application development times. They want a solution yesterday for today's problem. And did I mention they don't want to pay an arm and a leg?

Microsoft developers are given a wealth of tools to make their job easier. In fact, sometimes the number of them can overwhelm us and cause us to go into zombie mode as we try to figure out which ones to use. Using the .NET Framework and the advanced languages like C# and VB.NET, we can build amazing solutions that bring together other Microsoft components like Windows Workflow and Reporting Services. All this is great but they also all come with a big note that says "**_Some Assembly May Be Required_**". This means that these can each provide great value but it's left up to the developer to bring them together to build an application on top of or as I will refer to throughout this book to assemble an "Application Development Platform". Think of the Application Development Platform being like the foundation of a house, meaning it's what you build on top of.

An application development platform for our purposes is all the low-level functionality or "the plumbing" put together in one package that we could leverage time and time again. Look across the Microsoft developer division and what you see is a bunch of components, each providing great benefit and most designed to play well with other Microsoft components, but nowhere will you find a true application platform that comes pre-assembled.

Don't get me wrong, I like building infrastructure code; you know the stuff that glues together Reporting Services, Workflow Foundation, Error Handling and all the other products described by two or three letter buzz words. Today, businesses do not have the time or the patience to wait while we figure out how to put the parts together. Building that stuff is fun once every few years but not every time and with the pace of technology change, you need a large team doing that not two or three developers.

As we sit back and think about our perfect application development platform we would include things like workflow, reporting, integration with Outlook, an easily customized data model, and of course offline user support so our users can work anywhere. Oh sure the list could go on and we will explore more about what makes up a platform throughout the book but, the goal here is just to get you interested enough to read more.

In this book, we are going to explore using Microsoft Dynamics CRM 4.0 as an application development platform. I can hear your thinking "Oh great, I bought this book and it's talking about some contact management application and this guy is going to tell me how to use it as my Swiss Army knife of application development, I could have just bought a book on Microsoft Access". No worries, I wouldn't do that to you. I think after you hear some of the compelling features that are hidden behind the name CRM you too will agree that Microsoft has an "Un-Named" application developer platform.

I call it the "Un-Named" application developer platform because I think calling it Microsoft Dynamics CRM 4.0 causes developers to bypass it for non CRM solutions. You know, kind of like when I give my son a lecture on growing up, at some point his eyes just glaze over. That same thing happens to developers when you mention the acronym CRM. That happens for one of two reasons. Either they don't do CRM or they have no clue what CRM even stands for. I think as you understand a little more of the history of the product you will see how this problem was created. Originally, there was no application developer platform story and it was *just* a CRM tool. As CRM evolved, and the "plumbing" also evolved, a platform that could be used for more than just CRM solutions emerged. I thought about coming up with a crafty name we could call the plumbing or the Application Developer Platform but in the end I decided that was really Microsoft Marketing's job and I should focus on telling you why there were two parts to the Microsoft Dynamics CRM 4.0 product. The first part is the platform; the second is the CRM functionality that Microsoft built on that platform.

To bring you up to speed a little more on the thinking and to try to help you understand we aren't crazy, let's look back in history. CRM 1.0 came out and it was a basic CRM-type application having all the basic features you would expect in a contact management tool to help you with your customers. Then 1.2 followed and added some international support and other minor features. Still in 1.2, it was focused on managing customer relationships and really offered no generic application developer story. CRM 2.0 was in the works but midway into the development Microsoft decided to push harder and skip 2.0 in favor of a more robust CRM 3.0 release.

It wasn't until CRM 3.0 hit the street that we started to get something we could use to build more custom applications and not just a CRM tool. CRM 3.0 allowed the creation of custom entities and relationships which gave the ability to have a declarative data model that an administrator, developer or business analyst could customize to model real business problems. This data model was also exposed as a dynamic SOA web service interface that developers could use to interact with the data model. CRM 3.0 also introduced the integration SQL Server Reporting services as the reporting engine showing the CRM team's desire to start integrating with other Microsoft "best of breed" components and not build their own. This version showed the first signs of an application development platform being born, but it still had several pieces that needed polishing and was lagging a little behind in using the current version of things, including the .NET framework.

Microsoft Dynamics CRM 4.0, which is what we will cover in this book, represents a significant advance in the platform capabilities and introduces a number of new features. These features, while they make it possible to build CRM solutions, are more than enough that developers can use it as an application development platform for line of business applications. CRM 4.0 continues the evolution on a number of the core platform features but also brings the platform current with the latest .NET framework and tools. Other key features like converting from a proprietary workflow engine to Windows Workflow Foundation again showed how the team was willing to pick up and leverage other components. Throughout the book we will continue to paint the picture of how all the core platform capabilities come together to make it easy for you to build CRM solutions as well as any type of general business application on the platform.

When I first thought about writing this book, it was early on during the development cycle when CRM 4.0 was still referred to as code name "Titan". At the time, I thought that workflow was going to be the biggest change in the release and my writing plans were centered on the use of workflow (using Windows Workflow Foundation) in CRM. As the Beta of Titan progressed it became clear that significant changes were being made, not just to workflow. As I started passing around a draft table of contents for review and feedback it became obvious some expansion was needed. Shan McArthur, who I met when he attended one of the trainings I did on the Beta for Microsoft, pointed out that you can't cover work flow without touching on plug-ins which are another way to automate business processes. Plug-ins also are also the mechanism by which workflow is integrated into the platform. Taking that to heart I went back and revisited the table of contents and expanded what I decided I would cover. At the same time, I did a lot of thinking about what was out there for building more generic business applications. In CRM 3.0, those capabilities where there but it was a bit of a stretch to call it a generic application development platform. It was then I realized that a story existed about a developer platform that just wasn't being told. CRM 4.0 brings enough change though multi-tenant, offline, workflow, etc. the story had to be told and you had to decide for yourself if it was compelling enough to build applications upon. With that, I went back to the drawing board yet again and revised the contents to include enough to make sure developers beyond just the CRM developers would find plenty of information to leverage CRM 4.0 as a development platform.

So, the new and improved scope will cover a broader concept of what developers will find useful in developing custom solutions on Microsoft Dynamics CRM 4.0. We will not be covering the basic concepts of how to use Microsoft Dynamics CRM 4.0 from a user's perspective. Help documents and other books are available to help you understand basic operations and use – this book will focus on the developer topics.

The following are the key areas we will discuss in this book:

Understanding how to use CRM 4.0 to build line of business applications

What's new in CRM 4.0

The developer environment – how to effectively work as a developer

Client side development – a beyond the basics look at doing client side development – including advanced scripting and Silverlight integration

Web Services - web services provide a dynamic SOA interface to the platform – we will look at what's new and how to use them

Metadata API – you can now not only read the metadata but can update it using the API

Plug-ins – They used to be Callouts but now they're new and improved

Workflow – It's re-invented and a great way to automate processes

Keep reading to see a more complete list of the chapters and a synopsis of what you will learn in each.

Differences between this and the SDK

This book on Microsoft CRM 4.0 is intended to supplement the SDK documentation that is provided by Microsoft. Microsoft, in the SDK, will typically provide a detailed reference of all the classes related to the platform. This book does not attempt to provide that level of detail reference and in many cases will defer to the SDK. The SDK will also provide a very broad developer guide and samples for the platform In this case there may be some overlap in what we cover, but typically the samples will be different and we will go into more details and provide a consultant's perspective. What do we mean by a consultant's perspective? When writing documentation for a product you must be 100% on track with the capabilities and provide guidance that is broadly usable to the majority of users. In general, you never step away from what is 100% supported and concern about real word implementations are not always the first concern. In this book, we will attempt to give the consultant's perspective and ways to look for creative solutions. If we know something is not supported we will try to highlight that fact so you can make the determination if you want to use the approach.

Who is this book for?

The target audience for this book is solution architects and developers that are building applications inside their companies. It is also for those packaging up to resell as part of an ISV solution deployed on the Dynamics CRM platform. Finally, it is for the consultant who is the road warrior helping companies customize the platform for their business needs. One thing to be clear up front you do not have to be looking to solve a CRM (Customer Relationship Management) problem to benefit from this book. In fact anyone building solutions that will help automate and manage internal business processes can benefit from its insight. Non-developers, meaning system administrators, business analysts, and even project managers might find the book useful but will have to wander past any of the real developer-centered discussions.

How to use this book?

Read it cover to cover or simply skip and jump to the areas you need more details on – there is no single correct way to use this book. You could use it online or carry around the printed book to each of your client visits. Write on the pages, fold the corners and make notes of your own ideas. If you end up building something cool, drop us a note and tell us about it.

Contents overview

Chapter 1-What's new in CRM 4.0 – Microsoft Dynamics 4.0 has significant changes from the basic platform architecture to the tools developers use every day to create solutions. This chapter introduces the changes and sets the stage for developers to understand how to build applications.

Chapter 2- Building Line of Business Applications - Everyone thinks of CRM for managing Contacts and Accounts but Microsoft Dynamics CRM 4.0 can also be used to build line of business applications that are not just CRM. We explore how you can leverage the platform foundation to build applications without doing the "plumbing" yourself.

Chapter 3- The Developer and Team Workspace – One size certainly does not fit all when it comes to developers. This chapter, explore how developers can setup their development environments to maximize their productivity building applications. Included in this chapter are discussions on team development.

Chapter 4- Data Modeling in CRM – At the heart of any good CRM or line of business application is the data model. CRM allows developers to declaratively build the data model and work with it using all the power of the platform. Here we talk about defining the data model and the basic user inputs to manipulate data. This chapter is a must-read for a good understanding of the remaining chapters.

Chapter 5- User Experience Customization – We start with the basics and then move beyond to look at how to do client side development including leveraging some OO techniques with JavaScript (Yes, we said OO and JavaScript in the same sentence!).

Chapter 6- Client Scripting How To's – Having a basic understanding that we provided in Chapter 5 is great but here we dig into real world examples of common tasks you will want to do with the client side capabilities.

Chapter 7- Building Alternate UI's –   The built-in UI in the CRM platform is powerful, but in this chapter, we explore building alternate UI's using Silverlight.

Chapter 8- Exploring Metadata – Building on the data modeling in Chapter 4, we explore how you can programmatically access the platform metadata and use it as part of your development. New to Microsoft Dynamics CRM 4.0 is the ability to use an API to modify the metadata in addition to read access.

Chapter 9- Using the Web Services - Web services are the SOA extension of the data model and dynamically configure to implement and expose the custom data model. In this chapter, we learn the basics of working with the web services to interact with the platform.

Chapter 10- Web Services Common How-To's - Having a basic understanding that we provided in chapter 9 is great but here we dig into real world examples of common tasks you will want to do with the web services.

Chapter 11- Unified Event Framework - Building on our knowledge of the data modeling and the web services we embark to understand the Unified Event Framework (UEF) which is new to the platform in this release. The UEF sets the stage for how plug-ins and workflows are implemented into the platform. A basic understanding is essential prior to developing business logic extensions like plug-ins and workflows.

Chapter 12- Plug-in Basics - Plug-ins let you integrate your custom logic just like it was part of a platform operation. In this chapter, we explore how to build a plug-in and the different options that exist for getting it integrated to the execution pipeline.

Chapter 13- Plug-in Developer Framework - The "hello world" plug-in is easy, but what about real world plug-ins. Here we look at providing a consistent pattern for building platform plug-ins that includes a concept of a test bench for testing plug-ins outside the platform.

Chapter 14- Plug-in How-To's – Take a walk on the wild side and learn what type of problems developers are solving using the plug-in capability. In this section we look at real life examples of plug-ins.

Chapter 15- Workflow Re-Energized – It's not just upgraded, it's re-invented and based on Windows Workflow Foundation. Learn about the changes to workflow and how it makes workflow in the platform a powerful tool in your arsenal for business process automation.

Chapter 16- Workflow User Interface – You used to have to be an admin to manage and build workflows. Now, sophisticated business analysts and other non-developers can build them using the web interface. Learn what is there for users so when you build custom pieces that plug into it you will know how users can leverage it.

Chapter 17- Windows Workflow Basics – You don't have to be a workflow guru to take advantage of the workflow support in the platform but knowing the basics will help you get things done quicker.

Chapter 18- Custom Workflow Activities – Building custom activities really shows off the power of the platform allowing you to build activities that users can use via the web interface when building their own workflows. These can be simple or complex, and can be built to support development of more complex workflows as we will discuss in Chapter 19.

Chapter 19- Workflow Developer Framework – As we did in Chapter 13 for plug-ins this chapter looks at how to build a reusable pattern for workflow support including the concept of a test harness for running the workflow or activities outside the platform for easy development.

Chapter 20- Workflow Code Generation – In this chapter we explore ways that you could use code generation to make workflow development more drag and drop and extend on the dynamic SOA features of the platform to workflow by code generating custom activities based on the platform data model.

Chapter 21- Workflow How To's – In this chapter we look at some real world examples of how developers and users are leveraging the workflow capabilities of the platform.

Chapter 22- Building CRM Online Solutions – This chapter focuses on the specifics of building solutions that work with CRM Online. This includes looking at some techniques to work around some of the differences that exist between CRM Online and other deployments.

Chapter 23- Leveraging Multi Currency and Language These two features are at the heart of the global nature of the platform. In this chapter, we explore how to leverage them as part of your applications.

Chapter 24- Packaging for Deployment – Ready, Fire, Aim...oh wait we need to figure out how to deploy this to a real production site. In this chapter, we discuss just that and the features of the platform that help you get your solution deployed either to an internal host or from an ISV perspective in packaging up their application.

Chapter 25- Tracking Down Problems – Nothing is worse than getting the call that something broke and not knowing where to start. In this chapter, we explore techniques to prepare for production problems and what capabilities exist in the platform to help you solve problems.

Chapter 26- Performance Tuning – In this chapter, we look at some of the techniques to squeeze out a little more from your application. We also look at some of the platform metrics provided in performance counters that are used to help identify problems.

Where do I get the Source Code?

There's no need to re-type the examples in the book unless that's what you really like to do! You can download the source code and any other supporting files for the book from the book website at www.thecrmbook.com. Make sure to get on the e-mail list to get update notices if we make any changes to the downloads.

How is the Source Code Organized?

We tried to organize all of the sample code in a way that would be easy to use. The code has been divided into two major sections Framework and Chapters.

The Framework folder contains all the code for the common libraries that you might want to use over and over again. The license agreement EULA for the source code is flexible to allow easy reuse

The Chapters folder contains sub folders that try to group sample code based on the chapter we are covering. It's possible if an example from a chapter is from the Framework code there might not be a specific folder for that chapter.

What Software Do I Need?

In order to develop using the ideas and techniques presented in this book you will need access to a running copy of the CRM Server. The simplest way to obtain that is to download the demo VPC that Microsoft produces. Because the location of that changes from time to time here's a link that we know won't change http://www.thecrmbook.com/demovpc/.

In Chapter 3, we discuss different options in detail for setting up your complete development environment. However, the VPC will get you enough to get going quickly.

Some of the examples and concepts leverage capabilities that are part of Visual Studio 2008 and therefore to take advantage of them you will need access to Visual Studio 2008.

What about stuff we screwed up…You know Errata

In the process of writing, everyone sure wanted to make sure it was 100% accurate, but since nobody is perfect, we are sure you might find a few typos or other things that aren't correct. We would love to hear your feedback and will do our best to incorporate it into the next printing of the book. You can look at our website, www.thecrmbook.com for any last minute changes. Feel free to email us as well, info@thecrmbook.com if you find a typo.

1

What's New in CRM 4.0

Microsoft Dynamics CRM 4.0 represents a major upgrade to the platform and we will begin to explore some of the new features that are important to developers. For many of these features this chapter will simply set the stage for a much more detailed discussion later in the book where full chapters will be dedicated to a much deeper look at that feature.

From the 50,000 foot view, CRM 4.0 consists of a Server platform, a Client platform and e-mail integration capabilities. Since we are focusing on the developer's point of view, our discussions will mainly focus on the server and client platform and on features related to customizing it. We will however, highlight some of the user and operational features of the platform that have changed so that you understand the magnitude of the upgrade to the platform. A complete discussion of all new capabilities and changes is beyond the scope of this book, however this book, combined with other resources, will help build your CRM 4.0 knowledge.

When you look at the work done by the CRM product team in CRM 4.0 you will see that a significant amount went to the underlying infrastructure of the platform.

These investments were vital to allowing the platform to expand to support the larger on-premise deployments as well as a SaaS (Software as a Service) deployment by Microsoft and their partners.

Many of the investments, while infrastructure oriented like upgrading Workflow, are also exposed and directly usable and benefit both the developer and the user.

The Client

From the end user perspective, a number of UX (user experience) related changes start the process of closer alignment of the CRM UX to be more consistent with that of Microsoft Office. Some of these changes are simply layout oriented where things have been streamlined and consolidated. Many of the enhancements users will see are related to the customization capabilities.

Based on feedback, additional options were implemented to allow customizers to have more control on the navigational aspects of what the users see to allow it to more accurately represent their view of an application. For example, one of these navigational changes is related to having more control on how related entities show in the UI. You are now able to customize not only the labels but the order that the related entity shows. In Chapter 4, we will be diving much deeper into the various client side customizations.

The following is a screen shot of CRM 3.0 and then CRM 4.0. You can clearly see from these images and the following one of CRM 4.0 how the menu and the toolbars have been combined among other changes.

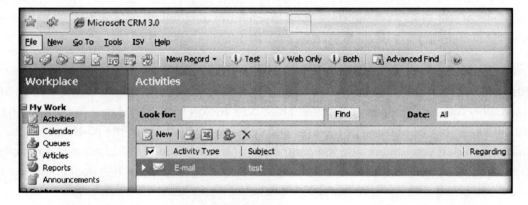

In addition to look and feel a lot of work was also done to streamline performance of both the web client and the Outlook add-in to try to optimize their network foot print.

The following is a screen shot from the CRM 4 web client..

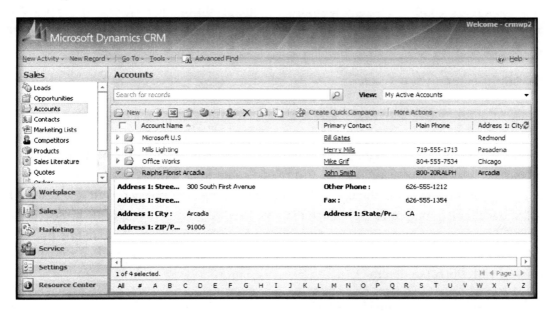

In CRM 4.0, the user still has multiple choices of how to access the server platform. One of the simplest choices is to use the Web Client that allows the user to access from any computer that has Internet Explorer 6 with SP1 or later. The Web Client is the simplest because it doesn't require any installation and can be accessed by the user from other computers as well as their own. Outlook users can take advantage of the CRM Outlook Add-In that integrates the CRM capabilities into the Outlook client.

The Outlook CRM Add-In has two configurations that you can install. The only difference is that the advanced one adds off-line support and installs its own instance of Microsoft SQL 2005 Express locally to store offline data and a web server that hosts then CRM platform logic while offline. When off-line support is enabled, the user is able to take a subset of their data offline, including many of the customizations developers can do. This allows the user to work while disconnected such as when traveling on an airplane. When the user connects back to the network their offline, changes are synchronized to the server.

From a developer point of view, the CRM Add-In handles all the data synchronization. New to CRM 4.0 is the ability to have access to the Web Service API on the Client. Prior to 4.0, this was only possible using unsupported techniques.

Additionally, developers can create plug-ins that also run on the client when offline. We will be discussing more on these changes later, but it is important to understand both client types and during testing, make sure your solution works in the offline configuration if you have users that will be taking advantage of that support.

E-Mail Integration and Tracking

E-mail integration is an important aspect of the platform because it allows e-mail communications to be tagged to platform data. This allows easy tracking of all interaction with a particular type of business data stored in the platform. For example, if you stored a list of projects or insurance policies in the platform you could track e-mails related to a specific project or policy. Then later when the user is looking at the project or policy record, the activity history will show all the e-mail correspondence that occurred related to that specific project or policy. E-Mail -integration is handled without developer intervention by the combination of the Outlook CRM Add-In and the CRM E-mail router service. E-mails sent from CRM are automatically tracked with the related item

Users are able to have more choices with respect to their e-mail integration with CRM 4.0. Users are now able to use the platform with Microsoft Exchange or a POP3 mail server. The e-mail router in CRM 3.0 only integrated with Microsoft Exchange and required being run on the same Exchange server where the associated CRM mailbox was located. In CRM 4.0 the e-mail router was re-written and in addition to supporting POP3, now no longer requires running on the Exchange server. In fact, in smaller environments or test environments the e-mail router can run on workstation O/S's such as Windows Vista. The CRM Outlook Add-In can, when configured, perform the functions the e-mail router would perform.

E-mails that are sent and received can now use Smart Tracking to associate the e-mail to a contact without having to add an e-mail Token Identifier. If you are new to CRM, the tracking function in previous versions added a token (e.g. CRM:123456) to the subject of e-mails to allow it to be matched to the original message when a reply is received. Using the token is still supported when enabled by configuration option and will increase matching but is no longer a requirement for tracking e-mail. When Smart Tracking is enabled, the platform will attempt to match an inbound e-mail to the related business data record automatically without user intervention. The matching will be heavily weighted on the subject and the sender of the e-mail to determine which related business record to tag as the related record.

TIP

Having subjects of e-mails that are unique will increase the effectiveness of the smart tracking. For example, "Your Insurance Policy" isn't as descriptive as "Your Insurance Policy A723" which will allow smart matching to be more effective.

From a developer's point of view, having e-mail integration built-in to the platform allows you to be able to provide 360° views of the business data in the system regardless of the type of solution you are building. This type of integration is often left to the user to perform manually due to the cost to build into each custom solution.

Mail Merge Enhanced

The Mail Merge capabilities for the users have been improved to allow custom data attributes and custom entities to be included in the Mail Merge. In addition to custom attributes you will now be able to include attributes from related entities.

The following shows the column selection dialog and how you can select related entities; in this case the parent account is selected. This would allow us to include data in the mail merge from the parent account as well as the contact.

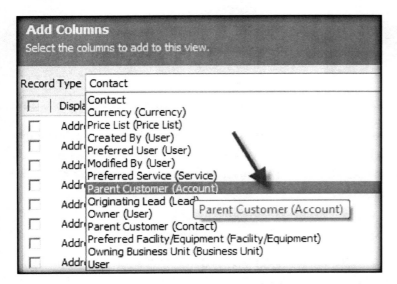

Templates are stored on the server for use with Mail Merge. They can be organization wide or user specific templates. By default, templates are provided for Contact, Lead, Quote and Account. You can create your own templates for custom entities and upload them to the server for use. It is also possible to start with a blank document and build it on the fly using the wizard.

Mail Merge can be used to create one page reports that are formatted in Microsoft Word.

Web client users now are able to launch a Mail Merge from the web client. Templates for the merges now are server based so they can more easily be shared.

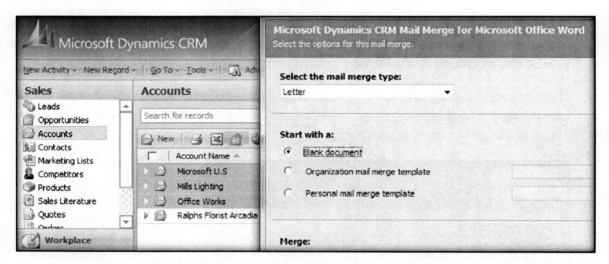

From a developer's point of view, the importance here is not that you will be interacting with Mail Merge capability via an API, but that your users can leverage the Mail Merge without your having to implement it directly in your solution. This includes the capability to store and share templates across the organization.

Auto Lookup Fields

One of the complaints we often hear from users with any system that tries to help them build relationships between their data is it takes too many clicks. In CRM 4.0 with the addition of Auto Lookup fields, building relationships among data is now easier because the lookup fields support auto resolution.

To use the auto lookup capability the user can simply type all or part of the information into the text box without having to open up a separate dialog. When the user tabs away from the field the system will attempt to locate the matching related record. In the event there is multiple matches found the lookup field will indicate that (by displaying the field in red) so the user can attempt to resolve to a single match.

Not all lookups are capable of the auto resolution. For example, on Activities setting the regarding will not use the auto resolution because it is possible for that to resolve to any number of entities and the performance would suffer as the system attempted to resolve all possible matches

In the following example, if you typed "ralph" and moved out of the field the system would look up and resolve to the correct parent account without the user having to look through a list.

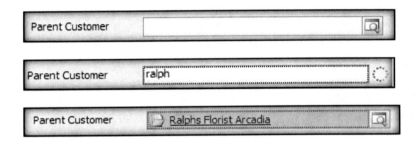

This is built for you without having to do custom AJAX style coding(techniques used for creating interactive web applications) just simply by adding a N:1 (many to one) relationship and putting that field on the form.

It is possible to turn this feature off on the Change Properties dialog when you are editing the form for the entity. For example, you might want to turn it off if you find it causes any performance impact due to high number of records.

Duplicate Detection

Duplicate detection is now included as part the platform and users with appropriate permissions are allowed to build custom detection rules.

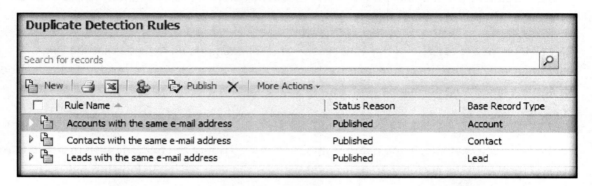

In the past, duplicate detection required writing custom code. Now one or more rules can be defined and you can schedule running duplicate detection jobs against your existing data. On the rule you can also identify if you want the rule to occur automatically when new data is added or updated. When that is selected the system will do the check in the background and the records are tagged as duplicates.

The following is an example of the dialog a user will see when a duplicate is detected. The user can then choose the action to take next.

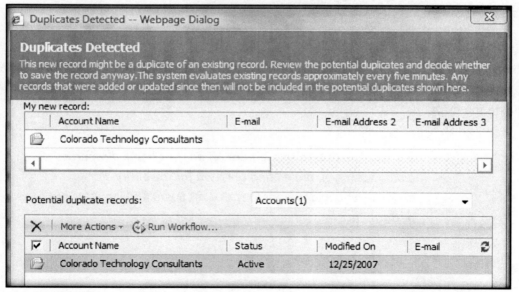

As a developer, you are able to also manipulate the duplicate detection rules using the platform API. Using this capability, you can define custom rules as part of an installation or provisioning process of a feature.

Using the client interface you can also define duplicate detection jobs that run against your data based on the rules defined and filters established. These jobs can be scheduled to re-occur without user intervention.

 *You must enable duplicate detection and create at least one rule for the entity in order for detection to happen.*

Report Snapshots

Report Snapshots allow the user to schedule creation of a report and save up to eight copies of the historical data. Using this new feature, a user could for example, schedule a daily, weekly or monthly type report.

The snapshot is stored and associated with the report in CRM so the user can view it by expanding the report in CRM. Access to the snapshot is controlled by the platform security and sharing model. One limitation of the snapshots is there is not currently an option to have the report snapshot mailed out to users. The limitation could be overcome by directly using SQL Reporting Services if needed.

Snapshots represents a nice addition to the reporting capabilities because it allows saving of historical perspective on data to be an automated part of the system.

Offline Reporting

One of the major limitations of reporting prior to CRM 4.0 was the fact that as soon as the user went offline they lost access to their reports. Now a user can produce reports on any of the data that they have taken offline with them. All that is required is the CRM add-in for Outlook.

Report Security and Sharing

Reports are now treated like other data records in the platform so they can have the same security capabilities. This includes the ability to share reports with users and teams.

Publishing Reports for External Use

Since reports are now published directly to CRM if you want to use a report directly from Reporting Services you can use this option. This option is found by editing a report on the actions menu. When you select this option a copy of the report is placed in Reporting Services.

Using this option you could easily make a report available in a SharePoint dashboard or schedule it to go out to users via the e-mail directly from Reporting Services.

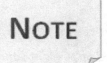

Check with your licensing expert! Make sure if you do expose the report in this manner you acquire proper licensing for each user that would be accessing the report.

Report Wizard

A common user frustration that is addressed is the creation of reports. Prior to CRM 4.0 reports used to require the assistance of a developer using Visual Studio to create a Reporting Services custom report. In CRM 4.0, users will be able to use a powerful Report Wizard to walk them through report creation.

The following is an example of a couple of the Report Wizard screens.

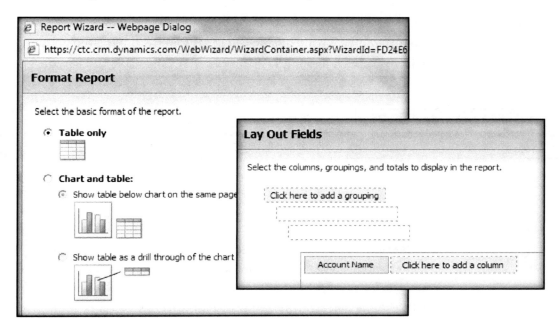

Using the Report Wizard users can create custom reports defining what should be reported on and how the report should be formatted.   You can also determine grouping and other summarization type options. Where appropriate, you can use charts to further illustrate the contents of the report. When you choose the Chart option you can allow the user to drill down to see the detail data.

The Report Wizard does a great job at empowering users to build reports. Developers still have the ability to take one of these reports and enhance it adding more complex capabilities to the report if needed. In this scenario, the user would first create the report using the report wizard. Then the developer would download it and modify it using Visual Studio's report designer to complete the more complex customizations.

Reports created by the wizard can also be used as templates for the user to create additional reports.

Related Data in Grids

In CRM 3.0 when we had a list of data, all of the columns came from the same entity. Now similar to how we saw with mail merge we are able to select attributes from related entities. In the following example we have included in our grid attributes that come from the parent account record.

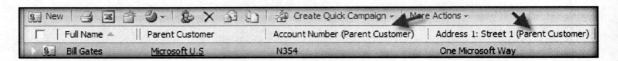

In CRM 4.0 you are not currently able to sort columns that come from related entities, only those from the primary entity are able to be sorted. The label for the column is also fixed to have the related entity name and is not currently changeable.

Improved Excel Integration

Exporting data from CRM using Excel continues to get more powerful. Similar to reports and mail merge you can add related entity attributes to the worksheet. There are three options you can choose when exporting to Excel.

- **Static** – this option creates an Excel spreadsheet that has the same columns and column order as the view that you are using. This is a static view, and does not have any connection to the data to be able to refresh as you work with the data

- **PivotTable** – This option is very helpful where you want to analyze data using a PivotTable. Using this option you are able to control which columns will be exported and available for use. You don't order the columns only select which will be used for the PivotTable. Once Excel is opened it will allow you to build the PivotTable from the columns selected.

- **Dynamic** – The dynamic option is similar to the static option, however, it allows you to modify the columns that are included and their order. Additionally, using the data refresh button users can update the selected data if it has changed recently in CRM.

Importing Data

The built-in import capabilities are improved and allow you to import data into both system and custom entities. Data must be formatted to a .csv or text file format to be able to be imported. Users are able to select the data delimiter and field delimiter as part of the first steps of the import.

Remember that even though .csv and text are the supported formats you can easily "save as" from Microsoft Excel to get data into that format.

The import can now be done in the background and the user is notified by e-mail when it is completed freeing the user to do other tasks while the data is imported. While the import is running the user is able to monitor progress as well as review any errors once it completes. Import also integrates with the platform duplicate detection capabilities and you can enable duplicate detection during import.

The data maps that are used to map the incoming data to the platform data record can be saved and re-used on subsequent imports. By being able to re-use the data mapping template it speeds up the import process by reducing the amount of user intervention required.

From a developer's point of view there is an Import API interface that you can leverage these import capabilities from code. For example, you can write your own import tool or use it to import data as part of a setup program. The following is a link to a sample that uses the Import API to allow you to export existing data and then uses the API to import (update) the data in CRM.

Download a complete sample using the Import APIs from CodePlex

http://www.codeplex.com/MSCRMimport

Data Migration Manager

Data Migration Manager is provided to help migrate data into the platform database. It offers several features that are not available in the Import tools that are accessible to users. The data migration capabilities have been improved in CRM 4.0 to handle several of the common scenarios. The following are a few examples of the capabilities.

- Able to customize entities including picklist value creation as part of the migration of data.
- Ability to use multiple source files that contain related data.
- Ability to assign records to multiple users.
- Ability to set the CreatedOn attribute from the source data – this allows historical dates to be set and is important for imports of older data from other systems.
- Able to create custom entities and attributes to accommodate source data fields.
- Complex transformations – including concatenation, splitting, replace, substring and other transformation capabilities.
- Auto mapping feature to allow quicker setup of mappings when the source have display labels similar to the attributes of the entity.

Data Migration Manager (DMM) now ties in with the platform Bulk Delete capabilities to make it easier to do test runs of importing data. From within DMM you can select Delete Data and a bulk deletion job will be triggered to remove the data imported. This allows for easier repeated testing of imported data.

DMM provides some sample maps now for various common imports from the following systems

- SalesForce.com
- ACT! 6
- Microsoft Outlook – Business Contact Manager 2003 and 2007

DMM is a separate install and is intended to run on the user's machine that is importing data. It does not require any server installation.

While DMM has the ability to create Entities and Attributes on the fly – I recommend manually creating these prior to the import using the normal techniques we will discuss in Chapter 4. This ensures the proper forms and other required setup is completed.

User Defined Workflows

In CRM 3.0 workflow definition was a complex process requiring administrative access to the CRM Server. Users had no easy way of creating a workflow, and when they did want one created, they would have to wait for the IT staff to fulfill even their simple requests. In fact, in most cases, workflows in CRM 3.0 were not a concept that end users, even power users really understood.

In CRM 4.0, users with security permissions can create workflow definitions using the client interface in addition to a full developer story using Visual Studio. In either scenario, Microsoft Windows Workflow Foundation is the runtime engine that manages and controls the workflow execution.

Standard platform security controls the ability for users to create, execute and monitor workflows. This means that you can control what workflows a user can see, invoke and monitor. Security also plays a role in what data changes will trigger the automated execution of a workflow created by a user. Each workflow has a scope associated with it that will determine in conjunction with the platform security what records will trigger the workflow to run.

Microsoft Windows Workflow Foundation as the runtime is completely integrated into the platform and not just a bolt-on addition. Using the hooks provided by the runtime, the platform is able to provide that tight level of integration.

An example of this is how you are able to monitor progress of the workflow as its execution progresses. This leverages the ability to tie into the tracking capabilities of Windows Workflow Foundation. You will see further signs of how tight the integration is as we explore workflow in greater detail in future chapters.

For developers, the ability for users to create workflows means that some basic automation will be able to be accomplished without requiring custom code development. One nice feature of the way workflow is implemented is it makes it real easy to combine custom code with the out of the box workflow capabilities. For example, developers can create custom workflow activities using standard Windows Workflow Foundation skills that show up to users in the workflow editor and allow them to be added to workflows created by the user. These custom workflow activities make it easy for developers to add custom capabilities to the workflow. CRM is able to provide the user interface to configure these activities in the workflow editor. CRM also provides monitoring of the execution of these activities in the user interface allowing users to see which step is currently processing and that includes the custom activities built by developers.

We have multiple chapters later dedicated to bringing you up to speed on the new workflow capabilities of the platform. The following is an example of the dialogue used to create and edit a workflow.

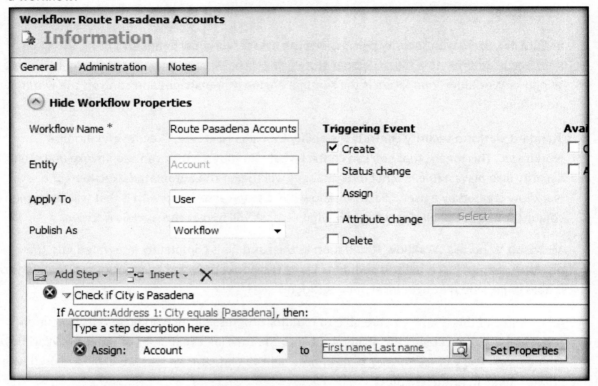

Another major enhancement in CRM 4.0 is the ability to trigger a workflow on detection of a change of data or update event. Previously, this required custom code to be developed and deployed because workflows could not be triggered by an update event.

 As you can see in the image above, the triggering events can be easily set. This includes the ability to specify which attributes changing should invoke the workflow. This support is possible thanks to a complete re-work of the platform event model. This re-work unified the event model that is used by workflow as well as other extension points developers can use. We will be discussing the new event model extensively later in the book.

| TIP | Workflows can be imported just like other customizations making it easy to move from one installation to another! |

Offline API and Plug-in Support

From a developer's perspective one of the major changes in CRM 4.0 is the ability to access the platform API from the laptop client when the user is offline. Specifically, the server side web services are hosted and made available on the local machine in offline mode. Most of the commonly used capabilities of the API are available including the fully customized WSDL for the organization. The main items that are not available are related to entity creation/modification and provisioning. The API will interact with whatever subset of data the user has defined as part of their local data rules. I talk about this being a big deal for developers but it is also a big deal for users too and they benefit heavily from the anywhere access to their data and customizations.

 This capability can also be used by developers to build completely custom interfaces that work both online and offline as well. For example, it would be possible to write a Smart Client application that accessed the server hosted API when the user was online and the client hosted API when the user was offline.

Plug-ins can also be configured to execute on the client when they are offline. Plug-ins are custom business logic you can create as a developer and register it with the platform to indicate which platform events should call and invoke your custom logic. We have a few chapters dedicated to discussing plug-ins in detail later in the book. When used on the client, the capability allows for business logic extensions to happen even when the user is offline. Several of the subsequent chapters will discuss plug-ins in greater detail.

The Server Platform

The CRM 4.0 server platform builds on top of and relies upon a number of other Microsoft products and technologies that are integrated together to provide a robust platform. The server components run on any version of Windows Server 2003 or later (See the Implementation guide for the complete list). Data management in CRM 4.0 now relies on Microsoft SQL Server 2005 as the database engine for managing all the platform data. SQL Server 2005 Reporting Services are used to support the reporting capabilities in the platform. It is expected that once Microsoft SQL Server 2008 is released it will be tested and supported by CRM.

In prior versions the server platform was a single install on each server, even if you had a web farm supporting your deployment. CRM 4.0 now further breaks down the server platform with roles that can be installed on separate servers(Enterprise Edition). Using these roles allows the server platform to scale out for larger deployments with each server(s) performing a role in the deployment. From a development point of view this is only important to understand the scale out capabilities of the platform, as it doesn't impact directly your coding of customizations.

Choices for deployment

CRM 4.0 now offers expanded choices for deployment including a hosted offering from Microsoft. For internal use within a company the traditional on-premise model is available and uses active directory for authentication. A hosted version of the platform can also be deployed and will use forms authentication and is intended for partners to offer CRM hosted services. New to CRM 4.0 is the CRM Online option, which is a hosted option and is hosted in Microsoft data centers. All of these deployment scenarios now use the same code base to minimize unexpected differences. This also allows for customizations, and data to more easily move between the different deployments if users change their mind. Each of the environments has some expected differences typically related to managing security and manageability of the environments. For example, CRM Online does not currently allow custom code to be deployed and provisioned for an organization. In that deployment scenario plug-ins and certain type of custom code based workflows can't be used. The core data modeling, customization and user experience of the platform though is very similar across all the deployment types. From a developer perspective, other than understanding limitations for custom code, developers do need to also interact with authentication differently in each of the environments and we will discuss this in more detail in Chapter 9.

Handling Multiple Tenants

CRM 3.0 was a single tenant platform. By single tenant we mean only one organization and one set of customizations and data could be installed on the platform application server. This led organizations that had either multiple internal installs or hosting companies to dedicate a lot of infrastructure to supporting CRM 3.0. One of the major goals of CRM 4.0 was to support the concept of multi-tenant or multiple organizations and customizations to be able to share a single install. To accommodate multiple tenants' major architecture changes were made under the covers in the platform in CRM 4.0. Some of these changes will affect developers in how they interact with the platform APIs. The multi-tenant capabilities are only able to be enabled in the Enterprise Edition. We will be discussing these throughout the book and it is important to understand even if you are not running the enterprise edition.

To help you get your head around what has changed here let's talk about some of the actual changes that were made to support multi-tenants. From a database perspective in CRM 3.0 there used to be two databases created on the database server when you installed a new organization. One of the databases contained the metadata and the other contained the data managed by the application. In CRM 4.0 each organization's metadata and data is stored in a single database named <OrganizationName>_MSCRM. The "deployment" or install also creates a database that is shared by the install with information about all the organizations that have been provisioned. This central database is named MSCRM_Config.

Probably one of the most important things to understand is the fact that each organization has its own database, and there is no sharing of data among the organizations. This high level of isolation will be a plus or minus depending on your specific scenario and your isolation requirements. No doubt, there will be solutions or customizations done to move data between organizations, but the key is to understand that the default is complete organization isolation

From an installation point of view, if you go through a standard install (not custom, it doesn't provision the default org), you will provision your first organization as part of that setup. Subsequent creation of additional organizations is handled using Deployment Manager -> Organizations - New Organization menu option - These additional organizations get created pretty quickly.

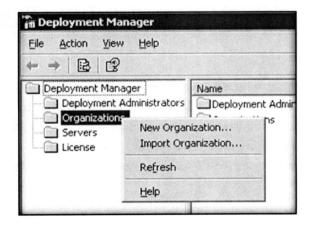

Another change that is a result of multi-tenant is you will find settings that used to be managed via the Registry or config files on the application server are now options that administrators can set and modify using the web client This is important because most of those options you want to be able to set on an organization by organization process . The following shows the settings portion of the settings that can be found at Settings - > Administration -> System Settings.

Custom menus and toolbars

Select the clients that will display custom buttons and menu items configured in ISV.Config.

Clients   Web Application;Outlook;Outlook Offline

Application mode

Set whether Microsoft Dynamics CRM can be opened in a browser window without menu, navigation, and command bars.

☐ Open Microsoft Dynamics CRM in Application mode

Another change you will notice pretty quickly is the url to access the site will now have the organization name as part of the url e.g. http://mycrmserver/myorgname/ The default (first org) can be accessed using the root without the org name but any additional will require specification of the orgname as part of the URL. The URL can also be prefixed with the organization name in the case of where you are using IFD (Internet Facing Deployment). In that case it would typically look like the following URL – http://myorgname.mycrmserver. IFD is a new authentication mode that allows users to access the CRM server without requiring VPN.

From a customization point of view each organization has its own data model and all the customizations that go along. This means that you can have one server support a number of organizations, each having their own custom entities and other customizations. So that if you need a custom entity in all organizations you need to either create it in each or import it into each organization. This can be automated using the Metadata API we will discuss later in Chapter 8.

Developers will also notice that if they are using the new 2007 web service end point they will need to provide the organization name to indicate which organization they are working with. Now is also a pretty good time to make sure that you understand that if you use the 2006 web service end point it does not allow you to access any organization other than the default organization. If you are building new code for the platform you will really want to target using the new 2007 web service end point.

To help with discovery needs developers can use the new Discovery web service to determine what organizations are provisioned and what the Web Service and Metadata Service URLs are.

In addition, plug-ins and workflows that we will be discussing are also provisioned (registered with each tenant in the multi tenant deploy) and execute specific to each tenant/organization that is configured. The nice thing here for developers is much of the complexity created by the multi-tenant environment is handled by the platform.

Multi-Currency Support

CRM 4.0 now has basic support for handling multiple currencies. This change allows an organization to define a default currency such as the US $ and then convert to and from other currencies for transactions. This capability allows for the concept of a transactional currency, which basically says that on a form, users can select from configured currencies and set the transactional currency for that form. All amounts input on the form are then input using that transactional currency. For example the base currency could be US $, but the user selected a transactional currency of Pound Sterling £. For purposes of discussion let's assume that one U.S $1 is the same as $ .50 Pound Sterling (yeah I know that's terrible!). When the form is saved the platform will save the Pound Sterling amount as the transaction amount, the U.S amount as the base amount, the Currency used for the transaction and the conversion rate.

If we dig deeper to try to understand more about what's happening we would start by understanding that there is a new Currency system entity. The Currency entity instances store the data related to each configured currency in the system and the conversion rate to the base currency that was identified during the setup of the organization.

The following is an example of the page where you can manage and configure currencies.

Currencies

Search for records

New | 🖨 | 🗷 | ✕ | More Actions ▾

☐	Currency Name ▲	ISO Currency C...	Currency Symbol	Exchange Rate
▶	Australian Dollar	AUD	$	1.0427000000
▶	Pound Sterling	GBP	£	0.5000000000
▶	US Dollar	USD	$	1.0000000000

 *It's important to note that this is not a real time currency exchange system that updates automatically as the published exchange rate is updated. The exchange rates must be manually maintained.*

The only time that the conversion rate is updated is if you manually update the value. Since Currency is a normal platform entity, you can use the platform API to modify it. For example you could have a nightly process that runs queries the financial markets and updates it based on the current exchange rates. This would be a good ISV product (hint, hint...).

Multi Language Support

The platform has had some multi language support for a while; however, you had to choose your language when you installed the platform. Once language was active in an organization, you could not allow users to specify their own choice. Further from a developer point of view there was no way to specify labels and such for each language.

All that changes with CRM 4.0 as it now will support the concept of a base language and allow for the installation of language packs that add additional languages. This allows a single organization to have multiple active languages and each user to pick from the list of installed languages for their personal preference.

The following shows that now users can also have control to pick their language preference.

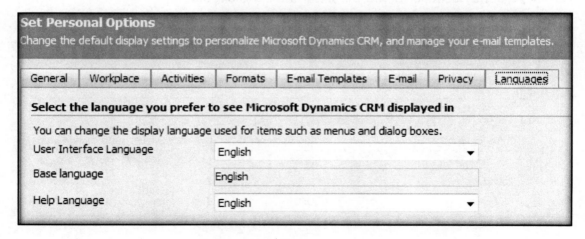

From a developer point of view this introduces a few things you need to be aware of. When accessing Display names using the Metadata API you will be working with a new object called CRMLabel. This object accommodates for the fact that a single description or label will have one value for each language defined.

It is also important for developers to know that in order to work with defining language strings for a given language that language pack must be installed on the development server they are using so that it can be added to the metadata. If you import or otherwise try to add a translated label for a language not installed it will be ignored or an error will be presented.

The multi language capabilities are targeted at handling the metadata. So things like labels and picklist values will have support for being tailored for each specific language. Things like reports and the data stored in the system are not covered by the current implementation.

We will discuss how to manage multi language transitions using the Metadata API later in Chapter 8. In Chapter 23, we will also be discussing the multi language capabilities in more detail as well.

Keep in mind the multi language capabilities allow users to change on the fly to any provisioned language

Data Management

CRM 4.0 provides a number of enhancements for working with the data model and managing the data. First, it's important to revisit the goal of data management in the platform. While under the covers Microsoft SQL Server is used to store all the data, developers and users are abstracted from that by using the data modeling capabilities of the platform. By creating custom entities which are similar to how databases would have tables, developers can create a data model for complex solutions. CRM 4.0 provides some additional capabilities such as new relationships to help handle the more sophisticated needs of these solutions. The Metadata API provides a programmatic interface to manipulate the platform metadata. In previous versions, the API was limited to read access, now in CRM 4.0 developers can use the API to modify the metadata as well. We will explore how this can be used later in Chapter 8.

Relationships

The ability to define custom relationships between platform entities both system and custom gives the platform the ability to model real world problems. CRM 4.0 adds several new relationship types to allow for expanding the creativity of applications. All existing relationship types that existed in CRM 3.0 have been maintained.

New relationships in CRM 4.0

The following are the key new relationship types that are supported.

- Many To Many – this is a true many to many that will work with both system and custom entities. In Chapter 4 we will contrast the new Many To Many capability to techniques used prior to CRM 4.0 to handle these types of relationships.

- Multiple Relationships between entities – this allows you to have more than one relationship to a particular custom or system entity. An example of this is where you want to have a primary and a secondary relationship. In CRM 3.0 you could only have a single relationship of this type.

- Relationships between system entities - This allows you to create multiple relationships between system entities - for example a secondary contact on an account.

- Self Referential - allows entities to relate back to them self to create hierarchical data.

The following diagram attempts to demonstrate some of the relationship capabilities that are available between entities in the platform.

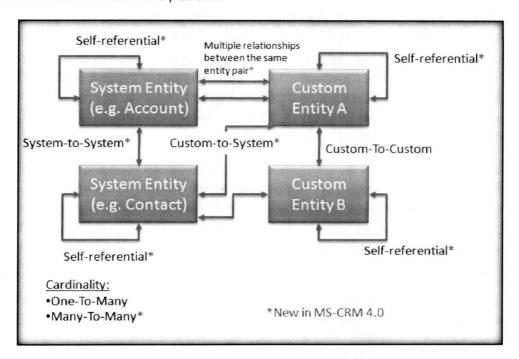

© 2008 Microsoft Corporation

The most reliable way to know what relationships an entity can participate in can be determined by the platform metadata.

When you query the metadata for an entity it will provide properties that indicate eligible relationship types.

In addition to providing more flexibility in relationship types a lot of changes have been made to how the customizer can indicate how the relationship can be used. For example, in the relationship editor interface you can now specify names for relationships as well as specify the order for how they will be included on the forms for the user interface.

For Developers, using the MetaData API you can now create all the different relationship types using API calls. This allows for creation of the relationships as part of a setup or provisioning type program.

Developer Extensibility

The CRM 4.0 server platform has significant enhancements around how developers extend the platform capabilities. In the prior version of CRM developers could implement callouts that were custom code that was invoked before or after a platform operation. callouts allowed the developer flexibility to introduce business logic like it was part of the core platform. CRM 4.0 continues that general concept but re-architects it to be a plug-in architecture. Plug-ins which will be fully explored later in Chapters 12, 13 and 14 provide the same capabilities as callouts but offer greater flexibility for the developer.

The workflow capabilities of the platform have also been re-energized and now integrate Windows Workflow Foundation as a replacement for the proprietary workflow that was in CRM 3.0. This change allows developers that already have Windows Workflow skills to use them with the CRM platform. With the move to plug-ins and a new workflow engine the CRM Team re-architected their implementation around a concept referred to as the Event Framework which we will discuss in great detail in Chapter 11.

Throughout this book we will be highlighting how developers can customize and extend the platform and where appropriate we will be calling out and explaining the new techniques.

Backward Compatibility

One of the goals of CRM 4.0 was to ensure that the new version didn't abandon users of the CRM 3.0 version. While we won't discuss much on upgrades or how the older capabilities migrate forward, it's important to note that extensive effort was put in to ensure where developers used supported techniques in CRM 3.0, they migrated to CRM 4.0 without a problem. Probably the best demonstration of this, is for developers who created callouts or Workflows in CRM 3.0, they are now migrated and still supported in CRM 4.0 even though those capabilities were completely re-written in the CRM 4.0 release.

Wrapping it up

In this chapter, we have taken a look at some of the new features of Microsoft Dynamics CRM 4.0 that would be interesting to the developer. Many other features and capabilities were also upgraded as part of the release. Some of them are more centric to the administrator and some are more user oriented. As we dig in deeper in the remaining chapters of the book we will be expanding on several of the topics discussed briefly in this chapter.

2

Building Line of Business Applications

What the heck is CRM? For someone who already is a CRM developer that might seem like a strange question but for someone who has never dealt with a CRM system this isn't that odd of a response. This book includes CRM in the text only because that is what Microsoft calls the platform. The reality is what we are talking about in this book can be used for building all kinds of line of business applications. Sure some of them might be CRM related – which in case you were wondering stands for Customer Relationship Management, but that certainly isn't the only type of applications you can build.

I'm not suggesting that all applications would be good to build on top of CRM 4.0 as the platform, but I do think that there are a number of applications where developers start from scratch and build a ton of plumbing (infrastructure code). If they had used CRM 4.0 as the platform the extra plumbing could have been avoided. Again, I'm not against building infrastructure code, I just think you should save that for where you build something unique or extend what is provided by the core platform.

I think that it could be argued that what Microsoft should have done with CRM 4.0 was separate its application development platform from the implementation as a CRM application. By doing that it could have established the CRM 4.0 platform as a solid application development platform for building line of business applications. Then they could market CRM 4.0 as being built on this application development platform. Then developers would be able to license just the platform portion and be charged a license fee that is appropriate for using only the application development capabilities. Maybe in the future, we will see that shift in thinking but currently the two are combined as Microsoft Dynamics CRM 4.0. That combination does not stop us from thinking of CRM 4.0 as an application development platform. In fact, even Microsoft is starting to talk about CRM in and it's broader capabilities. Ray Ozzie, Microsoft's Chief Software Architect referred to it as a rapid solutions platform in his keynote at Mix 08. Steve Ballmer, Microsoft's CEO further referred to it as being more like XRM in his Convergence 08 keynote.

In this chapter we will explore some of the capabilities that we believe make it appropriate for a line of business application development platform.

"First I need you to catalog each snowflake by size, shape, speed, and time it fell. After that, make a complete inventory of every fish in the sea. Then, after lunch…"

What is a Line of Business Application?

If you asked 10 developers what a Line of Business (LOB) application was you would get at least 10 different answers. The reason is this is a very broad category of applications. Sometimes the applications are pet projects like in the figure above, often times they are mission critical applications. In almost all cases, we are talking about internal applications used by a company to run their business.

They are critical applications that users inside the firewall or connected via secure networks use on a day to day basis. Using this definition, we exclude applications that facilitate e-commerce to the end consumer or other services to less trusted users outside the firewall. That said however, often these types of external applications can connect through integration or work in conjunction with one or more LOB applications at a company.

Often times LOB applications will be created to track a process, to track status, to coordinate or to facilitate other internal business process optimization oriented tasks. The data is often in high demand for reporting and analysis to find what works and what needs fixing. Flexibility to change is important, and even more important is the ability to evolve.

Surprisingly, you will even see some companies build their most critical LOB applications using Excel, Access or other end user tools (like the sticky note pad). These applications often times grow out of control and end up being shared and depended on by a large number of users at the company, yet lack the capabilities needed to support it as an enterprise LOB application. Often this happens due to lack of support from the IT side of the business by not providing a platform that is designed to support this type of rapid user application creation. At first, this creates immediate relief of a critical problem, but over time it can become a liability as it fails to grow and evolve with the company. With the gradual increase in the data captured and the absence of centralization, often times, useful data is not available when required.

For our purposes in this book, we do not need a more rigid definition of what a LOB is. As you learn more about the CRM 4.0 capabilities, you will also gain an increased ability to identify and propose where it could solve problems in your organization or in a client's organization.

What features do they typically have?

There is no such thing as a one size fits all when it comes to the features that an LOB application will use. In this section, we will explore some of the more common ones and specifically ones that are addressed well by the CRM 4.0 platform.

Custom Data Modeling

Clearly, at the heart of almost any LOB application is the need to be able to define a custom data model and have the ability to define relationships between the entities in that model. CRM accomplishes this using a declarative data model that sits on top of Microsoft SQL Server. We will explore more about these capabilities in Chapter 4 where we discuss Data Modeling in detail.

Customizable UI/UX

Having a data model is great but if nothing is there to let users search, view and modify the data then there is a problem. In the past we just focused on the User Interface (UI), today, we look broader than that at the complete User Experience (UX). Hundreds of hours can be spent just getting non-customizable forms in place in a LOB application. Typically the majority of these are not really complicated pages but take a lot of time up front. More often than not, time is not spent though, to allow the forms to be customizable by anyone but developers.

CRM accomplishes this by automatically creating a set of forms and views. Each data entity defined in our data model has a form built for it that the administrator or business analyst can customize for the user. Additionally, for the more sophisticated problems, the customizer can provide JavaScript that is invoked when events occur on the page such as on load or save of the page or when a field is modified on the form. This scripting allows for a number of problems to be solved ranging from validation to auto calculation of field values.

CRM provides for more customized UX by allowing integration of applications written in ASP.NET, Silverlight or for that matter any external application page inside a form frame. By modifying CRM's navigation structure these same applications can simply be navigated to by links.

CRM also is perfectly capable of having its complete UI/UX replaced by a custom application. This could be a Silverlight application, a WPF (Windows Presentation Foundation) application, a Windows Forms application or possibly a custom Outlook add-in. This is all accomplished by using the platform API directly.

Developer API

From an application point of view the requirement is to be able to access and modify the data stored using an API. In LOB applications this varies greatly in terms of how people typically implement it. Some are more elaborate and structured and others are inline and violate many of what we know to be good development principals. CRM 4.0 provides a dynamic Service Oriented Architecture (SOA) API that self modifies as you add custom entities to the data model. Developers can then access the API and use type safe classes and properties for interacting with the platform data.

Workflow

Workflow certainly is not a "required" element for a line of business solution but it's certainly one that can give the user a lot of power. The concept of workflow is being able to define rules that will run in the background and trigger based on events that occur. The triggering events are related to actions that occur in the system like when data is created, updated, deleted, or assigned. Sometimes the triggering event is the manual invocation by the user of the workflow.

Microsoft Dynamics CRM 4.0 greatly expands the workflow capabilities by introducing Windows Workflow Foundation as the replacement for their proprietary workflow solution that was in CRM 3.0. A benefit of this change is that not only does it greatly expand the developer capabilities allowing them to build custom activities and flows, but the users themselves can define, create and run workflows in the system.

Reporting

Reporting is another cornerstone of almost every internal LOB application. More than ever users want to view and analyze the data they have collected. To accommodate that CRM 4.0 comes with a Report Wizard empowering users to create reports using the client interface. Additionally, the developer story is still very strong enabling developers to build Microsoft SQL Reporting Services reports and upload them to CRM for processing.

Since CRM 4.0 data management engine is SQL Server it opens the door to also leverage the business intelligence capabilities of SQL Analysis Services. In fact, CRM Analytics Foundation provides a foundation for building robust business intelligence solutions using the platform's operational data. This opens the door to provide key metrics and measurements on the application data that can be used in Excel or integrated into a management oriented dashboard.

Offline Support

You might think in today's connected world that offline access to data was not important but simply put that just hasn't come true. While sales people and others that work outside the connected world would like to rely on things like cell phones' internet access, the reality is we have a way to go before that becomes reality. In the mean time having offline support is critical for sales people or other users to have access to their data 24/7 regardless of the fact that they are on a plane 40,000 feet in the air.

One of the features of CRM is that it provides an Outlook Add-in that provides for integration of the CRM capabilities with the Outlook client. When using the Add-In users also gain the ability to access the platform data and capabilities offline. This is accomplished by storing a local copy of the system metadata and selected parts of the user's data locally in a Microsoft SQL Express database. This is not a simple database replication solution; it's a true platform synchronization that ensures that transactions that occur offline go through the same business logic when the user synchronizes their data.

 New to CRM 4.0 is the ability to also write business logic extensions that run both on the server and on the client platform when the user is offline. These extensions use a version of the developer API that is available offline.

Often times applications provide some small amount of offline support but the offline sync of data is very challenging to do with full business logic integration. With CRM 4.0 supporting more offline capability it makes it easier to implement more than just the small amount of offline support.

Data Import/Export
It is very common to have some form of data import/export in LOB applications. Typically, these are added as ad hoc processes to support a specific area of the application. The yell and shout technique is very common – "Hey Joe, can you run that query again for me!"

CRM 4.0 provides support out of the box for users to export data into Excel. This exported data can be used for reporting or for bulk updating and then re-importing back into the platform. For example, you might send out a call list and then update the data based on the new information received back. Using the import capabilities, you can easily add new data into the platform from .csv files and .txt files. In addition, there are a number of import tools that also perform more complex data import capabilities by using the platform web services.

Security
Solutions need to ensure that only the right users have access to the correct data and services of the platform. CRM provides a role based security model that understands organizational hierarchy. This model provides protection to both built-in system entities as well as custom

entities unique to your solution. Each of which you can control the security needs of one or more users.

In addition to using roles to control security records that that are user owned can be shared with other users or teams. When shared, the sharing user can choose what level of access the shared record will have for different platform operations.

All platform operations, regardless if it originates from a user using the UI, or a developer calling an API, will go through the security logic to validate against the security permissions of the user. This provides a level of consistency you typically will not find in a homegrown security model used by most LOB applications.

If there were one area of deficiency, it is the lack of field level security. For applications with basic field(column) level lock down needs there are some options on how to handle this using some of the customization techniques.

Multi-Language/Currency

Many companies are serving not only a global customer base but often they find themselves with offices in more than one country. When this happens their systems are ill equipped to be expanded quickly to support the needs of their multi language colleagues not to mention the fact that they conduct business in a different currency.

CRM 4.0 provides all the hooks to handle both of these in an optional use fashion. Meaning that if you need them now or in the future you can take the time to setup the additional languages and currency but you aren't required to have multiple to get going. This saves a lot of complex planning in applications that decide to roll their own of these capabilities.

Going Mobile

Pick your favorite device (Windows Smart Phone, Blackberry, whatever is next) regardless the LOB applications are starting to be more important to have data on the go. The platform comes out of the box with basic mobile support but also is open to using the Web Service APIs so third party vendors can also create mobile applications that work with the platform.

"Growthability"

Ok, so maybe the word doesn't exist but the concept does. I'm talking about the ability to grow a platform with the company. This includes the ability to scale a platform out and up to support the growing needs of the organization as well as the growing reliability on the platform. More users cause more volume and in turn you need to run the application on more servers. As you have more users, and those users depend more on the system, reliability demands also increase. To satisfy reliability demands, you will need to be able to run the application on more hardware using concepts like load balancing, clustering and/ or mirroring to ensure that during problems users can still access the solution. Often time these aspects are not included in LOB applications and are only addressed when a crisis has occurred.

CRM provides a lot of flexibility in this area including the ability to start small on a single box running Windows Small Business Server and scaling up to a multi server deployment model including the ability to segregate and run certain system processes on different nodes to accomplish scale out.

Maintainability
A topic nobody wants to think about but one we all need to consider is maintainability. Using CRM 4.0 as a platform offers key servicing capabilities for the core platform. If you were to build your own plumbing, you become the plumber and are responsible for the upgrades to keep it working. With CRM 4.0 as the platform, you leverage the ongoing updates from Microsoft and their commitment to a shelf life for each release of the platform. They also expend an enormous amount of effort focusing on backward compatibility and how applications built on prior updates or versions will move forward as the platform evolves.Beyond just the basics of the core platform, the features like being able to add entities, attributes, views, workflows, reports quickly and easily is important. Often times LOB applications are outdated the moment they are finished so the ability to roll out incremental updates at the solution level is just as important as maintenance to the platform.

Operations
Another key aspect of an application development platform is its ability to play well with the operational staff.   Here we are talking about ability to monitor the platform for problems and overall performance. Since multiple applications might use the same logic, they want reassurance that updates to the core platform code is well tested and ready for prime time. CRM provides integration with System Center for monitoring of the platform health and performance. This capability comes out of the box and does not require developers to develop custom integration on their own.

Third Party Vendors
Ok, I agree this item probably wouldn't make the list if you were talking about building your own application development platform because no third party vendor would bother wasting time writing support for your internal proprietary platform.

In CRM's case though, there is a robust ecosystem of ISVs and value added resellers that focus on the CRM platform. Of course some of them focus on its CRM specific capabilities but a lot of them offer solutions that can work regardless of being a CRM solution or not. You can find more details about these type of products at http://pinpoint.microsoft.com.

Microsoft also has "connectors" that they create and are design to connect to other Microsoft products like Great Plains.

Wrapping it up

In this chapter we walked through what a LOB application is and what are some of the high level capabilities CRM has as a platform that can be used to build LOB applications. By leveraging CRM as your core application development platform you save hundreds of hours of infrastructure plumbing you would otherwise have to build for your application.

Besides just the initial building, when you build your own platform you sign up for ongoing additional maintenance rather than letting a larger development team at Microsoft provide that for you. Each release/update to CRM has brought significant, but incremental functionality and capability improvements to the platform. Upgradability is also extremely important to the CRM team and helps to preserve your investments across releases.

You are probably thinking at this point, boy that was a short chapter and the simple answer is yes it is. We set this concept aside as a separate chapter to make sure it received the focus and dedicated thought it deserves. As you are reading though the rest of the book or making decisions for your company on how to build your line of business applications, we want you to be including CRM 4.0 in the short list for the platform foundation.

3

Developer and Team Workspace

In this chapter we will look at how to prepare your individual developer workspace as well as discuss some of the things a team can do to be more productive.   You might be thinking, "don't I just download the SDK and I am ready to go?" In reality, developing applications that will run on the CRM platform is pretty straight forward compared to trying to glue all these components together yourself. The platform installation process hides much of the complexity of using all the combined products/components from you. For example, you do not need to configure all the options on Workflow or Reporting Services, this is done for you.   With that said there are things that can make you and your team more productive and this is what we will be discussing in this chapter.

From an individual perspective, you need to decide what version of Visual Studio you will use and where you will be pointing for your CRM server during development. There are a few approaches and options, but most of them boil down to personal choice and definitely are not a one size fits all solution. There are also some obviously different answers to the questions depending on if you are targeting an on-premise install versus developing an application deployed on CRM Online. Another big difference is how deep are the customizations you will be performing – if you will just be doing JavaScript or forms customizations or will you be doing deep code level plug-ins and workflow.

From a team perspective, we will explore some of the challenges you might face and some possible solutions. Teams need to handle multiple people making changes all at the same time.

This will include changes to customizations, scripts, and even custom code. How to approach and solve this will involve looking at the different phases from development to production. Finally, we will discuss an approach to setting up source control and a project structure for building your solution.

Much of what we discuss in this chapter is personal choice and there are multiple techniques to accomplish the same thing. This chapter will not be dictating a single approach, but give you ideas to develop your own path. Use this chapter to build ideas on how you want to tailor your specific environment to make you and your team the most productive.

Choosing your development machine OS

One of the things you need to decide is what operating system your development machine should be running. By development machine, I am talking about the computer that you sit at all the time doing your development work, not a team server, test server or the production environment.

The reason this is important is because it will affect how you go about debugging and doing other testing during development. If you are just doing customizations and scripting the choice of operating system really does not matter. If you are doing custom work flows or plug-ins to extend business logic where you will be writing .NET code, then the choice can be more important.

The reason really comes down to debugging. Currently, since CRM requires Windows Server as the operating system to run, if you want to interactively debug while running a custom workflow or plug-in deployed then you will need to have Windows Server as your operating system. Another option is to use Remote Debugging, but from past experiences I think it takes way too much effort for the rewards.

Personally, I'm of the opinion that the tradeoffs required for running Windows Server as my day to day machine are just unacceptable. Don't get me wrong, I think Windows Server is great when run on the server. However, on my desktop I prefer to run a desktop/laptop OS. In fact, just the thought of having Windows Server as my daily OS reminds me of doing MTS COM development years ago when that was the only way to go. I think the problem is the goals of a server OS are much different from a desktop/laptop OS especially when you start talking about doing development on a laptop.

In reality it's not so much an OS choice as a difference in philosophy on how I do my development. One of the things I do is to provide ways to do initial unit testing without needing to deploy to the CRM Server, but rely on deployment to a test server for full in platform testing. I then look for ways that I can make my local development environment more productive. For example by using a test harness for Workflow and Plug-ins I'm able to do debugging of them locally without having to have Windows Server be my desktop / laptop OS.

I will talk extensively about how to build a test harness like this later in the book in the respective workflow and plug-in chapters. I also establish a goal for myself that by the time my code works in the unit test environment I need to start thinking about production. What do I mean by that? A way too common development scenario is that developers rely on the debugger until the time that their code is deployed to production. That works great and they are pretty productive but once their code gets to production "where's the debugger?"

These developers are stuck trying to figure out what is going on in their code using a process I think is akin to walking blind-folded in a room and using the sound bouncing off the wall as a clue to where you are. I tend to like to start early thinking about how I will resolve problems in production. Like the CRM platform I have found that tracing is my friend and by building a robust tracing infrastructure and baking trace statements into my code I'm prepared for that call that we all get telling us something isn't working. Using the test harnesses, we will be discussing tracing extensively as we go through the workflow and the plug-in chapters.

So the bottom line is there is no single right OS for your development machine, it really comes down to personal choice. In fact, if you really get down to analyzing some of my reasons for not using Windows Server as the O/S, such as using test harnesses and tracing, they can all be done the same way using Windows Server. Regardless of your choice it is worth thinking about upfront.

If you are doing work with a 64bit client O/S keep in mind that there are not currently 64bit binaries for the client add-ins. That means some of the Outlook assemblies we talk about referencing require you to force the application to 32bit.

The Virtual Machine Approach

Another common approach is to use a VM (Virtual Machine) that runs either locally or on a remote server that you access for your development. When using this approach what you run locally as your base O/S really does not matter.

The nice thing about this approach is it does give you a lot of flexibility to maximize hardware. Using this approach you can build out virtual servers that support each project or client. You can also combine virtual servers with the Multi-Tenant capabilities of CRM to really have a flexible environment to support your development. When there are multiple developers virtualization can provide each their own sandbox to work in.

Using Pre-Built VMs

Microsoft makes available a pre-built virtual server with CRM pre-installed that you can just download and go. This is simply the easiest way, other than signing up for CRM Online, to get hands on experience using CRM. Other than the time to download, you should have a CRM Server up and running in a matter of minutes. If you're reading this book in order to get an idea of what the capabilities are of the platform and you want an environment to play with, while investing little, this is the way to go. Visual Studio 2005 will be pre-installed on it, so you will also have development tools ready to use.

 NOTE

Many of the examples in this book require Visual Studio 2008 to get the full advantage of the concepts. Using Visual Studio 2005 is still viable but you should understand that some things might not apply. For example, JavaScriptI IntelliSense is only supported in Visual Studio 2008.

If you are committed to the platform and are doing a real world project using it, it is highly recommend building your own virtual server(s) rather than using the pre-built server image.

Building your own virtual server image will require a bigger investment (typically a few hours of time) but you will have the following key advantages over using the pre-built image.

- No data will be there, just what you input after the install – you can always download the Adventureworks database from Codeplex if you need sample data later. Microsoft also makes available import files for most of the common built-in entities that you can import directly in as needed.

- o **http://www.codeplex.com/MSFTDBProdSamples**

- You will be sure there are no customizations already done to support the demo ware on the box.

- No "bloatware", you know what's installed and it's only what you need – If you need a demo version of something it will be you that installs it.

- Most important, you will understand the install process – even if it is a simplistic environment compared to what you will have in production. Knowing how the pieces fit together will help you when problems come up or more detailed knowledge is required.

The Disposable VM

In addition to using the pre-built images to get your feet wet quickly, they also are great if you need a disposable environment. Often times if you want to try a risky change or a 3rd party tool trying it first in a throw away server is always the best. You can also use the Differencing disk or Undo capabilities of Virtual Server/PC to do the same with the pre-built images or your real environment.

Virtual Server, Virtual PC or Hyper-V

All three work fine and in fact, you can share the VM easily between Virtual PC and Virtual Server environments. One thing to keep in mind if you are moving between different versions or flavors of the product, each have their own Virtual Machine Additions software to install. I have personally seen performance of both CPU and I/O be horrible (absolutely horrible) if the VM Additions software is mismatched.

Windows Server 2008 brings a new option called Hyper-V. Hyper-V is the next generation of the virtualization technology and is more tightly integrated with the O/S. Using Hyper-V would give you more flexibility because it offers features like snap shots that can be used to save copies of your VM at a point in time for later rollback. This feature could be very helpful if you are trying something risky or experimenting and want to get back to a stable point. You can accomplish similar things using undo disks with the older version; snap shots are just easier to manage.

Hyper-V also promises a number of performance improvements due to how I/O is handled. Startup and Save time for the virtual machines is noticeably faster on Hyper-V than on Microsoft's other products. Which of these flavors you pick really depends on your target OS for running it. Check the latest on the Microsoft site and I recommend using the newest version for your specific target OS.

Hardware Recommendations

There are just too many combinations and possibilities to give absolutes here but here is my rule of thumb for an all in one server environment. You will want at least 2GB of memory on the host OS. Quantity of memory and speed of hard disk makes the most difference. When possibly getting closer to 3-4GB will allow you to allocate a larger amount to your virtual machine and it will make a noticeable difference.

For laptops, I highly recommend 7200 rpm hard drives and on a desktop or server 10,000 rpm drives or faster make a big difference. Multiple drives also can provide an advantage because you can have your virtual server running on a separate drive from the host O/S.

For your own personal developer workstation – if you do not currently have a 10,000 rpm drive but you can get your hands on one then definitely get it . Earlier this year I upgraded my desktop machines and was amazed how noticeable of a change it was. If you have to choose, then buy a slower processor and spend more on faster disks!

MVP Tip: Microsoft CRM MVP Matt Parks added that the same is true of external enclosures and 7200rpm drives. Especially when using 2.5" drives, most are 5400 RPM. He also mentioned that the interface used by externals makes a difference also. He found that upgrading his to eSATA and an Express Card made a world of difference when compared to USB 2.0.

Building our own

Over the course of the next few sections we will set out to build our own VM environment from scratch. This will be a single server environment intended for development or testing.

The process here is intended to give you a basic idea of how to build the environment but will stop short of an elaborate step by step process for all the components.

The steps are intended for someone with basic system administration / network administration skills, otherwise you might need to look for more detailed instructions online where the process is not detailed in a systematic fashion.

The process here is intended to help get you going, it is not a replacement for the Microsoft CRM Implementation Guide that provides a wealth of detail on all the setup options.

Setup Windows

In VPC2007 or Virtual Server you should setup a new virtual computer and proceed to install Windows Server. The order of the various steps is important so follow them in order.

1. If you have two or more drives in your system try to place the virtual hard drive for the virtual machine on one other than your system boot disk. This will help slightly with performance. The faster the drive the better. If you are using an external drive make sure it is faster than your internal drives.
2. Allocate as much memory as you can to the VM without causing your normal machine to slow down too much. You can set it higher during the install and it will help it run faster and then just reduce it later.
3. If you haven't done an install like this before, you will use the CD/DVD menu in Virtual PC or from the Properties page in the Virtual Server to attach the machine you created to the Windows Installation ISO file or to the Physical CD drive on your host if you are installing using physical media. The Windows Server install ISO or CD/DVD is bootable and this will allow the VM to begin the installation when started.
4. Install the O/S
5. DO NOT join this machine to your domain! We will be setting it up as a standalone domain after we install some other software.
6. Once the O/S installation is completed, connect up to the Internet and apply any updates that your O/S is eligible for.
7. Once the installation is completed, you will want to enable Remote Desktop on the virtual machine. You can find this on the My Computer -> Properties option.

Promote the Virtual Machine To a Domain Controller

The next step is to promote the server to a domain controller and install IIS.

1. You can promote the server to a domain controller using either dcpromo from the command line or using the Configure Server wizard on the Administrator menu and selecting the Domain Controller role.
   o This will setup DNS, also make sure that you remember the password for restore.
2. Install IIS either via the Add Programs or the Add Application Server role. Make sure you enable ASP.NET.

Install SQL Server

Now we need to install SQL and get it ready to handle our CRM Data.

1. Install SQL 2005 (or 2008 once it's released and supported).
2. It is best to use Standard Edition or greater.
3. Make sure you choose to install Reporting Services otherwise CRM will not pass the validation checks
4. To make it easy to work with SQL from your host, I recommend setting Mixed Mode Authentication for this install. Typically, Windows Authentication only would be a better choice if this were a production server. Using Mixed will allow you to easily connect from the host that is in a different domain.

Install Visual Studio

The next step would be to install Visual Studio if you intend to use the server for debugging using it. This is not always required but if you prefer to debug locally you will want to install it now.

Be a little more precise on the options when doing the installation of Visual Studio to your VM. There is no reason to install options that you will never use as part of your CRM development. Remember, keeping your VM hard disk size as small as possible is the goal.

MVP Tip: Microsoft MVP Guy Riddle adds that he also installs Word, Excel and Outlook so he can test other components of CRM. He also finds it useful to add Adobe Reader and a zip product. It adds a little more to the image but you will miss them if they aren't there. You can read his blog at http://guyriddle.spaces.live.com.

Install CRM

We are now ready to install CRM.

1. Copy the CRM install file to the server and expand it into a local drive. That happens when you run the ".exe" file that you downloaded.
2. If you don't have Internet access to your VPC you will need the following downloaded before you begin. If you are using the physical media for CRM these are on the DVD but not in the download install.
   - The easiest way on these is to download each and install them prior to doing the CRM install.

   - Microsoft Application Error Reporting prerequisite can be found in the \Server\DW folder inside the CRM Server directory you expanded.

   - VC++ Redistributable is a challenge because it doesn't detect that it's already installed if it is so we have to accommodate for that. To do that we will create a \Redist folder and place the install files there so CRM Setup can handle forcing an install. Download and place the files in the following folders inside where you expanded the CRM Server install files
     - <CRMInstallFileFolder>\Redist\i386\VCRedist\vcredist_x86.exe
     - <CRMInstallFileFolder>\Redist\i386\VCRedist\vcredist_x64.exe
     - <CRMInstallFileFolder>\Redist\amd64\VCRedist\vcredist_x64.exe

 *You can download the trail from the public Microsoft Downloads or you can download from MSDN as well if you are a MSDN subscriber.*

Install CRM (Continued...)

3. Inside the folder where you expanded the CRM files create an ifdconfig.xml file and add the following content. (replace $OrgName$ and $DomainName with the appropriate values).

The following is an example of the setup xml configuration file.

```
<CRMSetup>
  <Server>
    <ifdsettings enabled="true">
      <internalnetworkaddress>
          192.168.1.1-    255.255.255.255
      </internalnetworkaddress>
      <rootdomainscheme>http</rootdomainscheme>
      <sdkrootdomain>$OrgName$.$DomainName</sdkrootdomain>
      <webapplicationrootdomain>
          $OrgName$.$DomainName
      </webapplicationrootdomain>
    </ifdsettings>
  </Server>
</CRMSetup>
```

- The ifdconfig.xml will enable the Internet Facing Deployment capabilities. We want this enabled so we can test our applications using that as an option as well as Active Directory. You can disable and enable this at will by changing a registry setting, more on that later in this chapter.

- Now start the CRM install, running from a command prompt (Start – Run – cmd) the following command o   Setupserver /config ifdconfig.xml.

- Once the install has completed, your server is setup.   It's a really good idea to re-boot your VPC, even if you are not prompted to do this by CRM.

- Once rebooted, try to access the server and make sure it works correctly. Unless you specified a different URL or port other than the default you should be able to point your browser to http://localhost:5555 to verify.

Enabling IFD is not required; however, it can be very helpful to have this available for testing.

Install and Configure Loopback Network

Now that we have setup a standalone Windows Server, our next step is to build an isolated network. To accomplish this we are going to install a Loopback network adapter. Unlike a regular network adapter this network adapter will only allow communication between our host computer and the virtual machine.

On your Host Machine, not on the new server VM, perform the following.

1. Launch Add Hardware Wizard from Control Panel (From Windows Vista this is easier to find using the Classic Control Panel view). Click Next to start it.
2. Do not select Search for and install, instead select the second option – Install Hardware that I manually configure.
3. From the list, choose Network Adapters.
4. It should show you a list of Manufacturers, select Microsoft.
5. On the right side list, select Microsoft Loopback Adapter, and click next to allow it to install the adapter.
6. From the Network and Sharing Center select View Status on the newly added connection

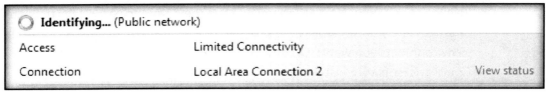

- On the dialog that shows, select Properties to modify the adapter settings.
- Select the Internet Protocol Version 4 in the list, and click Properties.
- Change the IP address to 192.168.1.2 and the DNS IP to 192.168.1.1

On the New Server VM, Not on the Host perform the following

- Change the IP Address of the Server to 192.168.1.1.

In Virtual Server or Virtual PC2007 perform the following

- On the properties for the new Virtual Machine that you created there will be a Network item. Edit that and select the Loopback Adapter.

At this point you have created an isolated network between your host and the virtual machine that we are creating. This is good as it will allow you to have a sand box that can't do things like send out e-mails to external people by accident!

Prepare for Reuse

The next set of steps are not required to be done, however will make it so if you need another VPC or kill this one by accident that you have a base copy that you can reuse. It also uses a technique called differencing disks. Differencing disks are a feature of Virtual PC/Server to allow you to start with an original VHD and then the differencing disk only stores what is different from the original. That means you can setup 10 CRM VPCs each having their own differencing disk that points to our disk we built in the above steps and all that would be stored would be the delta of the data for the drive. For example, a complete copy for each would take 7-12gb, but a differencing disk might only take 1-3gb depending on use.

1. If you would like, create a bunch of accounts for testing in the Active Directory. This will allow them to be available on all copies and will save you time later.
2. Shutdown the VPC and mark your existing VHD file read only. This will be our base image (keeping a copy of it on DVD or external drive isn't a bad idea either!).
3. Create a new Virtual Hard Drive – select type of Differencing. For the parent point to your base image that we just marked read only.
4. Now create a new Virtual Machine and use the differencing VHD (Virtual HardDrive)as its hard drive – you can repeat this process for as many developments or testing environments you want! Or after you accidentally destroy your current one with too must trial software installations – no worries just build a new one!

Using, Enabling, Disabling IFD

Using the following steps, you can access your server from the Host machine using either IFD or Active Directory.

1. To access CRM via IFD from the Host OS you will need to add the IFD URL to your hosts file (c:\windows\system32\drives\etc\hosts) and map 192.168.1.1 to $OrgName.$DomainName (or whatever you decided to call your deployment).
2. The above step should be repeated for each new organization you create if you are using the multi tenant capabilities to have multiple organizations. Multi Tenant is the new feature in CRM 4 that allows one installation of the software host multiple organizations.
3. By default with our setup, while we enabled IFD, we set a subnet mask that will treat our host as being internal and use Windows Authentication.
4. The IfdInternalNetworkAddress registry key allows us to switch that in our environment. When the caller's IP address fits inside the network IP range and subnet mask provided we will be considered internal and get the "Windows Experience" for login. This means we will use Active Directory.
5. If we modify that value to not include our Host IP then we will get the "IFD Experience" and will see the IFD login page.

This registry key can be found at the following location:

[HKEY_LOCAL_MACHINE\SOFTWARE\Microsoft\MSCRM]\"IfdInternalNetworkAddress"

Set the following values depending on how you want authentication to work.

- IFD Experience = "192.168.1.1-255.255.255.255"
- Windows Experience = "192.168.1.1-255.255.255.0"

That is the short version of toggling IFD on / off. The Implementation Guide and the IFD Setup document have much greater detail on all the options that can be setup.

Wrapping up VM Building

A big Thanks to Philip Richardson from the Microsoft CRM product team. The VM install was adapted for the book with permission from a couple of blog posts by Philip on his blog at http://www.philiprichardson.org/blog.

In this section of the chapter, we have looked at how to build out a reusable virtual machine environment that you can use as your development environment for building numerous solutions.

Test Servers

Another topic that you should spend a few minutes on your test environment. Depending on the formality in your organization, a test environment could take a number of different forms and we will only be touching on some concepts here. Your first decision really has to do with real physical servers or virtual servers. If your goal is simply functionality testing it really is not a big deal either way if you use virtual or physical machines. If you plan to do any performance or volume testing you will want to use physical servers and avoid virtual servers.

Your next decision is one server or multiple servers, each with their own role. Typically for us, when we get to testing we go the multi server route. This means separate domain controller, separate SQL Server and finally a separate server to run CRM. New in CRM 4.0 is the ability to further separate out the roles that the CRM server performs. We typically do not separate that out in test unless we are doing performance related testing.

Testing on production

One question I am often asked right after talking about the multi tenant capabilities is can we put test and production on the same install. I always nervously answer "technically yes, but....." followed by a discussion on how just because you can, does not mean you should.

I do not think it is a good idea to mix test/production because while multi tenant gives you a good amount of isolation at the data and configuration layer, it does not protect you at the O/S layer. The purpose of testing is to prove an application is ready for production and often requires hammering on the environment to work out any quirks. In addition, often you will have hotfixes or updates that update either the O/S, its associated software or CRM itself. These type of updates are best tested in an environment with your application but isolated from the production site.

I do however think that if you have the enterprise edition where you can use multi tenant it is a good idea to have a spare organization configured on the production hardware that you can use for verification. When I say spare, I'm saying basically another organization on the same CRM installation that has a different organization name but all the same customizations as your production instance installed. By verification, I mean that you can test to see if something that is not working in your production environment also does not work in another organization. That is a great way to isolate organization issue from a hardware or an operating system related issue.

Controlling Dev/Test Server E-mails

One of the new features of CRM 4.0 is the ability to have e-mail sent/received directly via Outlook rather than requiring the centralized e-mail router and an outbound SMTP host.

When this feature is enabled, e-mail activities created by the user or on behalf of the user (e.g. via plug-in or workflow) will be set in a "pending send" status until the CRM Outlook client connects and deals with sending them out. This is a great feature and I think it will work much better than having the router for a number of different deployment scenarios.

So what's the issue with e-mails on your dev or test systems? Imagine this scenario; you have a copy of production data and you're doing testing of some enhancements. Your solution uses workflow or plug-ins etc. to generate e-mails or perhaps your testers create them as part of their testing. This is especially true if sending e-mails or automated e-mails is a key part of your solution. Prior to CRM 4.0 you could simply make sure you didn't have a viable way for the e-mail to go out, e.g. point to a bad mail server. CRM 4.0 allows you to configure the install without specification of an e-mail server. This leads you to think that no e-mails can go out if I don't have an e-mail server configured right? Wrong...

Here's how this can happen. You start testing and generate a bunch of pending e-mail activities. Then, someone says "hey let's test inside Outlook and make sure things work there too!" so they or the unsuspecting network admin installs the Outlook client. Assuming that Outlook client is connected to a valid e-mail account, soon Outlook starts and the CRM Add-in connects up to the CRM server. Surprise...all those queued up e-mails will be sent. If all you had was some test e-mail addresses in the data no problem, but what if you had some valid e-mail addresses sitting around... Usually about 5-10 minutes after this happens and panic sets in "Hey Joe, did you just e-mail a buy 1 get 5 free offer out?"

How can you avoid this? Well there are a few options. First you could just use the word of mouth approach along with hope and pray and just tell people to not turn on that option. When you create CRM Users the user is configured by default to route via the CRM Outlook client. So you could go change that option to route through a nonexistent e-mail router. You could also do a mass modification of contacts, and users etc. to invalidate the e-mail addresses. That approach is not perfect either because all it takes is someone adding a new valid e-mail address and then another user sending to it. The reality is you may actually want some e-mails to go out but want to make sure it is to a "white list" of e-mail addresses.

In a normal .NET app we control this by using a common set of code to send e-mails and then it has a white list as well as an always "CC" list so we can ensure we never have an accidental e-mail leakage. Applying this same thinking to CRM 4.0 requires a little more thinking because a user could create the e-mail via the UI or it could happen from the web service.

Import Organization / Redeploy

Another common method of handling setup of a testing environment is to use a copy of a production organization and restore it to a test environment. In CRM 3.0 this was accomplished using a redeploy process. In CRM 4.0 it has changed a little and is now part of the capabilities of Deployment Manager. Inside Deployment Manager when you right click on the organization node you can select Import Organization.

Prior to using Import Organization you would perform a database backup of the production or source CRM organization database and restore it on your test SQL Server. Once you have done that, when you enter the Import Organization process you will be able to select that database from those available on the server for importing.

The Import Organization wizard will walk you through mapping user accounts that exist in the CRM database being imported. You will have a few options on how to handle the mapping including mapping users to other users in your target domain. During these initial steps, you will also specify the new organization name. Once all that is input the process will import the data and the new organization will be ready for use.

Using this approach you can pretty quickly pull data back to the test environment. If your test environment is hooked up to a viable network you may want to keep in mind some of the discussion earlier in this chapter on Test Server e-mails.

Now that CRM import/export of customizations supports additional items like reports, workflows and roles you might find some times where redeploy/import would be used you can just move the customizations between the environments.

What version of .NET

For building any server side custom code Microsoft CRM 4.0 requires all development to be done using the .NET 3.0 Framework. This would include developing plug-ins and custom workflow activities as well as ASP.NET applications, if they will be deployed in the same address space (IIS Application Pool) as the CRM code.

If you're building a standalone ASP.NET application in a separate address space or a client application, or for that matter a standalone executable / service that will just access the CRM Web Services then you don't have the same limits on the version of .NET.

CRM 4.0 and .NET 3.5 Framework released within months of each other and as a result CRM was not fully tested with .NET 3.5 at the time of initial release. The .NET 3.5 Framework release consists of new capabilities plus a hotfix to the .NET 2.0 runtime to allow it to support the new capabilities. In fact, many of what would appear to be new runtime changes are really compiler changes related to the C# or VB.NET language.

As of the release of this book, we have done CRM related work that used .NET 3.5 on the CRM server. That said, the official guidance offered by Microsoft is to use .NET 3.0 until the .NET 3.5 testing has been completed. Keep your eye out for updated information on this either on the book site or from Microsoft.

What version of Visual Studio

Visual Studio 2005 or 2008 is required if you are doing any code level development. If you are just doing client script or form customization neither is required but can be helpful as you will see later in the book. Visual Studio 2005 works fine for developing solutions however, our recommendation is to use Visual Studio 2008 if possible. A few of the key features of Visual Studio 2008 that we believe are useful.

- For client side script development JavaScript coloring and IntelliSense is supported – in fact we leverage the IntelliSense in this book's examples to customize it with the platform meta data.
- If you're building any ASP.NET customizations you can take advantage of the improved visual design features of Visual Studio 2008 like split view between source and design view.
- Multi targeting lets you use .NET 3.0 for CRM deployed components and .NET 3.5 or .NET 2.0 for other using the same tool.

- Improved debugging support

Referencing the CRM Assemblies

Several of the assemblies provided with the SDK are essential for your CRM development. You will be referencing these often when you build your applications.

Microsoft.CRM.Sdk - This assembly contains the base classes you will use for building Plug-ins, workflows and other extensions.

Microsoft.CRM.SdkTypeProxy - This assembly gives you access to the proxy classes – this is particularly important when you are accessing the CRM services or Metadata Services as the proxy classes live in this assembly. Also included are the Request / Response classes for each built-in entity and platform message.

You will notice that this assembly also includes some of the standard entity classes that the web service exposes such as contact or account. These are provided for internal use and could be removed in the future by the product team. It is recommended you use Dynamic Entities when working with the CrmService from this assembly. More on that in Chapter 9.

If you install the client for Outlook then these assemblies will be placed in the GAC on your machine. This is also true if you are developing on a server that has the CRM Server installed. Otherwise, we typically find a common location such as a folder in a project and reference these assemblies from there so it is consistent on all developers' machines.

Microsoft.CRM.Outlook.Sdk – This assembly is provided to help you if you are building solutions to run on the client and access CRM when the user is offline. Using this assembly you are able to detect the state of the Outlook add-in and know if you are on or offline. By default this assembly is not available on the server.

Referencing the Web Services

While it's possible to do all development using the type proxy classes in the CRM assemblies we just discussed and not directly referencing the CRM Web Service, you will be missing out on some of the power of the platform. One of the things that happen is as you add custom entities to the system; the CRM Web Service is dynamic and adjusts to provide an interface to your newly created custom entity. This is designed to allow you to have typed access to all the properties on your CRM custom entity.

If you are building an ISV solution or a custom solution that will work in various installations that may or may not have specific custom entities you're better accessing the CRM Services using the type proxy classes instead of referencing the Web Services. In this case you will be doing all of your work using Dynamic Entities.

One of the things you will want to do is adopt a standard name for the reference to the CRM Web Service and Metadata Service. The reason for this is simple. It just makes it more predictable and you do not have to guess what the name space will be.

Downloading the WSDL Files

New in CRM 4.0 is the ability to easily download the WSDL files for the web services. The following figure shows that you can find those off the customization menu.

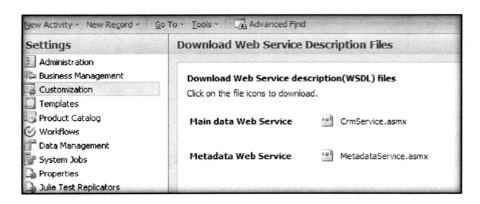

I recommend saving a copy of the WSDL to a local file ideally in your project that will be version controlled. That way you can keep a history of prior WSDL files if needed.

Referencing with Visual Studio 2005

Referencing the web services is pretty simple using Visual Studio 2005. From the project you will be referencing from select Add Web Reference as you see in the following figure.

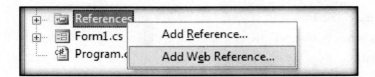

You should then see the following dialog that will prompt you for the URL of the web service. It's not obvious but if you did store the WSDL on your local file system you can give a file path like "c:\mywsdl.wsdl" instead of a URL.

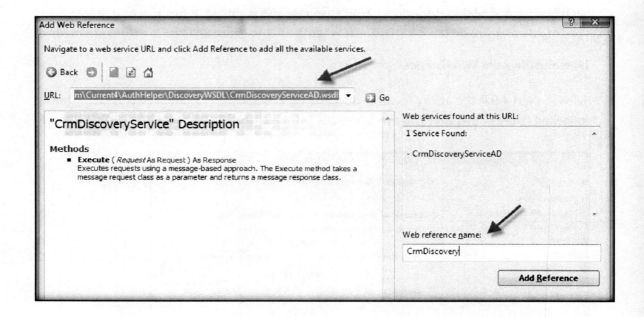

Before you click Add Reference you will want to modify the name of the web reference to be something meaningful. For example, by default it tried to name the discovery service "WebReference". As you can see we changed that to be CrmDiscovery which simply gives a more meaningful name to reference later.

The process would be the same for doing references to the CrmService as well as the MetadataService.

Referencing Web Services with Visual Studio 2008
Since Visual Studio 2008 supports multi targeting of the framework version it is possible to use Visual Studio 2008 for doing CRM development. If you are doing that and using a target

framework of 3.0 or below, the experience of adding a web reference for the CRM service or Metadata service are similar to what you would do in Visual Studio 2005. If you're using .NET 3.5 as the target framework when you right click on references and are looking for the "Add Web Reference" menu item you might be surprised to not find it. Instead you see a new "Add Service Reference" menu option. That's because Visual Studio 2008 introduces a lot of new features, one of which is improved tooling for managing and configuring Windows Communication Foundation (WCF). Since the CRM web services are ASP.NET ASMX services you need to handle adding the reference a little different.

The following example shows the Add Service dialog.

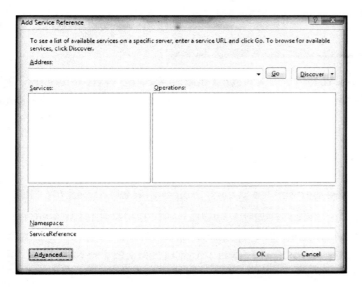

If you were to proceed with the above dialog, it would work and add the reference but you would likely find yourself with a set of class proxies that don't match any of the SDK documentation or examples. To add a Web Reference to the Web Service that CRM exposes you need to do a couple more steps.

When you select the advance button you will see the following..

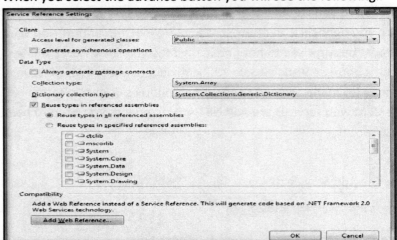

At the bottom of the Advanced Settings dialog you will see a button for Add Web Reference. By clicking on that button you will see a familiar page that allows you to add the reference the same way you did in Visual Studio 2005.

Using a Common Project for References

You can certainly do the reference to the web service in each project that will access the CRM services; however, you might want to strongly consider creating a common project to share. Using this approach you create a new project in Visual Studio that will exists for the sole purpose of holding the web reference. Then later as you build other projects that need to reference the web service you simply reference this common project. Because web references expose as public classes you will have visibility to the CRM services.

This approach is also helpful as we talk about helper classes that the SDK provides because you can add them to this common project as well. Later in this chapter we will be discussing building a full solution file that will contain the multiple projects that you will work with in building a solution, keep in mind this approach and add that to your list of projects to create.

TIP

This common project makes a great place to also store any common logic for accessing the CRM platform and performing common processing.

CRM helper Classes

One of the features that was enhanced in the CRM 4.0 SDK is some additional C# helper classes that make the platform web services easier to use. These helpers leverage some of the newer language features that were not available in .NET 1.1 such as partial classes. Using partial classes, the helpers augment the web services adding things like name indexed properties that are not possible to do with just a standard web reference.

The helper classes are located in the SDK under the <sdkroot>/server/helpers/cs folder. Copy the files from that folder into your project. If you are using the common project to hold the reference as we recommended earlier in the chapter you will only need to do this once.

Once the files are copied into your project you will need to modify the namespace that is used in the files. The reason for this is for the partial classes to work, they must have the same namespace as the Web Reference you added. The Web Reference will have a namespace of <ProjectName> .<web reference name> . The web reference name is whatever you input when you added the reference for the name. So if you used CrmSdk and your project name was MyCRMServiceLib then you would change the namespaces from Microsoft.Crm.Sdk to MyCRMServiceLib.CrmSdk using replace all or replace all in files option in Visual Studio.

Installing the CRM Debug Visualizers

One of the samples that is provided in the book sample code is a Debug Visualizer specifically designed to work with some of the CRM data types like Dynamic Entities. Using this you will be more productive at debugging problems. We will explore the full capabilities in Chapter 25, but here we will focus on installing the visualizers.

 In case you are not familiar with Debug Visualizers they basically are custom code you can create that interacts with the debugger and allows you to examine data. When you build a custom one you can make it understand your custom application types. The following is an example of the Dynamic Entity Visualizer and how it looks in Visual Studio.

```
DynamicEntity entity = new DynamicEntity("contact");
CTCDEPropHelper.AddStringProperty(entity, "FirstName", "John");
CTCDEPropHelper.AddStringProperty(entity, "LastName", "Doe");
```
⊞ ☑ entity 🔍 ▾ {Microsoft.Crm.Sdk.DynamicEntity}

✓ Dynamic Entity Visualizer

To install the CRM Debug Visualizer you should open up the code samples from the book and look in the Assemblies folder. Copy the CRMDebugVisualizers.dll assembly to the folder for your version of Visual Studio.

Typically the following are the folders for version 2005 and 2008.

```
C:\Users\<your user Name>\Documents\Visual Studio 2005\Visualizers
```

```
C:\Users\<your user name>\Documents\Visual Studio 2008\Visualizers
```

Once you have done that you should be able to use the Debug Visualizers. In Chapter 25 we go into detail on how to use each of the visualizers provided.

Simple debug visualizers are not that hard to create and are a great way to make debugging more productive. Creating additional ones for the CRM specific types or more complex objects you use internally can pay back quickly.

Managing and Tracking Customizations

Depending on what type of customizations you are doing to the platform, you will have to make some decisions on how to manage the changes. Version control or tracking of customizations is not a feature that CRM provides. It does provide a few hooks and places to help with the process but for the most part it's up to you to implement your own processes and procedures to track customizations.

The extent to which you formalize the tracking depends on the type of solution you are building. The following illustrates the progression from an internal solution designed for internal use to the other end of the spectrum which would be an ISV (Independent Software Vendor) solution.

Often times for internal solutions, having a more informal process is typical and that is leveraged to allow the platform to be more nimble and facilitate rapid development. As you move to the other end of ISV solutions, the need becomes more critical to have repeatable processes and a concept of a "release". In that case being more formal about change tracking and how customizations are managed becomes critical.

While there is no single answer on the best approach here are some ideas on the various types of customizations and where you might want to store them.

Customization Type	Where / How
Data Entities, Form and Layout	Having one master server works well for this and allows a central point of change. Often times depending on team size you may want to appoint a librarian or keeper of all or certain entities. In Chapter 4, we discuss using the Description field to track a version number for the entity.
JavaScript for Form Events	Store this in a Visual Studio Team Project with version control – so you can not only track changes but also take advantage of the improved editing capabilities. We will explore more of this in the upcoming chapter on scripting. This allows for easy viewing of history and details on changes.
SiteMap/ISVConfig	Store these in the same Team Project as JavaScript but in a separate folder. This ensures consistent navigation each time deployed. You will need to refrain from making some changes in the web editor for this to work – this is not ideal for informal, but recommended for ISV solutions.
Plugins/Workflow Activities and other Code related items	In the Team Project, we will break that out more in detail later in the chapter, these should be version controlled. To allow for easy deployment, they should be in their own class libraries.

Customization Type	Where / How
Reports	Reports built with the Report Wizard are best stored as part of your master server. But those that are customized in Visual Studio should be in a report project as part of your Visual Studio projects.
Security Roles	Best kept in the master server – and moved around via import/export.
Workflows – Web Created	Best kept in a master server and moved around via import/export.

In the next section of the chapter, we will elaborate more on the Visual Studio Project concept and what project types you might use.

Setting Up a Team Project

Like most things in life, there is usually not just one right way to do things and setting up a project for working with a team is certainly no exception. The ideas presented here are just to give you an idea of how you might want to organize and manage source control in your project.

Let's first cover our requirements.

- Must be able to use Visual Studio 2005 or greater
- Must be able to support managing one or more Visual Studio Project types
- Must be able to integrate with some type of Source Control

Let's cover our nice to haves.

- Source Control structured so we can branch (create versions) as we evolve
- Have ability to automate our building of our software

In the example we are going to walk through here, we are going to use Visual Studio 2008 and use Team Foundation Server for our source code control.

Since we are going to use Team System for our source control, we have created a new Team System Project called CTCRECRM. Do not confuse the Team System project with a Visual Studio project, as they are separate concepts. Team System projects are designed to be a container for Source Control, Work Items (Bug / Issue Tracker), Document Repository (SharePoint), Team Builds and more. We won't go into detail about how Team System works anymore than is necessary for you to understand this project's organization.

Creating the Solution

The first thing we do after we create the Team Project is establish some folders in our source control tree to store our project files. To enable branching of our code as we do development we typically create a high-level folder that will be the container for all our project files so we can branch at that level if we want. In our example, we are creating a Current and a Released folder. Current will contain our active development baseline and Released will be our baseline that will contain our released files once we go live. Code will be promoted from the Current folder to the Released folder as we deploy to the live system. The following shows what our source control tree looks like at this point.

In the example, the branching folders of Current and Released are just examples. More complex projects or products can have additional folders added to allow multiple versions to be tracked.

The strategy you use for organizing your projects really depends on if you are building an internal solution or an external product. Internal solutions typically won't have to support as many active releases that are deployed out at customer sites that might need quick fixes. On the other hand, even for internal solutions it's good to give a little extra thought to how your code might be used.

You may find after some thought that certain parts of your code will be reusable by other CRM projects and should be separated out and referenced. Keep in mind it's easier to start out with a little extra organization and projects than it is to have to try to separate one project into multiple projects later. One thing to be aware of is too many projects and too much organization can be cumbersome to the developers and slow things down. The key is to find the right mix that gives you flexibility without adding too much overhead due to a complex project structure.

Next, in Visual Studio, navigate to the File - > New Project dialog and you should see the dialog we see in the figure. We are going to expand the "Other Project Types" category because that is where they have hidden the creation of blank solutions.

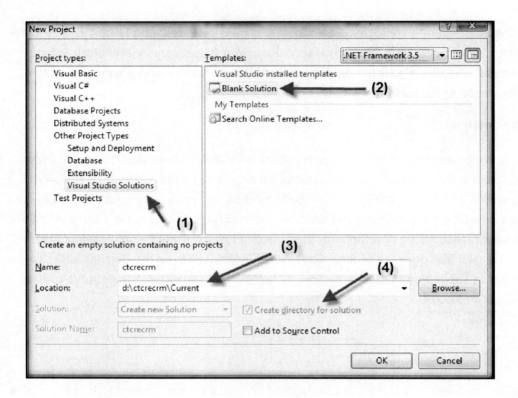

1. Expand Other Project Types, Select Visual Studio Solutions.
2. Select the Blank Solution, this template creates us an empty solution file because we are going to add our own projects to it.
3. For the location select the folder where you have "got latest" from source control of the Current folder.
4. Notice we cannot keep it from creating a directory for the solution. This typically drives me nuts because I really don't want another layer deep, so I normally cheat here and let it create the folder because I don't have a choice and then go move the solution file back to the Current folder and then I create all my projects based in the Current Folder and they become sub folders.

Next, I normally close the solution using the File -> Close Solution and I proceed to move the ctcrecrm.sln file from the new folder it created to the current folder and then delete the solution folder it created. I do this just because otherwise it creates an unnecessary layer. In reality, I want the .sln file to end up in the root of the Current folder and all my projects I create to fall nicely under the current folder in their own subfolders.

```
Directory of D:\CTCRECRM\Current

11/18/2007  01:27 PM    <DIR>          .
11/18/2007  01:27 PM    <DIR>          ..
11/18/2007  01:27 PM    <DIR>          ctcrecrm
               0 File(s)              0 bytes
               3 Dir(s)  45,098,463,232 bytes free

D:\CTCRECRM\Current>move ctcrecrm\ctcrecrm.sln ctcrecrm.sln
        1 file(s) moved.

D:\CTCRECRM\Current>rd ctcrecrm /s
ctcrecrm, Are you sure (Y/N)? y

D:\CTCRECRM\Current>
```

Next, if I re-open up the ctcrecrm.sln file from the current folder I will want to add it to source control. To do that I select the File -> Source Control – Add Solution to Source Control menu option.

Adding Web Site to Store CRM Customizations

In Chapter 5, we will discuss in detail how to use a web project for storing customizations so I will not go in to great detail now. The idea here is that the web project can act as a container to store, and version control your customizations such as JavaScript files and isv.config type files. Since the web project template already offers a new item template for xml and JavaScript files it is the best choice. It also is setup if you want to create some test pages to experiment with how your JavaScript will work. To add this project you will do a Right Click on the solution file in the Solution Explorer and click Add ->New Web Site. On the dialog that comes up I recommend picking the Empty web project because we don't plan on using any of the files the other templates create. Typically, we will call this web project CRMCustomizations so it's clear what its intent is.

Adding Web Site to Store CRM Custom ASP.NET pages

If you plan to do any custom ASP.NET pages to use with your CRM site, you will want to create another web type project to hold those files. You want to keep them separate from your customizations. You can choose between a Web Site, which is just a folder, and a Web Application, which has a project file similar to Visual Studio 2003. We typically will name this project CRMWeb.

Later in the deployment chapter we will discuss how to add a Web Deployment Project where you will setup the assembly name to be more specific so you don't collide with other applications when deployed.

You also should keep in mind, that since you will likely be running in the CRM web scope, you will want to ensure your pages have a namespace added and not just depend on using the global namespace that is the default when adding new pages to a web folder project. If you use the global and anyone else deploys an application that also depended on global you will have a name conflict with the Default class existing in more than one assembly. To avoid that simply make sure your pages have a fully qualified namespace that is unique to your project.

Adding Common Class Library Project

I always end up with some common code I want to share. Every time I skip the step of creating a common library I always end up regretting it and going back and creating it and moving my common code to it. A common class library will give you a place to store reusable code and encourage creation in there instead of inline in a project file where it can't be shared. I typically recommend creating one project file that is common to the project / product you are creating and another that is intended to be used across projects / products.

Adding Plug-in Class Library Project

If you plan to have plug-ins as part of your project, you will want to create a separate class library project file to support them. The reason for this is typically for production deployment you will deploy this project file into the CRM Database. Therefore, there is no reason you want to have a bunch of extra code as part of this assembly that is created and registered with CRM.

From the dialog, select a new Class library. You might want to include Plugin in the name so you know what it is when you are looking at your project in solution explorer.

Adding Project for No Code Workflow

We will talk about this in more detail in the workflow chapters; however, if you plan to do workflows in Visual Studio you need to make a few decisions. If your workflows are going to be deployable to CRM Online as well as on-premise, they need to be "No Code" workflows. If your target is only on-premise, you can have workflows that have custom activities and both can have custom code as part of them.

In our example, we are going to setup both, so we will create two separate projects to be clear where we are suppose to maintain and develop each type.

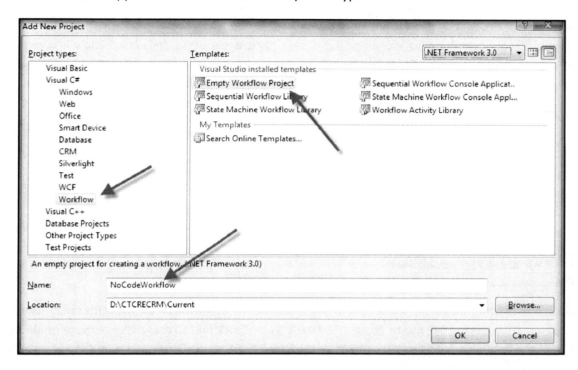

As you can see above there are a few different types of templates. There is not one specifically for a No Code workflow project so the easiest is to pick the Empty Workflow Project.

Official support for no-code workflows built in Visual Studio has not been released - the core components are in the platform just hasn't been through complete release testing. Building Custom Workflow Activities is fully supported and discussed in details in later chapters.

Adding Project for Custom Code Workflow

If you are going to be building any custom activities or workflows that include managed code, you will want a place to store them. Technically, you could store them as part of your Plug-in class library but for clarity, we think putting them in their own assembly is cleaner. For example, you might create another empty workflow project and name it CRMWorkflow. Notice I do not call it just Workflow because what happens if later you decide you want to do some non-CRM workflow as part of the solution.

Where are we?

So if we were to look now in Solution explorer we would see that we had created 6 projects to support our product or project we are working on. This gives us some good isolation so if different team members are working on different parts we are less likely to collide with their efforts. You can see from the following figure what solution explorer should look like with our projects.

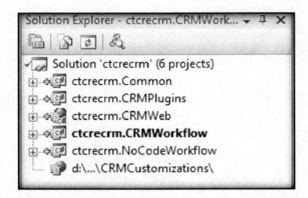

Notice that while we named some of the projects initially Common or CRMPlugins in Solution Explorer they are prefixed with "ctccre.". That's a little trick I do to make things more readable. I want the folder to be called CRMPlugin or Common but I want the project namespace , assembly and project file to be qualified with the namespace for clarity and to avoid collisions with other projects.

 Imagine if everyone named something Common and produced an assembly Common.dll how high the risk of collision is. To accomplish this after the project is added I rename the project file in Solution Explorer and I modify the project name space and assembly defaults on the project properties page before I check it in for the first time. Again, this is not required but something I do to make it cleaner and more clear what you are working with in a large solution. There are other options like leaving the name alone and modifying the name space.

Now with our projects setup, our source control established we are prepared to being development and can easily share our projects with a number of team members. In the chapters that follow, we will be discussing more about how to use each of these projects and how they are deployed to a production environment.

It is important to keep in mind that the project structure presented here represents a single idea and not a directive on how it should be done. In fact, there probably isn't a single right way to organize solutions and projects within them because of how much it depends on the team, the project and the organization that is building the solution. The important thing is to adopt some structure that works for you and your team.

Automating with Snippets

Code Snippets are a great way to package up things you do all the time so just a few keystrokes can be used to add code to your application. If you haven't heard of Snippets they were new in Visual Studio 2005 and have continued to be used to make it easier to do simple tasks.

An example of a common snippet is the property snippet. By typing prop <tab><tab> in to the Visual Studio editor while editing a source file it will walk you through creating a property in a class.

What might not be as obvious is that you can create your own snippets for your custom code. While there are not currently any CRM specific snippets included in the CRM 4.0 SDK, you can create your own library.

In our sample files, we have included a couple to get you going inside a web folder project named CRMSnippets. We have added a few examples to get you started.

Before you can use snippets you must register or import them into Visual Studio. To accomplish that use the Snippet Manager from the tools menu

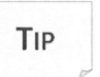

You can also use the Ctrl+K, Ctrl+B key sequence to bring up the snippet manager if the menu option isn't showing. That menu option will not always show depending on your settings you chose when you first started Visual Studio.

From the Snippet Manager select Add and navigate to the sample files folder CRMSnippets and click Select Folder. You will now see the folders added.

Using the Snippets

Using the snippets is easy. You can use the shortcut if one is assigned to the snippet. In our example the Auth snippet, which is designed to help you connect to CRM, we assigned a short cut of crmauth. So when we type in the editor crmauth <tab> <tab> we get the following inserted into our source code.

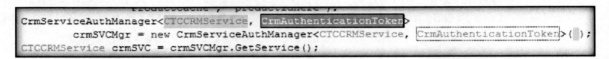

```
CrmServiceAuthManager<CTCCRMService, CrmAuthenticationToken>
        crmSVCMgr = new CrmServiceAuthManager<CTCCRMService, CrmAuthenticationToken>();
CTCCRMService crmSVC = crmSVCMgr.GetService();
```

The highlighted areas require us either to overtype them with the correct values or tab past them to indicate the value should keep the default.

Not good at remembering the shortcut keys? Don't worry you can right click and select Insert Snippet from the menu and then you will see the following to help guide you to the CRM snippets.

Once you click CRMSnippets, all the snippets in the folder will be there to choose from as you can see in the following example.

Regardless of which approach you took, shortcut or insert snippet, what is put into the source code is the same.

Building your own snippets

A complete discussion of snippet building is well beyond the scope of the book. However , we wanted to give you an example of how easy it really is to do one. As you will see in the source example of our snippet – they are just XML files.

Visual Studio comes out of the box with a bunch of Snippets and you can download a number of them from the Internet community sites to add on for common items. Similar to how Visual Studio settings work, they don't automatically share with a team – so when you start thinking about building some custom snippets you should also identify a location such as a common project to store them in.

There's not a specific Visual Studio Project Template for creating a library of Snippets – but using a simple Empty Web folder will work fine because then you get XML Intellisense as well as the ability to version control the snippet files.

Snippets are simply XML that explain to Visual Studio what to do when the snippet is invoked. At the top of the snippet is the header where you basically put the author information along with the title and description that will be used to explain how the snippet can be used.

Also in the header is the shortcut. This shortcut is what lets us do the crmauth <tab><tab> earlier. You will notice in the markup the actual shortcut is crmauthgetservice but since nothing else matched to crmauth it was able to resolve that for us.

As you start building your own snippets try to find names that are easy to remember but also try to keep them from conflicting with other existing snippets.

The following is an example of the xml required to build our auth helper snippet we used in our prior example.

```xml
<?xml version="1.0" encoding="utf-8" ?>
<CodeSnippets
xmlns="http://schemas.microsoft.com/VisualStudio/2005/CodeSnippet">
      <CodeSnippet Format="1.0.0">
            <Header>
                  <Title>crmauthgetservice</Title>
                  <Shortcut>crmauth</Shortcut>
                  <Description>Code snippet for an automatically
implemented get of crm service</Description>
                  <Author>We Speak You Learn, LLC</Author>
                  <SnippetTypes>
                        <SnippetType>Expansion</SnippetType>
                  </SnippetTypes>
            </Header>
            <Snippet>
                  <Declarations>
                        <Literal>
                              <ID>CrmServiceType</ID>
                              <ToolTip>CRM Service type</ToolTip>
                              <Default>CTCCRMService</Default>
                        </Literal>
                        <Literal>
                              <ID>CrmAuthTokenType</ID>
                              <ToolTip>Auth Token type</ToolTip>
                              <Default>CrmAuthenticationToken</Default>
                        </Literal>
                        <Literal>
                              <ID>ConnectionInfo</ID>
                              <ToolTip>Optional Connection
Info</ToolTip>
                              <Default></Default>
                        </Literal>
                  </Declarations>
                  <Code Language="csharp">
                        <![CDATA[CrmServiceAuthManager<$CrmServiceType$,
$CrmAuthTokenType$>
                        crmSVCMgr = new
CrmServiceAuthManager<$CrmServiceType$,
$CrmAuthTokenType$>($ConnectionInfo$);
                        $CrmServiceType$ crmSVC =
crmSVCMgr.GetService();]]>
                  </Code>
            </Snippet>
</CodeSnippet></CodeSnippets>
```

As you can tell, snippets are pretty straight forward to build. As you start thinking about how to keep everyone on the team doing things the same way, consider snippets as a technique you can leverage to help out.

Import/Export Customizations

Assuming you have one CRM server that acts as the master for customizations – import/export is one way to move them to other developers local machines , test or production. Import/Export allows you to pull the data model, the web form and view layout, workflows, reports, security roles ad extract them to a zip file. The contents of the zip file is a xml file named customizations.xml. You can export one or several entities at a time depending on the export option you choose. Export is located at Settings -> Customizations -> Export Customizations.

You can save yourself and others some time by using helpful names to indicate what is in the file that you exported. Sure you could open it up later and try to figure it out, but if it's all customizations then just put that in the name. Remember, you may end up with several of these files lying around and the more you know about its contents and creator the better.

In a dispersed team or where you have outside consultants or partners you may find yourself e-mailing and otherwise moving these files around. I have seen numerous scheme's for encoding the name of the file so you know what's in it, some type of version number or other useful bits of information. One example might be MyOrg-AllCust-1-11-08.zip. In the name I have indicated the org name, the contents and when.

Using the zip file, you can re-import that into the target CRM server. The following are some things to keep in mind about the Import process that are important.

- Import is cumulative – meaning that it will not remove entities or attributes from the target system just because they aren't in the import file.
- If you need to remove entities or attributes, you need to remove it using the web client, or the Metadata API.
- Things like Forms and Views are replaced – there's no partial on them. So if the import file removes a bunch of attributes from a form or view that another person had added the last one in wins.
- Less is better than more, meaning if you can import one or two entities that's less risky and less likely to make hard to find problems than just doing an import of all customizations.

That should get you started with Import /Export, and we will be discussing customizations again in the deployment chapter.

Wrapping it up

Taking the time to make sure that not only your individual development environment is setup for your team can save a lot of time on your project. A lot of the things discussed in this chapter can be addressed and solved using multiple approaches. Many of these approaches are personal choice and not a one size fits all solution. Use the suggestions in this chapter to help you develop your own best practices that you evolve and use on all your projects.

4

Data Modeling

In this chapter, we will discuss how to use the data modeling capabilities of the platform to layout how data will be managed for your solution. It is important for developers to understand how this works as the following chapters will build on and use this data and the model we build. Under the covers, Microsoft Dynamics CRM 4.0 stores all data in Microsoft SQL Server providing a layer of abstraction shielding developers and business analyst from low-level data modeling complexity.

We will start this chapter discussing some fundamentals of how the platform manages and works with data and some of the terms that are important. We will then move on to how to create custom definitions for both entities and attributes. Then using those building blocks we will explore the different entity relationship types and how they can be used to model your real life situations. Our final stop will be a deep dive into how things work under the covers in Microsoft SQL Server so you can have an understanding of what is going on behind the scenes.

Don't load up SQL Studio yet, as most of the work we will be doing in this chapter will be done using the web client. The web client allows for managing the data model for the platform instance using the Settings-> Customization menu area. Using these pages we will be able to manage the out of box definitions and the custom ones we build.

Basic Concepts

Before we get too far, let's get some basic concepts out of the way. If we were discussing data modeling for a database, we would be talking about tables and columns. From a CRM platform perspective the equivalent to a table is an Entity and the entity has Attributes. Attributes are the same as columns in database tables. They define the characteristics for the data elements that will be stored as part of the Entity. In some cases, CRM will physically store multiple columns in the SQL database for a single Attribute. An example of where that would be the case is attributes of type money. In this case CRM creates two columns on the physical SQL table, one for the base currency and one for the transaction currency. If this is the first money attribute, a column is also added to track the currency for the record. This allows CRM to provide multi currency support without burdening that on the developer directly. When a user interacts with the platform user interface, each Entity has a form associated with it. When the user saves the form, the platform creates a record for the given Entity in the database.

To further paint the picture of what an Entity is, an entity is a template for a specific type of record. An entity is a definition that includes all the attributes, forms, views and other related items that make up what is called an Entity from a CRM platform point of view. So for a developer an Entity is roughly analogous to a Class. An **Entity *instance*** is an object. An object saved to the database is a record.

All access to the data is done through the client user interface, the web service API or using what is referred to as Filtered Views. Filtered Views are normal Microsoft SQL Server views that are created and maintained by the platform. The view exposed is a view that ensures consistent data security. Developers typically will use the Filtered Views for reports where they are retrieving a lot of data from the platform. Most interactive or business logic extensions that developers will code will do all their data access using the web service API. Direct access to data stored in SQL Server by developer code is unsupported and definitely not recommended.

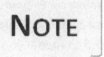

If you were to directly access the database, you would be bypassing any plug-ins registered and all of the platform security. Additionally, as Microsoft evolves the platform you are more likely to break if they make a change to the physical database implementation.

Each entity defined to the platform also has forms and views and attribute mappings associated with it. From a form perspective, the most common form that a developer will modify is the main form. This form is shown to the user to allow input, modification and viewing of the entity's attributes. Developers can modify the contents of the form to add tabs and arrange how the attributes are shown. A complete discussion of form design and editing is not included in this book as it is pretty straight forward.

Views define what attributes are shown when a user is viewing a list of records for the entity. Views can be either system views or user views, meaning that users can also define their own views of the data. A typical reason for doing that is to have custom filters to show things like Top Accounts or Active Accounts.

MVP Tip: Microsoft CRM MVP Nythya Balasubramanian added that if you're trying to customize a view but can't select a column from the list displayed you should add 'about:blank' to your Trusted Sites list in Internet Explorer. Nythya's blog can be found at niths.wordpress.com.

New in CRM 4.0 is the ability to include attributes from related entities. Take where you have created a relationship from Account to Contact to indicate the Primary Contact. In a view you could include fields from the Primary Contact in a view created on the Account entity.

Attribute mappings exist to make it easier when a user is creating an instance of an entity that is a child to another entity. It allows fields to be pre-filled based on the data that is on the parent entity. This mapping only occurs when the record is created by navigating from the associated view because this gives the context to know what the parent record is.

When you are adding and removing entities and attributes, it is important to note that these changes occur immediately. This means that if there is existing data stored for those items it will be removed and it is not an undoable operation. There is a confirm delete to help you from shooting yourself in the foot In the case of attributes if they are in use on a form or view, you must remove that attribute from the form prior to being able to delete the attribute. The exception to the immediate rule is forms and views, changes to these items only happen when you click on the publish operation.

Custom Entity vs. Custom Database

One of the choices you will need to make when you customize or build add-ons to work with the platform is where to store custom data. For example, if you built a custom ASP.NET page to integrate and add some custom features and it required some configuration data – where would you store that configuration data? Often times the immediate reaction is you need to create a separate database to store the data and not in the platform as custom entity.

Later in this chapter we will have a full discussion of custom entities but with all the capabilities in CRM 4.0, including offline access using the API, the reasons for creating a separate SQL

Database for custom processing becomes less desirable. By having separate databases developers are required to create their own access methods as well as administrators are now required to manage another database. You would also need to handle any multi tenant support in your separate database. Strong consideration should be given to using custom entities.

> **TIP**
>
> *Using a custom entity you are able to take advantage of activities, notes, attachments, mail merge and more. This includes the full data access that is dynamically added to the web service for your custom entity.*

How to change the Data Model

There are three ways to alter the data model of the organization. Most important is do not go directly into SQL Server and perform modifications to the data structures unless instructed by Microsoft Support. Making those types of changes will most likely cause your system to stop functioning correctly.

The following are the supported ways to change the data model.

Technique	Description
Web Editor	Using the CRM web Interface via the settings - > customizations section you can modify the data model using a series of web forms that we will discuss in more detail in this chapter. This method is typically used to establish the initial data model and for ongoing maintenance. This can be done by any user that has been given the customization security role.
Import/Export	Most of the data model can be exported to a compressed zip file that contains an xml file using the settings -> customizations -> export customizations menu item. This produces a file of the selected items that can be later imported into another CRM organization. This is often used to move changes between a development and a test/ production type environment. We will be discussing this option in detail in Chapter 24 when we talk in detail about deployment.
Metadata API	New to CRM 4.0 is the ability to use the Metadata API to manipulate the metadata in addition to simply being able to query it. This technique is typically targeted to ISVs that will be installing their solution repeatedly. Unlike the import technique, the Metadata API can be used to automate the removal of items from the data model. You are also not able to

manipulate the forms for the entity using the Metadata API currently. We will cover technique of using the Metadata API in detail in Chapter 8.

If you need a place to store your own tables and other custom database objects and are not using CRM entities for them, use a separate database.

What comes out of the box

When you install CRM, or when you provision a new organization, an initial set of entities are created for you by the installation or organization provisioning process. These entities that are created are the core system entities that either support the basic operation of the platform or are entities that would be typically found in a CRM solution.

The following table has some of the core system entities that are used to support the basic operation of the platform and therefore you should be familiar with what they are.

Entity Name	Description
Async Operation	This entity is used behind the scenes to track Plug-in and Workflow execution – You will not be updating this directly but might want to browse its contents for debug or more creatively to use it to detect change in data. More on that later in the CRM Online chapter where we use it to drive an external workflow.
Entity Name	Description
BusinessUnit	The Business Unit entity is used to model real world organization structure. It is used in combination with the security roles to help partition access to data in the platform. Each User in the system is

	assigned to a single Business Unit. The Business Unit entity is not currently customizable.
Currency	Currency in which a financial transaction is carried out. This entity is used to store information about currencies configured to the organization and their current exchange rate. If you add a Money field to any entity in the system an automatic system relationship will be built from that entity to the Currency entity. The schema name (internal name you will use when programming with the API) for this entity is transactioncurrency.
ISV Config	This represents the isvconfig customizations; it stores things like what to show on an edit page for a given custom entity including custom buttons and menu items. The contents stored in the ISVConfig entity are changeable, but the entity itself is not customizable. More details on ISV Config later in this chapter.
Organization	Top level of the business hierarchy. The organization can be a specific business, holding company, or corporation. It has a ton of attributes assigned to it that deal with system configuration options for that organization. Everything from the next invoice number to the xml that is used for the Site Map. This is not a customizable entity so you can't add more to it, if you need system level configuration settings you will need to store them in your own custom entity.
Queue	Queue is a powerful entity that gets involved in the handling of work. You can use a queue to route inbound e-mail. For example, using the e-mail router you can have e-mail pulled from Exchange or Pop e-mail accounts and placed in the queue without user intervention.
Entity Name	**Description**
Role	Grouping of security privileges. Each role has a name, and exists within a business unit. Roles cascade down though lower business units and can be assigned to users in any of the children business units. Each role has a dynamic set of permissions that expand as you customize the system with new custom entities. Users are assigned roles which give

	them cumulative access to system services and data.
User	This is the user in the system. Often you will use this to set the ownerID of a record. It also plays heavily into the security model determining if the user has the ability to read or modify data. A user exists inside a business unit and has roles, both of which work together along with record ownership to determine a users data rights. The schema name for this entity is systemuser.

In addition to these, there are a number of other entities provisioned as part of the organization setup that are more solution related and depending on the type of solution you need you may or may not find them helpful.

Nothing says that you have to use them and you can hide them using platform security if you want to not use them or to create your own variation. There are 50-60 entities initially created so a complete discussion of all of the entities is beyond the scope of this book. The SDK is your best reference for getting more detailed information on each of the built-in. Check out the Entity Model section in the SDK.

The following table lists some of the common out of the box entities that have special capabilities and their purpose.

Entity Name	Description
Account	Account represents the company you are working with and is often called Company. But like others you can re-purpose it to have other meanings like Hospital, School or anything else that has meaning in the organization.

Entity Name	Description
Contact	Used to represent a person at a company or account that you interact with. This can be re-purposed to be all kinds of things like Students, Parents , Client or whatever makes sense in the organization vocabulary.

Lead	Lead is intended to be someone who has interest in your offerings but you do not yet have a relationship with. It's used to track early interest, for example those guys that come to your trade show booth and say "mail me some more info". Lead is different than opportunity because a Lead is typically someone you don't know commonly called a Prospect. For example, if you got a list of trade show attendees you might import them as Leads and then further qualify them before promoting them to contacts. Leads typically do not appear on an organizations sales pipeline.
Opportunity	This is used in the sales process to represent a tangible opportunity that you are chasing. Think of it as the deal the car sales person is working with you on to get you to buy your new car. It might have a lot of history of his activities trying to inform you on the cars they have and learning what you want and don't want all associated with the concept that "You want a Car". In this example "You want a car" is the opportunity and the opportunity tracks the sales person's efforts to win the sale. Remember you can rename it, so if Want/Need or something else makes sense in your solution just change the name. Opportunities make up your sales pipeline and a subset of those will be your forecast for sales.

Activities

Another set of built in entities are provided to help with tracking and managing activities. Out of the box, the platform supports the following type of activities (appointment, service activity,email, fax, letter, phone call, and task). These activities can be related to your main data entities using a concept referred to by the platform as "regarding". By setting the regarding on an activity you cause a relationship to be created to the item regarded.

When you create a custom entity, you have the option of enabling activities. When you first create the custom entity, you have the option to turn off this feature. After that, there is no easy, supported method of enabling this. In general, if you think you might use this capability you are best to enable it. Often times, you will find that you thought it was not needed but find out later that you needed it enabled. When you turn on the option (more on that later) it creates a relationship between the activities and your entity for you.

Activities are special in that they all inherit fields from a common parent entity called ActivityPointer. This special inheritance is only supported and used on the activity entities. When you create a task, an e-mail or any of the other activity type entities you are creating a row in the ActivityPointer entity as well in the specific task or e-mail entity. This special inheritance relationship is important to understand because you will need to use it at times when retrieving data.

Activity types are fixed, meaning you cannot create your own special task or other activity that uses the same inheritance model. You can however, rename the display side of any of the existing activities to be used for your own purpose. For example, you could rename Letter to be called Status Report

ActivityPointer itself is not customizable, but you can however modify each of the inherited activity types. You can customize the views for ActivityPointer which are used when displaying lists of all different types of activities. Each activity can be customized to add fields and customize the forms/views. For example, if you wanted to add an attribute like Billable to each activity, you can't just add it to ActivityPointer you would have to add it to Task, E-Mail, Letter, etc., each individually.

Another thing related to Activities that is important to understand is their role in the integration with Outlook. When the Outlook add-in is used users can be enabled to have their activities show up and synchronize with their Outlook calendar, tasks etc. Using this capability is a powerful way to integrate the data from CRM to the user's day to day workspace.

Data from Outlook can also easily flow to CRM using the Track In CRM feature. For example, while reading an e-mail a user could decide to track it in CRM and associate it with a Contact, Account or really any custom entity you create and turn activities on for. What happens then is CRM takes a copy of that E-mail and makes it a CRM E-mail Activity and relates it using a relationship to the Account or Contact. After completed, if you were to look at the history of activities for that Contact or Account you would see that e-mail in the list.

Customizable Entities

A number of the out of the box entities can be customized to add additional attributes or modify labels to make them more appropriate for the application that you're building. You can also find all the entities that are customizable by using the drop down on the Settings-Customization-Customize Entities list. You can find a table in SDK documentation that lists all the out of the box entities that are customizable and what aspects of them you can modify. The following is an example of that list and you can see on the column type that it shows customizable on many of them. Of course your custom entities are fully customizable.

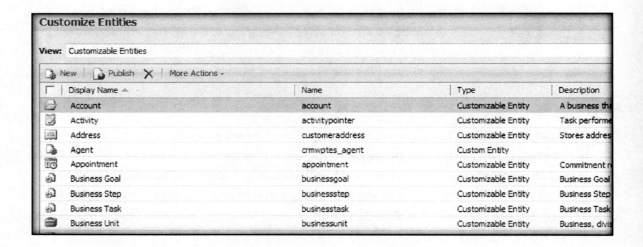

If we were to select Account from this list for modification, we could change things like the name of it to Company instead of Account because that's more meaningful in the solution we are building. Keep in mind that even though we change the display name the schema name and the name we use when doing development stays account, but from the users perspective they will always see Company.

If you can keep the names similar, you avoid the developer calling it a "Transaction" and the business user calling it a "Deal". In other words, leverage this capability when it makes sense but do not just have different names because you can.

The following is the entity edit form used to create and modify both built-in and custom entities.

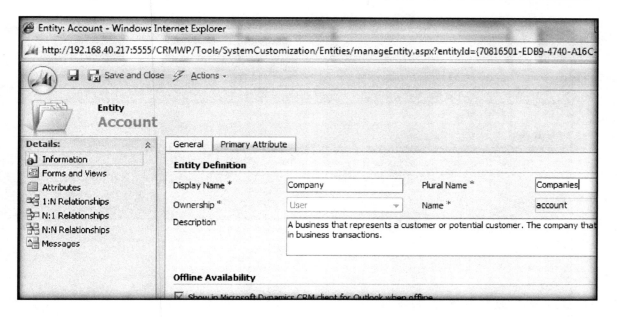

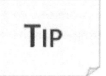

Account is one of the more common customizable entities to change the name to make sense. You can call it Company, Account, Hospital, Owner or whatever makes sense in your solution.

In addition to modification of labels in most of these customizable entities you can add additional attributes and often times additional relationships.

Exploring More

Another way to get your hands around the entities that exist in the system is to use the List.aspx page that exists on every server. This page will show you a list of all the entities defined and allow you to drill down into the details of each one.

You can find this page at http://<YourServerName>/sdk/List.aspx

The following is an example of what you will find at that link after you drill down into the account entity.

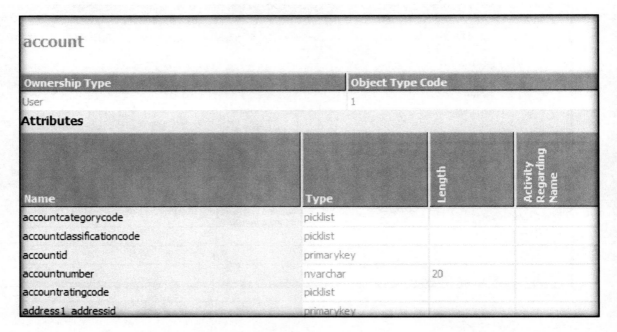

account

Ownership Type	Object Type Code
User	1

Attributes

Name	Type	Length	Activity Regarding Name
accountcategorycode	picklist		
accountclassificationcode	picklist		
accountid	primarykey		
accountnumber	nvarchar	20	
accountratingcode	picklist		
address1_addressid	primarykey		

Using this tool you can learn a ton of information that will help you when customizing and developing on the platform. Here are some of the key things you can determine from here.

- What attributes an entity has and its type/capabilities.
- Ownership, Object Type Code, Customizable, Valid for Advanced Find.
- What relationship each entity has and their relationship type and relationship behavior settings.

Another helpful tool is provided, but buried in one of the SDK sample folders. It's called the Meta Data Diagram sample and it generates Visio diagrams using the platform meta data. This is a great way to help visualize the entities. The diagram could then be included in documentation or printed and posted for your team to discuss during meetings.

Since it's in the SDK, the source code is there so it's possible to customize it for any documentation type needs you have. You can find it in the following folder <sdkroot>\server\fullsample\metadatadiagram

The Metadata diagram utility uses the Metadata API to retrieve all the information and is a great way to see how you can use the Metadata API

Custom Entities

The real power of the platform is the ability to define completely new entities that are custom to the application you are building. These custom entities can be one time for a single solution or can be reused time and time again when you have an ISV type solution delivered to multiple customers.

Custom Entities have almost all the capabilities that the built-in system entities do with the exception of any special system capabilities. For example, you can add attributes, customize the forms, and even add relationships to other entities in the system. Custom Entities are also eligible to have activities and notes allowing you to easily reuse the activity tracking capabilities of the platform. That means for example, if you create a custom entity called Project, and then a user creates a Task associated with that project, the task will flow down and show up in the users Outlook Task list without any custom coding.

Each custom entity and attribute that is added is prefixed with a schema prefix name. This name is intended to help identify your custom entity and attributes and keep them from colliding with other companies' customizations. For example in all of our custom entities and attributes we prefix them with ctccrm.

Display names of entities must be unique so if you decide to name yours similar to a built-in entity e.g Order you would first need to change the name of the built-in entity before the system will allow you to create your new custom Order entity.

You can modify the prefix that is used by visiting the Settings -> Administration –> System Settings –> Customization Tab. By default the prefix is set to "new" and should be modified before building any custom entities or attributes.

The following example shows the dialog that allows you to modify the name and it gives you a preview of what entities or attributes will look like with that prefix.

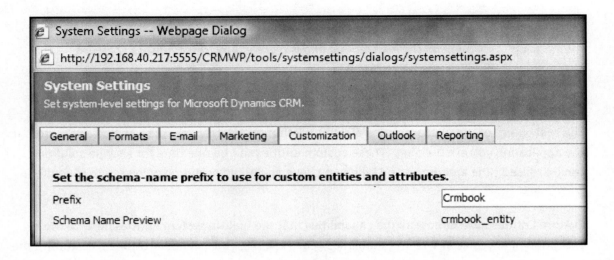

This setting typically only needs to be modified the first time you use a new organization and then it should be good to use for all customizations going forward.

Make sure you try to pick a prefix that has the least likely hood of colliding with other companies customizations. Using common terms like "common" or "new" increase the chance that something you create will collide with a vendor package you want to install in the future.

It is possible to change the prefix at any time to allow you to manage multiple prefixes that you do customizations under. One reason you might do this is if you use a prefix tied to a product and you have multiple products you are developing under a single organization. Multiple organizations can be used to accomplish the same thing.

The following is the dialog that you will need to complete to add a custom entity. This dialog is reached from Settings - > Customizations -> Customize Entities and the by clicking the new button from the toolbar.

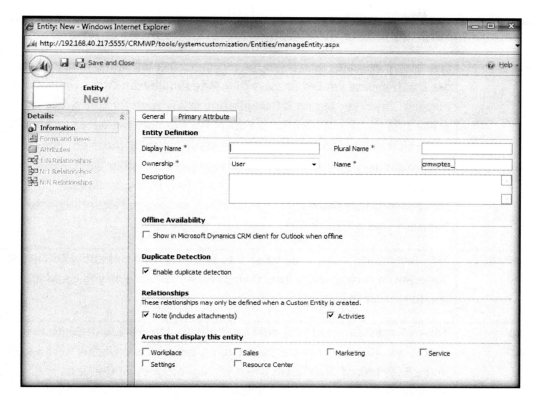

While a pretty simple form to fill out there are a couple of trick questions on there that could impact you later if you make the wrong choice. In fact, a few of the choices you make on this form can't be changed unless you delete and re-create the entity.

If you give access to customizations to a user that is not as technical it would be a good idea to make sure you have given them some guidance. In addition to the items on the next page, thinking through the name of the entity is important.

The following table will walk you through each of the items.

Field	Description
Display Name	This is the singular name that the user will see when they work with this entity. This is not the name that developers will use but an end user name. For example for a real estate system you might put Property in to refer to the real estate property.
Plural Name	This is the name used when there is a list or a grid of the entity. Using our same real estate property example you might put the word Properties in

	the plural to show to the user.
Ownership	Ownership indicates who owns the instances created of the entity. If you are creating data related to users that they should own User ownership is correct. The other option is Organization this is great for config data or other data that is not specific to a user. For example, we wrote an import utility that needed some configuration settings having those entities be organizationally owned made a lot of sense. On the other hand, if you want to have a record owned by a specific user, then user based ownership makes more sense. This cannot be changed after the entity has been created
Offline Availability	This determines if users will be able to pull data from this entity Offline. If you want to restrict users from taking certain data offline you could use this to restrict that option.
Enable Dup Detection	This indicates if the entity should be configured to work with duplicate detection. This does not create any rules, but makes it eligible to show up in the Base record drop down when you define rules on the Data Management -> Duplicate Detection Rules page. This setting can be modified at anytime.

Field	Description
Relationship – Notes	This indicates if you want to allow notes and attachments to be saved with this entity. This is a system level relationship that will be created for you and you can only enable this at entity creation time. If you fail to turn this on there is currently no supported way to add it later so make sure when you create your entity you make this choice carefully. Often times if you aren't sure it's better to have it enabled and not use it, then to wish you had turned it on.
Relationship – Activities	This allows you to have activities such as tasks, emails etc. associated with the entity. Like Relationship – > Notes this must be decided at entity creation time.
Areas that display this Entity	These control the sections on the left navigation that will show this entity. These can be changed at any time and it's not required that the entity show at all in any of these areas. An example of that would be an internal entity used by your application might not need to show to any users of the system.

Description Field

One thing I like to do for common entity definitions that will be shared in multiple CRM installs is to use the description field to indicate version information. For example, let's take the Trace Config custom entity that we use later in the book as an example. If you have this custom entity installed in 10 different systems wouldn't it be nice to be able to quickly glance at the list of entities and know by seeing the version string in the description field that the entity is not the latest version?

You can develop your own content that you like but here's an example of what I like to put in the description field.

V1.1-02-25-08 – this is the trace config entity

Then when I modify any aspect of the custom entity I make it a point to increment the version and the date. The version number is incremented separate from the date because you can at times of rapid change modify the entity multiple times in a single day. If you aren't familiar with the list of custom entities and the contents, the description field shows in the list. So by filling this out you can quickly scan the list to see what version each item is.

I have seen other people do things like include the name or initials of who changed the entity as well. Remember, the goal here is to try to find ways to make it easier to identify possible problems or where a change needs to be made. Ideally, in the future CRM would provide more details like this in the grid list, so that human intervention isn't required.

Primary Attribute

An often overlooked key part of creating a custom entity is the primary attribute. By default, if you don't do anything special this will be created as a attribute called "<prefix>_name" and will be of type NVarchar. The primary attribute will show up in a few places with special meaning such as the Title of the window when you view a record of that type. You cannot change the primary attribute after the initial creation other than the description and the constraints.

The Built-In Attributes

You must save the form before it will allow you to add more attributes and relationships. When you complete the form and the system creates the custom entity it also creates a few attributes for you by default. These are used by the platform to manage instances of the entity and can't be removed. The following table shows the attributes that are created by default each time.

Attribute	Description
CreatedBy	Unique identifier of the user who created the record.
CreatedOn	Date and time when the record was created.
ID	Unique identifier for entity instances, the real name for this is <prefixname>_<entityname>id. This is a Guid and is used to reference this entity in the future using the API.
Importsequencenumber	Sequence number of the import that created this record. This is useful if you are doing research on how data was input into the system to determine if it was an import problem.
ModifiedBy	Who did the last modification to this record?

Attribute	Description
ModifiedOn	When was the last modification done?
Ownerid	This is the id of the user that is the current owner of the record. The user can only be an owner of records that security provides access to. Owner ID is changed when a record is assigned to another user. Records that have an ownership type of Organization will not have this attribute added during creation since there is no user that owns those records.
Owningbusinessunit	The business unit that owns this record. This attribute will be automatically set by the system based on the owner of the record.
Statuscode	Status of the entity instance maintained by the system.

Custom Entity Implementation

If we were to peer into the entity we would see that the system had created two tables for us in the organization database. If our entity was called TraceConfig and our prefix was CrmBook then the two tables would be crmbook_traceconfigBase and crmbook_traceconfigExtension in the SQL Server database for the organization after the custom entity create completed.

crmbook_traceconfigBase

This table holds all the standard platform attributes that are part of every entity. The following shows what you would see.

```
Columns
    CreatedBy (uniqueidentifier, null)
    CreatedOn (datetime, null)
    Ctccrm_traceconfigId (PK, uniqueidentifier, not null)
    DeletionStateCode (int, null)
    ImportSequenceNumber (int, null)
    ModifiedBy (uniqueidentifier, null)
    ModifiedOn (datetime, null)
    OrganizationId (FK, uniqueidentifier, null)
    statecode (int, not null)
    statuscode (int, null)
    TimeZoneRuleVersionNumber (int, null)
    UTCConversionTimeZoneCode (int, null)
    VersionNumber (timestamp, null)
```

Not all entities will have two tables, several of the system entities only end up having a single table. All customizable entities will have two tables.

In addition to adding physical tables to the database, the platform also does some updates to other tables for various things. For example metadata must be updated to store all the details about the custom entity. Additionally, a default user interface is created and stored in the database.

Crmbook_traceconfigExtension

For any custom attributes we add that would be stored on this table. You can see from the following image each of the custom attributes we have created. These are unique to our custom entity

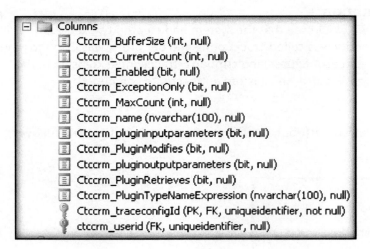

You should never work with these tables directly. They are there to support the working of the platform. If you need to create, modify or retrieve data you should do it through the platform Web Service interface that we will be discussing in Chapter 7. If all you want to do is query data you do have one additional option which is using a filtered view. Filtered views are created for each custom entity as well as each system entity. They are simply SQL Views that give you a single view of both the Base and the Extension part of the table for an entity and combine that together with implementing the platform role-based security model to ensure that the data you are able to query is data that should be visible to the authenticated user.

Custom Attributes

Adding additional attributes to an out of the box entity or adding a new one to a custom entity is the same so this section will apply to both. Attributes that are added to an entity are then available to be added to the entity's main form to allow the user to modify and view the contents. It is not required that all attributes are added to the entity form, in fact it is common to have attributes that are used by custom business logic extensions and never show to the end user.

When you create a new attribute the most important decision is the type of attribute. The only way you change the attribute type is to delete and re-create the attribute.

The following are the types of attributes supported by the platform.

Type	Description
bit	Represents a Boolean field that is either true or false
datetime	Represents a Date or a Date and Time. On the database a Datetime column is used regardless of if you specify Date only on the CRM side.
int	Represents a whole number value between -2,147,483,648 and 2,147,483,648.
float	Allows setting of precision as well as a min/max value for the data value.
Lookup	This is not one you can create on the form, it's created when you create a relationship and this represents the lookup field that will be put on the form to allow you to assign a value. You can also access these attributes via the API to set their values. On the database a lookup field is stored as 4 fields as you can see from the following image. ctccrm_userid (uniqueidentifier, null) ctccrm_useriddsc (int, null) ctccrm_useridname (nvarchar(160), null) ctccrm_useridyominame (nvarchar(160), null)

Type	Description
money	For tracking of currency values. In SQL table this will cause two columns to be added; one for the transaction currency and one for the base currency. Crmbook_ListingPrice (money, null) crmbook_listingprice_Base (money, null)
nvarchar	For shorter string based data; lengths between 1 and 4,000
ntext	For longer string data; lengths between 1 and 100,000
picklist	Picklist allows you to have combobox list of items. From a SQL perspective, only the integer value of the Picklist is stored on the table.

Important things about Custom Attributes

The following are a few key things you need to know about attributes that might cause you some pain later.

- You can't change the type of attribute after the initial creation – for example if you later decide that 4,000 is too short for your NVarchar field – you can't just change it to a NText later.

- On items like NVarchar that have a format type such as Text or TextArea – you can change that at creation but not during an update of the attribute

- You can however, change the attribute length or min / max values during an update of the attribute. Keep in mind it is possible to cause problems with existing data if you later reduce those values in conflict with your data already stored.

What is a Picklist?

Think of a picklist as a super drop down list. Simply put a Picklist is associated with a set of values and corresponding labels that can be picked by the user. Unlike a drop down in a simple custom application, a Picklist is fully integrated with the multi language capabilities of the platform. So for each configured language you can specify a display label that will show for that selected value. Using the attribute edit form, you can modify the list of items for the Picklist as well as order and set default values.

Picklist changes in CRM 4.0

One of the changes that occurred in CRM 4.0 was the handling of picklist values on out of the box entities. Prior to version 4.0 you could add additional Picklist values to attributes that came out of the box. The value for the item was determined based on the next sequential number. For example, if the picklist had 5 items the next value would be 6. In CRM 4.0, if you attempt to add a new item the value will start at 200,000. Without having a lengthy discussion on why the change was made, let's just leave it at it provides for a consistent way to know what is a system value and what is a custom value.

This change probably has the biggest impact on existing customizations that occurred prior to version 4.0. To accommodate for that, the import of customizations will allow values < 200,000 to be imported to provide for support of legacy configurations. All new values after the import would then be above the 200,000 mark.

Picklist or Relationship

One of the choices you should give some thought to when needing some type of list lookup is which technique should you use a Picklist or a Relationship. Both can easily provide the ability to provide lookup from a list and associate it with the data record you are editing. There are some distinct advantages and disadvantages of using either depending on the scenario. Here are some specific thoughts around each approach.

- When you need the list of data to provide support for multiple languages Picklists provide that capability without any extra work. Using a relationship simply provides a way to lookup and associate records from the associated entity, but no multi language capabilities exist.

- Picklists provide a combobox style selection if you have a large number of items the list could become lengthy and hard for the user to find the correct item. The relationship approach on the other hand would allow the user to quick find by typing in the text box on the form, or using the standard lookup dialog experience. Using the lookup they would have access to doing searches for the desired item as well as seeing the results of the search showing one or more columns of data to help make selection easier.

- Picklist values cannot be filtered based on the users security. The relationship approach on the other hand will only allow the user to associate the record to data that they have access to – so this gives the ability to create lookups that contain a filtered list of values based on the user's role or other security preferences.

- Picklists only provides for a single value to be selected and stored on the record. Relationships on the other hand can be configured to be many to many and allow multiple items to be related. For example if you wanted to track all the languages spoken, using the Picklist approach only one language could be stored. Using the relationship and a many to many relationship you could have as many languages as possible.

- Picklist items can only be added by someone with customization security access and require publishing of the values before they are visible to other users. Alternatively, with the relationship approach you can grant non admin type users the ability to add new values by giving them the appropriate security. Using this approach the list could be built by the users dynamically as they use the system.

- Picklist items have only a value and a label associated with it. There is no place to store additional data. The related entity approach can have additional attributes and show them on the lookup field to make it easier to choose the right item. This is also important for building Views, Reporting or exporting of data to Excel where you can include the related entity's data in the output.

While that is not a complete list of all the things to think about when choosing to use a Picklist or a related entity via a relationship it should get your thinking started. The important thing is to go through the process of making sure you choice is correct. As you will see in the next section with some of the expanded relationship types in CRM 4.0 this makes the choice even more important.

Relationships

Relationships are an important part of the data modeling capabilities of the platform because they allow you to further model real world situations. Relationships connect one entity to another and define the characteristics of the relationships. In addition, by defining behaviors automated actions can be configured to occur in conjunction with platform operations. Without this capability, our data would just be islands of information without meaningful connection.

In addition to just symbolic connecting of the dots between entities, relationships also provide some level of user interaction. As an example, users will see this as they interact with Lookup Fields on forms, which are a result of a relationship between two entities. They will also see changes take place to navigation and to their ability to view data all because of the relationships that exist. CRM 4.0 now provides a lot more opportunities to allow custom ordering and determination of how relationships are shown in the user interface.

From a developer perspective, relationships are also important because they define the navigation paths that you can use to query and find related data. Looking at relationships from a database perspective you would accomplish a similar thing with foreign keys.

Relationships can be one of the more challenging areas of the platform to understand. Unlike other platform concepts, relationships have their hands in several places and at times it can be challenging to understand why they work the way they do.

The following diagram illustrates the various types of relationships that are possible in CRM 4.0.

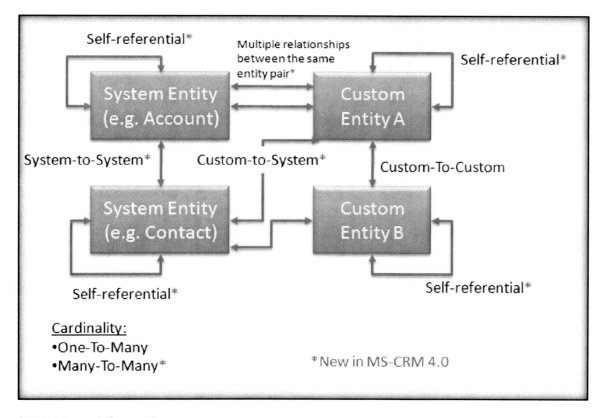

As you can see from the diagram all relationships have a cardinality of either One to Many or Many to Many. Many to Many is new to CRM 4.0.

One to Many

One to Many relationships are hierarchical in nature and define a parent / child relationship. These relationships are often referred to as 1:N where N is the child. If you looked at it from the child perspective it would be N:1, but either way describing the same relationship just from the child's perspective.

Relationships with a cardinality of one to many are commonly used in solutions. For example, if we were modeling a hospitality solution (e.g Hotels) you might have a Hotel entity and it would be related the Hotel Room entity. Each Hotel could have multiple Hotel Rooms but a Hotel Room only exists in a single Hotel. Or in relationship speak it has a single parent.

Many to Many

Relationships that are many to many allow the ability to relate one item to multiple items, and that one item to be linked to multiple items of the same entity type.

For example, we could define a custom entity called SpokenLanguage and it would contain all the possible languages people could speak. If we were to relate that to the Contact entity we could then be able to relate to a contact all the languages they spoke. One person could speak English, French and German and still be accounted for.

Using the many-to-many we could look at this relationship both ways – meaning we could ask the question what languages does this contact speak? Or the other direction what people speak this language?

Using the built-in many to many relationship cardinality there is no joining entity or place to store data (additional attributes) about the relationship. For example, it's not possible to track how long the person has spoken the language or how proficient they are.

Many-to-Many Link vs. Built-in Many-to-Many

Prior to CRM 4.0 if you needed to model a many-to-many relationship your only option was to use a "linker" entity. In this pattern a custom entity is created with the sole purpose to have relationships to the other two entities that you want to have the many-to-many relationship between. The advantage of this pattern is that you can also add additional attributes to the "linker" entity that describe the relationship. For example you could indicate time frames that the relationship existed or a date the relationship expires. The disadvantage of this pattern is that it is much clumsier for the user to establish the relationship because there's no specific built in UI to handle this type of many-to-many.

The many-to-many relationship that comes with CRM 4.0 provides a similar capability to relate two entities but does not have the ability to store any additional attributes that describe the relationship. The advantage of this implementation is that there is a UI experience built into CRM 4.0 that makes it easier for the user to establish the relationships. The disadvantage of this is there is no ability to decide later that you need to add additional attributes.

Careful consideration should be given during establishment of many-to-many relationships to think about how it will be used in the future. Once in use the only way to convert built-in many-to-many to a "Linker" pattern is manual, there is no automation provided.

Allowable Relationships

The following are an overview of the combinations of the relationships between different entity types.

Type	Description
System to System	Describes relationships between two system entities such as between account and contact. As an example by default a primary contact exists for the account, but you could add a secondary contact relationship.
System To Custom	In this scenario you are mixing one of the built in entities as the part with a custom entity as a child.
Custom to System	An example of this type of relationship would be creating a link from the User Entity which is a built-in system entity to our Hotel. In that scenario our Hotel would be a lookup field from the user form. The only constraint here is the Custom entity can't be defined as being a parent. We will cover parent and other relationship types later in the chapter.
Custom to Custom	This scenario you are relating two custom entities together.

Type	Description
Self Referencing	Self referencing allows an entity such as our Hotel Room to be related to other Hotel Room entities. To take that example further using self referencing you could relate Hotel Rooms in a self referencing type relationship to indicate which rooms are adjoining each other.
Multiple Relationships	New to CRM 4.0 is the ability to allow creating multiple relationships between the same types of entities. For example, using our Hotel Room example I could add a relationship to a user called Housekeeper and another one for Maintenance Person. This basically creates the two relationships between our Hotel Room entity and the system user entity.

Special Relationships

The following are some special relationships that exist to help allow some of the CRM related functionality to work.

Type	Description
Activity	This relationship is created by the system when you check the activity check box on the custom entity form at the time of creation. It is used to relate activities like Task, Email etc to your custom entity. This is system created and there is no way to create multiple activity type relationships.
Notes	Note relationships are created by checking the Notes check box on a custom entity when you create it. The relationship allows tracking notes related to that custom entity. This is created by the system and you can't create your own extra notes type relationships.
Customer	The customer relationship type is used on the Opportunity entity to allow you to relate it to a contact or a company. This is a pre-defined system relationship and there is no way to add more "customer" type relationships.

Relationship Behaviors

The following are the different types of relationship behaviors and explain some automatic behaviors that get configured with each type.

Type	Description
System	These relationships are created by CRM and can't be modified or removed.
Parental	This creates a parent child relationship. An entity can only have a single relationship marked as parent but can have other relationships that are referential. Using our Hotel example, the Hotel would be the parent to the Hotel Room entity. This makes sense because a Hotel Room would never exist without a hotel. If the Parent is deleted, assigned or shared then the child records are also affected. So if we deleted the hotel all hotel rooms would be deleted.
Referential	Referential relationships are common where the data is related but you don't want actions on the related record to affect the other. For example, where we related a User to a Hotel room as the house keeper. If the Hotel Room was removed we don't want to remove the User we just want to remove the link. The same is true of assignment and sharing – they will not cascade to referential related records.
Referential Restrict Delete	Referential Restrict Delete allows you to prevent deletion of a primary record as long as related data exists.
Configurable Cascading	Configurable Cascading is the most flexible in that it lets you fully configure all the options that happen when the primary record is affected. See the following table on Cascade types for the detail options that must be chosen for this type of behavior.

Configure Cascading Actions

The following are the different types of platform actions that can occur and allow you to specify a cascade type for each. These are used in conjunction with the Configure Cascading option above.

Action	Description
Assign	This action occurs when you change the owning user of a user owned entity. A common example of assign is changing the owner from Dave to Mary. Specification of cascade types on this option can control things like if all related data should be transferred as well.
Share	This action occurs when data is shared with another user.
Unshare	Opposite of Share, it allows specification if an unshared operation should cascade.
Reparent	Allows specification of how Reparent should be controlled.
Delete	This is an important one because it controls how cascading works during a delete. This option can give you a lot of power to allow the platform to cascade operations for some entities and not for others.
Merge	Merge occurs when you combine multiple records together and what should happen to the children.

The following cascade types are used in conjunction with the actions above. For each action when using Configure Cascading you will pick a cascade type to use for that particular action on the specific entity.

Cascade Type	Description
Cascade All	This causes application of the operation to the current entity and all related entity rows
Cascade Active	This only cascades the operation to related records that are active. This is common when using the Assign action above to allow only accounts that are active to be assigned. Any retired account would stay with the prior owner.
Cascade User Owned	This is powerful because it allows cascading the action against only records owned by the same user. For example, I might want a user to re-assign only the child records automatically with assignment of the parent if that user was the owner previously
Cascade None	Cascade None prevents any of the actions for cascading down to related items.
Restrict	This is the same as specifying Restricted Referential. Basically it keeps a delete from happening as long as there is related data. This only applies to use on the Delete action dropdown.

Relationship types and behaviors can be complex but with a little thought ahead of time you can find the right mix to ensure the entity reacts the way your users would expect.

Relationship Limitations

Like all relationships, the concept does have some limitations. In this section we will try to highlight some of the limitations, not to point out limitations in the platform but to help save you time. The best way to find other occurrences to this is using the metadata relationship flags.

Entity	Description
Business Unit	Can't participate in many-to-many relationships Can't be a child of another entity N:1, it can only be a 1:N
Opportunity Product	This is an example of a built-in entity that can't be customized to add additional relationships.

Sharing Across Organizations

One of the common questions that comes up in larger deployments that involve multiple platform organizations is around sharing across those organization instances. There are two levels people typically want to share. The first thing people want to share is customizations – typically they have the same custom entity that they want to use in multiple places. On that question, the answer is yes. You can either export it then re-import it into the other organization. Or if you want to be more sophisticated use the Metadata API to create it as part of an install program in the other organization. The next common question is can I share data? The simple answer is no, by default and by design each organization is intended to be stand alone. With that said you can of course do your own synchronization either using a 3rd party product or rolling your own. If you're building your own, you want to think about opportunity to do it using the import capabilities or for lower level control consider using the Web Service API to do the data synchronization process. For companies with large number of instances that share some lookup type of lookup data you might want to consider designating one source for the data.

While not data, the same answers apply to other customizations and that's good to keep in mind. For example, plug-ins and workflows are registered to a single organization and do not cross that boundary in any of their actions. You certainly though can "register" a plug-in or workflow with multiple organizations on the same server.

Wrapping it up

Having a good understanding of the data modeling capabilities is important because it is part of the foundation we will use throughout this book. Using custom entities, custom attributes and relationships give you the ability to model and implement real world problems.

In the packaging and deployment chapter we will be discussing how you can import and export the data model and re-use it or deploy it to other systems. Also a lot of what we did here using the user interface can also be done using the Metadata API. We will explore the Metadata API in more detail in Chapter 8.

5

User Experience Customization

In this chapter, we will look at how you can customize the user experience by adding custom client side scripting and other techniques to tailor the user experience for a solution. Typically, these capabilities are used to add validation and other types of user interaction that is more complex than can be provided out of the box or are driven based on other choices the user makes on the form in real time.

We will start by taking a brief tour of the capabilities the CRM platform provides out of the box so that you understand what you have to start. Since the basic form creation is not typically something a developer will be involved with we won't go into a lot of detail on the specifics but just a survival guide so you understand the basics. Then we will dive into client side scripting with JavaScript by hooking into the CRM platform events that are exposed. Let's face it, JavaScript can be a pain and not fun to work with. So we will look at how to make it less painful by looking at some techniques that make it more object oriented and easier to maintain. Finally, we will explore client Trace code that you can plug in to get some real diagnostics going without resorting to debugging using alert().

Navigation clearly is part of the user experience so we will look at what changes you can make to the CRM platform navigation and use it to stitch your external applications so they look like they were built as part of the platform. From a CRM platform perspective this means we will be discussing how to modify the SiteMap and the ISVConfig files.

One of the nice things about the CRM platform is that we can also integrate application parts built using ASP.NET or other standard web development technologies and have them appear as part of the CRM application using what is referred to as IFrame integration. We will explore how this can be used to build custom forms using ASP.NET as well as how those IFrames can include Microsoft Silverlight content.

When looking at these type of customization from a CRM SDK point of view these are all wrapped up under the concept of Client Extensions.

Form Basics

A basic data input form is created for each entity that is defined in our data model as we discussed in Chapter 4. Using the web form editor a business analyst, customizer or developer will go in and move the contents of the form around, add tabs, add sections to the tabs and allocate the entity fields to the form section.

The following is an example of the basic form editor, by selecting items on the form and using the navigational arrows items can be adjusted on the form surface.

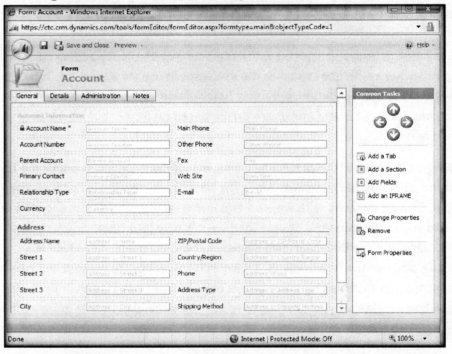

Currently, CRM only allows one main form per entity, however you can always create custom ASP.NET or Silverlight pages to accommodate for any custom needs you have. There is also a preview form that is used in conjunction with views to allow an expanded view of the data in a view's grid control.

Global Variables

The following Global Variables are new in CRM 4.0 to support the multi tenant and multi language capabilities.   Please see the SDK for a complete list of all global variables.

Variable	Description
SERVER_URL	This is the URL to the server including the http or https prefix and the organization name. For example http://myserver/myorg if accessing an on-premise. For IFD this URL would be http://myorg.myserver.com . The main difference being that the org name is the first part of the URL. When offline this will contain the local host address – e.g http://localhost:2525.
USER_LANGUAGE_CODE	Language code for the active user – e.g 1033.
ORG_LANGUAGE_CODE	Base Language code for the organization. This represents the language chosen as the default language at installation time.
ORG_UNIQUE_NAME	Unique Name assigned to the organization. Remember, organizations have a Unique Name and a Friendly Name. Unique name might be "MyCo" and the Friendly Name might be "My Company". This property is more intended to help integrate with other applications than for end user consumption.

These variables can be easily accessed from any of your scripts you will be writing since they are global variables. The following is a simple example of accessing the variables.

```
if (ORG_LANGUAGE_CODE != USER_LANGUAGE_CODE)
{
    alert('this user has selected language code ' + USER_LANGUAGE_CODE);
}
```

Probably the most common usage scenarios for these are when you are integrating external pages or building custom URLs. For example, if you are setting the source for an IFrame on the fly, you might want to include the Organization Name, and Language codes so the custom page has access to that information. This allows you to accomplish the same thing that CRM does when it automatically appends the ID to the URL. Having access to these will allow you to build the same type of URL on the fly without having to parse complicated URL strings.

Global Functions

The following Global Functions are available to help allow your JavaScript to react to the current state of the client as well as to leverage the pre-done authentication if you need to call back to the platform web services.

Function	Description
IsOnline	Allows you to check if the form is being accessed in On-line mode.
IsOutlookClient	Allows you to determine that the form being accessed from the Outlook Client. This doesn't indicate if you are online or offline at the time.
IsOutlookLaptopClient	True if the client has offline capabilities. You must check IsOnline to determine if you are on or offline at the present time.
IsOutlookWorkstationClient	True if Outlook client but no capability to go offline.
GenerateAuthenticationHeader	Helper method that returns an authentication string necessary to authenticate back to the CRM web services from the client. Using this allows you to make SOAP requests back regardless of how the client authenticated to the server and without you having to roll your own authentication code. We use this method extensively in our CTCCrmWebService helper that we will be discussing later in the book.

We take advantage of the IsOnline and IsOutlook functions in our CTCCrmFormTab.js that you can find in the ClientScripts/Common folder. We use those methods to determine if we should show a tab based on the mode the form is in and if the user is online or offline. The following is a quick example using those methods.

```
if ( IsOutlookClient() )
    {
        if (IsOnline())
        {
```

```
if (!this.ShowInOutlookOnline)
    this.HideTab();
```

Form Object Model

To allow developers to interact with the contents of the form and help make the user experience more interactive, each form exposes a crmForm element that serves as the wrapper that can be used to access and manipulate fields (attributes) placed on the form. The crmForm object exposes a handful of properties that can be evaluated as well as a few form level methods that can be invoked. The following table shows the properties that can be accessed on the crmForm object.

Property	Description
IsDirty	This is a Boolean property that indicates true if any fields on the form are dirty. This is an easy way to quickly do a check to determine if you need to do more custom validation or other processing. If it's set to false the user did not change any of the fields on the form
FormType	FormType is important because it can tell you if you are in a Create(=1), Update(=2), Read Only(=3) , Disabled(=4), Quick Create(=5), or Bulk Edit(=6) type of form. The obvious reason you want to know this is to adjust your scripting to accommodate. For example, you might want to make certain fields read-only during edit or not run your script at all when displayed on a read-only form.
ObjectId	This is the object id or the key for the record you are editing. This is great to have if you need to pass it along to anything else. For example, you might add a button that launches a new window and passes along the ID to allow that new window to pull up the same data or related data.
Property	Description
ObjectTypeCode	This is the entity type code used to identity what type of object you're working with. Where possible use ObjectTypeName as it is less fragile because ObjectTypeCode can change from install to install.
ObjectTypeName	A character representation of the object name, e.g systemuser or new_mycustomentity. Using the type name where ever possible will

	result in your solution being less fragile compared to using the ObjectTypeCode that can change from install to install.
all.{field name}	Each field on the form can be accessed and should be accessed via the .all collection property that is exposed on the crmForm object. By using this instead of directly accessing the HTML DOM you are less likely to be impacted by the CRM team providing hot fixes that change how things are rendered on the form.

In addition to the above properties, the crmForm object also exposes two methods that you can call directly. The following table has the methods that can be called directly from the crmForm object.

Method	Description
Save	This method will cause the form contents to be saved but to not close the form. Typically you would use this where you had added a custom button to a toolbar and when the user clicked it you wanted part of the logic to be similar to the user pressing the save button.
SaveAndClose	Just like Save but it will also close the window. You should ensure the user won't be surprised when the form is closed. Using this option without the user expecting it can lead to extra support calls.

Form Field Object

For each field that is placed on the form it can be accessed using crmForm.all.<name of field>. By using this method to access the field you get access to the following field level properties that can be set and evaluated by your JavaScript.

Property	Description
DataValue	This is how you get/set the value the field currently has. Each data type can have a different way to express the value property. For example, the string simply provides a reference to the string object, while a field with a data type of lookup has a DataValue set to an object with several

	properties. The SDK has a good set of information on the data types and what their specific properties are so we won't repeat in this chapter unless we provide some specific tip or trick for working with it.
Disabled	Allows you to get/set if the field is disabled. A common use of this is to disable or mark a field read only to start with, then based on the user selecting another field on the form, using JavaScript you can set this to enable/disable the field on the form for the user. This allows for much more dynamic control that can't be done by a simple check box on the form editor.
RequiredLevel	This is simply there to allow you to interrogate if the user is not required or recommended to input the field. This is a get only property. You can call crmForm.SetFieldReqLevel(field,true) if you need to mark as required – however it's not an officially supported method and could change without notice.
IsDirty	This makes it easy for you to check if a field has been modified. Often times this can be used for checking if you need to do a calculation or further validation or possibly confirm with a user that they intended to modify that particular field.
ForceSubmit	CRM only submits changed values back to the server. This attribute specifies if the field must be submitted to CRM. By default read only/disabled fields will not post back their value to the server. Often times to support custom scripts we place disabled fields on a form and then update the contents in our scripting methods. If we don't set this property the value will not be transmitted back to the server during the save operation.

The following is a simple example of using the ForceSubmit property. Imagine you have a flag that is read only or disabled on the form that you use for scripting purposes. If you modify that attribute without setting the ForceSubmit = true it will not be sent to the server. The following sets the value and then turns on the ForceSubmit property for the attribute modified.

```
crmForm.all.crmbook_newcustflag.DataValue = 1;
crmForm.all.crmbook_newcustflag.ForceSubmit = true;
```

The following are the methods accessible from each Field Object.

Method	Description
SetFocus	This causes the form to give focus to this field. The most common use of this is in support of validation where you detect an invalid value in a field. You could also use this during the form OnLoad event to set focus to an alternate field.
FireOnChange	This simulates the user changing the field and causes the OnChange event for the field to fire. The typical reason you would do this is to ensure the OnChange gets called after you modify the value of the field's DataValue property using scripting. By using default scripting you can modify the DataValue and it won't be treated like the user changed the field, allowing the script to silently operate in the background unless this method is called.

MVP Tip: Microsoft MVP Ronald Lemmen adds that you can set the focus to another tab by using SetFocus method and set the focus to the first field on the tab. You can read Ronald's blog at http://www.ronaldlemmen.com.

Form Events

Form events provide a way for the developer to gain control during certain phases of the form processing. Using the events the developer can provide JavaScript that gets run when the event occurs. This JavaScript essentially becomes a registered event handler, in fact behind the scenes the JavaScript is registered using the attachEvent() method. The custom JavaScript is added using the web form editor by clicking on form properties and selecting the event you are interested in providing custom JavaScript for.

The following is an example of the input form for the OnLoad event.

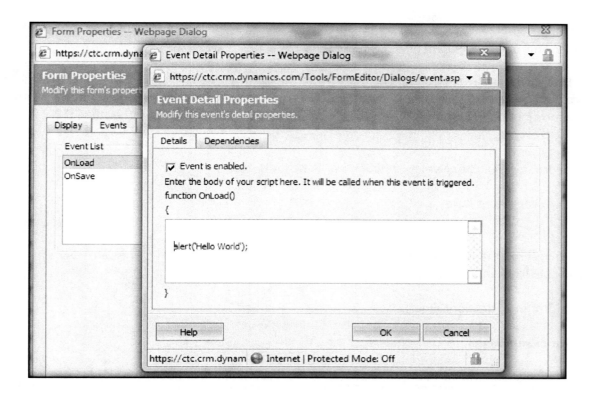

It is also possible to programmatically manipulate the JavaScript using the web service API. You might want to consider this approach if you want to integrate the process with a setup program. We will touch on this later in Chapter 24 when we talk about deployment options.

When the platform renders the form to the browser it will take care of getting the script you provided for your events onto the page. It will also take the necessary steps to invoke your script at the correct time.

External JavaScript Files

It is possible that instead of placing all of your script inline in the event dialog that you include it from an external file. That external file then needs to be hosted on a server that the client can access. The challenge you run into is when the client is offline you need to ensure that the location you retrieve the script from is still available or that you take appropriate steps to handle that condition. Otherwise, the user will receive errors because the file is unavailable. It is also important to note that technically this approach is unsupported by Microsoft. This is however, a possible technique you could consider during development and then later move the code inside the events once development is completed.

In that scenario, the code should be moved into the event as the final step. That solves the problem of accessing the code while offline. Once you know it is working – why not move it into the form? To do this, you need to associate the functions to the crmForm rather than the onLoad event:

```
crmForm.my_FunctionName = function my_FunctionName()
{
        Logic goes here
}
```

Then paste all the functions from your external file into the onLoad event. They are now available from any event. You call them like this:

```
crmForm.my_FunctionName();
```

Form Level Events

The following are the form events that you can add custom JavaScript to at the form level.

Event	Description
OnLoad	This is called after the form is loaded (So it's too late to try to stop it!). We will be using this event later to load up all of our JavaScript in one place. Read more on this later in the chapter.
OnSave	This method is called after the user presses Save or Save and Close or the methods have been called on the crmForm object. The most typical use of this is to validate data and if necessary you are able to stop the save from happening.

The OnSave event is a great place to trigger your final client side validation as the user has indicated by clicking save that they are prepared to persist the data. Often times you want to defer as late as possible for that type of processing but want to catch it before you have to wait for a page post back to occur.

Field Level Events

You can also add custom JavaScript at the field level using the following event.

Event	Description
OnChange	This is a field level event that is available to be used on each field that is placed on the form. Using this you can gain control if the user modifies the contents of the field. The event is only triggered once control is lost so you won't be called for every keystroke on the field.

On the other hand, using field OnChange events you can cause more real time JavaScript to run and perform calculations or other validation. Often times OnChange is used to set defaults. For example, if I were on a real estate property and the Property Type lookup is set, there might be certain form defaults I would want to establish based on that field data value.

As we get further in the chapter, we will explore some techniques to tie these events in with a scripting strategy that is more manageable and allows integration with source control.

Use the Preview Form button to launch the form directly from the edit page so you can test out your script. No need to publish the form yet, just try it there so if you have an obvious error you can fix it before leaving the edit page. Some features are limited but it can help speed up some of your initial testing.

Understanding some of the Scripting Challenges

Now that we have identified the type of events that can be specified, we need to tackle some of the challenges to manage all of this JavaScript we are creating and plugging into the events on the forms. The the interface for editing the JavaScript on events is very simplistic. This simplicity works great for very simple custom scripts of a few lines but gets out of control quickly when the scripting gets more complex and/or a team is involved in the development.

The first thing you need to understand is that event JavaScript is stored along with the form, so when the form is imported or exported so is the event JavaScript. This is important in a team environment because it can be very easy to step on other people's customizations. The other challenge here is there really is no version control or tracking of changes. Once you hit the save button or import a new customization file containing this entity it will overwrite your custom script and there's no "View history" button to click like you would in a typical source control product. We will explore some options for how to improve this later in the chapter.

One of the other common things that occurs frequently is field OnChange event scripts being repeated over and over again. This is easy and simple until you have to go find the 5 or 10 places that you put the same 5 lines of code just to correct a bug. All the fun and games end when you forget to fix one of them.

In case you haven't guessed yet you don't get much in the way of IntelliSense or code coloring on the JavaScript using the built-in web client form editor. In fact Visual Studio is typically my editor of choice and now that Visual Studio 2008 has JavaScript IntelliSense and code coloring I do almost all of my scripting using Visual Studio 2008. The techniques I'm going to discuss don't require Visual Studio 2008 but are enhanced by using it.

The final thing that's important to understand and probably one of your questions, can't you just put some common script somewhere and let CRM manage it. Currently there isn't any support in the platform for central storage of JavaScript for use on the forms. It's something the CRM team knows developers would like but it didn't make it into CRM 4.0. You might be wondering why a developer couldn't just store client-side script on the server. Well, that's fine if the client is online, but if the user is offline those scripts would not be available.

Using a web project

One of the things that can help a lot when you have a team involved is to treat the JavaScript customizations more like you would files in a web project. So what we commonly do is create an empty Web Site project that we will use as a container to store and organize our JavaScript. To make it easy to find our scripts, we typically will create a folder for each entity that we will do custom scripting for. Then for each event that we have script for we will create a JavaScript file to store the script in.

The following is an example of what the web site project file structure would look like if we had customized the Account entity.

```
$/
$/Account
      Account_OnLoad.js
      Account_OnSave.js
      Account_OnChange_name.js
      Account_OnChange_new_mycustomattribute.js
```

As you can see we have mirrored the files based on the events that we want to capture on the form. This makes it easy to find a customization you are looking for. By storing them in JavaScript files we can take advantage of any editing smarts the editor has – such as how Visual Studio 2008 can provide IntelliSense and color coding to make it easier to read. By storing them in separate files, it makes it easy to grab and upload them manually into the CRM web editor. The names of the files have been chosen to make it possible if we wanted to write a tool to automate the upload to CRM process we could use the name to infer the form, event and attribute to apply the change to.

Keep in mind this is just one idea on how to organize files, but the goal is to get you thinking about more creative ideas than just simply storing them in CRM.

Integrate with Source Control

Another benefit of storing your JavaScript outside of CRM is that you can leverage more of the development tools used for typical web site development. In the example above using the Web Site project we can now connect that to a source control product like Visual Source Safe or Team System Version Control to track changes to those files. When working on a team or a project with larger amounts of customizations the extra tracking capability can be very useful throughout the project. It is also very critical if you're an ISV maintaining multiple versions of your product.

Understanding JavaScript

Before we dive in and discuss some ideas on how to rewrite our JavaScript to be cleaner, let's first cover some JavaScript language concepts that will make it easier to understand what we suggest later in the chapter. Most people, if you asked them, wouldn't think of JavaScript as an object oriented language. Now don't worry I'm not going to go comparing language features here but I will highlight some capabilities of JavaScript that have only recently become more popular.

First, let's talk about how we can create the equivalent of a class or a grouping of related JavaScript methods. JavaScript does not have a formal class keyword as part of its syntax, but that does not keep it from being able to support some level of encapsulation. Let's take a look at how we can build a JavaScript class.

The first step is to setup what is referred to as a constructor function. This function is responsible for setting up the new instance of the object we will create. We can pass parameters to this constructor to provide some initial values. If you are familiar with classes in managed code (e.g. C# / VB.NET) this is very similar to a class constructor method.

The following is a simple example of a JavaScript class.

```
function PersonClass (firstName,lastName)
{
    this.FirstName = firstName;
    this.LastName = lastName;
}
```

This sets up the definition and establishes two properties FirstName and LastName, and then initializes them based on the values passed to the constructor.

To create an object instance using this we would do the following:

```
var myPerson = new PersonClass('John','Doe');
```

We could then reference the properties using the following syntax:

```
alert(myPerson.FirstName);
```

The next thing we need to think about is how to include some more functions as part of our object. For example, let's try a simple method like GetFullName that would simply concatenate the First and Last name together. I realize it is a simple example, but the point is to understand the concept, not the complexities, you could create. The following shows a modified constructor that adds a method GetFullName.

```
function PersonClass (firstName,lastName)
{
    this.FirstName = firstName;
    this.LastName = lastName;
    this.GetFullName = function() { return this.FirstName + ' '
                    + this.LastName; }
}
```

Then we could use the class and call the method GetFullName as you can see in the following example.

```
var myPerson = new PersonClass('Dave','Yack');
alert(myPerson.GetFullName());
```

Using this approach each instance of PersonClass will get its own copy of the GetFullName method. JavaScript has a lesser known capability that can help so that we only have one copy that is shared with all instances. This is accomplished using a built-in property named "prototype".

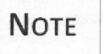

Don't confuse the prototype capabilities of JavaScript with the Prototype JavaScript library that some use for implementing AJAX web applications. They are separate and the prototype we are talking about is part of the core JavaScript syntax.

To use the prototype with our function definition we would change the following line:

```
this.GetFullName = function() { return this.FirstName +  `    `
                 + this.LastName; }
```

to be:

```
PersonClass.prototype.GetFullName = function() { return this.FirstName
             +  '    ' + this.LastName; }
```

The change is that we replaced "this." With "PersonClass.prototype." and that will cause the method to be available on all instances but only one copy exists.

Using this approach, while not exactly like using a managed language, we can write more manageable JavaScript and make our code easier to read. We will be using some of these techniques in our example scripts as we move forward in the rest of the chapter.

Our End Goal

So you will have an idea of what we want to accomplish, let's discuss our end goal before we get into the step by step example. The first part of the goal is to minimize having to change different events each time some code changes. To accomplish that, we will put the bulk of our code into the OnLoad event and simply reference it from any of the other events. In fact the other events, the OnSave or the OnChange of any of the fields should only have one line of code. That one line of code should call back into code that we load during the OnLoad event. By doing this the only time we touch an event other than OnLoad is if we are setting it up for the first time. This goes a long way to help avoid pasting the wrong code in the wrong event handler (not that I have ever done that!).

The other big thing we want to do is start building some reusable code that we can use form after form. The CRM platform out of the box provides some of this functionality, but by creating our own abstraction layer we can add and make available some of the capabilities that are missing from what is provided out of the box. To accomplish this we will use a base class that we put all of our common code in, and then include that in each of our forms. We will also package into that common base class some tracing capability that we can use to improve our debugging and stop using alert() as our debugging technique.

Defining a base class

One of the things we are going to try to accomplish is to establish a more formal structure for our JavaScript that will promote easy reuse of common functions. We also want to make it easier to plug-in any form specific logic. Our first step in trying to accomplish this goal is to define a base class for our solution. The following code snippet simply defines a class called MySolutionClass that in subsequent examples we will add more capability to.

```
MySolutionClass=function()
{

}
```

Now this class is probably best stored in a separate JavaScript file maybe in $/Common or some other obvious place. We will be re-using this base class over and over again as we customize each form.

In this class and in the file in our common folder we want to put any function that would be useful to all our forms. A good example of that is possibly some helper functions like the following that checks to see if we are on an Edit Form.

```
MySolutionClass.prototype.IsEditForm = function()
{
    var CRM_FORM_TYPE_EDIT = 2;
    if (crmForm.FormType == CRM_FORM_TYPE_EDIT)
        return true;
    else
        return false;
}
```

One of the other common things we do on forms is to have logic that we want to run during load of the form. Often times we want to do different things during load of a Create form versus an Edit form. Not to mention most of the time we want our script to ignore Quick Create and the other types of forms.

Rather than always packaging up if / else logic on our pages to do these checks on form types we could add the following common function that would do the check for us and call our method if we chose to override it. We will discuss how to override and implement custom logic later, for now let's look at our example of our common method that handles OnLoad processing.

```
MySolutionClass.prototype.HandleFormOnLoad = function()
{
    CTCTrace('HandleFormOnLoad','Starting');
    var CRM_FORM_TYPE_CREATE = 1;
    var CRM_FORM_TYPE_EDIT = 2;

    switch (crmForm.FormType)
    {
        case CRM_FORM_TYPE_CREATE:
          CTCTrace('HandleFormOnLoad','Calling OnFormLoadCreate');
          this.OnFormLoadCreate();
          CTCTrace('HandleFormOnLoad','Done Calling
OnFormLoadCreate');
          break;

        case CRM_FORM_TYPE_EDIT:
          CTCTrace('HandleFormOnLoad','Calling OnFormLoadEdit');
          this.OnFormLoadEdit();
          CTCTrace('HandleFormOnLoad','Done Calling OnFormLoadEdit');
          break;
```

```
    }

    CTCTrace('HandleFormOnLoad','Ending');
}

MySolutionClass.prototype.OnFormLoadCreate = function()
{
    CTCTrace('OnFormLoadCreate','Default implementation called - no
action taken');
}

MySolutionClass.prototype.OnFormLoadEdit = function()
{
    CTCTrace('OnFormLoadEdit','Default implementation called - no action
taken');
}
```

So what we have accomplished in the above example is created a method that will be called during OnLoad, it will decide if we are in Edit or Create and call OnFormLoadCreate or OnFormLoadEdit.

If we don't override those OnFormLoad methods then no processing will happen, but if we do override them our code will run without doing all of the if checks we would have had to have done without this structure.

We can also apply the same concept to OnSave. In the case of save, what you are choosing between is if the form has anything dirty on it or not.

The following example adds to our base class the methods for processing OnSave.

```
MySolutionClass.prototype.HandleFormOnSave = function()
{
    CTCTrace('HandleFormOnSave','Starting');
    if (crmForm.IsDirty)
    {
        CTCTrace('HandleFormOnSave','Calling OnFormSaveDirty');
        if (!this.OnFormSaveDirty())
        {
            CTCTrace('HandleFormOnSave','OnFormSaveDirty setting return
value to false, since onsavedirty returned false');
            // Cancel the save operation.
            event.returnValue = false;
        }
        CTCTrace('HandleFormOnSave','Done Calling OnFormSaveDirty');
    }
    else
    {
        CTCTrace('HandleFormOnSave','Calling OnFormSaveClean');
        this.OnFormSaveClean();
        CTCTrace('HandleFormOnSave','Done Calling OnFormSaveClean');
    }
    CTCTrace('HandleFormOnSave','Ending');
}

MySolutionClass.prototype.OnFormSaveDirty = function()
{
    CTCTrace('OnFormSaveDirty','Default implementation called - no
action taken');
}

MySolutionClass.prototype.OnFormSaveClean = function()
{
    CTCTrace('OnFormSaveClean','Default implementation called - no
action taken');
}
```

Now at this point we have built up our base class and have added common logic to make handling OnLoad and OnSave in a cleaner fashion. In the following we will start to discuss how to use this class in our actual forms.

Compressing the script

Since this is common code it will not change that often, so one suggestion is to compress it using a tool like W3c or other JavaScript compression tools. These tools should reduce the script above down to a long one line script that we then include in each of our pages. This keeps things clean and also helps improve performance slightly. The following is an example of what this would look like when included on our form OnLoad JavaScript file.

```
//MySolutionClass V1.0 - Start
MySolutionClass=function(){MySolutionClass.prototype.IsEditForm=func...
//MySolutionClass V1.0 - End
```

You might notice we wrapped our long line of code with a name and version tag. This version tag makes it easier to look at one of our OnLoad.js files to see if we have the latest code included. If you are manipulating the scripts as part of your installation or upgrade process of your solution, you might consider taking this even further. For example, you could include in the comment line a check sum of some sort to allow you to confirm that your script has not been altered.

The full file of the compressed version can be found in the samples as file name MySolutionClass_compressed.js

Using on our form

Now let's move on to how to use this with our form. The first step to accomplish this is to modify our Account_OnLoad.js file to have the compressed one line like above and the following that creates an instance of MySolutionClass. We then make a simple call to the HandleFormOnload to begin our common code processing of the OnLoad event.

```
//create new instance of MySolutionClass
document.MySolution = new MySolutionClass();
//call the necessary on load functions
document.MySolution.HandleFormOnLoad();
```

Now let's modify our example to override and provide our own OnFormLoadCreate function. The following overrides and implements a very simple version of that.

```
//create new instance of MySolutionClass
document.MySolution = new MySolutionClass();

//our custom onformloadcreate
document.MySolution.OnFormLoadCreate = function()
{
     Alert('hello!');
}

//call the necessary on load functions
document.MySolution.HandleFormOnLoad();
```

To take this a step further, let's look at how we would hook into the OnSave. In the OnLoad.js file we would add the following code that would override the OnFormSaveDirty method.

```
document.MySolution.OnFormSaveDirty = function()
{
     Alert('hello from Save');
     return true;
}
```

Obviously a real world implementation of that would include a lot more JavaScript but for example purposes "Hello" is plenty! Next, we need to add our script that will be in our OnSave event. Remember, this code we will put there once and don't need to change because all changes will be done via our code in OnLoad that is all centrally loaded. The following example shows what the code would look like that we would put in the OnSave event area.

```
//Call the standard HandleFormOnSave
document.MySolution.HandleFormOnSave();
```

Adding Tracing Support

One of the most common challenges with developing JavaScript for use with the forms is handling debugging during development. One of the more common approaches is to leverage the built-in JavaScript alert() method to assert some type of message. The following is what we often run across demonstrating this "advanced" debugging technique.

alert('I am Here');

At runtime, this will then produce the following popup message:

Imagine hitting "OK" twenty or thirty times as you progress through your logic on the page. This results in a very tedious debugging session.

To help improve on that technique we have provided with the book a Trace class similar to using Trace from a .NET managed code application. The trace class is simply included as part of your JavaScript that you are developing. The following are some of the benefits of using this helper script.

- Can be turned on as needed – no need to remove the trace statements from the code like you would have to with alerts.

- Great for complex scripts because you can take time to study the pattern after the processing is completed.

- Can help find performance problems because it omits time since last trace statement was printed.

- Opens in a separate window so it does not interfere with the standard form you are testing.

We have compressed it to a long single line to make it easier to include and not clutter up your file.

The following shows the line that you would put in your JavaScript to use trace.

```
//CTCTrace - Start
var CTCTraceWindowHandle=null;var CTCTraceLastTrac
//CTCTrace - End
```

You can find the actual line to include in the ClientScript/Common/TraceOptimized.js file.

The other thing you need to do to activate it is set a variable to indicate that you want it active on the page.

```
var CTCTraceWindowEnabled   = true;
```

In the above example we don't get very creative on how we enable it, so you could obviously use some additonal logic and only set it for certain users or sessions as you saw fit.

Now the next step is to actual call the trace as part of your JavaScript code. Using it is very similar to using the alert() method but the output is much more useful. The following is an example of calling the CTCTrace method.

```
CTCTrace('OnFormSaveDirty','Default implementation called - no action
taken');
```

You might have seen the above line in our earlier example. That is because in our common code we have included several of these trace statements to help you in using them.

The method takes two parameters. The first is the category that you are tracing, this is output in front of each line of trace simply to make the trace easier to read and know where you are. Typically I would recommend putting the method name or some other useful tag in that parameter. The second parameter is the message you want output to the trace window.

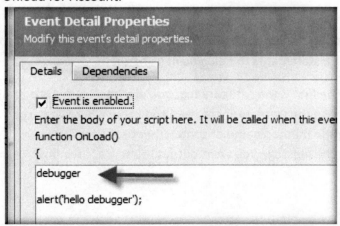

```
http://localhost:65285/CRMWeb/Tracing/ShowTrace.htm - Windows Internet Explorer

Clear Window
Tue Nov 27 12:24:15 MST 2007(426) :OnFormSaveDirty:Starting
Tue Nov 27 12:24:15 MST 2007(5) :OnFormSaveDirty:Calling User Method
Tue Nov 27 12:24:18 MST 2007(2397) :OnFormSaveDirty:Done Calling User Method
Tue Nov 27 12:24:18 MST 2007(7) :OnFormSaveDirty:Ending
```

As you can hopefully see in the above example of the output from the trace calls, it is much easier to read than seeing one alert after the next.

You may also notice that in addition to the category and message we also output the Date / Time and the elapsed milliseconds since the last call to trace. This time stamping is a great way to isolate places where your script might be taking too long to perform processing. For example, if you look at the above trace output carefully you will notice that the user method called took over two seconds to process. With that knowledge it would be easier to track down the offending code and get it fixed.

You will see the trace utility methods used throughout many of our examples.

Debugging Script with Visual Studio

Another technique you can use to track down problems in your client script is to use the debugger built into Visual Studio. Visual Studio 2008 improves on the capabilities of the debugger so we will be focusing on the steps for that version. There are a few different ways to get into the debugger but the most effective is to use the "debugger" keyword in JavaScript. As you can see in the following example we have added the "debugger" keyword at the start of our Onload for Account.

Event Detail Properties
Modify this event's detail properties.

| Details | Dependencies |

☑ Event is enabled.
Enter the body of your script here. It will be called when this eve
```
function OnLoad()
{

debugger

alert('hello debugger');
```

What that will do is cause the form to stop on that line and prompt if we want to use a debugger. You should at this point see the following form when you load the account form. If it doesn't work, check your IE options to ensure that debugging is not disabled which is the default setting in IE.

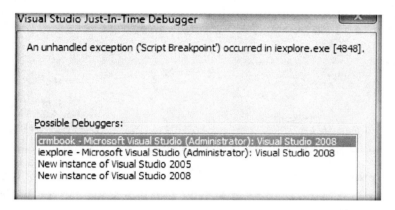

This form allows you to pick which debugger you want to use and if you already have Visual Studio up it will allow you to choose an existing instance. If you choose New Instance it will load up a new instance of Visual Studio and start the debugger. I tend to prefer that option rather than using the one that has my CRM project. In the above example, you will notice Visual Studio 2005 come up in the list – that's because on this particular machine I have both Visual Studio 2005 and 2008 installed. Visual Studio 2005 will still stop on the "debugger" keyword, however, it will not give you near the same debug experience. After selecting either New Instance or an existing instance you should see the debugger load up and stop at our "debugger" keyword. The following shows you an example of stopping on the keyword.

```
function crmForm_window_onload0()
{

if (event.returnValue != false)
{
try
{
debugger

alert('hello debugger');
}
catch(e)
{
    displayError("window", "onload", e.description);
```

At this point , you could browse around to see what different values are on variables. The easiest way of doing that is using quick watch ctrl-alt-q to bring up the Quick Watch Window as you can see below.

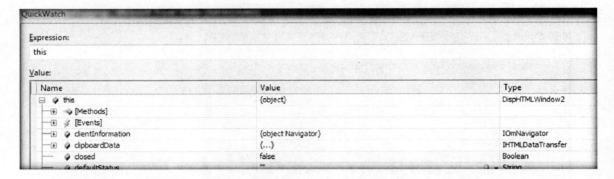

In the above example, for the expression we input "this" which will give you the context for the current page. From there you can look at any method or variable that is in scope and see and/or modify the value of the item. This is one area that is greatly improved in Visual Studio 2008.

If your goal was to step through your script code the easiest way to do that is to set the next statement that will run. You can do that by right clicking on the line after the "debugger" keyword or wherever you want to start and selecting the Set Next Statement menu option as you can see in the following image.

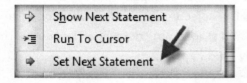

Then you can step line by line through your script code.

Another big difference between Visual Studio 2005 and Visual Studio 2008 is the view from Solution Explorer. In 2005, you would only see the current file that you are debugging and wouldn't really be able to navigate to other scripts that were loaded or see the page markup. In Visual Studio 2008, the Solution Explorer will show you a list of all the files for the current browser session and allow you to navigate around them. This can be real interesting to see what all the CRM script is and what other code is currently running on the form.

The following is an example of the Solution Explorer view.

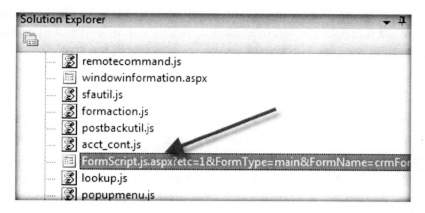

Notice the highlighted item is the form script for the account page we modified.

The debugger is great when you know a specific portion of script is having problems and you want to be able to stop there and walk through it. It's not a good production diagnostic approach because it would cause an interruption for all users. The type of trace that we discussed earlier works better for production use because it can be dormant until needed. In general, both techniques should be used when developing script. Debugger when you want to look at specific lines and Trace when you want to be able to review all the processing by looking at the trace window.

Calling Web Services from Client

Using JavaScript as we discussed earlier in the chapter provides an easy way to provide a more interactive user experience. As an extension of that technique you can access the platform web services from the JavaScript. There are a number of reasons to do this, but for a simple example let's assume you have two dependent lookups on a form. If the user selects item "A" on the first lookup, you want to default the value on the second lookup. Let's assume that entity related by the first lookup has an attribute that tells you what the default should be for the second lookup. Using normal client scripting techniques there isn't an easy way to accomplish this. When the user picks the value for the first lookup by selecting item "A" the only data available to you is the ID and the Name from the lookup field. By using that ID and calling the platform web services to retrieve the default value you would be able to set the default for the second lookup. This is just one example, the bottom line is by being able to call the platform web services from the client side script you can access much more data from the platform. In addition to accessing data, you could create, update, delete and even do things like start a workflow on demand from the client script code.

By default, calling the web services from client side scripting is a little more challenging than we will discuss in the web service chapter. The reason for this is you need to navigate the syntax of calling a Soap service. There are a couple of ways to work around this and make it real easy and we will cover those in more detail than the raw Soap example you will find in the SDK.

Using Server Side Proxy

If the solution you're building will only ever run in the on-premise or partner hosted deployment model you can choose to call the CRM web services by creating your own ASP.NET web service that you invoke. The custom web service you build and deploy to the server would proxy the request to the real CRM web service. By doing that you don't have to worry about making a generic web service interface, you would simply just expose the method calls that you need for your particular solution. Because this approach requires you to deploy server side code to proxy the request to the real CRM platform web services it wouldn't be appropriate if you wanted to be able to deploy your solution to the CRM Online platform since custom server deployed code is not allowed. As a simple example, if you needed to query from a CRM form the default unit of measure for a product you could expose a web service that simply took ProductID and returned the Unit of Measure ID. To accomplish this you would create a custom ASP.NET web service that would proxy the request to find out the default unit of measure for a product. In this scenario we pass in the product ID and expect to get back the ID of the default unit and its name so we can set the default value of Unit lookup.

In this approach we have pushed much of the work to the server ASP.NET code. If you are making a large number of platform calls to accomplish something, this approach would be more efficient because the server application is closer to the platform API than the client is so the cost of the round trips are less. This approach can also simplify the call from the JavaScript because it doesn't need to deal with the generic platform interface. It's making a simple method call to the GetDefaultUOMByProductID exposed by the custom ASP.NET web service. The GetDefaultUOMByProductID method will then turn around and make the necessary CRM calls to retrieve the Default UOM and return it.

Using this approach you will also have to do some extra work to handle offline clients. With offline clients you have to assume they are offline because they don't have access to the server host so expecting them to talk to the server host to access your proxy probably won't work well when they are offline. In CRM 4.0 since the offline client does expose an almost identical copy of the web services and has a local web server running it would be possible to have a copy of your server side proxy that also resides and runs on the client. Doing this you introduce some deployment challenges because you now have to get your server side proxy deployed to the client. If you are heavily reliant on using the sever side code offline this approach could be considered , but if client side web service access is a small part of your overall solution you would be better off using the next approach of calling the services directly via JavaScript.

Using JavaScript

Another option would be to invoke the platform web service calls from the client. To make this approach easier we have built some helper classes to make calling the platform web services from the client a lot easier than navigating the Soap protocol. To make the helper classes familiar to you, we have modeled them to be very similar to how the web services work if you were invoking them from a server side application. In the next chapter we will discuss this helper in detail and show you how to use it to make the client more responsive.

Make sure you check out the CTCCrmService helper routines in the next chapter as they will save you a ton of time getting calls to be made to the web service.

Client Script IntelliSense

One of the new features of Visual Studio 2008 is support for JavaScript IntelliSence and coloring. By default both of these are enabled and used just by editing a file that has a ".js" extension. In addition to support for the languages basic syntax, Microsoft has added the ability to provide hints to make JavaScript IntelliSense pickup your custom code as well.

Out of the box, the IntelliSense is able to detect and show methods and variables that are defined inside the script file, but if you have any external utility scripts by default they are not known about by the IntelliSense engine. This is true also of dynamic script that is injected by the page rendering engine. An example of this type would be the crmForm object hierarchy that is used to access form fields and methods. By default IntelliSense has no ability to help because it doesn't know about it.

In this section we are going to look at a technique of adding hints into your file to help JavaScript figure out how to provide IntelliSense for your crmForm fields. In fact, by combining that with the platform meta data it's possible to make the IntelliSense even recognize custom entities and attributes as well.

To accomplish this we have created a utility that will query the meta data and generate a ".js" file for each entity found.

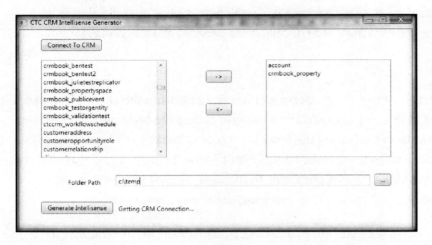

In the generated file, we define a shell class that implements crmForm and has properties for all the attributes on the entity.

The following is an example of part of the generated file for the account entity. Notice that each property is created using the type of the attribute –this is done by pulling information from the platform Metadata API.

```
crmForm.all.defaultpricelevelid =  new CRMLookupProperty();
crmForm.all.address1_shippingmethodcode =  new CRMPicklistProperty();
crmForm.all.originatingleadidname =  new CRMStringProperty();
crmForm.all.industrycode =  new CRMPicklistProperty();
crmForm.all.statuscodename =  new CRMVirtualProperty();
crmForm.all.address2_fax =  new CRMStringProperty();
…more
```

This file will never be executed and will only be used to give hints to the Visual Studio 2008 IntelliSense engine for what fields are available on the account entity.

We have pre-generated one of these files for each of the built-in entities in the system. You can find that in the sample code under the ClientScript/CrmFormIntelliSense folder.

We have also provided in the samples the utility that generates these files so you can re-run them against your specific customizations. That will allow generation of the files with any custom attributes and entities. You can find this tool in the sample files under CRMIntelliSenseGen.

Using these generated files is simple. All you need to do is include one line at the top of your JavaScript file that you are using for adding custom script to the entity events. If you are following our suggested file scheme then you would just add the following line to the Account/account_OnLoad.js file to be able to use the IntelliSense.

```
/// <reference path="..\\CrmFormIntellisense\account.js" />
```

This line is only interpreted by Visual Studio 2008 and can be left in at deployment time as it is treated as a comment by the browser. The IntelliSense engine however will parse it and use it to help you as you try to write your JavaScript code.

 **NOTE**   *The ///reference only works with a web project approach and will not provide IntelliSense with the built-in form editor.*

The following is an example of what will show once you start typing crm into the account_onload.js file.

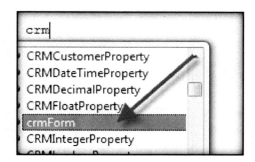

Note: It may take a few seconds after a file is opened or you add the reference tag to the file before the editor will re-parse and IntelliSense will start working.

I know that seems simple but keep reading it gets better. As you type crmForm.all. it will start showing you all the attributes that entity has and allow you to select using a name. This is a huge benefit for someone new to the CRM platform or your custom entities so they don't have to have memorized all the field types. Even for an expert, the IntelliSense will save you time as it reduces the required typing.

The following shows IntelliSense drilling down to the field level.

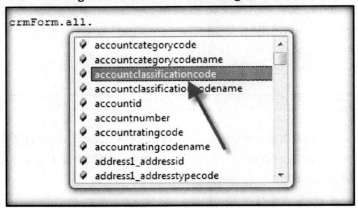

If you recall above when we defined each of the attributes we used the Metadata to determine the type of the attribute and set the JavaScript property to the corresponding attribute type. We did this because each Attribute Type has certain properties and methods that are available.

The following shows an example of showing the methods and properties list for address1_city attribute.

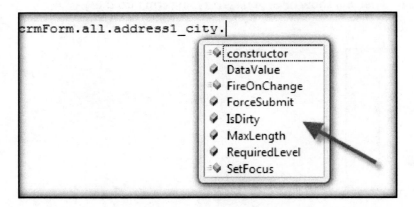

As you can tell it has shown the properties that exist for a String attribute and makes it real easy to know what is available to use in your JavaScript.

The code generation application is pretty simplistic and hopefully by including it in the sample code you can customize it if needed to add additional capabilities or use it to generate custom script for other purposes that are driven by Metadata of the platform.

SiteMap / ISVConfig

A critical customization to any solution is the ability to modify the navigation of the client interface. The CRM platform uses two xml files to control overall site navigation. Much of this is done for you as you modify or customize entities and make selections of where you want that form to show. However, editing the SiteMap and ISVConfig directly can provide complete control to customize your site navigation.

Prior to CRM 4.0, the ISVConfig was a physical file stored on each server. In CRM 4.0, it is now stored as part of the organization database along with SiteMap. Both of these are modified by exporting the XML and then re-importing them back into the organization. There is not a user interface or an API to supporting modifications of either of these configuration files. The SiteMap is also modified by the system when you select an area in the entity editor that you would like it displayed.

The following image shows an example of an entity showing in multiple areas and the ISVConfig, so we won't re-cover any more than necessary of the basics here.

If you do decide to make changes to the XML files directly, I recommend storing it externally in version control and avoiding using the above check boxes except when adding an entity for the first time and testing it. Always using the external file and importing it will lead to more consistent repeatable results.

You should think of SiteMap as controlling the overall navigation of the site. By modifying SiteMap you can move, remove, and rename areas that are in CRM as well as their sub areas and items that they contain. For example, The "Workplace" might be more appropriately called "My Work" in a solution and that can be changed by modification to the SiteMap.

The ISVConfig on the other hand allows you to modify the form navigation for each entity in the system both built-in and custom entities you create. Using this you can add buttons; customize grids as well as the navigation on the entity form.

In order to use ISVConfig you must enable that in each organization using the Settings - > System Settings - > Organization Settings page.

Editing the Files

Both the SiteMap and the ISVConfig extract to a simple XML file that looks like the following.

```
SiteMaps/SiteMap.xml
<ImportExportXml version="4.0.0.0" languagecode="1033" generatedBy="OnPremise">
    <Entities>
    </Entities>
    <Roles>
    </Roles>
    <Workflows>
    </Workflows>
    <SiteMap>
        <SiteMap>
            <Area Id="Workplace" ResourceId="Area_Workplace" ShowGroups="true" Icon="/_im
                <Group Id="MyWork" ResourceId="Group_MyWork" DescriptionResourceId="My_Wc
                    <SubArea Id="nav_activities" Entity="activitypointer" DescriptionResc
                    <SubArea  Icon="/_imgs/area/18_calendar.gif" Id="nav_ctcactviewer" Pa
```

As you can see in the above example of a SiteMap it's part of a larger XML Import/Export file. In this example, I only exported the SiteMap but you still get the empty tags for other things like Entities, Roles, Workflow, etc.

Typically what I like to do is take this file, add it to my CRMCustomizations web project so I can version control it. I then use Visual Studio to be able to edit it and get IntelliSense.

To recover from importing a bad SiteMap file use the following URL along with your backup sitemap file

<serverurl>/tools/systemcustomization/ImportCustomizations/import Customizations.aspx

Enabling IntelliSense in Visual Studio

By default you would get the basic IntelliSense you get with every other generic XML file which isn't enough to make it easier for us. To improve on that we can inform Visual Studio of the SiteMap/ ISVConfig schema so it can use that to inform IntelliSense what is valid in the XML.

 If you look at properties for our exported SiteMap or ISVConfig you would see the following dialog.

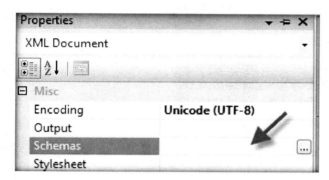

Notice how the Schemas location is blank. What we want to do is click the browse button and add a reference to the CRM SDK provided schema for the import/export format.

The next dialog you will see is the XML Schemas list which shows the schemas currently registered.

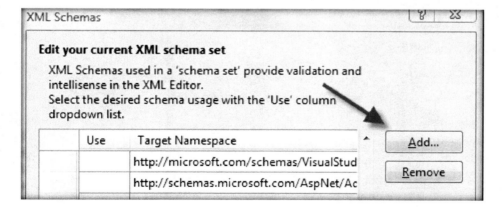

If you had done this before for the project, then the CRM schemas might be on the list we will cover that later in the chapter how to enable it. If this is the first time, click the Add and it will bring up an Open XSD Schemas dialog to allow you to find the schema file you want to add.

The CRM schema files are located in the SDK folder $sdkroot/sdk/server/schemas. The specific one we are looking for is customizations.xsd located in the importexport subfolder as you can see below.

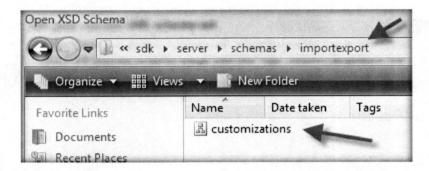

After selecting the customizations.xsd file it will return us to the list of XML schemas. Now when you get back to your XML file for the ISVConfig if you start typing you should see the IntelliSense pickup showing the valid tags and attributes for the ISVConfig.

The following is an example of the IntelliSense.

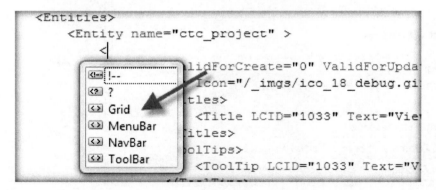

Now to configure IntelliSense for the SiteMap file, all we have to do is browse to XML Schemas again and our customizations.xsd will already be on the list. In the left hand column, we use the drop down to select "Use this schema" from the list.

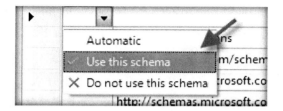

Using these steps you can enhance your edit experience in Visual Studio and reduce the chance that you will introduce an error in either of these files.

Passing Parameters

When using the Url property on SiteMap subArea element to specify the application to be target of invocation you can optionally have CRM pass some parameters to it. Using the PassParams you can have CRM automatically include the following as part of your Url. This also works with Buttons, MenuItem and NavBarItems when working with the ISV.Config file. The following table will highlight the different parameters passed

Parameter	Type	Description
orgname	ISVConfig SiteMap	The unique name of the CRM organization. Remember the unique name is the one without spaces and not intended to be necessarily friendly for display. The orgname can be used by the target page to ensure they interact with the correct organization in a multi-tenant installation.
orglcid	ISVConfig SiteMap	This indicates the base language code for the organization e.g. 1033 is English.
userlcid	ISVConfig SiteMap	This is the language code for the user's current settings. Remember a user can choose from any of the provisioned languages of the organization to use that language. They can switch using the Tools- Options menu from the client interface at any time even during an existing session. Using this, a target application could help ensure consistency in the users

		language on the external page that is being invoked.

Parameter	Type	Description
typename	ISVConfig	This passes the name of the entity e.g. crmbook_project. The target page could use this along with the id property to retrieve or modify the record.
type	ISVConfig	This is a numeric number to indicate the type – avoid using this as much as possible as it can change from install to install depending on the order that custom entities are imported or created in the system. Use typename instead where possible.
id	ISVConfig	This is the GUID for the record currently being worked on by the parent form.

Vary by Client and Online/Offline

Since the user can interact with different type of clients and those clients can be on or offline at any given point in time it's important to be able to use that information to customize navigation of the site. The platform provides the ability to control when the lowest level of navigation shows based on the "Client" attribute. For example if you add a button to a toolbar you can specify the "Client=" attribute to indicate that it should only be viewed in some client environments.

You can further indicate if you want an item available if the client is offline by using the "AvailableOffline" attribute.

This is important for a couple of reasons, first, you might have some items that link to things that are not available when the user is offline. By setting this you can hide those items from the user when they are offline. Additionally, you could use this to vary the link or other settings on the item depending on if the user is online or offline.

The following example shows a button that specifies both the Client and the AvailableOffline attributes.

```
<Button Title="My Button"
            ToolTip="This is a simple do nothing button"
            Icon="/_imgs/ico_18_debug.gif"
            JavaScript="alert('Hello From Button');"
            Client="Outlook,Web" AvailableOffline="true" />
```

The following are the valid values for the Client attribute: All, Outlook, OutlookLaptopClient, OutlookWorkstationClient, Web - These can be comma separated to allow specification of multiple.

Supporting Multiple Languages

If you plan on supporting multiple languages you will want to consider how to handle that on your navigation elements as well. The platform provides support for that by allowing you to specify a title for each language ID.

```
<SubArea Id="nav_dashboard" PassParams="1"
         Url="/dashboard/dashboard.aspx" >
<Titles>
    <Title Title="CRM Dashboard" LCID="1033" />
    <Title Title=" Tableau de bord de CRM" LCID="1053" />
</Titles>
</SubArea>
```

Customizing Left Navigation Areas

One of the things you can do to personalize an application for the particular user segment is to modify the areas that are displayed in the left navigation.

The following is an example of the areas. Notice you don't see "Sales" there. That's because "Sales" has been modified to be "Manage Contacts".

This type of change is done by modifying the <Area> elements in the SiteMap. You can also add groups within each of the areas to further divide the links. A group is added using the <Group>element inside an <Area>. When you add a group by default there's no divider shown the links are just concatenated together. On the Area element you can specify ShowGroups="True" and then a divider with the name of the Group will be shown.

The following is an example of what it looks like to have multiple groups and turning ShowGroups="True".

Another thing you can do is allow users to personalize the Workplace area. When a user goes to Tools - > Options and then the Workplace tab, they see the following.

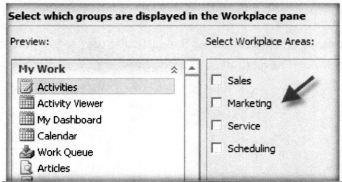

The area on the right where it says "Select Workplace Areas" can be customized. What shows up there is any group that is in the Workplace Area and has its IsProfile="true" enabled on the group. The IsProfile attribute is at the Group level and only effects Groups that are inside the Workplace Area. Using the IsProfile option you give the user the ability to decide if that group will show up in their Workplace area or if it will be hidden.

Don't forget if you do change the name of any of the Areas from the standard Sales, Marketing etc. You must also change the duplicate group that is in the Workplace section otherwise your users will still see those names on the options page.

IFrame Integration

Integrating external applications can be done using the IFrame capability of the CRM forms. Using this capability, you can identify a section on a tab to contain an IFrame and then point that to any external application you desire. Here are a few ideas of things you could do with IFrames.

- Include a SharePoint document workspace that is associated with the CRM entity form.

- Integrate mapping with your form – show where the contact , account or whatever is located. Even better, show what else is located near there. We have an example of integrating mapping later in the chapter.

- Any external URL – really, you can even vary what it points to based on data that the CRM entity contains.

- A custom ASP.NET web page to allow custom input or display. This approach could be used to integrate non-platform data, or since you can be passed the entity Id, you can reach back and pull data from other entities to display.

The URL that is used for the IFrame can be static and defined when the IFrame is added to the form, or it can be dynamically set. In the following chapter, we will be going over a helper script that makes it easier to set the URL for an IFrame.

There are a few key things to keep in mind when you're working with IFrames. One of the common things you will need to think about if your IFrames are dynamic is what type of data you will want to pass back and forth between the parent form and the child IFrame. You do have access to the standard techniques using DHTML to pass things back and forth between the parent and the child. That said, you have to keep in mind that there are strict security restrictions in place if the page in the IFrame is not from the same domain as the hosting page. This isn't likely to cause problems in on-premise installations but will cause some problems in partner hosted or CRM Online configurations.

You can also easily host Silverlight content within an IFrame. Using Silverlight you get the rich .NET programming model without having to do as much AJAX Javascript. See Chapter 7 where we show a couple of Silverlight examples.

Let us look at an example of using IFrame to integrate Virtual Earth Mapping into the form for the Contact entity. Our first step will be to add a Tab to the form, followed by adding a section to the new tab.

For our example, we will be naming both the tab and the section "Map". Next, we will click on the Add IFrame link and we will see the following dialog.

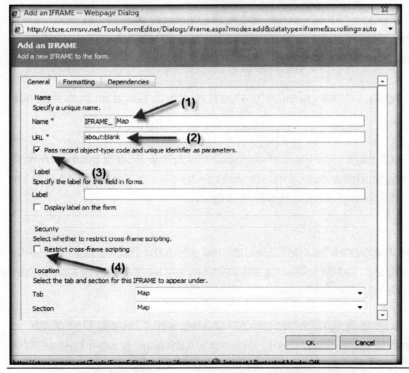

On this form we will be configuring how the IFrame will behave and where it will point.

1. This gives the IFrame its name. This will be used later when we need to set the IFrame URL.

2. The URL property allows us to establish the URL that the IFrame will point. For our purpose we have intentionally used "about:blank" which will cause the IFrame to be blank initially until we set the URL. In some cases you might want to point it to a fixed place so in this field you could put a full URL like http://crm.davidyack.com .

3. This option tells the form to pass the typename and the ID to the URL that is being put in the IFrame. The reason you would do this is the application in the IFrame might want to retrieve or otherwise manipulate the object.

    For example, we could allow the user to click on the map, and then use the Object ID to update the geo code for that entity. You can see an example of what is passed in the figure below.

4. This enables or disables cross site scripting. If you don't control the target page leaving this checked is advisable. Even with this turned off there are some limitations on what will work for talking back and forth with the parent form and the IFrame.

```
/VEIFrameMap.aspx?type=1&typename=account&id={85F31707-BF7D-DC11-8D49-001B787660A2}
```

Before we save the Add IFrame dialog, click on the Formatting tab and we need to make a couple of changes. We want the IFrame to expand to take the entire tab so we check the "Automatically expand to use available space" checkbox. We also want our Virtual Earth map to flow with the tab so we uncheck the "Display Border" checkbox.

Setting up the ASP.NET Page

Now let us turn our attention server side and look at how we can build out our page to host the map. Some of our choices including how we will interact between the IFrame and the server page will be based on the fact we want this to work in CRM Online as well as on-premise. CRM Online because we cannot host pages on Microsoft's servers will increase our challenge a bit.

The ASP.NET page we are showing parts of here and the associated helper Javascript is located in the sample CRMWeb project in the Mapping folder.

```
<script type="text/javascript" src="http://dev.virtualearth.net/mapcontrol/mapcontrol.ashx?v=6"></script>
<script type="text/javascript" src="CTCVEMapHelper.js" ></script>
<script type="text/javascript">
        var ctc_Map = null;
        function GetMap()
        {                                              (2)
            ctc_Map = new VEMap('ctcMap');
            ctc_Map.LoadMap();              (3)                                      (1)

            var CTCVEMapHelper = new CTCVEMapHelperClass(ctc_Map);

            var QS = GetQS();              (5)
                                                   (4)
            pinLabel = GetQSValue(QS,'Label','');
            pinDesc  = GetQSValue(QS,'Desc','');

            if (QS['AddressLine'] != null)
            {
                var addressLine = GetQSValue(QS,'AddressLine','');
                CTCVEMapHelper.OnGeoCoded =              (6)
                    function(latitude,longutide)
                        { CTCVEMapHelper.AddPin(pinLabel,pinDesc,latitude,longutide);}
                CTCVEMapHelper.GeoCodeAddressLine(addressLine);
            }
            if (QS['LatLong'] != null)              (7)
            {
                var latLon = GetQSValue(QS,'LatLong','').split(",");
                var zoom = GetQSValue(QS,'Zoom',14);
                CTCVEMapHelper.AddPin(pinLabel,pinDesc,latLon[0],latLon[1]);
                this.ctc_Map.SetCenterAndZoom(new VELatLong(latLon[0], latLon[1]), zoom);

            }
        }
```

Most of the work to interface with Virtual Earth is using JavaScript. The above figure shows the steps we take to integrate. Many of these use helper methods of an included class to make life easier.

1. This includes the Map Control JavaScript that is required to get the Virtual Earth functionality.
2. This includes a helper JavaScript class that makes it easier to interface with Virtual Earth and packages up calls like GeoCodeAddressLine.
3. Here we are setting up the Virtual Earth Control, ctcMap is the name of a Div tag on our page that will be taken over by Virtual Earth to show the map.
4. On this line we are creating an instance of our map helper and giving it a reference to the map control.

5. Using a simple Query string parser we are getting what is passed. CRM will be passing the address as a query string to the page.

6. Many of the Virtual Earth functions are asynchronous and use callbacks. Here we are setting up what we want done when our helper is done getting a geo code for the address – in this case we simply want to add a pin to the map.

7. Same logic as for Address but here's a helper to add a pin if we have the Lat/Long.

Now we have our basic ASP.NET page that will host our map control. We could do a lot more processing server side, for example go find other data to show on the map, but for now we will keep it simple.

Connecting the Form IFrame to the ASP.NET Page

Now that we have the server side all ready, let us go ahead and hook up the form so when the user clicks on the Map tab it loads the map page. To do this we are going to modify the OnLoad event for the form and include the following code.

```
//CTCTraceWindowEnabled = new Object();
//CTCTrace - Start
var CTCTraceWindowHandle=null;var CTCTraceLastTrace=new Date();functi
//CTCTrace - End


// CTCCrmIFrame   V 1.0 11/17/07
function CTCCrmIFrame(iframeName,defaultServerURL,targetPagePath){thi
// CTCCrmIFrame   V 1.0 11/17/07


// CTCCrmFormTab V1.0 11/17/2007
function CTCCrmFormTab(tabNumber){this.ShowInOutlookOnline=true;this.
// CTCCrmFormTab V1.0 11/17/2007
```

The above helper classes will be used to make the coding shorter and more supportable for managing the tab and the IFrame which require some technically unsupported manipulation to get this to work. Using these helper classes isolate the small amount of unsupported code. In reality, it is sometimes required to use unsupported methods, but when possible it is always best to use the supported methods if they exist. When doing something unsupported like this, try to isolate it to a single place or a common place so it could be easily replaced in the future. That helps you mitigate risk compared to sprinkling it all over the place. In most cases, unsupported typically means that if you have a problem in that area, you will need to show that it is still broken without the unsupported code being used.

The following example shows the code that implements the RegisterOnClick method.

```
var tab4 = new CTCCrmFormTab(4);                                    (1)
tab4.RegisterOnClick(
  function()                                   (2)
  {
    CTCTrace("TabOnClick","Starting - About to create instance of IFrame");

    frame = new CTCCrmIFrame("Map","http://ctcre.crmsrv.net","/ctcreweb/Mapping/VEIFrameMap.aspx");

    CTCTrace("TabOnClick","About to build QS");
    var qs = new Array();
    var addr = new Object();
                                                       (3)
    addr['Name'] = 'AddressLine';

    addr['Value'] = crmForm.all.address1_line1.DataValue+ ',' + crmForm.all.address1_city.DataValue + ','
    + crmForm.all.address1_stateorprovince.DataValue + ','+
    crmForm.all.address1_postalcode.DataValue ;

    qs[qs.length] = addr;
                                                  (4)
    CTCTrace("TabOnClick","calling Set URL");
    frame.SetURL("/ctcreweb/Mapping/VEIFrameMap.aspx",qs);
    CTCTrace("TabOnClick","Done");
  }
);
```

The code above uses the helper classes to hook up to the OnClick event of the tab and set the url and the parms we are going to pass.

1. Create a new instance of our Tab Helper and reference the 4th tab.

2. RegisterOnClick wraps around some unsupported code to add an Event handler to the tab to call our provided method when the user clicks the Map Tab.

3. We simply concatenate the CRM fields for address to pass on the query string. Obviously some additional error handling if this was a production application.

4. Using our Frame helper we set the URL and pass the parms that we want to be on the query string.

The following is our end result with our map integrated into the IFrame.

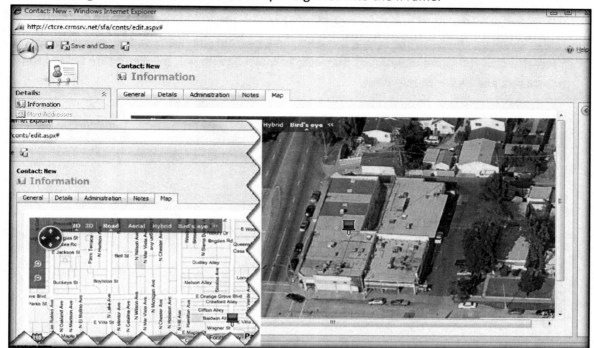

As you can see from the above example the Virtual Earth map is now integrated as a tab on our contact. The user is able to switch between views on the map by interacting with the map controls in the IFrame.

This is a great example of the power of integration using the CRM Forms and the IFrame capabilities. Not only did we leverage server side integration we also pulled in some existing capabilities from another SaaS platform by integrating Virtual Earth.

Silverlight

Microsoft Silverlight is a cross-browser, cross-platform implementation of the .NET Framework allowing development of rich interactive applications for the web. Sliverlight can be integrated as part of the CRM platform user experience to provide a richer interface for certain types of customizations. We cover SilverLight in much greater detail in Chapter 7.

Wrapping it up

We have covered a lot of ground in this chapter talking about everything from form basics to more advanced concepts like calling the web services from client side script. More important we have also covered some techniques that help to make developing the client side script more productive and easier to maintain.

6

Client Scripting How-To's

In the previous chapter, we looked at what you can do to customize the client interface. This included looking at the built-in object model that is exposed by CRM to allow custom client scripting. In this chapter, we will be looking at some tangible examples of how you can leverage client side scripting to make the user interface more interactive. Using client side scripting you can easily make the difference between what the user perceives as an off the shelf solution and one that is custom for how they perform their work.

These examples can be single lines of JavaScript that you place in the form event handlers or they can be more complex. (We have created some reusable libraries for you to use.) As you are looking through the chapter to find something to help with a specific requirement, you may not find an exact match, but should find you ideas on how to take it and customize it for your particular need.

If you are working with CRM Online, you may find that you leverage client scripting a little more than you would in an on-premise type installation where you can deploy your own managed code. Often times, using client script you can accomplish some of the same things that required deployment of code to do in the past. For example, using the CRM Web Service helper class we include in this chapter you can easily do things like retrieve default values, update values on other entities and more.

Supported vs. Not Supported

One of the things to keep in mind when doing client side script is around supportability. There is a fine line on the client side script between 100% supported and not supported. As a rule of thumb we try to encourage where possible to stay as much on the supported path as possible.

That said, you will likely encounter scripting that you will need to or will want to do that will take you a little outside the supported changes. I always encourage when that happens that you do so knowingly and with a plan. If you pick-up code from the Internet, make sure you know what it does, some will be fully supportable others will not.

What are the risks? You can look at the risks a couple of ways. The first risk arises if you have to call Microsoft support for a problem. You will need to reproduce the problem without your unsupported changes. For script, most of the time that can be as simple as removing or disabling the offending logic. The other area of risk is around upgrades and hotfixes. When you step outside the supported scripting, it's possible that things you depend on might not exist or will have changed after a hotfix or an upgrade is completed. A good example of this, is from CRM 3.0 to CRM 4.0 several of the fields HTML markup changed due to changes in the platform. If you were dependent on the structure of that markup you would have to update it before moving to CRM 4.0.

Calling Web Services using JavaScript

To start this off we will be looking at how you can call the Web Service from the client directly via JavaScript. The helper class that we present in this chapter and make available in the samples make it much simpler to interact with the web services from JavaScript. Using this technique allows you to do a lot of different user related custom processing without installing any code on the server. This can be particularly helpful in the CRM Online environment since you can't deploy custom code to the server.

What that means is our helper classes take care of handling all the details of the Soap protocol and you only have to worry about calling the helper classes. We have implemented three key JavaScript classes that you will interact with. First is the CTCCrmService class. This class provides the methods you will invoke to access the platform web service calls. To be able to pass and retrieve data we have a client side data container that emulates a Dynamic Entity and is implemented by the CTCCrmDynamicEntity class. Finally, to support doing complex queries from the client, we have implemented a CTCCrmQueryExpression class that will simulate the QueryExpression class used on server side to specify your criteria for retrieves of data.

To use these helper classes as part of your JavaScript you need to include them at the top of your script. You can include the above classes by including the $/Framework/ClientScript/Common/CTCCrmWebServiceOptimized.js file.

```
// CTCCrmWebService 1.2 - 2/12/2008
```

```
CTCCrmConditionValue=function(){this.Type='guid';this.Value='';CTCCrmC...
// CTCCrmWebService 1.2 - 2/12/2008
```

By including this it will define all the necessary classes for working with the web services from JavaScript.

By using this helper class it will shield you from having to do a lot of the heavy lifting required by the Soap calls. Additionally, it will do the work for you to determine the correct host and authentication header to send so you can focus on simply calling the web services and your business logic.

As part of that method, it creates a global variable CTCCrmService that will be used to ineract with the server web service.

CTCCRMService Methods

The following are the current methods supported by the version included in the book.

WhoAmI

Simply returns the Guid of the current logged in user. Great for testing to make sure things are working!

```
GUID (as string)   CTCCrmService.WhoAmI()
```

RetrieveMultiple

This method takes a CTCCrmQueryExpression class and returns a collection of dynamic entities. We will discuss more on QueryExpression and Dynamic Entity Collections later in the chapter.

```
CTCCrmDynamicEntityCollection
CTCCrmService.RetrieveMultiple(CTCCrmQueryExpression)
```

Example using Retrieve Multiple

In this example we are looking at what it would take to call Retrieve Multiple directly. The first thing we need to do is construct a CTCCrmQueryExpression. The following logic shows that plus calling the retrieve method.

```
var qe = new CTCCrmQueryExpression();
var crit = new CTCCrmCriteria();
qe.Criteria = crit;
var c1 = new CTCCrmCondition();
crit.Conditions[0] = c1;
c1.AttributeName=keyName;
var v1 = new CTCCrmConditionValue();
v1.Type="guid";
v1.Value=keyValue;
c1.Values[0] = v1;
qe.EntityName=entityName;

entityCollection = CTCCrmService.RetrieveMultiple(qe);
```

RetrieveBySingleKey

This is a helper method that will take your simple parameters and build the CTCCrmQueryExpression for you and then call the RetrieveMultiple and return you the results as a dynamic entity collection.

```
CTCCrmDynamicEntityCollection
        CTCCrmService.RetrieveBySingleKey(entityName,keyName,keyValue)
```

RetrieveFirstBySingleKey

This is another helper method to net down the results of a query to a single dynamic entity that is the first returned. The return type for this is a single Dynamic Entity.

```
CTCCrmDynamicEntity
    CTCCrmService.RetrieveFirstBySingleKey(entityName,keyName,keyValue)
```

Example calling Retrieve Single

The following example shows the code to get the defaultuomid for the product selected on a lookup.

```
//get the lookup value from the field
lookupItem = crmForm.all.productid.DataValue;

//call WS and get the Product
dynProduct =
    CTCCrmService.RetrieveFirstBySingleKey("product",
        "productid",lookupItem[0].id);
alert(dynProduct.GetStringValue("defaultuomid",""));
```

Compare this example to the example in the SDK for calling Web Services from the client and you will see how streamlined this approach is from an end developer point of view.

Create

Allows you to create an entity instance from the client side by passing in a Dynamic Entity object. The method returns the Guid of the record that was created.

```
GUID        CTCCrmService.Create(CTCCrmDynamicEntity)
```

Update

Update allows you to pass the fields desired and update an entity instance. You must pass at least the key field in order to have the method work.

```
CTCCrmService.Update(CTCCrmDynamicEntity)
```

Delete

The Delete method requires you to pass the entity name and an ID to delete a record.

```
CTCCrmService.Delete(entityName, entityID)
```

Using Create, Update and Delete

The following example demonstrates using the Create, Update and Delete methods:

```
var de  = new CTCCrmDynamicEntity();
de.EntityName ='contact';
de.AddProperty('firstname','StringProperty','Dave');
de.AddProperty('lastname','StringProperty','Yack');

entityID = CTCCrmService.Create(de);

var de2  = new CTCCrmDynamicEntity();
de2.EntityName ='contact';
de2.AddProperty('contactid','KeyProperty',entityID);
de2.AddProperty('lastname','StringProperty','Denver');
de2.AddProperty('firstname','StringProperty','John');

CTCCrmService.Update(de2);

CTCCrmService.Delete('contact',entityID);
```

Example using LinkEntities as part of a Query

The following example gives a more complex example of using the Query Expression object to specify criteria that involves more than one entity. In this example, we are filtering on values of related entities to reduce our result set to only those records that match.

The crmbook_property entity is our main entity that has a 1:N relationship with crmbook_propertyagent. Our crmbook_propertyagent entity is further related to System user. The following example uses the LinkEntity capabilities of the API to do a retrieve multiple that gets all system user records associated with the crmbook_property via the crmbook_propertyagent entity.

```
var qe = new CTCCrmQueryExpression();
var crit = new CTCCrmCriteria();
qe.Criteria = crit;
qe.EntityName = "systemuser";

var c1 = new CTCCrmCondition();
crit.Conditions[0] = c1;
c1.AttributeName="internalemailaddress";
c1.Operator = c1.OperationNotEqual;
var v1 = new CTCCrmConditionValue();
v1.Type="string";
v1.Value="";
c1.Values[0] = v1;

var links = new CTCCrmLinkEntityCollection();
qe.LinkEntities = links;
var l1 = new CTCCrmLinkEntity();
links.LinkEntities[0] = l1;
l1.LinkFromEntityName = "systemuser";
l1.LinkFromAttributeName = "systemuserid";
l1.LinkToEntityName = "crmbook_propertyagent";
l1.LinkToAttributeName = "ownerid";

var links2 = new CTCCrmLinkEntityCollection();
l1.LinkEntities = links2;
var l2 = new CTCCrmLinkEntity();
links2.LinkEntities[0] = l2;
l2.LinkFromEntityName = "crmbook_teammember";
l2.LinkFromAttributeName = "crmbook_propertyidid";
l2.LinkToEntityName = "crmbook_property";
l2.LinkToAttributeName = "crmbook_propertyid";
var crit2 = new CTCCrmCriteria();
l2.LinkCriteria = crit2;
```

```
var c2 = new CTCCrmCondition();
crit2.Conditions[0] = c2;
c2.AttributeName="crmbook_propertyid";
var v2 = new CTCCrmConditionValue();
v2.Type = "guid";
v2.Value = window.opener.document.crmForm.ObjectId;
c2.Values[0] = v2

var entityCollection = CTCCrmService.RetrieveMultiple(qe);
```

The result of the web service call would be a Dynamic Entity list of matching system users.

GetUserRoles

The following example demonstrates using GetUserRoles to get a list of the roles that a user has. You could use this to alter the behavior of the form and your script.

```
var roles = CTCCrmService.GetUserRoles();
for (i=0; i<roles.length; i++)
{
    if (roles[i] == "System Administrator")
        alert('you are a system administrator');
}
```

IsInRole

The following example demonstrates using IsInRole to check if a user is in a specific role.

```
var isSysAdmin = CTCCrmService.IsInRole("System Administrator");
```

Wrapping up CTCCRMService

In the above examples we looked at how to use the CTCCRMService class to make calls back to the platform. Using this as part of your client script code you can do any type of platform action you would typically do from server side custom code.

Defaulting a Lookup Field

One of the things you might want to do is default the value of a lookup field on a form. Lookup fields DataValue property is an array of LookupControlItem objects that represent the selected value(s). To set a default, you need to have the Guid, the type and the label you want to show for the item. We have included a method GetDefaultLookupValue in our base class that we suggest you use for all forms. The following is a quick look at how the method works. It basically creates an array, and then creates an instance of LookupControlItem and adds it to the array.

```
MySolutionClass.prototype.GetDefaultLookupValue =
function(guid,type,label)
{
    var lookupItem = new Array();
    lookupItem[0] = new LookupControlItem (guid, type, label);
    return lookupItem;
}
```

To use this, you would call the method and set the DataValue property of a lookup. The following is an example of using the GetDefaultLookupValue method.

```
crmForm.all.crmbook_userid.DataValue   =
     document. MySolution.GetDefaultLookupValue(
              crmForm.all.ownerid.DataValue, 8, "John Doe");
```

Defaulting a Lookup Field from Web Service

Taking our prior example a step further, we might want to default the value by retrieving the default value from a web service call. In the following example we combine the use of GetDefaultLookupValue we already saw with a call to get the value using our Web Service helper class. As you can see below, we are retrieving a product entity based on the product ID a user selects on a product lookup. Then using that product entity we retrieve the defaultuomid from its dynamic entity object that was returned from the web service call. Using that ID we do another call to retrieve the unit of measure object. Using the uom dynamic entity that is returned we can build out our default value and set the lookup on our Unit of measure lookup.

```
if (crmForm.all.productid.DataValue == null)
     return;

//get the lookup value from the field
```

```
lookupItem = crmForm.all.productid.DataValue;

//call WS and get the Product
dynProduct = CTCCrmService.RetrieveFirstBySingleKey("product",
                "productid",lookupItem[0].id);

//call WS and get the Unit
dynUOM = CTCCrmService.RetrieveFirstBySingleKey(
      "uom","uomid",dynProduct.GetStringValue("defaultuomid",""));

//build out the default lookup and set the unit value
crmForm.all.uomid.DataValue = MySolution.GetDefaultLookupValue(
        dynUOM.GetStringValue("uomid",""), 1055,
              dynUOM.GetStringValue("name","")
```

Using the approach in this example we are able to drive our default values from the data record not a hard coded value in our script.

Working with IFrames

As we saw in the prior chapter IFrames are powerful because they allow us to integrate external applications inside the platform forms. Using this approach we can give users a more seamless experience when interacting with the form. Often times a user will never know that there are multiple applications involved.   In this section we are going to look at how to work with an IFrame and dynamically set and control some of the properties on the fly.

The CRM Form object model exposes each IFrame defined on a form as part of the crmForm.all collection using the name you give the IFrame. For example, if you add an IFrame named "Map" then you can access it via crmForm.all.IFRAME_Map similar to how you would access a field on the form. To make it easier to work with the IFrame to do common tasks we have created a helper JavaScript class that you can use called CTCCrmIFrame. The following are some of the things you can do using it.

- Set the URL using a SetURL method or when constructing the helper class.
- Determine when the IFrame should show based on Type of Form.
- Determine when the IFrame should show based on Type of Client and if the client is Online or Offline.
- Set the IFrame to display related Items in an IFrame instead of on the Left Navigation of the Form.

To use the CTCCrmIFrame helper class we need to include in each of our OnLoad events where we plan to use it the following compressed/optimized script. The script can be found in the book sample code in the following location:

$/Framework/ClientScript/Common/CTCCrmIframeOptimized.js

```
// CTCCrmIFrame  V 1.1 4/24/08
function CTCCrmIFrame(iframeName,defaultServerURL,targetPagePath)
// CTCCrmIFrame  V 1.1 4/24/08
```

If you need to make changes to it the non-optimized script can be found in the CTCCrmIframe.js file.

Referencing our IFrame

To use the class you would first create a reference to the IFrame by creating a new instance of the CTCCrmIframe class as you can see in the following example.

The constructor for the class takes the following parameters.

```
CTCCrmIFrame(frameName,defaultServerURL,targetPagePath);
```

The following creates a new instance of CTCCrmIFrame referencing the "Map" Iframe on our page.

```
mapFrame = new
CTCCrmIFrame("Map","http://serverurl","/crmbookweb/Mapping/page.aspx");
```

Configuring IFrame Visibility

Now that we have our reference to mapFrame let's explore some of the things we can use our helper class for. One of the features is to help control IFrame visibility. To be up front, there is no 100% supported way to hide an IFrame other than setting it's source to about:blank which will simply cause it to not show valid data but the frame itself will still be on the page.

Because the IFrame is just a HTML element you can use the standard item.style.Display="none". Technically speaking, that would not be 100% supported code and could break in future releases. In our helper class we use that technique but we centralize and hide it as part of the helper class in hopes that if the technique changes for doing it, we can simply update our helper class.

Using the helper class you can control visibility based on type of form and type of client. The following are the properties you can set to control visibility based on type of form. The values shown below are the default values if you don't set them.

```
mapFrame.ShowFormTypeCreate = true;
mapFrame.ShowFormTypeUpdate = true;
mapFrame.ShowFormTypeReadOnly = true;
mapFrame.ShowFormTypeDisabled = true;
```

As you can see those are just properties on our mapFrame object .

You can also control the visibility based on the type of client interface being used. For example, you might not want an IFrame to try to load when the user is offline in the Outlook interface. The following are the properties that control visibility by client type and their default values.

```
mapFrame.ShowInOutlookOnline = true;
mapFrame.ShowInOutlookOffline = false;
mapFrame.ShowInWeb = true;
```

To give you a more complete example, imagine if you want to show the IFrame at all times with a couple exceptions. In our example, we don't want to show on the Create form because we have nothing to pass to the external application because the user hasn't input any data yet. Additionally, since our external application is only available when the user is on-line we want to turn off showing it when the user is in the Outlook client and is offline.

The following creates a new reference to our "Map" frame and then sets the values.

```
mapFrame = new
CTCCrmIFrame("Map","http://serverurl","/crmbookweb/Mapping/page.aspx");

mapFrame.ShowFormTypeCreate = false;
mapFrame.ShowInOutlookOffline = false;
```

The rest of the work is then done by the CTCCrmIFrame helper class. Notice we allowed the other properties to take their default values and only needed to specify the ones we specifically want to modify.

Finally, you can also manually call the show and hide methods to control visibility directly from your script as you can see in the following example.

```
mapFrame.HideIFrame();
mapFrame.ShowIFrame();
```

Setting the URL to a Page

The next thing we will look at is setting the URL. For the most basic needs you can do this without using the helper class by just setting the "src" property on the IFrame. Using that approach your code would look similar to the following example.

```
crmForm.all.IFRAME_Map.src = "http://myserver/page.aspx";
```

The helper class provides the SetURL method that can be called to set the URL to an external page. The following is the method signature for this method.

```
SetURL(targetPagePath,qsArray)
```

The target path is the path to the page on the external server. Remember we specified the external server on the constructor for our helper class, so it's not needed at this point. The second parameter is an Array object of parameters. These parameters are appended to the target page path.

The following example code shows how to build the query string parameters to pass into the SetURL method.

```
var qs = new Array();
var addr = new Object();

addr['Name'] = 'AddressLine';

addr['Value'] = crmForm.all.address1_line1.DataValue;

qs[addr['Name']] =  addr['Value'];
```

The above code basically creates an array of Name/Value objects. The SetURL method will then append each of these when it builds the full URL string. The full URL string will be used to modify the IFrame's "src" property.

In addition to appending the array of parameters passed to the SetURL method a few standard CRM form variables will also be appended as well without you having to do any custom code to make that happen. The following will be appended for you.

Parameter	Form Variable	Description
type	crmForm.ObjectTypeCode	The type code for the current item being displayed in the form. Applications should use typename parameter instead when possible.
typename	crmForm.ObjectTypeName	This is the type name for the entity being shown in the form e.g "account".
Id	crmForm.ObjectId	This is the ID of the record being shown in the form.

Setting the URL to a Related View

Another common request is to have the grid of related items show up on a tab instead of from the navigation in the left hand side. The easiest way of accomplishing this is to use an IFrame that would point to the same page the left navigation icon does. It turns out all links on the left navigation of an entity form use the Areas.aspx page to display and based on the "tabset" property they vary the contents. Our IFrame helper class has a method to wrap this up into a one line method call passing only the relationship name to the method. While not 100% supported this encapsulates it into a common method. The following is an example of placing open activities and history of activities into IFrames on a form tab.

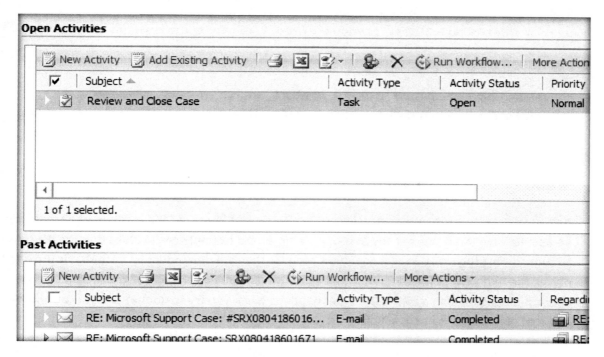

The code to accomplish the above is really simple as you can see in the following code sample.

```
historyFrame = new    CTCCrmIFrame("History","","");
historyFrame.SetRelatedView("areaActivityHistory");

openFrame= new    CTCCrmIFrame("OpenActivities","","");
openFrame.SetRelatedView("areaActivities");
```

The above assumes we have already created two IFrames using the form editor, named them History and OpenActivities. Make sure you turn off the Restrict Cross Scripting on those IFrames otherwise none of the links inside the IFrame grid will work.

You can use the same method to handle displaying of related data. For example if you had an entity crmbook_Project that was used to track projects and it was related to crmbook_ProjectMilestone, you could display the milestones in an IFrame.

The code to accomplish this is also really simple as you can see in the following code sample.

```
msFrame = new    CTCCrmIFrame("ProjectMilestones","","");
msFrame.SetRelatedView("crmbook_crmbook_project_crmbook_milestone");
```

The relationship name passed "crmbook_crmbook_project_crmbook_milestone" is the relationship name you used when you created the 1:N relationship between the two entities.

Working with Form Tabs

As you start getting into more complex customizations of forms in CRM it becomes desirable to be able to have them show at the appropriate time. For example certain tabs don't make sense to show during the creation of a new item because they are dependent on data that is provided during the first save of the data. Another example is if you use an IFrame to pull up a custom application page within a CRM form what happens when you try to do that and you are offline and that application is not available?

One common workaround (which is technically unsupported) is you can use JavaScript and on each form that you need these custom rules hard coded to the specific form. For example you can address the first tab on a form by doing the following call to document.getElementById('tab1Tab'). If all you wanted to do is hide it then you simply modify the display property and set it to none as you can see in the following example:

```
document.getElementById('tab1Tab').style.display = 'none';
```

That's only if you always wanted to hide it, then you could also hand code the check to determine what state the form is being invoked in. The CRM form (crmForm variable) has a FormType property that you can check to determine the mode the form is being invoked in, for example, Create or Update form etc. The form types are documented in the CRM SDK.

The other issue that needs to be handled is web vs. Outlook client, and in the Outlook client online vs. offline. CRM provides you the IsOutlookClient() method that you can call from the forms Onload to determine what client you are being invoked by. If you are in the Outlook Client – you can then further evaluate the IsOnline() method to determine if you are online or offline at that particular time. Again, on each form you could hard code the checks for these and hide or show the appropriate tabs.

I'm going to take a little different approach because what I want to do is package this up as some reusable JavaScript that could be put inline on each OnLoad, but represent the same reusable code. You might be asking why don't I just simply reference it from the OnLoad and not have it redundantly placed inside each Onload? The reason for this is I need the logic to run offline while the sales guy is sitting in the airplane at 30,000 feet. If you were dependent on the host CRM server that wouldn't work too well. So instead we sacrifice some of the convenience when we need to cut and paste that section into each OnLoad. But we don't need to hand code a separate version each time.

To optimize things I typically like to use W3cCompiler – a utility that compresses Javascript. Using its most basic options it strips comments and white space from the JavaScript and turns it into one long line of text. I then usually take that output and store it for re-use – and when I add it to each of the OnLoad event's it's in a compressed form.

```
// CTCCrmFormTab V1.0 11/17/2007
function CTCCrmFormTab(tabNumber){...removed for readability ...}
// CTCCrmFormTab V1.0 11/17/2007
```

As you can tell from the above example I also wrap the long line with the Date and a letter version for that date in case I changed it multiple times. This gives me an indication of what version a specific OnLoad might be using in case I had fixed a bug or two previously. Using this technique it reduces the amount of data being sent to the client, but it also makes the OnLoad event a little easier to read rather than having a few hundred lines of extra Javascript.

Ok enough about good deployment practices. Let's jump into looking at how this tab utility works! Inside the form OnLoad event after you paste in your copy of the utility script you can define how the tabs on that form should work.

The following example shows defining two tabs: one locationTab and the other dashboardTab. The first line of each creates a new instance of my utility script and passes the index number of the tab I want to work with. From that point forward all my work will be done using the published interface on my utility class and by using the name of my variable and not an index number of the tab. This makes for much more readable code.

```
locationTab = new CTCCRMFormTab(4);

locationTab.SetOnLoadVisibilty();

dashboardTab = new CTCCRMFormTab(0);

dashboardTab.SetOnLoadVisibilty();
```

The second line for each tab above does the auto setting of the visibility during the load of the form. For example by default the tab will not show if it is offline in the outlook client. Also the tab won't show if the form is in create mode. Those are just the defaults, but they could be overridden by specification of the properties before calling SetOnLoadVisiblity().

The following shows an example of modifying them before calling the SetOnLoadVisiblity() method.

```
locationTab.ShowFormTypeCreate = false;

locationTab.ShowFormTypeUpdate = true;

locationTab.ShowFormTypeReadOnly = true;

locationTab.ShowFormTypeDisabled = false;

locationTab.ShowFormTypeQuickCreate = false;

locationTab.ShowFormTypeBulkEdit = false;
```

This example also shows the default settings for those items that I decided to use for my utility class.

I also packaged up a HideTab() and a ShowTab() method on my utility class that can be used anytime after the instance is created to manipulate the tabs manually.

You may be wondering what this is doing under the covers to hide and show the tabs. To hide a tab a reference to the tab is retrieved from the form and then the style.display property is set to 'none' causing the browser to hide the form.

```
this.TabControl.style.display = "none";
```

To show the tab again the script cheats and forces the CRM logic to work by invoking the click() method on the tab. This is the same process that happens when the user clicks on the tab, and under the covers it causes the tabs to switch and takes care of the housekeeping that CRM requires for managing the tabs. Here's what the invoke of the click() method looks like.

```
this.TabControl.click();
```

If you're curious and want to know how the tabs are managed the secret can be found by looking in the _nav folder on the server and dive into the tab.htc and tab.css files.

In the end we end up with a good utility that can reduce the amount of redundant code we have to custom write for each form. This packaging into a utility also can setup a level of abstraction in case CRM changes how tabs are managed on forms in the future. In fact for the most part this does not use any deep interaction with non published items to work. It does require a modification to the style property and calling of the click() method just like the user would do by clicking on a tab. While those could be considered officially unsupported customizations, by wrapping it in a clean utility class you encapsulate the unsupported code into a clean wrapper that can be modified when the next version of CRM releases.

Tab On Click handling

Another tab related thing you might want to do is have some script run when a tab is selected by the user. There's no 100% supported way that you can accomplish that but by attaching to the "onclick" event of the HTML you can register your script to be called when the tab is selected. To help encapsulate that concept into a reusable set of code our Tab helper provides a RegisterOnClick method that you can call. Under the covers it does the same as the attach to onclick method but by having it isolated into a helper class allows you to modify its implementation if the CRM team changes how form tabs work.

The actual method in the CTCCrmFormTab class is pretty simple as you can see in the following code sample.

```
CTCCrmFormTab.prototype.RegisterOnClick = function(methodToCall)
{
    this.TabControl.attachEvent("onclick",methodToCall);
}
```

To use this method, we first create an instance of CTCCrmFormTab and then call the RegisterOnClick method. In the following example we pass it a reference to an existing JavaScript function.

```
var myTab = new CTCCrmFormTab(4);

tab4.RegisterOnClick(MyCallBack);
```

Another way this could be used is to create the callback function inline. The following demonstrates what that approach would look like.

```
var myTab = new CTCCrmFormTab(4);
tab4.RegisterOnClick(
    function()
    {
        alert('tab clicked');
    }

}
```

Regardless of which approach you take, the result is the same, a method that gets called with the form tab is selected.

Client Side Snippets from Stunnware.com

As I started thinking about some of the client side scripting how-to's I wanted to include, I couldn't help but think about pointing people to Stunnware.com. The site is run by Michael Hohne, a CRM MVP, and has to have the largest collection of CRM client side script snippets.

I had the privilege of meeting Michael when I was doing a CRM training class in Munich, Germany during the early Beta days of CRM 4.0. Michael was gracious enough to allow me to include some of his snippets in the book. These are only a small sample of the large collection on his site – and I encourage you to visit it to find additional CRM related how-to's. You can find his site at www.stunnware.com.

Changing the title of a CRM form

```
document.title = "Hello World!";
```

Changing the color of a single option in a picklist

You can change the color and background color of an option element using the following syntax.

```
//TODO: Replace <name of your picklist field> with the schema name of
//the picklist in question.
var list = crmForm.all.<name of your picklist field>;
//using the first option here, you need to find the one you need.
var option = list.options[0];
//Set the background color to red.
option.style.backgroundColor = "#FF0000";
//Set the text color to white.
option.style.color = "#FFFFFF";
```

Retrieving the text of a lookup control

```
var lookup = crmForm.all.<lookupfield>.DataValue;
if (lookup[0] != null) {
    var theText = lookup[0].name;
}
```

Getting notified when the user selects a another tab on a form

Put the following in the OnLoad event of your form.

```
crmForm.all.tab0Tab.onclick = function() {
    alert("Tab 0 clicked");
}

crmForm.all.tab1Tab.onclick = function() {
    alert("Tab 1 clicked");
}
```

Initializing a date field with the current date

```
crmForm.all.<attribute>.DataValue = new Date();
```

Displaying a picture in a CRM form, using a text field to store the data source

Let's say you have a custom field storing the image name called new_picturename. Then in the OnLoad event do the following.

```
if ((crmForm.all.new_picturename != null) &&
(crmForm.all.new_picturename.DataValue != null)) {
    document.all.IFRAME_<name of iframe>.src = http://server/dir/images/
+   crmForm.all.new_picturename.DataValue;
}

In the OnChange event of the new_picturename place the following:

if (crmForm.all.new_picturename.DataValue != null) {
```

```
      document.all.IFRAME_<name of iframe>.src = http://server/dir/images/
+
crmForm.all.new_picturename.DataValue;
}

else {
      document.all.IFRAME_<name of iframe>.src = "about:blank"
}
```

Disabling the time selection of a date/time field

You can dynamically enable or disable the time selection box of a date/time field using the following syntax.

```
var dateField = crmForm.all.<name of datetime field>;

//Check the existence of the time field. It is null if the control is
setup to only display the date.
if (dateField.all.time != null) {

    //Disable the time field
    dateField.all.time.disable();

    //Enable the time field
    dateField.all.time.enable();
}
```

CRM automatically enables the time selection box if the date value changes to a non-null value, so in order to always disable the time selection box, you need to add the following OnChange event script to the datetime field.

```
var dateField = crmForm.all.<name of datetime field>;

//Check the existence of the time field. It is null if the control is
setup to only display the date.
if (dateField.all.time != null) {
    //Disable the time field
    dateField.all.time.disable();
}
```

To initially disable the time field, put the following into the form OnLoad event.

```
var dateField = crmForm.all.<name of datetime field>;

//Check the existence of the datetime field. It may not be included in a
quick create form!
if (dateField != null) {

    //Call the OnChange event handler
    dateField.FireOnChange();
}
```

Getting notified when the user enters a form field

The OnChange event of a form field is fired when you are leaving a field (and of course have changed the field value). If you want to perform an action when the user enters the field, use the onfocus event.

```
crmForm.all.your_field.onfocusin = function() {
    alert("Received focus");
}
```

Changing the available entity types in a lookup dialog

Use one of the following in your OnLoad event.

```
//Allow only accounts to be selected
crmForm.all.regardingobjectid.setAttribute("lookuptypes", "1");

//Allow only contacts to be selected
crmForm.all.regardingobjectid.setAttribute("lookuptypes", "2");

//Allow accounts or contacts to be selected
crmForm.all.regardingobjectid.setAttribute("lookuptypes", "1,2");
```

It does not change the behavior of the form assistant, but the lookup dialog will not display any other entity. The attribute values are entity type codes and are documented in the SDK help file. You can use the code for any field allowing multiple entity types (usually customer fields and the regarding field).

Hiding a single field

```
crmForm.all.<fieldname>_c.style.display = "none"; //hides the label
crmForm.all.<fieldname>_d.style.display = "none"; //hides the field
```

Getting notified when a user changes a checkbox value before leaving the field

The OnChange event of a bit field is fired when you leave the field. Often you want the event to be triggered as soon as the user clicks on a checkbox before tabbing out.

In the OnLoad event create a new event handler like this.

```
crmForm.all.your_checkboxfield.onclick = function() {
    crmForm.all.your_checkboxfield.FireOnChange();
}
```

Obviously the onclick event is raised when clicking on the checkbox. Not so obvious is the fact that it also fires when you change the value using the keyboard (space bar). The above code calls your OnChange event handler after the value changed but before the control loses focus, so OnChange will be triggered again when you tab out. If that's a problem, place the existing OnChange event handler into the onclick event.

```
crmForm.all.your_checkboxfield.onclick = function() {
    //add existing OnChange implementation here
}
```

Now you can deactivate your OnChange event.

Maximizing a form

Put the following two lines of code into any OnLoad event to maximize the form.

```
window.moveTo(0,0);
window.resizeTo(screen.availWidth, screen.availHeight);
```

moveTo moves the window to the specified location and resizeTo resizes it. screen is a global object and gives you the available screen width and height in the corresponding properties.

Using a toolbar button to open a referenced entity

Let's say you have added a lookup field to a form referencing one of your custom entities and you have added a toolbar button in isv.config.xml. When clicked it should open the entity shown in the lookup field, which basically is the same as clicking the link in the lookup itself.

Here's the code.

```
var lookup = crmForm.all.your_lookup_field;

if ((lookup != null) && (lookup.DataValue != null)) {
    var objectTypeCode = lookup[0].type;
    var objectId = lookup[0].id;
    var url = '/userdefined/edit.aspx?id=" + objectId + '&etc=' +
objectTypeCode;

    window.open(url);
}
```

Note that when using a system entity, you have to replace /userdefined/edit.aspx with the appropriate edit URL of the system entity. The code first checks for the availability of the lookup field. If it's not included on the form (lookup will be null) or no data value has been set then no action is performed; otherwise the complete edit URL is stored in the url variable and passed to the window.open method.

Setting lookup values

The following is an example of how you can get the value from a lookup.

```
var lookupItem = new Array;

// This will get the lookup for the attribute primarycontactid on the
//Account form
lookupItem = crmForm.all.primarycontactid.DataValue();
// If there is data in the field, show it in a series of alerts
if (lookupItem[0] != null) {
    // The text value of the lookup
    alert(lookupItem[0].name);
    // The entity type name
    alert(lookupItem[0].typename);
    // The GUID of the lookup
    alert(lookupItem[0].id);
    // The entity type code of the lookup: 1=account, 2= contact
    alert(lookupItem[0].type);
}
```

Here's the code to set the primarycontactid on the account form.

```
var lookupItem = new Array;

var referencedItemId = "{c7717ce0-67a4-da11-9372-001438b86853}";
var referencedItemObjectTypeCode = 2;
var referencedItemDisplayName = "Höhne, Michael";
lookupItem[0] = new LookupControlItem(referencedItemId,
referencedItemObjectTypeCode, referencedItemDisplayName);

crmForm.all.primarycontactid.DataValue = lookupItem;
```

The only problem is that you need to find out the correct values to set. Of course, the Guid assigned to referencedItemId will not work on your system and even on mine it doesn't make sense to hard-code it. But if you have this information available, these few lines will do the trick.

Wrapping Up

In this chapter, we have looked at some more advanced techniques to use what we learned in the prior chapter about JavaScript coding. In each of these examples, we tried to package up some logic that would give you ready to use code. We also hope that some of the ideas presented here give you ideas to implement your own.

7

Building Alternate UI's

Often times when packaged platforms are used to implement solutions there can be complaints that the user experience just does not fit the way the user thinks and does their work. Many of the customization capabilities in the core platform attempt to address that and provide ways to customize to meet the needs of users. That said, it is impossible to predict all the needs a user will have and sometimes they are just too specific to a small set of users to have that capability built-in to the platform.

To address that, we saw in the prior chapter where you can use integration capabilities like IFrames and links to external applications. While powerful, they don't fully explain and encourage the full set of out of the box thinking that can be done to replace or enhance the user experience with one that fits your specific needs.

To get you in the right mindset, you have to think of the UI that CRM provides as just one of the services that the platform offers. Other services are things like Data Management, Workflow, Security, Reporting and many others. The UI that CRM provides uses all the other services to render the pages that the user interacts with. That means that you can replace all or part of the existing built-in UI with your own custom interface. To do this you would just leverage the platform APIs to access the metadata, services and data.

A good example of this is some of the 3rd party mobile applications that extend the platform to mobile devices. These applications transform the platform to work on a small screen device. Another example would be replacing the user interface with a custom Smart Client application. Here you might build a WPF or Silverlight application that interacts with the platform. It is possible when doing this type of customization users have no idea that CRM is the platform under the covers. They just see a completely tailored application that provides them the access they need.

In this chapter, we are going to look at a few example applications that try to demonstrate how you can use alternate user interfaces with CRM. In each example we will highlight the goals of the application and why the approach was chosen.

Silverlight and CRM

In this section we are going to begin to look at how Silverlight can be used to easily add a rich user experience to CRM. We will discuss techniques of adding just a small piece to existing forms to completely building a Silverlight component that replaces some built-in capability. At the time of this writing Silverlight 1.0 is released and Silverlight 2.0 Beta 2 was just released. Much of our discussion will focus on Silverlight 2.0 Beta 2 and therefore is subject to change by the time it releases to manufacturing (RTM) later in the year.

Silverlight 2 allows developers to use .NET managed code that is downloaded and runs in the Silverlight browser plug-in. This powerful combination allows developers to use .NET languages and tools like Visual Studio to build rich internet applications. These applications are simple to deploy and run inside the Silverlight plug-in sandbox on the client machine.

At the time of this writing, the CRM product development team hasn't discussed anyways they might use Silverlight in the future. I suspect though as you look at some of the demonstrations in this chapter you too will start to see many of the opportunities for not only you to use Silverlight but where it might fit with the CRM product strategy.

Some history on Silverlight

Microsoft announced at the Mix conference in 2007 that they were building a new technology called Silverlight. At the time, Silverlight was explained as a browser plug-in that would be Microsoft's next generation cross browser web runtime. Allowing developers to implement rich internet applications (RIAs) that brought to the web some of the capabilities that could only be done using applications deployed as smart clients, ActiveX or Flash.

Originally, Silverlight was code named WPF/E for Windows Presentation Foundation (WPF) Everywhere. WPF/E at the time presented a plug-in that would load up a user interface described using XAML (Extensible Application Markup Language). This XAML described user interface could be manipulated at the time using JavaScript running in the browser.

The Future of XAML

In explaining XAML, Microsoft started down an important path to change how applications are built both on the web and on the desktop. As we look forward to the future XAML will be used to commonly describe the look and feel of user interfaces that can be deployed to the desktop using WPF, to the web and mobile devices using Silverlight. Silverlight, using a subset of the WPF XAML capabilities, will allow developers to leverage their WPF skills across the different types of platforms.

A big part of XAML is the separation of the user interface specification and layout from the code that implements the business logic of the application. This separation is key to establishing a workflow where designers can focus on the layout and developers can focus on the business logic. Layout and manipulation of XAML can be done using Microsoft Expression Blend or Visual Studio 2008. Both of these tools are capable of working on the same solution and project structure allowing the developer or designer to choose the tool they are most productive in.

Using the Power of .NET

It was at Mix 07 in Las Vegas that it was announced that what was viewed as a Javascript browser plug-in was being evolved in Silverlight 2 to bring a subset of the .NET framework to the plug-in to be able to run .NET code on the client browser. This announcement made clear how powerful the sharing of XAML between the desktop and the web would become. The shared XAML combined with the ability to build the business logic of the application using .NET immediately provided a consistent toolset between the desktop and the web application.

Beyond just the UI

At first glance you might think that Silverlight is all about the UI and moving widgets around. But the reality is when you start peeling back parts of the onion you will find a number of things that provide a ton of power. Silverlight 2 implements a subset of the .NET runtime that focuses on critical components needed to support the UI and connecting that UI to services in the cloud. In the cloud being either your internal services that are exposed or third party services.

The following are some of the key components that are part of the subset.

- A subset of WPF used to implement the UI experience.

- WCF – To include the ability to reference services and do things like syndication feed consumption.
- LINQ – Core support for LINQ to objects and LINQ to XML are available.
- Isolated Storage – ability to store data locally on a client machine from a web application to make things faster.

What this means for CRM developers is that you can build applications that extend CRM using Silverlight and connect up to the CRM platform webservices for working with data and services.

Getting Started with Silverlight

Your first step in building Silverlight is to get the Silverlight SDK and get that installed - you should visit www.silverlight.Net. Notice I put ".NET" not ".com" if you end up at the .com you won't find the SDK! You will find the SDK under the "Getting Started' section, of the .net site.

Once there make sure you grab the Silverlight 2 SDK and not the SDK for 1.0. While I believe you can do some basic things with CRM with the 1.0 SDK, the real fun starts with Silverlight 2. As of this writing the best thing to download is "Microsoft Silverlight Tools for Visual Studio 2008" that contains both the project templates as well as the SDK and Silverlight 2 runtime. While you can use other variations, for simplification that is what we will be covering in more detail as we move forward.

In addition to the Tools for Visual Studio, you might want to grab Microsoft Expression Blend 2.5 while you are there. Expression Blend provides you a richer design surface at this time for doing things like recording storyboards or other things where you want to visually design your Silverlight elements. Storyboards in case you aren't familiar with them allow you to define animation sequences that act on UI elements. Expression Blend is designed to work in conjunction with Visual Studio 2008 and you can share the same project files between the two environments.

 With the Beta 2 version of the Tools for Visual Studio , the design time experience in Visual Studio renders the Silverlight control but does not allow you to manipulate the designer surface. You can only modify the XAML directly or drag elements from the toolbar to the XAML view. Blend however does allow you to use the full designer surface. It is expected that the Visual Studio designer will move toward allowing a similar experience in the future, remember it is still Beta 2! That said, it has amazed me some of the things can are easier to do in Silverlight compared to other traditional ways of accomplishing similar tasks.

Your next step is to create your first application. You can follow the next tutorial that is CRM specific or use one of the generic tutorials you can find on Silverlight .net.

Hello CRM World in Silverlight

So assuming you followed the getting started and have the tools all installed, the next step is to create your first Silverlight application that connects to CRM. The first thing you will do is a File-New Project. When you installed the Visual Studio tools you installed a template designed to work with Silverlight.

In the following image of the File – New Project dialog, notice I have selected the .NET Framework 3.5. If you select any other version you will not see the Silverlight templates. On the left hand side of the Project types you should see Silverlight – this will show up under the C# and VB.Net, so choose the language that is your preference.

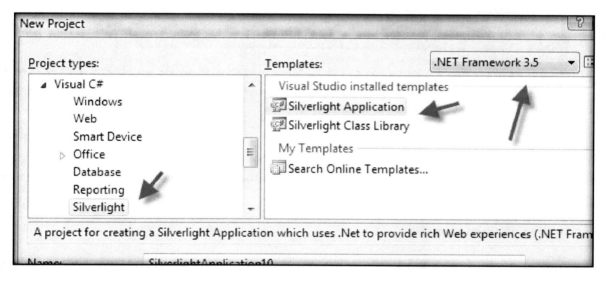

You will notice in the above dialog there are two project types. Silverlight Application is what you will use to create your actual visible Silverlight component and as you will see it helps you by creating a Web project to hold the Silverlight page. The class library is for building reusable assets that will be used across multiple Silverlight application projects. We will be using the Silverlight class library later in our example where we talk about the CRM Discovery service.

Next, you will be shown the following dialog that will ask you how you want to test this new Silverlight application.

As you can see you have three choices. If you have an existing web project you can actually "link" this to the existing web site. This will create a ClientBin folder in the existing website and build the necessary build actions to copy the output from your Silverlight project to your existing web project.

For our example, we are going to use the Add a new Web to the solution option. This will create a web folder with a couple of test pages we can use to kick the tires of our Silverlight application.

Once you click ok on this dialog, don't be surprised when you see Visual Studio start opening windows and adding things to your solution. That's the wizard at work adding the web site and connecting it to your new Silverlight project.

Adding our first control

Looking at the Toolbox you will see one of the big changes from Silverlight Beta 1, there are now numerous controls that we can use. In fact, if you are curious you can even download source code for the controls and look at how they were built. They are also licensed under a pretty liberal license if you want to extend them and use them to build your own custom controls.

The following is a look at the tool box view of controls available with Silverlight Beta 2.

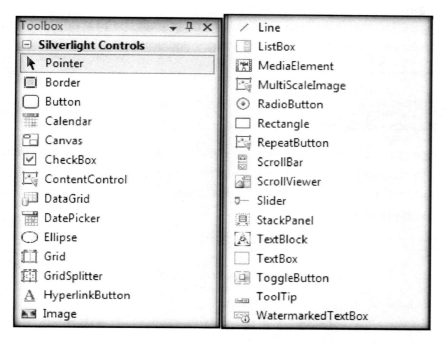

In the current beta, one thing to keep in mind is the design surface in Visual Studio is read only, however, Expression Blend has full designer surface support.

For our example, we are going to use the DataGrid control to load up some data from CRM. So from the Toolbox, using your mouse drag a DataGrid control to your XAML design area at the bottom of your Page.xaml. It should look like the following once you have added the control.

```
<Grid x:Name="LayoutRoot" Background="White">
    <my:DataGrid></my:DataGrid>
</Grid>
```

You won't see anything on the design surface yet at this point. The next thing we are going to do is add a Name attribute to our grid so we can reference it in our C# code to set the data. We are also going to set the AutoGenerateColumns attribute to true so it will add a column for each property in our data.

```
<my:DataGrid x:Name="crmDataGrid" AutoGenerateColumns="True" >
</my:DataGrid>
```

Next, let's add a button that we will use to trigger us to fill the data grid. Try just typing into the XAML area of the editor and see how well the IntelliSense works.

You will notice as you type Click- that IntelliSense will kick in and prompt you to create an event handler to handle the Click event. For now let it create a new handler for you.

About now you will notice that the button has completely filled out design surface and we now have a giant button! To fix this problem, let's just wrap our controls with a StackPanel which is one of the layout controls. Modify the XAML to look like the following. With StackPanel wrapped around both existing controls.

```
<Grid x:Name="LayoutRoot" Background="White">
    <StackPanel>
        <my:DataGrid x:Name="crmDataGrid" AutoGenerateColumns="True" />
        <Button x:Name="buttonGetData" Content="Get Data"
                Click="buttonGetData_Click"></Button>
    </StackPanel>
</Grid>
```

Accessing CRM Data

Our next step is to access CRM and retrieve some data. If you recall, we indicated that Silverlight has the ability to use WCF. Originally, I thought we would simply access the CRM service using WCF. When I first attempted to do that I ran into a few challenges. Some of those challenges were overcome, as we understood the differences related to using WCF in Silveright. However, a few have not.

As of our current testing, WCF in Silverlight 2 Beta 1 did not seem to be passing the headers in the SOAP request to the CRM server. Another thing we noticed was the size of the runtime files created when the CRM Service was referenced via WCF. Unlike an application that is installed once, a Silverlight application will be downloaded more often. So the smaller the size of the runtime assemblies the better performances clients will see. Just referencing the CrmService because of its rich object model increased the compressed size of our output assembly to 750K. To make that size more meaningful, the approach we are about to discuss created an assembly with a compressed size of 17K. With these two key challenges in mind we decided to approach this more similarly to how we approached accessing the CRM service from Javasript and developed some code to use the HttpWebRequest post method to interact with the CRM server.

An alternate approach that you might consider is exposing a web service from a server that is more specifically designed for how your Silverlight application will interact with it. Using this approach would cover both problems discussed above. The only negative of this approach is it does require special code to be deployed to each CRM server.

So the approach choice taken for this chapter is to build a helper assembly that has a Silverlight specific implementation of some of the CRM common classes. These classes are modeled after the normal CRM Service and associated query classes. It also is designed to allow the results to be easier to use with LINQ to further refine and render on the Silverlight output.

In the sample files, we included an assembly ctccrm.SilverlightCommon. You should add a reference to your project to that assembly. Once that is completed you should add the following using statements to your code behind.

```
using ctccrm.SilverlightCommon.CrmWS;
using ctccrm.SilverlightCommon.DynEntity;
```

Now we are ready to build a query to go retrieve data for our grid. You will see the following code as part of our buttonGetData event handling method.

```
private void buttonGetData_Click(object sender, RoutedEventArgs e)
{

    CTCCrmQueryExpression qe = new CTCCrmQueryExpression();
    qe.EntityName = "activitypointer";
    CTCCrmCriteria criteria = new CTCCrmCriteria();

    CTCCrmService svc = new CTCCrmService();
    svc.ServerURL = "http://ctcvs1";
    svc.OrganizationName = "crmbook";

    svc.RetrieveMultiple(qe, svc_RetrieveMultipleCompleted);

}
```

In the simple code above we begin a retrieve request for all rows of the activity pointer entity. If you are familiar with doing RetreiveMultiples using the CRM web services this should look pretty familiar to you.

One part that might look odd is the second parameter to RetrieveMultiple. The reason for this is all Silvelright networking calls must ensure that they don't block the UI thread so to accomplish that all requests for network resources are done using an async paradigm. This async paradigm will take you a little work to get used to but it's definitely workable in most cases. The "svc_RetrieveMultipleCompleted" references the method below that is called when the retrieve request has been completed. The following is a simple implementation of this method that binds the results to our data grid.

```
void svc_RetrieveMultipleCompleted(object Sender,
                    CTCCrmRetrieveMultipleResult e)
{
    if (e.EntityCollection.Entities.Count > 0)
        crmDataGrid.ItemsSource = e.EntityCollection.Entities;
}
```

We now have enough that we could execute our sample. One problem we will run into is the fact that by default RetrieveMultiple will return Dynamic Entities or in our case CTCCrmDynamic entities which represent our Silverlight implementation of the built-in CRM Dynamic Entity object. The Dynamic Entity is more geared toward being a generic bucket of data and really isn't well suited for binding to a UI data element or working with LINQ. In fact if we bound it to our grid here's an example of what the output would look like.

	Properties	EntityName	
▶	System.Collections.Generic.Dictionary`2[System.String,ctccrm.SilverlightCommor	activitypointer	
	System.Collections.Generic.Dictionary`2[System.String,ctccrm.SilverlightCommor	activitypointer	

Making results LINQ Friendly

LINQ stands for Language Integrated Query and provides an easy way to work with collections of objects. To get the most value out of LINQ though you want to be able to do things like have typed properties on an object for example myContact.FirstName instead of myContact.property["FirstName"].Value. By having explicit properties you are able to write queries that evaluate them and fully leverage IntelliSense. To modify our solution to better allow the use of LINQ, we made a small change to the RetrieveMultiple method. In the following example you can see we added specification of a type DEactivitypointer.

```
svc.RetrieveMultipleBeginRequest(qe,
        typeof(DEactivitypointer), svc_RetrieveMultipleCompleted);
```

The DEactivitypointer class is one we code generated from the metadata of the CRM Server and it inherits from our CTCCrmDynamicEntity class. The code generation then added properties for each attribute and the property basically was a pass though to the base dynamic entity that was storing the data. You can see an example of one of the properties below.

```
public string addressused
   {
           get
           {
               if (this.Entity == null)
                   return null;

               if (CTCDEPropHelper.PropertyExists(this.Entity,
                               "addressused"))
                   return CTCDEPropHelper.GetStringValue(this.Entity,
                               "addressused");
               else
                   return null;
           }
           set
           {
               if (this.Entity == null)
                   return;

               CTCDEPropHelper.AddStringProperty(this.Entity,
                           "addressused", value);
           }
   }
}
```

The DEactivitypointer class is included in the ctccrm.Silverlight assembly for convenience, but you can easily generate one of these for any entity in your CRM including your custom entities using the DataEntityGen application included in the book code framework.

So I have modified the retrieve completed method to take advantage of the fact that the results will be of type DEactivitypointer. I'm now using LINQ to build a smaller subset of the results into my own "display" class called ListItem.

```
void svc_RetrieveMultipleCompleted(object Sender,
CTCCrmRetrieveMultipleResult e)
{
    //if (e.EntityCollection.Entities.Count > 0)
```

```
//     crmDataGrid.ItemsSource = e.EntityCollection.Entities;

    var listItems = from DEactivitypointer item in
                    e.EntityCollection.Entities
                    where (item.createdon != null)
                    && (item.createdon < DateTime.Now)
                    orderby item.createdon
                    select new ListItem
                    {
                        Title = item.subject,
                        CreatedOn = item.createdon.Value
                    };

    crmDataGrid.ItemsSource = listItems;


}

public class ListItem
{
    public string Title { get; set; }
    public DateTime CreatedOn { get; set; }
}
```

Server Setup

One thing to keep in mind is in order for our application to be able to connect with the CRM server we will need to deploy a couple of files that are related to networking security, Silverlight uses a crossdomain.xml and clientaccesspolicy.xml file to determine if it is ok to connect and exchange data with a target server. These files are used by Silveright for WCF as well as lower level network interactions. A complete discussion of these files is beyond the scope of the book, however, we will cover a couple basic examples that will allow you to build applications that target a CRM server. The examples are as of Silverlight Beta 2, so check with the Silverlight documentation if using later releases.

The first file is crossdomain.xml

```
<?xml version="1.0"?>
<cross-domain-policy>
  <allow-http-request-headers-from domain="*" headers="*" />
</cross-domain-policy>
```

The second file is clientaccesspolicy.xml

```xml
<?xml version="1.0" encoding="utf-8"?>
<access-policy>
  <cross-domain-access>
    <policy>
      <allow-from http-request-headers="*" >
        <domain uri="*"/>
      </allow-from>
      <grant-to>
        <resource path="/" include-subpaths="true"/>
      </grant-to>
    </policy>
  </cross-domain-access>
</access-policy>
```

The above two files both setup very open access to the server from a Silverlight client. For production use you might want to consider reducing the access granted.

These files need to be placed in the root of the CRM web server. The same is true if you want to use Silverlight from the CRM client while offline.

Now when you run the application and click the get data button the results grid looks a little more refined as you can see in the image below.

	Title	CreatedOn	
	Finish Chapter 7	3/8/2008 6:43:26	
▶	E-Mail publisher about deadline	3/8/2008 6:45:17	

So with that we successfully built a small Silverlight application that accessed the CRM server and presented the data using the new Silverlight 2 Beta 2 controls.

Why Silverlight, When Silverlight

Now that you have completed a basic Silverlight application you should be starting to think about why and when you would use Silverlight. As you can probably tell from the example Silverlight isn't that hard to develop for. As a client side technology it is well suited to augment the standard CRM interface because it can provide a replacement as a small part of the page using the IFrame integration CRM offers or can be used as a full page CRM application.

As you start thinking about places you might invest and write the customizations in Silverlight, think about applications that can leverage the client side execution. Using that combined with the ability to still call back to the server web services can make for a very responsive application.

Additionally, using the Isolated Storage capabilities of Silverlight, it would be possible to pull down some information for the user and store it locally and then re-use it time and time again when the user visits that page. A good example of that might be some of the CRM metadata. For example, if you were to want to make your Silverlight application Multi-lingual, you could pull down and cache the Metadata in isolated storage so you don't have to retrieve it each time the Silverlight component is used.

Office as the User Experience

We have talked earlier in the book about how CRM has a Microsoft Outlook Add-in that extends the functionality into Outlook. In addition, there are a lot of opportunities to build custom integration with the Microsoft Office products that implement specific business functions. Microsoft Visual Studio Tools for Office (VSTO) have been around for a while now and offer a number of templates for building integration with the Microsoft Office Products. If you're not familiar with VSTO, it used to be a standalone product that you had to purchase but is now part of Visual Studio 2008 Professional and higher editions.

VSTO makes building Microsoft Office add-ins and workbooks much simpler by providing a managed wrapper around the non-managed components exposed by Microsoft Office Applications. Our goal of talking about this in the book is not to teach you VSTO, but to give you an example of integrating with CRM using VSTO. There are a number of books published that only cover VSTO so we won't attempt to cover that topic in detail here. We will however highlight how you can make calls to CRM and how that works. To demonstrate, let's walk through an example of building a Microsoft Word 2007 add-in using Visual Studio 2008 / .NET Framework 3.5.

In this example, we will build an add-in that connects to CRM and allows a user to build a simple real estate flyer for a property using data pulled from CRM. We will add a custom ribbon control that will show how easy it is to plug-in to Microsoft Word. The custom ribbon will control turning on / off a custom task pane that will allow us to lookup and insert data from CRM into our word document. We will demonstrate using control templates that can be placed in a document and act as place holders allowing us to easily insert data into a document without having to parse through a document or relying on a user to place a cursor at a specific location in a document.

In our example, we are going to re-use some of our framework components such as the connection dialog, and ability to connect when we are both on and offline. We will also leverage some of our common service manager routines to make calls to the CRM server to retrieve and work with data. You will notice that we don't spend a lot of time making this "pretty" as its goal is to walk you through how easy is to build a simple add-in.

Adding a Word Add-In Project

Our first step is to choose a project template for our new add-in that we are going to create. You will notice that with the .NET 3.5 Framework there are a number of new templates available for us to build Office related add-ins , templates and workbooks. For our example we are going to select Word 2007 Add-In.

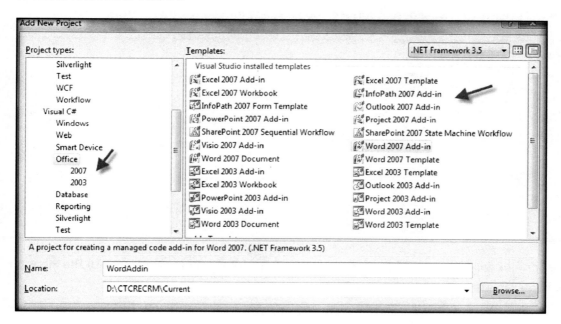

Once the project wizard is completed you will see the following in our solution explorer view.

Adding our own Ribbon Tab

One of the new features of VSTO 3 that comes with Visual Studio 2008 is a Visual Ribbon Designer. In the past, you used to have to edit the XML file by hand. Now you can just drag and drop controls from the toolbox onto a Visual Ribbon Designer. To use the Visual Ribbon Designer simply click add new item and select Ribbon (Visual Designer) from the new item templates listed under the Office category.

You will see the following design surface appear ready for you to add controls.

The Toolbox will have a number of controls specifically designed for working with the Ribbon that you can drag onto the design surface.

The following is a subset of the available controls.

The control Id properties determine how the Tabs on the Ribbon will be merged with Words ribbon. As you can see in the following example it specifies ControlIdType of Office and TabAddIns as the OfficeId. That indicates that this tab will merge with any other tabs using the same name.

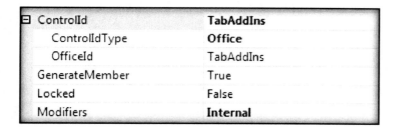

By changing that to Custom we can then specify our own ControlID as you can see in the following.

We can also change the Label that is displayed on the tab by updating the Label property.

Since all this is visually designed you can now see the label change takes effect instantly.

Using the tool bar, I added three more groups and modified their labels. I also started putting some buttons on each group to enable showing/hiding of a content panel we will be discussing later. The following is how the Ribbon looks after doing all those changes.

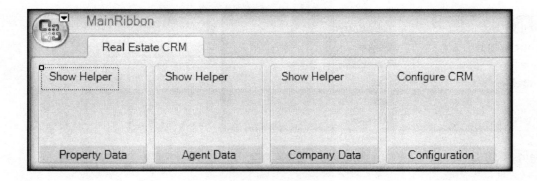

The above Ribbon Buttons are simple and no attempt was made to style them with icons and such as you would probably do in a real solution. The key message here is how simple it is to build applications that integrate with office and to focus on how to tie it to CRM.

Referencing the CRM Assemblies

The next step is to add references to our project to the CRM specific assemblies. From the CRM SDK assemblies I need to reference Microsoft.Crm.Outlook.SDK, Microsoft.Crm.Sdk and Microsoft.Crm.SDkTypeProxy. Additionally, because I want to leverage some of the book sample code I will also reference ctccrm.AuthHelper and ctccrm.PluginCommon. If I have them included in my solution then those will be done via Project references. You should also add a reference to the System.Web.Services assembly.

AddIn State Helper Class

We are going to add a utility class to our project called AddInSharedState. This class could be called, anything it's just a place to hold some state data and common methods we will be using in various parts of our add-in.

Configure CRM Connection

We are going to use the Windows Form that is in the ctccrm.AuthHelper assembly to collect user information necessary for login. Our first step is to catch the button click event on the Ribbon for the Configure CRM button.

Our code in the handler looks like the following and simple calls the GetCrmConnectionInfo method from our helper class. The true is passed to this method to force it to always show the dialog to collect information from the user.

```
private void buttonConfigureCRM_Click(object sender,
                    RibbonControlEventArgs e)
{
    AddInSharedState.GetCrmConnectionInfo(true);
}
```

The GetCrmConnectionInfo method uses the FormCrmConnectionInfo class from the helper assembly to show the login form. Once the user has saved the information it will be encrypted in a local file using the DPAPI encryption.

The following is the code to launch the form if saved credentials are not available.

```
public static CrmConnectionInfo GetCrmConnectionInfo(bool force)
{
    FormCrmConnectInfo formCRM = new FormCrmConnectInfo();
    CrmConnectionInfo connInfo = formCRM.LoadSavedLogin();
    formCRM.AllowSaveLogin = true;
    connInfo.AllowOfflineUse = true;
    if ((!formCRM.HasSavedLogin()) || (force))
    {
        if (formCRM.ShowDialog() != DialogResult.OK)
            return new CrmConnectionInfo();
        connInfo = formCRM.GetConnectionInfo();
        formCRM.SaveSavedLogin(connInfo);

    }
    return connInfo;
}
```

The following is the login dialog that the user will see and be able to provide the type of connection and do things like pick the correct organization.

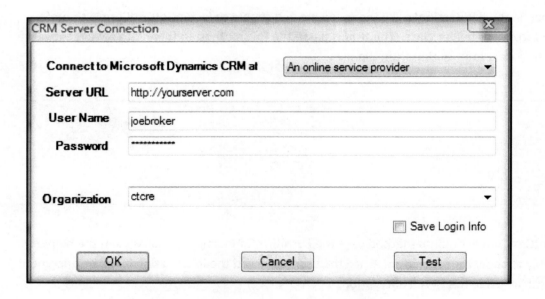

Adding a Task Pane

A Task Pane is really just a Windows form User Control. It's called Task Pane because that's what it is when used in the Word context and we will be adding it to the TaskPanes collection. Our user control will be very simple, just a drop down list of our Real Estate properties from the CRM system and as you select one we will show the details on the panel.

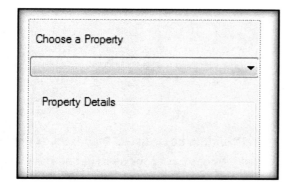

Hook up the Task Pane

Our next step is to hook up the Task Pane to Word and show it can become visible to the user. The following code adds a property for the user control and the CustomTaskPane that holds it and then adds it to the collection of CustomTaskPanes.

```
public partial class ThisAddIn
{
    ContentPanelPropertyHelper m_PropHelper =
            new ContentPanelPropertyHelper();
    public ContentPanelPropertyHelper PropHelper
         { get { return m_PropHelper; } }

    public CustomTaskPane PropHelperPane { get; set; }

    private void ThisAddIn_Startup(object sender, System.EventArgs e)
    {
        this.PropHelperPane =
            this.CustomTaskPanes.Add(m_PropHelper,"Property Helper");
        this.PropHelperPane.Width = m_PropHelper.Width;
        this.PropHelperPane.Visible = false;

    }
. . . other code removed for simplification..
}
```

Controlling Visibility

Now that we have told Word about our control, we need to have our Ribbon button toggle its visibility. To do this we double click on the toggle button we added to the Ribbon and add the following event handling code.

```
private void toggleButtonPropertyHelper_Click(
        object sender, RibbonControlEventArgs e)
{
    Globals.ThisAddIn.PropHelperPane.Visible =
                toggleButtonPropertyHelper.Checked;
}
```

You might notice in the above code the use of Globals.ThisAddIn being used. That is an example of how Visual Studio Tools for Office (VSTO) tries to make things easier for us to get all the pieces working together.

Getting Data For the Combo Box

For the most part, working with our Custom Task Pane is just like working with a normal Windows Form, however, I want to spend a couple minutes talking about how we are retrieving the data because we are using a few tricks.

Our first stop is filling the combo box. We aren't really doing much special here other than using a helper method in the AddInSharedState class called SearchFor. That method basically turns our parameters into a QueryExpression and calls Retrieve Multiple.

```
private void comboBoxProperty_DropDown(object sender, EventArgs e)
{
    if (comboBoxProperty.DataSource == null)
    {
        List<SearchForItem> items =
            AddInSharedState.SearchFor("ctcre_property",
                    "", "ctcre_propertyid", "ctcre_name");

        comboBoxProperty.DisplayMember = "Name";
        comboBoxProperty.ValueMember = "EntityID";
        comboBoxProperty.DataSource = items;
    }
}
```

The following is part of the SearchFor method so you can see that we are using DynamicEntity objects and converting them to our SearchForItem.

```
RetrieveMultipleResponse resp = service.Execute(req) as
      RetrieveMultipleResponse;

List<SearchForItem> items = new List<SearchForItem>();

foreach (BusinessEntity be in
    resp.BusinessEntityCollection.BusinessEntities)
{
    DynamicEntity de = be as DynamicEntity;

    SearchForItem item = new SearchForItem();
    item.EntityID = CTCDEPropHelper.GetKeyValue(de, keyAttr);
    item.EntityName = entityName;
    item.Name = CTCDEPropHelper.GetStringValue(de, nameAttr);
    items.Add(item);
}
```

By using a DynamicEntity our SearchFor method can be generic and work with any target CRM schema and it converts it to a developer friendly SeachForItem object that is easy to bind to a results grid or drop down. I highly recommend building up a library of these type of common routines that you can use over and over to speed up development.

Getting the Selected Property Data

I took a different approach with getting the property data from CRM. Here I want to use a typed object that had a property for each CRM attribute instead of the DynamicEntity generic methods. Instead of using a web service reference though, I generated a typed data class using our utility CTCWorkflowEntityGen which can in addition to generating workflow activities can generate typed data classes. The DEctcre_property is an example of one of those classes. It is built by encapsulating a dynamic entity inside and wraps it with typed properties built from the Metadata.

The following calls the GetProperty method and it returns a typed DEctcre_property instance that you can see how we are using the typed properties to set the label values for the Property Details section.

```
public DEctcre_property CurrentProperty { get; set; }

private void comboBoxProperty_SelectedIndexChanged(
        object sender, EventArgs e)
{
    if (comboBoxProperty.SelectedItem == null)
        return;

    SearchForItem item = comboBoxProperty.SelectedItem as SearchForItem;

    this.CurrentProperty = AddInSharedState.GetProperty(item.EntityID);

    labelPropertyName.Text =
            this.CurrentProperty.ctcre_name;
    labelPropertyStreet.Text =
            this.CurrentProperty.ctcre_address1_street;
    labelPropertyCityStateZip.Text =
        this.CurrentProperty.ctcre_address1_city + ","
      + this.CurrentProperty.ctcre_address1_stateorprovince +
      " " + this.CurrentProperty.ctcre_address1_postalcode;

}
```

If we look inside the GetProperty method we are going to see that it basically does a retrieve and gets a BusinessEntity back but wraps that with our typed class DEctcre_property by setting the Entity property.

```
internal static DEctcre_property GetProperty(Guid propertyID)
{
    CTCCRMService service = GetCrmService();
    CrmServiceManager svcMgr = new CrmServiceManager(service);

    BusinessEntity beProp =
            svcMgr.RetrieveFirstBySingleKey("ctcre_property",
          "ctcre_propertyid", propertyID);

    DEctcre_property deProp = new DEctcre_property()
            { Entity = beProp as DynamicEntity };
    return deProp;
}
```

Using this approach we don't require a web referece and we only have the baggage of the typed classes we plan to use. They are flattend out using nullable properties to be a little more data binding friendly as well.

Testing our Progress

Before we go to populate more of the document content let's test our progress to see what we have working. As you can see in the following image our Ribbon integrates nicely with the Word Ribbon and our options we added all are there.

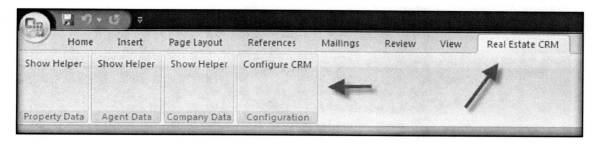

Clicking on the Show Helper in the Property Data group will cause our Property Helper to show on the Right Side of the document window as you can see below. Clicking on the dropdown list we get our list of properties from CRM.

Finally, upon selecting one of them from the list we get the Property Details area populated.

Now that we have our basic data retrieval we are ready to move on to building a document template that we can populate with our data.

Turning on the Developer tab

In order to do things like add Content Controls to our document and other things like that we need to turn on the developer tab. If you go to Word Options you will see the option like below to enable it.

Once turned on you will see the following on the Developer Tab

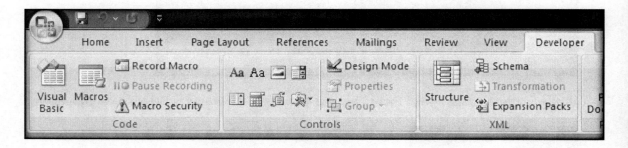

The icons in the center of the tab starting with "Aa" are the Content Controls that allow you to add place holders or fill in the blanks on the document. Using these we are going to put place holders we can use to pre-fill from our CRM data.

Not sure what Word API method to call for something? Use the Record Macro and then look at the code. It generates to help you find the right methods to call to modify the document. Often times it will help you get to the right spot in the help docs!

Adding Content Controls

My next step was to add a number of content controls to the document. Each of these content controls can then be easily accessed from code and populated with content from CRM. As you can see in the following image the Tag name I have used the CRM attribute name to make it easier.

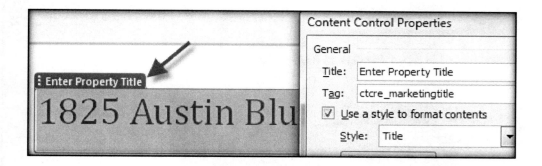

Our Final Output

Once we populate a few of our content controls we get the following as an example of our output. Now the user could print it, PDF the output or move things around and change the design. The important thing is we made CRM data easy for them to use. In fact, if I hadn't put CRM in front of some of the titles, the user would never have known CRM was even involved in the process.

Going Mobile

For years now technology people have been trying to heavily using mobile technology to do everything from e-mail to quick viewing of documents. What's changing now is mobile devices are starting to be viewed as indispensible by the common business person. Mostly, people are using the devices for some form of messaging capability, but we are starting to see more people interested in having access to some subset of their data and applications from their phone. For whatever reason, mobility for CRM has not been one of the areas that Microsoft has aggressively pursued; instead leaving it up to partners for the most part to implement. Microsoft did release a Mobile Express client as open source; it is currently in the process of being converted to work with CRM 4.0.

Prior to the release of CRM 4.0, I did a lot of travel for giving training to ISVs on the features of the CRM platform. One of the companies that had people in one of my classes was CWR Mobility (www.cwrmobility.com). Their product CWR Mobile CRM intrigued me because it leveraged the CRM platform and wrapped it with a new face that ran on a mobile device. This extended the CRM application to a mobile device using CRM as the central storage platform. It wasn't until Convergence when I was talking with them at their booth that I realized they also had an SDK that allowed you to further extend the mobile interface. That combination solidified my decision that I wanted to include a few pages about how their product allows for an alternate or additional user interface to the platform.

Configuration

The first step when you install the product is to configure it for use. Here you will indicate among various things what data will be made available and what users will have access to the mobile interface. CWR Mobility's configuration process integrates in with the platform and as best as possible provides a similar interface to some of the built-in CRM customizations.

One could easily assume with a product like this that you should just show all the data that's available but when you think about it, does that really make sense when you're mobile? On a mobile device you have a small screen and often times are after only very specific information. CWR Mobility took the approach of using the platform Metadata as the starting point to build a mobile view but allows you to customize it for the mobile view. This includes what data shows in views and on the forms in the mobile client. This is a great example of using the configuration information that's available as a starting point but not letting that become a limiting factor.

The idea of building your configuration of an add-on into the CRM navigation makes a lot of sense and is a good suggestion for others who are building add-ons. I think it's also a good idea where possible to follow a similar theme or look and feel. The following is an example of the mobility forms editor that is used to configure what the mobile form will look like.

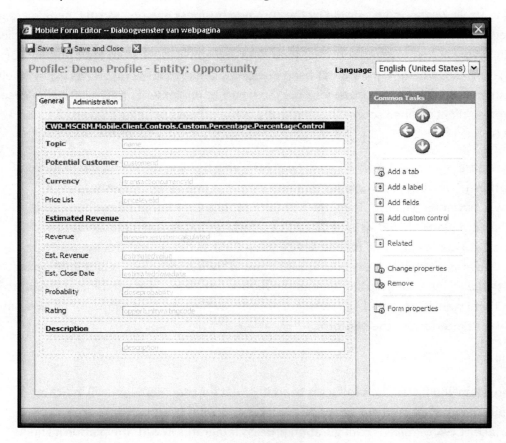

If I didn't tell you it was for the mobile client you would probably think it was the built-in form editor.

Mobile Client Interface

The real fun starts when you get the mobile client installed on your mobile device. It supports Windows Mobile 5.0 and Windows Mobile 6.0. I have it running on my Treo 750 which is nice because it provides a full touch screen interface as well as the keyboard navigation. The mobile client uses the phone's connectivity to install and to connect to the CRM server and during the first connect retrieves the necessary information about what data the mobile client will have. The client can run in an online mode where it directly hits the CRM server and also in an offline mode that is great for traveling outside the range of your cellular service. For example, from a plane you could lookup information about the hotel you were staying at when you landed. To support offline, the mobile client uses a SQL Server Mobile database to store the data locally, and then synchronizes back with the server.

When you open up the client you see a simple list of the areas that have been made available offline. In the following examples, you can see how you can easily navigate and drill down into an item. In the image on the right you can see a similar view that you might configure on the CRM client interface but this one is designed specifically for the mobile client.

 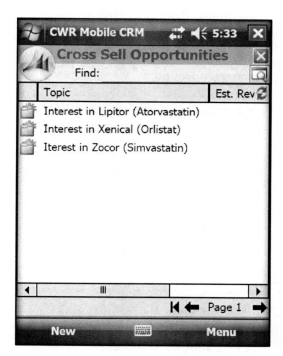

You might notice words like Leads and Sales and think this is just a customer management specific tool. But like the CRM platform it really depends on how you configure it and use it. You could hide any CRM like entities and configure it to be a project management tool, or a tool for an inspector to use when he visits project sites. As I said early in the book, I think often times we get too hung up on the fact that the product has "CRM" in the name and don't look at some of the broader types of applications that can be built.

This is also the reason that CWR Mobility likes to refer to their product as a "Mobile application development platform", because based on the CRM metadata you can build virtually any mobile application you want (see also "Extending with the SDK").

Take a 5 minute break, go grab a clean sheet of paper or your nearest whiteboard and write down 5 ideas for applications that would be easier to build if all the "plumbing" had already been built.

When you drill down further you get the data in forms that were customized for the mobile client. Using a tabbed interface you are able to still have a fair amount of data that is pretty easy to navigate around.

The following is an example of the data viewing and input form that we configured on the server and was pulled down to be used on the client.

To continue to get you to think a little about the type of applications you can build, I included a snapshot of the signature page. You could also do the same thing with a Windows Forms, WPF or SilverLight front end to capture the user's input using ink.

It's probably also important to point out that it supports all the major CRM v4 features, like multi-currency, multi-lingual (10 languages) , the new relationship types and multi-tenency. It also provides basic integration with pocket outlook.

Extending with the SDK

One of the nice features of the mobile client is that they have an SDK that you can extend and customize it with custom controls and mobile callouts. These custom controls and callouts are written using the .NET Compact Framework. The nice thing here is you only have to write the custom control and not the whole mobile client. Using this approach you leave all the server interaction including synchronization to someone else to deal with.

Custom controls are placed on a form and are typically used when you need some interaction with the user and/or the form. The following are a few examples of things you could do with custom controls:

- You could create a custom control that links two existing controls together and adds validation to those controls(in the CRM web client you would use client-side javascript to do this)..
- You could create a custom control that integrates with a route navigation application and uses values from existing controls as input.
- You could create an (invisible) custom control that fills default values when the form loads.
- You could create a custom control that presents another input method for an existing control, thereby overriding that existing field. E.g. a control with a large numeric keypad for easier entry of numbers.
- You could create a custom control that represents a "toolbar" from which you can start several actions on the form (e.g. a Resolve/Cancel/Reactivate Case button).

In addition to the custom controls you can also hook into the processing on the forms using the mobile client's Callout capability. If you used Callouts in CRM 3.0 you will find the interface very similar and gives you the ability to do things like capture Pre/Post event conditions and have custom code run.

Common uses for client-side callouts are:

- Offline calculation of order header values when adding/deleting order details.
- Integration with backend systems, e.g. credit card validation and processing.
- Validate data in a Pre event callout and abort the action when validation fails.

You may or may not need the extensibility the SDK offers but having that option makes it possible to build more complex solutions.

Wrapping up CWR Mobility

I included the mobility client in this chapter because I really feel it demonstrates that you can completely put a new front end on the platform. I also think CWR Mobility does a great job of using the standard platform extensibility points to provide their own interface, but behind the scenes they rely on the platform to still do things like workflow, reporting, security and more.

Leveraging SharePoint

Microsoft SharePoint offers a number of opportunities to act as a portal for CRM related data or can be integrated and used within the context of the CRM interface. As a portal, SharePoint can aggregate and display data from CRM using web parts or reports to give the user a dashboard type view of their CRM data. Depending on the version of SharePoint you are using, additional capabilities like Business Data Catalog (BCD) and search can offer additional features to help tie CRM data into an enterprise portal. Business Data Catalog allows you to expose CRM data to SharePoint by establishing a mapping to the data in CRM. Users can then access CRM data from SharePoint to leverage SharePoint features like search against the CRM data.

SharePoint is really good at managing unstructured data like files and includes some rich functionality like versioning to make users more productive. As it turns out, those type of features are not provided by CRM, as CRM is better at managing structured data and the relationships that exists among them. Often times, SharePoint can be used in conjunction with CRM to provide access to these additional features. A common integration is to tie a document workspace to a particular data item in CRM. For example, if you had a custom entity named "project" it would be possible to have each project have its own document library in SharePoint that was shown in an IFrame when you view the data in CRM.

As CRM and SharePoint continue to evolve we will hopefully see more integration between the two products as we have seen Microsoft do with other products. For example, SharePoint

Services is completely integrated and ships with Microsoft Team Foundation System (TFS) allowing TFS to take advantage of the extra features without requiring the users to do the integrating the together. I believe that the same type of integration would make sense with CRM and SharePoint and would like to see that in future releases.

Wrapping it up

In this chapter, we just touched on the surface of the possibilities of ways you could leverage the core platform to build custom interfaces. Speaking of "Surface", can you imagine sitting down using the new Microsoft "Surface" that allows users a touch interface to applications. What type of solutions can you build using that? Think about how you might leverage a unique interface like that to provide a Management platform and to think of ways you can innovate using the other services the platform offers. For example, Dashboard type view of all the CRM data controlled by the user dragging around items on the "Surface". Another emerging user experience that will become more popular is automobile computing. There have been some basic announcements about Microsoft Sync and their integration with cars. Here the opportunity exists to extend the platform to interact and provide more real time value. Imagine you're driving along and you pass a client's office that you had scheduled for a follow up in the next week. Having an application running in the car that interacts with the platform it could advise you "Excuse me, you're about to pass John Smith's business address you have a follow-up for him next week- would you like me to call him now?". Today, these types of integrated applications are still more concept than reality but they are tomorrow's opportunity. The goal of this chapter was to get you to start thinking outside the box of the standard user experience that comes with the CRM platform.

8

Exploring Metadata

At the heart of the platform is the metadata that exists and describes all entities including both system and custom. It also helps to facilitate the multi language capabilities of the platform by keeping track of the metadata by language code allowing multiple languages to exist simultaneously.

Most important to developers is the fact that you can use the Metadata API to discover and explore what exists in a particular organization. This allows ISVs and other developers to program against the platform without having any knowledge of what custom entities and attributes have been added.

New in CRM 4.0 is the ability to use the Metadata API to modify the platform metadata. In the past this was only accomplished either though the Web Client interface or importing a customizations file into the system. Now using the API you can do things like create custom entities, add attributes and even use it to manage multi language settings on the various metadata in the system. In this chapter, we will look at some of the capabilities of the API, including both the retrieving and the new modification capabilities.

Using the Metadata Service

The Metadata service can be accessed using a web reference or the class object that is part of the SDK assembly. Using the metadata service reference you will then make request/response calls to get information from the platform.

The API can be called when the caller is both on-line and off-line. When you are off-line you are limited to being able to use the Retrieve oriented calls. You must be on-line to use any of the "write" methods that will result in changes to the platform metadata.

 TIP

Metadata retrieval can be slow so for best performance you might want to consider caching a copy of the data you need and only going to the server when you need updated

Security Roles for Metadata Access

Access to read and update an organizations metadata is controlled by the security roles. By default most roles do not have access to read the Metadata. Both the System Administrator role and the System Customizer role both have read and update by default. If you are planning on having normal users access the metadata you would need to grant access to those users roles. For example, if you were going to write an Office application add-in and were going to pull from the metadata via the API those users would need access to read the metadata. On the role edit panels the Customization tab controls access to the metadata. The following shows the default rights most roles have and as you can tell they don't have read to Entity, Attribute and Relationship.

You can modify that by simply clicking on the circle to grant access to read to that specific role.

Using the Metadata Service without a Web Reference

One of the things that may not be as obvious is that you can actually access the metadata web services using the MetadataService class that is part of the type proxy assembly (Microsoft.Crm.SdkTypeProxy) in the Microsoft.Crm.SdkTypeProxy namespace.

Keep in mind that unlike the CRMService that is dynamic based on the custom entities that you add to the CRM organization, the Metadata Service is static and does not change.

The following shows the minimal code to use the Metadata Service via the proxy.

```
CrmAuthenticationToken authToken = new CrmAuthenticationToken()
authToken.OrganizationName = "myorg"
MetadataService ms = new MetadataService();
ms.CrmAuthenticationTokenValue = authToken;
ms.Credentials = new NetworkCredential("myuser", "mypass");
ms.Url = http://myserver/MSCRMServices/2007/MetadataService.asmx
RetrieveEntityRequest req = new RetrieveEntityRequest();
req.EntityItems = Microsoft.Crm.Sdk.Metadata.EntityItems.EntityOnly;
req.LogicalName = "ctccrm_traceconfig"
RetrieveEntityResponse resp = ms.Execute(req) as RetrieveEntityResponse;
```

We will be discussing authentication and connecting to all types of deployments in detail in Chapter 9.

Using the Metadata Service with a Web Reference

You can also use the Metadata service by referencing it using a web reference. There really isn't anything gained by doing this instead of using the class that comes with the SDK assembly. In the next chapter when we are talking about the CRM Service and referencing it using a web reference that will make more sense because it dynamically configures based on the entity data model.

One scenario that would take advantage of the fact that you can reference it using a web reference is if you were accessing the service from a non .NET language. For example, if you wanted to access the metadata service from php.

Understanding the API

The Metadata API uses a Request/Response object model. Interaction with the API is done by passing a "Request" to the Execute method on the API and it will return a "Response" object.

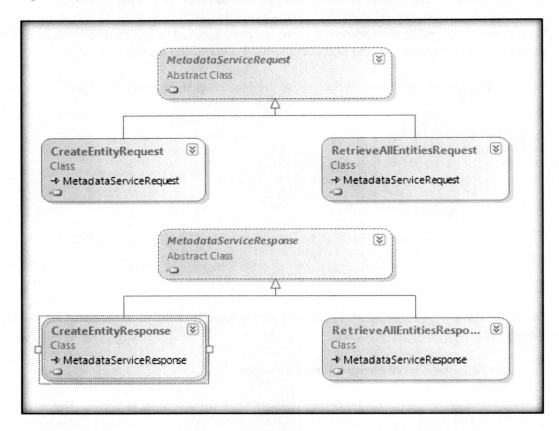

There are about 20-25 different request / response object pairs that you will be working with when you make calls to the Metadata API. Each of the pairs is designed to accomplish a specific task. This architecture also makes it easy for enhancements to be added later to the API.

Error handling is accomplished by the throwing of exceptions the same way that you will read about in the Chapter 9. The guidance provided there will also apply for your calls to the metadata service.

The following is an example of one of the simpler ones that retrieves all the entities.

```
RetrieveAllEntitiesRequest req =
          new RetrieveAllEntitiesRequest();

req.MetadataItems = MetadataItems.EntitiesOnly;

RetrieveAllEntitiesResponse resp =
          (RetrieveAllEntitiesResponse)service.Execute(req);

foreach (EntityMetadata entity in resp.CrmMetadata)
{
    EntityDisplaySchemaName info = new EntityDisplaySchemaName();
    info.DisplayName = GetDisplayName(entity.DisplayName);
    info.SchemaName = entity.LogicalName;
    list.Add(info);
}
```

In the above example, we make the request, get the response, then iterate through all of the entities returned. Notice that we set MetadataItems to be EntitiesOnly. That informs the API that we only need the basic details about the entity and things like attributes will not be fetched.

If you just need the data for a single entity don't use the RetrieveAllEntities use the RetrieveEntity as it will perform significantly better.

Common Request/Response Objects

The following are the common Request/Response objects you will be working with when dealing with Entities, Attributes and their associated picklists.

Each of these has corresponding Request/Response pairs.

Message Names	Description
CreateEntity DeleteEntity RetrieveEntity RetrieveAllEntities UpdateEntity	This set of request/response messages all work with the Entity. In the case of Create, Retrieve and Update in addition to the basic entity information you can also modify some of the children items like attributes using the same calls.
CreateAttribute DeleteAttribute RetrieveAttribute UpdateAttribute	These all work on one attribute at a time. These methods you will use to surgically add/remove or update individual attributes. These messages are less overhead than working at the entity level when performance matters.
DeleteOptionValue InsertOptionValue OrderOption UpdateOption	These options allow you to manipulate picklist entries. This is particularly important when you want to do simple changes to a system that already has some data in it. This avoids having to try to import the complete entity just to change a simple value.

In addition to the basic entity /attribute and option manipulation relationships are also a key part of what you can do with the Metadata API. The following are related to handling of relationships.

Message Names	Description
CanBeReferenced CanBeReferencing CanManyToMany GetValidReferencingEntities GetValidReferencedEntities	This set of messages can be used to determine what type of relationships entities are eligible for. If you are building any type of a tool that helps setup relationships these would allow you to filter your list of eligible entities based on what relationships could actually be created.

Message Names	Description
CreateManyToMany CreateOneToMany DeleteRelationship RetrieveRelationship UpdateRelationship	These messages let you retrieve, create, update and delete relationships.

Retrieving Information

Using the metadata service to retrieve information will allow you to build more generic solutions that can be reused. As you start planning how to use the metadata it's important to think about optimizing access. Retrieving all the metadata from the platform can take much longer than just retrieving the information for a single attribute.

One common strategy for optimizing access is to enable some form of caching of the metadata for use by multiple users / requests. If you think about it, once you finish your initial development, the rate of change of metadata will slow quite a bit. So you should be able to do some significant caching of it for typical use. The exception to that is if you are working on a solution that will modify the metadata; I recommend always working with a live copy to avoid any conflicts.

If you do cache the metadata, keep in mind the multi tenant capabilities and the fact that a user could connect to multiple organizations. Each organization has its own metadata that is unique. Make sure any strategy including cache keys or file names takes that into account.

Using the metadata service you can retrieve a timestamp string that you can use to check to see if the metadata has changed for that organization.

The following code shows how to retrieve the timestamp.

```
public string GetMetadataTimestamp()
{
    MetadataService service = GetMetadataService();

    RetrieveTimestampRequest req = new RetrieveTimestampRequest();
    RetrieveTimestampResponse resp =
                (RetrieveTimestampResponse)service.Execute(req);
    return resp.Timestamp;
}
```

The easiest way to use this is to retrieve it when you retrieve your metadata information and then simply do a compare to see if the value has changed to determine if you need to retrieve it again.

Retrieving Entity Information

We saw earlier in the chapter our example of retrieving the metadata for all the entities defined in the organization. A typical use for that is when you don't know what entities you will be working with and need to provide the user a complete list of entity names. The RetrieveAll is also the method you will probably use if you want to cache all the metadata in one call. There are not a lot of options that you can provide, but one property that does affect performance is the EntityItems property. This property informs the platform how much of the details of the entity metadata you want retrieved. This property is available on the Retrieve All as well as the Retrieve that returns a single entity metadata. The following are the options for the EntityItems property.

Option	Description
All	This is the catch all, "give me everything you got" option. It will perform the worst of all as it pulls all of the data available for the entity back in one call.
EntitiesOnly	This is the lightest weight message that can be used when for example you need a list of entity names that exist. It retrieves the simple properties on the EntityMetadata object (SDK has full list), but does not retrieve any of the related child objects (e.g. attributes).

Option	Description
IncludeAttributes	Pulls EntityOnly plus all the data about the attributes in the form of AttributeMetadata objects in the Attributes property.
IncludePrivileges	Pulls EntityOnly plus the privilege information – this is a less used option.
IncludeRelationships	This pulls down the ReferencesFrom and ReferencesTo in addition to the basic entity data.

We saw earlier that we can simply set this to a single value like below.

```
req.MetadataItems = MetadataItems.EntitiesOnly;
```

You can also combine these together to get multiple of the "include" options in one call. For example I could request Attributes and Relationships using the following code.

```
req.MetadataItems = MetadataItems.IncludeAttributes
          | MetadataItems.IncludeRelationships;
```

The less information you can request the faster the API call will be. You should consider whether you can retrieve only the minimal information and then do separate calls as needed for the deep details, or if you are better to just get all the details in the first call.

Retrieving Attribute Information

In addition to getting information at the entity level, you can drill directly into an attribute using the RetrieveAttributeRequest. The following is an example of what that code would look like.

```
RetrieveAttributeRequest req = new RetrieveAttributeRequest();
req.EntityLogicalName = "contact";
req.LogicalName = "firstname";
RetrieveAttributeResponse resp =
        service.Execute(req) as RetrieveAttributeResponse;
```

As we start talking about updating the metadata, the changes to the Metadata schema take place immediately. That would be things like adding, updating and deleting entities and attributes which would be considered schema related. As we talk later about changes to PickList options, those changes are not considered schema changes. That means in order for them to be visible they must be published.

If you have made changes to a Picklist options for example and haven't published it by default the retrieve methods we have been talking about will return the published values without your changes. You can get the unpublished changes by setting the property RetrieveAsIfPublished on all the Retrieve requests we have been talking about. Using that option you will get the unpublished picklist values returned. In the future it is possible that more types of changes will require a publish before they become visible, so a good practice would be just to publish after making any metadata change.

TIP

Using the RetrieveAttribute request can be more efficient than retrieving the entity with all its attributes. Where possible if you only need a couple attributes consider using this request.

Create, Get, Delete Custom Entity via API

One of the new features of CRM 4.0 is the ability to not only read from the platform metadata but to be able to modify it through the API as well.

If you are familiar with CRM 3.0, you were only able to do these type of changes though the web client, or by importing existing customization files.

There are lots of things you can do with this capability, but for this chapter, I'm just going to use the API to create a custom entity, read it back and finally delete it to cleanup.

To Create the Custom Entity, we need to do a CreateEntityRequest .

```
CreateEntityRequest createReq = new CreateEntityRequest();
EntityMetadata entityInfo = new EntityMetadata();
entityInfo.Description = CreateSingleCRMLabel("Property Entity");
entityInfo.DisplayCollectionName = CreateSingleCRMLabel("Properties");
entityInfo.DisplayName = CreateSingleCRMLabel("Property");
entityInfo.DuplicateDetection = new CrmBoolean(true);
entityInfo.IsAvailableOffline = new CrmBoolean(true);
entityInfo.SchemaName = "Ctccrm_MyProperty";
entityInfo.OwnershipType = new
        CrmOwnershipTypes(OwnershipTypes.UserOwned);
createReq.Entity = entityInfo;
createReq.HasActivities = true;
createReq.HasNotes = true;
```

NOTE

The LogicalName property on the EntityMetadata object is read only and will be created by the system from the schema name. If specified, it will be ignored by the create or update request.

Before you call the Execute there's one more required step, you must setup the Primary Attribute. In this case I'm going to use Name as the primary attribute.

```
StringAttributeMetadata primaryAttrib = new StringAttributeMetadata();
primaryAttrib.DisplayName = CreateSingleCRMLabel("Property Name");
primaryAttrib.Description =
        CreateSingleCRMLabel("This is the name attribute");
primaryAttrib.AttributeType = new
        CrmAttributeType(AttributeType.String);
primaryAttrib.MaxLength = new CrmNumber(100);
primaryAttrib.SchemaName = "Ctccrm_Name";
primaryAttrib.Format = new
        CrmStringFormat(Microsoft.Crm.Sdk.Metadata.StringFormat.Text);
primaryAttrib.DisplayMask = new
        CrmDisplayMasks(DisplayMasks.PrimaryName);
primaryAttrib.RequiredLevel = new
        CrmAttributeRequiredLevel(AttributeRequiredLevel.Required);
createReq.PrimaryAttribute = primaryAttrib;
```

 *If you do not set all the required properties you will get an Unexpected Exception from the API. Since the update portion of the Metadata API is newer, these type of errors are more likely to happen here. If you encounter this, double check your request object for required properties and then check with the debug chapter for tips on how to best debug the problem.*

request.

```
CreateEntityResponse createResp =
          ms.Execute(createReq) as CreateEntityResponse;
```

Now at this point we could jump over to the web client and check the list of custom entities and we should see the new entity on the list. The other thing we could do is use the RetrieveEntityRequest and do the same check using the API.

```
RetrieveEntityRequest req = new RetrieveEntityRequest();
req.EntityItems =
    Microsoft.Crm.Sdk.Metadata.EntityItems.IncludeAttributes;
req.LogicalName = "ctccrm_myproperty";
RetrieveEntityResponse resp = ms.Execute(req) as RetrieveEntityResponse;
```

Finally, using the API, I will just delete the new custom entity I just created.

```
DeleteEntityRequest delReq = new DeleteEntityRequest();
delReq.LogicalName = "ctccrm_myproperty";
DeleteEntityResponse delResp =
          ms.Execute(delReq) as DeleteEntityResponse;
```

TIP

Delete also deletes all of the data, so don't get too carried away with doing deletes without making sure that your users know you are deleting data also!

Properties on both the Entity and the Attribute I did it by calling a helper method called CreateSingleCRMLabel. Those properties are of type CrmLabel that is designed to support the multi language aspects of CRM 4.0 and allow you to set one or more language strings for each of the properties.

I will elaborate more on how you can use the CrmLabel later but for now here's a simple code snippet for the helper method. The CreateSingleCRMLabel method prepares an English(That's what the 1033 indicates, it's the Language Code) version of the label.

```
public CrmLabel CreateSingleCRMLabel(string labelText)
{
     return CreateSingleCRMLabel(labelText, 1033);
}

public CrmLabel CreateSingleCRMLabel(string labelText, int lcID)
{
     LocLabel[] labels = new LocLabel[1];
     labels[0] = new LocLabel(labelText, new CrmNumber(lcID));
     CrmLabel label = new CrmLabel();
     label.LocLabels = labels;
     return label;
}
```

So with the ability to do metadata modifications using the API, you can now do things like automate the creation of your custom schema as part of your install or provisioning program. It also makes it so in the uninstall routine you can remove attributes or entities if you want to completely remove your solution from a schema and from being installed in a system. Previously, this could only be done by manual intervention using the user interface and there wasn't a way to automate it.

Understanding Attributes

When working with entities you will also be working with their attributes. Attributes all inherit from AttributeMetadata as the base class.

When you retrieve them as part of an entity or one by one they will come back as the specific type. For example, if you retrieve the account name from the account entity it will come back as a StringAttributeMetadata object. That's great if you want to work with the specific type but you can also access it generically like it's an AttributeMetadata object. The following is an example of looping through an entity's attributes using the generic AttributeMetadata reference.

```
foreach (AttributeMetadata attr in entity.Attributes)
{
    fileWriter.WriteLine("Attribute: " + attr.LogicalName.ToString()
               + " is type " + attr.AttributeType.Value.ToString());
}
```

You might be surprised how often code like this is helpful, typically where you just need the name and possibly the attribute type.

When you are creating a new attribute or modifying one, you will almost always want to use the specific type. The reason for this is each of the attribute types have special properties related to their type. For example, a StringAttributeMetadata it has a MaxLength property but on an IntegerAttributeMetadata object is has a Min/MaxValue property.

You might find also that some Attributes will simply come back as AttributeMetadata – these typically are system types. A good example of this is a Virtual, while you will see it in the list, it's not one that you can manipiulate using the SDK.

A great way to gain a better understanding of how the attributes work is to retrieve an entity in the debugger and look at each of its attributes. You will be able to see what type of properties are set compared to what you input on the web client when you created them. Early on when the documentation was pretty thin on the Metadata API that was how I fumbled around to get it to work.

Modifications to Attributes on an Existing Entity

Often times you will have the need to modify an existing entity like Contact, Account or Opportunity. Since those are existing entities you can't assume that you can just import your own customization file and overwrite what is already there. Prior to CRM 4.0 if you needed to add or update a single attribute you really didn't have any great options. Now you have the ability to perform actions at the attribute level to an existing entity.

A great example of this is Opportunity. We have a set of standard fields we like to add to help simplify follow-up. In that scenario we can just use the CreateAttribute to add those on.

Another scenario that might play out here is if you wanted to do customizations of the display labels based on the client's preferences. You could have an Excel file that contained all the attributes and their display names and then the client just went through and made any changes. If you fed this Excel back you could do an update on any of the names that changed simply updating the attribute one at a time.

Updating an Attribute

The following code sets up changes to an attribute and then calls the helper method on our utility class MetaDataManager to apply the change to the platform. Only the properties that are going to be modified are specified.

```
StringAttributeMetadata attr = new StringAttributeMetadata();
attr.DisplayName = CreateSingleCRMLabel("Property Description");
attr.Description = CreateSingleCRMLabel("This is the Description
attribute");
attr.MaxLength = new CrmNumber(100);
attr.RequiredLevel = new
CrmAttributeRequiredLevel(AttributeRequiredLevel.None);

using (MetadataService srv = this.GetMetaService())
{
    MetaDataManager mgr = new MetaDataManager(srv);
    mgr.UpdateAttribute("ctccrm_myproperty", attr);
}
```

The following code is from the MetaDataManager UpdateAttribute method and packages up the attribute for a call to the Metadata Service API.

```
UpdateAttributeRequest req = new UpdateAttributeRequest();
req.EntityName = entityName;
req.Attribute = attr;
req.Attribute.EntityLogicalName = entityName;
req.MergeLabels = false;
UpdateAttributeResponse resp =
         service.Execute(req) as UpdateAttributeResponse;
```

Deleting an Attribute

Using the DeleteAttribute method on our MetaDataManager helper class you can easily remove a single attribute from an existing entity.

The following code shows the call to the DeleteAttribute Method.

```
MetaDataManager mgr = new MetaDataManager(srv);
mgr.DeleteAttribute("ctccrm_myproperty", "ctccrm_description");
```

Looking inside the DeleteAttribute method you will see that it's building up the DeleteAttributeRequest with the information passed and making the call to the Metadata API.

```
public void DeleteAttribute(string entityName, string attrName)
{
    MetadataService service = GetMetadataService();

    DeleteAttributeRequest req = new DeleteAttributeRequest();
    req.EntityLogicalName = entityName;
    req.LogicalName = attrName;

    DeleteAttributeResponse resp =
            service.Execute(req) as DeleteAttributeResponse;

}
```

Cloning an Attribute

A useful technique when working with metadata is to clone an attribute that already exists. We will be looking at a more complete example of this later on in the chapter with a tool to replicate attributes.

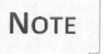 *Some system attributes can't be cloned and can only be created by the system when a new entity is created. Attempting to create those attributes will generate an error.*

The following is a code snippet pulled from the MetaDataManager class in our common helper library provided with the book. This method assumes that you have retrieved or otherwise built the AttributeMetadata prior to calling and it just simply helps you package up the request and get the response back.

Example of our AddAttribute Method from MetaDataManager.

```
public Guid AddAttribute(string entityName, AttributeMetadata attr)
{

    MetadataService service = GetMetadataService();
    CreateAttributeRequest req = new CreateAttributeRequest();
    req.EntityName = entityName;
    req.Attribute = attr;
    req.Attribute.EntityLogicalName = entityName;
    req.Attribute.MetadataId = null;

    CreateAttributeResponse resp = service.Execute(req) as
CreateAttributeResponse;

    return resp.AttributeId.Value;

}
```

Prior to calling the above method it is assumed that you retrieved a property from an existing attribute or created it by hand as you can see in the following example.

```
StringAttributeMetadata newAttr = new StringAttributeMetadata();
newAttr.DisplayName = CreateSingleCRMLabel("Property Highlight");
newAttr.Description =
        CreateSingleCRMLabel("This is a property highlight");
newAttr.AttributeType = new
        CrmAttributeType(AttributeType.String);
newAttr.MaxLength = new CrmNumber(100);
newAttr.SchemaName = "ctcre_PropertyHighlight";
newAttr.Format = new
        CrmStringFormat(Microsoft.Crm.Sdk.Metadata.StringFormat.Text);
newAttr.RequiredLevel = new
        CrmAttributeRequiredLevel(AttributeRequiredLevel.Required);
```

Using the attribute created above we would simply make a call to the MetaDataManager class.

```
mgr.AddAttribute("ctcre_property",newAttr);
```

We will see more of using this approach when we dig deeper into the Attribute Replicator example later in the chapter.

Updating Language Strings using the API

Supporting one language at a time is easy, because you only have one set of definitions active at the same time. When you start having multiple languages active, you need to be able to track each languages display strings, plus be able to determine when to show the right one. The platform accommodates for that by using a composite object (CrmLabel) to represent strings such as Display Name, Description and other fields that are displayed to the user. This allows you to customize them for each language you want to support.

Understanding CrmLabel

CrmLabel has two key properties that you will be working with. LocLabels which is a collection of all LocLabel's that are defined with that particular string. A single LocLabel object instances represents the combination of a Language Code and the text of the Label that a user would see for that Language Code. UserLocLabel represents a single LocLabel object that is the specified LocLabel for the user that is authenticated. This is very helpful because it keeps you from having to first determine the user's language, then rummage through the list of available languages to find the right one. UserLocLabel also handles the situation when the language of the user is not available, it will downgrade to the default language of the install.

```
CrmLabel(Microsoft.Crm.Sdk.LocLabel[], Microsoft.Crm.Sdk.LocLabel)
CrmLabel()
LocLabels
UserLocLabel
```

You saw earlier in the chapter the CreateSingleCRMLabel helper method that is part of the MetaDataManager class. The GetDisplayName method is also helpful because you can simply pass it a CrmLabel instance and it will give you back the user preferred label or fall back. In theory the fallback should happen for you, however under certain conditions we found it easier to wrap this access into a helper method. It also provides a single place where if we ever need to do additional checking or the implementation changes we can easily accommodate by updating our helper method.

TIP

As a general rule of thumb, most of the properties in the Metadata classes that will be able to be seen by a user are represented by a CrmLabel object so they can support specification in each language code.

The following is a helper method to get the DisplayName from a CrmLabel object.

```
public string GetDisplayName(CrmLabel lab)
{
    if (lab.UserLocLabel != null)
        return lab.UserLocLabel.Label;

    if (lab.LocLabels.Length < 1)
        return "";
    return lab.LocLabels[0].Label;
}
```

You will find when working with the metadata properties that about half of them are CrmLabel and half of them are just standard strings. As a good rule of thumb any that contain data that will be shown to a user will almost always be a CrmLabel because it accommodates the need for supporting the multi language capabilities of the platform.

Updating Picklists

The most common reasons you will use the Metadata API to modify Picklist attributes on an entity will be to accomplish one of the following:

- Inserting a new item into an existing entity – the API allows you to insert the new item without disturbing the existing items on the list.
- Removing one or more Picklist items that are not going to be used in your solution.
- Adding language strings for multi language support on the Picklist. Using the update capabilities you can insert a single language or replace all values for a given Picklist option.
- Reordering the options on a Picklist.

Changes to Picklist Values in CRM 4.0

Prior to CRM 4.0, if you added additional options to an existing system entity Picklist the value would start at the next sequential number. For example, if the last entry had a value of 5, adding another would assign a value of 6.

In CRM 4.0, the product team made a change to require additional values on system entity Picklists to start at 200,000. So in our scenario where the last one is 5, adding another would start at 200,000. This change is true on the client as well as the Metadata API.

The only exception is when the Picklist is imported using the customization import capability. In this scenario to ensure backward compatibly values lower than 200,000 will be still allowed.

Adding a Picklist Option

Picklist options are added using the InsertOptionValueRequest/Response. The following is an example of adding an option input by the user into a Windows Forms grid.

```
MetadataAuthManager<MetadataService, CrmAuthenticationToken> metaMgr =
    new MetadataAuthManager<MetadataService, CrmAuthenticationToken>();
using (MetadataService svc = metaMgr.GetService())
{
  MetaDataManager mgr = new MetaDataManager(svc);
  e.Row.Cells[2].Value = Guid.NewGuid();
  string curKey = e.Row.Cells[2].Value.ToString();
  Option opt = new Option();
  opt.Value = new CrmNumber(int.Parse(e.Row.Cells[5].Value.ToString()));
  opt.Label = mgr.CreateSingleCRMLabel(e.Row.Cells[4].Value.ToString());
  m_Options.Add(curKey, opt);
  InsertOptionValueRequest req = new InsertOptionValueRequest();
  req.Label = opt.Label;
  req.Value = opt.Value;
  try
  {
      svc.Execute(req);
  }
  catch (SoapException ex)
  {
      MessageBox.Show(ex.Detail.OuterXml);
  }
}
```

NOTE

This new option will appear at the end and you will need to use the order capabilities we discuss later in this chapter to place the new option in the correct place.

Updating a Picklist Option

The update capabilities of the API for Picklist options can be used to update a label value or to add a language variation. Using this approach you can easily add additional labels. An example of using this might be to add labels for a Dutch version of your solution.

The following is an example of the helper method in MetaDataManager for updating a Picklist option.

```
public void UpdatePicklistOptionLabel(string entityName,
          string attributeName,int LCID, string label, int value)
{
   MetadataService service = GetMetadataService();
   UpdateOptionValueRequest req = new UpdateOptionValueRequest();
   req.AttributeLogicalName = entityName;
   req.AttributeLogicalName = attributeName;
   req.Label = this.CreateSingleCRMLabel(label, LCID);
   req.MergeLabels = true;
   req.Value = value;
   service.Execute(req);
}
```

The MergeLabels property above that is set to true allows us to specify only the Labels and Laguage you will be changing with this request. So for example if English and Germany were already on the Option, and you did a update on English this would merge our update for English with the existing German. Otherwise, without that option set if you called update and only passed English that would be the only left on the Option after the update completed. This allows you to do "Language Updates" where the goal is to simply add a variation of another language without caring what is already stored on that Option already.

Replacing a Picklist Option

You might have noticed on the update Picklist Option that it is using the value property as the key to locate the Option to update. That means if you want to change the value you need to take a different approach. I have included a simple replace option that basically calls the add / delete as part of the samples.

The following method shows how to replace option using the Delete/Add methods.

```
public void ReplacePicklistOption(string entityName,
    string attributeName, string label, int newValue,int oldValue)
{
    DeletePicklistOption(entityName, attributeName, oldValue);
    AddPicklistOption(entityName, attributeName, label, newValue);
}
```

The method above only works well when there is only one language specified on the existing item. If you wanted to handle multiple, you would be best to retrieve the Attribute and update the value and use the UpdateAttributeRequest instead.

Deleting a Picklist Option

Deleting a Picklist option is pretty easy, the following is an example from our MetaDataManager helper class provided in the examples.

```
public void DeletePicklistOption(string entityName,
        string attributeName, int value)
{
    MetadataService service = GetMetadataService();

    DeleteOptionValueRequest req = new DeleteOptionValueRequest();
    req.AttributeLogicalName = entityName;
    req.AttributeLogicalName = attributeName;
    req.Value = value;
    service.Execute(req);
}
```

Ordering Picklist Options

One of the frequent things you might need to do with the options on a Picklist is re-order them. Using the client interface you can do that using the Move Up and Move Down buttons on the edit page as you can see in the following image.

The following is an image of the sample application that performs ordering.

Now with the new capability of the Metadata API you can now do the same thing using the API. Using the API, you can create your own ordering utilities or perform order changes as part of provisioning of your solution.

Using the OrderOptionRequest/OrderOptionResponse we can provide and save a specific order for the options on the Picklist.

The following shows an example of a Windows Forms application that duplicates the capability of the Web Client using the Metadata API.

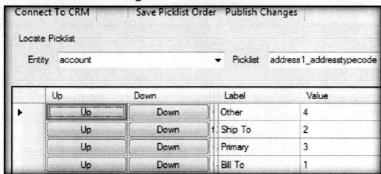

When the user clicks Save Picklist Order in the above form the following code executes to make the request to save the order.

```
List<int> values = new List<int>();
foreach (DataRowView row in m_DV)
{
    values.Add((int)row["Value"]);
}
OrderOptionRequest req = new OrderOptionRequest();
req.EntityLogicalName = comboBox1.SelectedItem.ToString();
req.AttributeLogicalName = comboBox2.SelectedItem.ToString();
req.Values = values.ToArray();
MetadataAuthManager<MetadataService, CrmAuthenticationToken> metaMgr =
    new MetadataAuthManager<MetadataService, CrmAuthenticationToken>();
```

```
using (MetadataService svc = metaMgr.GetService())
{
    try
    {
        OrderOptionResponse resp =
                svc.Execute(req) as OrderOptionResponse;
        MessageBox.Show("Reorder Completed");
    }
    catch (SoapException ex)
    {
        MessageBox.Show(ex.Detail.OuterXml);

    }
}
```

NOTE

The above example shows MetadataAuthManager which is part of the book samples and will be discussed in more details in the next chapter.

Ideas on how to use Metadata

You might not have realized it at the time but you have already seen examples of using the metadata to drive utilities. When we built the client script IntelliSense reference files in Chapter 5 we used the entity and attribute metadata to be able to generate the script files.

I guess you could say we have done this type of stuff for years using SQL Server and scripting out and reusing scripts. In fact, we even could query some of the system catalogs of the database and use it to generate things in utilities we built. I think what's different in the CRM metadata is not only does it encapsulate the data definitions it also includes the labels and things the user will see and interact with. By doing this it is able to hide and help with some of the complexity of implementing things like multi currencies and languages.

Also in this book in Chapter 20 we will be using the metadata to help build custom workflow activities and data classes to wrap around dynamic entities to make them easier to work with.

Another application that we have used internally we call the Attribute Replicator. The Attribute Replicator was created to save time moving attributes around form one entity to another. In the past, we used to have to hand input those on each entity. If you are cloning 10-20 attributes again and again that can become very time consuming. Imagine Picklists that have 50-100 values on them, doing it by hand you would have to manually one at a time add those values to the picklist attribute. Using the attribute replicator you can copy or clone that picklist from an existing entity. In addition, the replicator allows you to save Attribute Packs which are just saved versions of the attributes you want to be able to clone. The Attribute Packs can then be reused over and over to add the same sets of attributes.

The Attribute Replicator uses the metadata read API to retrieve information and then allows the user to select which attributes to replicate. The user can then using the screen below to modify the prefixes for the attributes. The last step is for the user to select which entities to copy these attributes to. Finally, the selected attributes are applied to the one or more selected targets using the metadata write API capabilities.

The following is a screen shot from our Attribute Replicator utility.

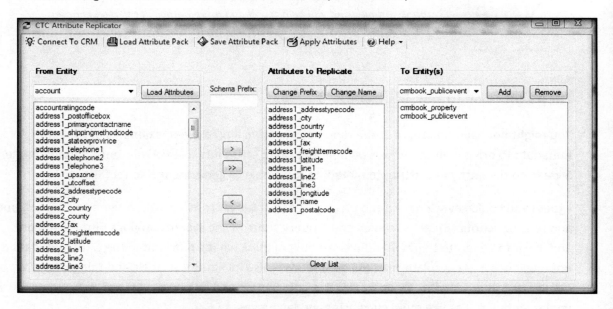

In addition to real time copying of attributes the Attribute Replicator allows you to save off the selected attributes into an "Attribute Pack" that can be reused over and over to apply common attributes.

These are just a few ideas and samples of using the metadata and the API capabilities.

Avoiding Trouble!

How does the saying go? With great power comes responsibility.[2] The same is true when you start using the Metadata Service to modify the metadata. By thinking ahead, you can avoid not only headaches for yourself but for your users. Here are a couple of thoughts to get you started.

Deleting Entities or Attributes

If you decide to use the delete capabilities of the API you should make sure that the application informs the user and the user understands that what they are doing will remove data. This can really be a problem if you decide to do it during the uninstall of your program where typically users expect it to remove the program data only.

Frequent Backups

Frequent backups are a great way to have a safety net in case something goes wrong. This can apply to changes you make during a setup program or to your development environment as you're building your solution. The important thing to think about when you design your backup strategy is to make it multi level. By multi level, I recommend doing more than just a database backup, as that requires extra time and energy to recover. It is a great parachute, but if you also do things like export your customizations frequently and keep a copy, you can use that to recover from minor problems without using the sledgehammer approach of a backup/restore.

Internally, we use a windows service configured to call the export customizations on all our development organizations on a regular schedule. We then save a handful number of copies of the export in case we need to determine what has changed.

What you can't do with the API

The one area that would have been nice to make it into CRM 4.0 was dealing with manipulation of the forms and views using the same API. Currently, those are not modifiable via the Metadata API.

---

[2] http://en.wikiquote.org/wiki/Stan_Lee

For new custom entities, that you need to get into a target system, the easiest method is using the import xml capabilities of the CRM Service API. Since it is a new entity being added you do not have to worry about stepping on some other customization.

For existing entities, your choices are a little more challenging. Of course you can use the Metadata API for adding/changing attributes on the existing entity and then use the Web interface to manually add them to the forms and views. Alternatively, you can export to xml the entity after you have made your metadata changes and then manipulate the XML to add in the new or changed fields. Finally, you could also do updates to the OrganizationUI entity which is where the forms customizations reside. With any of these approaches you need to keep in mind that other customizations may already be in place and you should ensure you don't corrupt what was already in place.

Metadata API or Import/Export

One of the choices you will make if you are trying to package up your solution is how much do you do with the Metadata API and how much do you do via the Import /Export. Metadata API is good for adding one attribute at a time to existing entities because you can surgically do it without impacting any of the other attributes. Import/Export works well in the case where you control the complete entity typically a custom entity you defined for your solution.

In that case, you can import the whole entity including forms and views without worrying about stepping on changes made by another vendors.

One thing you might consider doing as part of your install / upgrade process is to validate that your custom entities contain what you expect. You can do this by keeping track of a hash or checksum value of your customizations and then comparing it on subsequent updates. This would allow you to alert your customer that one or more of their changes they made may be lost during an upgrade of your product.

Wrapping it up

Metadata is an important part of the dynamic nature of the platform. By exposing it along with a rich API that you can modify it provides a lot of power. Think about how in your solution you can leverage the Metadata APIs to make your development tasks easier. Often times as we discussed in this chapter you can leverage the metadata to build some interesting tools.

9

Using the Web Services

The platform exposes a dynamic Web Service interface that developers use to interact with the platform and data. This interface is dynamic because it adjusts to the data model defined to a specific organization. Each organization's Web service definition (WSDL) is customized to reflect that organization's specific data model customizations.

Developers can then interact with the organization's data either using the typed classes that are customized or using a more generic interface called Dynamic Entities that are simply a generic object presentation of the data. We will be exploring both these approaches in more detail but simply put the typed interfaces are best where you are working with a known domain. The Dynamic Entity is more appropriate for ISVs and others developing logic that is intended to be more generic and discovers the data model at run time.

The CRM 4.0 platform exposes two versions of the Web services. A 2006 end point is provided to ensure backward compatibility with CRM 3.0 and a 2007 end point is provided to support the new capabilities of the platform including multi tenancy. All new applications should be using the 2007 end point as it provides the ability to leverage the new version features.

What we learn in this chapter regarding Web services will also help us in future chapters as we look at plug-ins and workflow. When coding for those you will also leverage the Web service to interact with any of the data.

The Basics

The Web services expose CRUD (Create, Read, Update, and Delete) methods that can be used for each of the entities defined in the data model. These provide typed properties for working with their attributes but require a Web service reference to be added to a specific set of CRM customizations.

The following are examples of using the typed objects to do the CRUD methods. This assumes you have already created a Web reference and somehow completed authorization to the target CRM server. In Chapter 3 we covered how to setup the Web reference to use the CRM Web service. We will be discussing authorization in more detail later in this chapter.

Create

Creating a new instance of an entity is pretty straight forward. You create a new instance of the entity type e.g. contact, populate the properties and then call the Create method on the service.

```
contact myContact = new contact();
myContact.firstname = "Dave";
myContact.lastname = "Yack";
Guid id = svc.Create(myContact);
MessageBox.Show("GUID = " + id.ToString());
```

Once the call is completed, it will return the GUID for the new instance of the entity that was created.

Update

Update is very similar to Create, in that you only specify the properties that you want to modify. It is also important that you must have the ID of the entity and set the Key property to the ID you are updating.

```
contact myContact = new contact();
myContact.contactid = new Key(m_ID);
myContact.firstname = "John";
myContact.lastname = "Smith";
svc.Update(myContact);
```

One thing to consider about Update is how you want to handle any form of concurrency. By minimizing the fields passed to only the ones modified you do reduce the footprint of what could possibly collide with other changes occuring to the same entity. It is the calling applications responsibility to only pass fields that have changed to the system.

Fields not set are not modified by the update call. If you want to clear a specific field you must pass it and set the IsNullSpecified property on the field to true to indicate you are specifically wanting to update it to a null value. For strings you must pass an empty string.

Retrieve

The only thing different about Retrieve is that you need to know the name of the entity in addition to the ID value. You will also need to specify which columns you wish to retrieve. The columns are passed using a ColumnSet object instance that includes the specific fields you wish to retrieve.

```
string[] colNames = {"contactid","firstname","lastname"};
ColumnSet colSet = new ColumnSet(colNames);

contact myContact = svc.Retrieve("contact", m_ID, colSet) as contact;

MessageBox.Show("Contact ID is " +
        myContact.contactid.Value.ToString() + " Name is " +
        myContact.firstname + " " + myContact.lastname);
```

Notice that when we specify the columns we are going to be interested in working with – only these are returned from the call. It is possible to specify that you want all columns, however, that would not perform as well. The following shows how to specify that all columns should be retrieved.

```
ColumnSet colSet = new AllColumns();
```

Since Retrieve can return any of the entities , it is necessary to cast it to the specific type we are working with.

Keep in mind if you pass an ID that doesn't exist the Retreive will throw a SoapExcepetion with the following details <detail><error <code>0x80040217</code> <description>contact With Id = 063cc145-76af-dc11-87ca-0003ff23671c Does Not Exist</description> </error></detail>". You might want to do a Retreive Multiple if that is an exepected condition it handles it without an exception.

There are other options for retrieving multiple records at once using RetrieveMultiple, Fetch and even directly using SQL FilteredViews.   Some of these we will discuss later in the chapter.

Delete

The delete operation is probably the simpliest of all the CRUD commands, it does however require the entity name (which is always the logical name) in addition to the entiy ID.

```
svc.Delete("contact", m_ID);
```

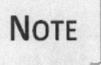

Delete can also delete records of related entities when the entity being deleted is the parent or cascading options are configured to cause that to happen. For example, if you delete a contact all activities associated with that contact are deleted as well due to the parental relationship that exists.

By understanding the basic CRUD methods you are able to work with all the entities. Later in the chapter we will discuss more advanced methods including using Dynamic Entities to work with entities when you don't know what they are beforehand.

Authentication

Authentication can be simple or complex depending on the type of solution you are building. Microsoft Dynamics CRM 4.0 supports three distinct authentication types that depend on the type of deployment you are talking to. In this section we are going to attempt to bring you up to speed on the different types and some of the details that are important.

Depending on the type of solution you are building you might not ever encounter all three, or if you are building a product to sell, it's possible you will have to support accessing the Web service in each type of deployment. Regardless, the information here will start to build your understanding of what is required to interact with each scenario.

Once we cover some of the basics we will introduce you to our authentication helper library that is included in the samples. The helper library is designed to help hide some of the implementation details. When you use the library it will work with on-premise, partner hosted and CRM Online and eliminate the need for you to figure those out on your own.

The following are the different types of authentication currently supported.

- **Integrated Authentication** – Using active directory credentials of either the currently authenticated user or of the user passed on the credentials property on the Web service. This is used in on-premise deployments.

- **IFD (Internet Facing Deployment) Authentication** – This uses a type of forms authentication from the caller's perspective. The user and password are of an active directory user behind the scenes. The interaction during authentication is intended to not leverage the active directory capabilities on the interaction between the caller and the server which removes the need for VPN connections. For developers, this means that you will pass different parameters to the Web service calls to indicate the user. This style of authentication will be used in on-premise where the site is also exposed for access outside the active directory controlled environment as well as in partner hosted installations.

- **Live ID Authentication** – This uses the Windows Live ID (WLID) for authentication and requires interaction with the Live ID servers during the course of authentication to CRM. This is used only when interacting with sites hosted on Microsoft CRM Online.

In addition, there are special case scenarios that you must account for depending on the type of application you are building. The following highlights some of these special cases.

- **Outlook Offline** – While not really a different type of authentication, it does require some special handling during the authentication process. Authentication to the CRM Offline API that is exposed by the CRM Outlook add-in is handled very similar to an Integrated Authentication / Active Directory scenario. The main difference is detection that you are offline and modification of the URL used for the services to the local version of the API. Additionally, the Discovery Service is not used. In fact the Discovery API is not running on the local offline copy of the Web services.

- **ASP.NET Deployed on CRM Server** – If you are writing a server side ASP.NET page/application that will be used in the CRM application and want to leverage the pre-authorization of the user that is accessing the page on the CRM Server you must use a special CrmImpersonator class. To use this class you must deploy your application in the ISV folder of the CRM Web site. CrmImpersonator is used because depending on which authentication type the user is accessing the site with, you would otherwise have to handle user identification and authorization uniquely for each type. By using CrmImpersonator CRM handles that for you. We will discuss how to accommodate for the CrmImpersonator later in the chapter.

- **ASP.NET Deployed to the Client** – ASP.NET applications deployed to the server only will not be available to the user when they are offline unless you make special accommodations. To work offline, the ASP.NET page must be installed on the client machine, more on that in the deployment chapter 24. From an authentication point of view, the user will always authenticate using Active Directory / Integrated Authentication and you shouldn't need to call the CrmImpersonator as you would when deployed on the CRM Server. So basically your application must detect or know where it is running and handle that appropriately. We will discuss later using our AuthHelper library included as part of the samples to help simplify this process.

Each of the above scenarios, if used by your application, would require slightly different code to be able to run against each of the scenarios. Our goal as we progress through this chapter is to explain what is happening in more detail and provide a concept of a AuthHelper library that will allow you to connect to all of the above using the same class with similar metaphors for each scenario.

Steps to Authenticate

At a high level each of the authentication scenarios goes through the following steps.

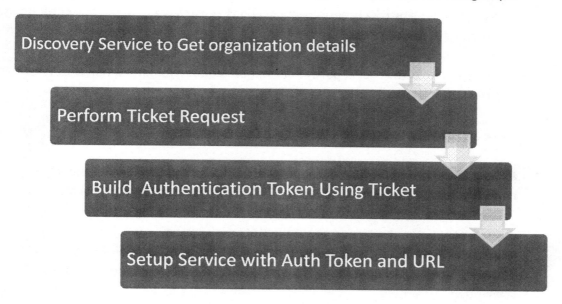

When using the services from within a workflow or plug-in these steps are handled by CRM and you are not required handle authentication as long as you use the methods provided on the context as we will discuss later in the book.

As we continue forward we will start to unravel what is unique to each type of authentication.

Understanding the Discovery Service

Before we explain our simplification process let's dig in deeper into what the platform offers as building blocks so you understand what our proposed black box does. The first stop is the Discovery Service. This is a new Web service end point that was created to help handle the multi-tenant aspects of the platform. Additionally, it also is involved with helping to facilitate some of our authentication scenarios mentioned previously.

While it's possible to build an application that never uses the Discovery Service to connect to an on-premise deployment your application would not be as flexible.

The following are the primary goals of the Discovery Service.

- Allow applications to query a CRM deployment to discover what organizations a user can access. Without a discovery service, applications would have to hard code or otherwise determine this on their own.

- Allow applications to request policy information required for interaction with Windows Live ID authentication.

- Allow applications to retrieve a ticket for IFD authentication

- Allow applications to retrieve the appropriate URLs for the CRM Service and the metadata service for each organization. This allows flexibility to the CRM deployment to determine how best to provision the roles on the server and the scale out of the environment without worrying about the URLs the application is using. Applications could do without this by hard coding the service URLs or using other techniques but the Discovery Service packages this up to work with all the different authentication scenarios.

There are three end-points exposed by the platform depending on the authentication type you are using. You access them using the Server URL plus the following:

- **Integrated / Active Directory** - /MSCRMServices/2007/AD/CrmDiscoveryService.asmx

- **IFD** - /MSCRMServices/2007/IFD/CrmDiscoveryService.asmx

- **Online** - /MSCRMServices/2007/passport/CrmDiscoveryService.asmx

At the time of the release of CRM 4.0 these three end points WSDL are identical. It is possible that each evolve differently over time as the product matures. Therefore, if you are writing code that uses all three scenarios you might want to consider using three separate Web references. This is handled for you if you use the ctccrm.AuthHelper assembly.

The following is an excerpt from some of the code we use in our common class to work with Discovery Service. In this example we setup a new instance of the Discovery Service Web Service and setup the URLs to call it. Then we proceed to make a request and iterate through the response.

```
DiscoAD.CrmDiscoveryService disco =
          new DiscoAD.CrmDiscoveryService();

disco.Url = BuildDiscoURL(connInfo.Server,
          "/MSCRMServices/2007/AD/CrmDiscoveryService.asmx");
DiscoAD.RetrieveOrganizationsRequest orgRequest =
          new DiscoAD.RetrieveOrganizationsRequest();


DiscoAD.RetrieveOrganizationsResponse orgResponse =
          (DiscoAD.RetrieveOrganizationsResponse)
            disco.Execute(orgRequest);


DiscoAD.OrganizationDetail orgInfo = null;

foreach (DiscoAD.OrganizationDetail orgdetail in
                    orgResponse.OrganizationDetails)
{
    if (orgdetail.OrganizationName.Equals(connInfo.Organization,
        StringComparison.CurrentCultureIgnoreCase))
    {
      orgInfo = orgdetail;
      break;
    }
}
```

This type of call would be used to find a particular organization details or to build a list of possible organizations that a user has access to so they can select the correct organization.

Making the Ticket Request

One of the other services performed by the Discovery Service is to facilitate getting a ticket to use as part of the authentication token that needs to be set on the CRM Service prior to use.

The following is again an excerpt from our Discovery Service common class that demonstrates how to make a call to get the ticket.

```
//Retrieve a CrmTicket from the CrmDiscoveryService Web service.
DiscoIFD.RetrieveCrmTicketRequest ticketRequest =
                    new DiscoIFD.RetrieveCrmTicketRequest();

ticketRequest.OrganizationName = orgInfo.OrganizationName;
ticketRequest.UserId = connInfo.User;
ticketRequest.Password = connInfo.Password;

DiscoIFD.RetrieveCrmTicketResponse ticketResponse =
            (DiscoIFD.RetrieveCrmTicketResponse)
                disco.Execute(ticketRequest);
```

While not required to make a call to get a ticket for an Integrated / Active Directory scenario, you can make the call. That's one way to make your code more consistent across the different authentication types.

Building the Authentication Token

Once you have discovered the organization details, and have done the ticket request you can now setup the CrmAuthenticationToken that needs to be used with the Web service calls. This object is basically a SoapHeader in disguise and allows the token to be passed with each Web service request to the server.

The following is an example of the code that would be used to setup the CrmAuthenticationToken instance.

```
CrmAuthenticationToken authToken = new CrmAuthenticationToken();

authToken.CrmTicket = ticketResponse.CrmTicket;

authToken.AuthenticationType = 2;

authToken.OrganizationName = orgdetail.OrganizationName;
```

Notice, we are taking the ticket from the Ticket Response and the organization name and populating them on the token.

The values for AuthenticationType are as follows.

Type	Description
0	Integrated / Active Directory
1	IFD (Internet Facing Deployment)
2	Windows Live ID

Final Service Setup

At this point we have discovered our organization. We have gone though the ticket request process. We have built our authentication token that will be used by our service. The next step is to configure our Web service instance to use this information. In the following final step before we can do real work, we need to populate these values on our service instance.

For the CrmService

```
crmSvc.CrmAuthenticationTokenValue = authToken;
crmSvc.Url = orgdetail.CrmServiceUrl;
```

For the Metadata Service

```
metaSvc.CrmAuthenticationTokenValue = authToken;
metaSvc.Url = orgdetail.CrmServiceUrl;
```

Notice that in the above code examples we show the same process applies for both the metadata service as well as the CrmService.

Authentication From ASP.NET Pages

Before we get too far from how authentication works with the built-in capabilities, I want to touch on how things work if your writing an ASP.NET page that will run on the CRM server and access CRM data. To give a more concrete example, if you create a form that is designed to be included in an IFrame and will be passed an ID of the active account being viewed. That page, if it accesses CRM, will want to do so using the credentials or with the rights of the user accessing the parent form.

Now that CRM supports multiple authentication models for clients to access the site there are some special considerations that you must take when building the ASP.NET page to impersonate the user. For example, if the user is accessing the site using Active Directory, it would be pretty easy for you to just use the same and everything would work. However, if the user was accessing the site using IFD and you assumed the Active Directory pattern your page would fail because it would attempt to connect to CRM most likely using the user that the IIS application pool is running under.

To accommodate for this the CRM team has provided a new class called CrmImpersonator that you can use to allow your page to impersonate the user regardless of how they authenticated to the CRM site. This approach currently applies to on-premise and IFD authentication and does not apply to CRM Online because no custom code can be deployed to the CRM Online servers.

To use the CrmImpersonator it must wrap around any calls you make to the platform. You wrap it with the "using" statement as you can see in the following example.

```
using (new CrmImpersonator())
{

//Setup CRM service and make calls to the methods here.

}
```

The using statement should be used when you use an IDisposable object to ensure that the Dispose method on the object is called. It also causes the object to go out of scoop as soon as Dispose is called. Using also makes sure that Dispose is called even if an exception occurs while you are calling methods on the object.

I'm not going to include all the code here and in fact looking above it looks simple, in reality it's not and you need to write about 100+ lines of code each time because you need to check if you're running offline and other conditions. Check out the sample in the SDK (Authentication from an ASPX Page) so you see what I mean. Also, if you want to debug your applications running on the normal Visual Studio host if you use CrmImpersonator like the example in the SDK it will throw an exception. So what I am going to do is recommend that you look at the AuthHelper library that we provide with the book and how it handles this same concept without requiring as much code. We will discuss that in detail later in the chapter.

What We Didn't Tell You

We covered the basics in going through the authentication process using the out of the box capabilities. There are a number of items we didn't cover in detail that if you were going to write code that worked with all three environments you would need to consider and implement in your authentication logic. The following are some of those ideas to think about.

- We really did not touch on how to get the user/ password from the user. In the AuthHelper library we provide a form that will collect as well as persist securely on the caller's computer.

- When working with Live ID, there's calls required to the Live ID authentication process that take a policy that is requested from the CRM Discovery service and the users credentials and give you back a Passport ticket that is required to be passed to the CRM Ticket Request.

- We really didn't discuss how you know what environment you are talking to- is it IFD, is it on premise, or Online? Stay tuned for how our AuthHelper provides a process for determination.

- This only applies to code using the 2007 end point. If you need code that works with the 2006 end point you would need to also handle that separately from the steps above. In that case only Integrated/ Active Directory would matter and you are limited to the default organization.

- Code that is designed to run on the CRM Server or the CRM Client has a slightly different authorization pattern since we are running inside the CRM Address space. More on that as we get further in the chapter.

- Outlook Online / Offline detection logic was not included in the above. If you want your code to work with the CRM Outlook client when it is offline then you have more special processing to be done and would use the Microsoft.crm.outlook.sdk.dll to make calls to determine the state of the client, and using that vary the URL and authentication technique accordingly. For example, when the user is online it could be IFD to the server, but offline would always be Integrated / Active Directory. The AuthHelper assembly hides a lot of that complexity so you don't have to detect and handle each condition.

There are probably other things we didn't cover in detail. But the best way to understand them is to dig into the code for the AuthHelper assembly we are about to discuss.

The AuthHelper Assembly

As you probably gathered by now there is a little bit of complexity involved if you are writing code that works with all three authentication types and the various related scenarios. As we got closer to release of CRM 4.0 we started looking for patterns in how we were doing authentication code. The biggest realization was we kept copying little snippets of code from project to project. So we really needed to get a first class authentication assembly that wrapped the built-in capabilities and simplified them.

The AuthHelper assembly and code that is provided as part of the samples for this book are designed with one main goal in mind – make it simpler to authenticate to the platform. The service instance returned from the GetService() call on the AuthHelper library will be ready to use, no complicated environment logic required. As we set out to build the helper assembly the following are some of our guiding concepts for design.

- Must abstract the process of authenticating as much as possible making the calls required by an application just a few lines of code.

- Allow for heavy reuse of the assembly across all types of CRM client applications ranging from a windows client to code running on the server.

- Allow to work with the built in Proxy classes (CrmService) from the SDK assembly as well as CrmService when it is added as a Web reference. The helper library is accomplished using generic types – stay tuned for more details.

- Identify and implement a few of the common usage scenarios and facilitate helping with the collection or storage of user credentials / configuration options in those environments.

- Hide as much of the Outlook on-line/off-line, URL determination and differences in authentication types as possible. From a caller perspective, all I really want to configure is if I will allow offline connection if the client is currently offline.

- Hide as much of the differences running in the CRM Web site, on the client, or in a standalone Web application. This includes making sure you can still debug your ASP.NET application locally that you intend to be deployed on the CRM site and will require CRM Impersonator. In that scenario CrmImpersonator will error if called from the debug Web server on your local machine otherwise.

There were probably a few others, but it really came down to the simple idea that if you want to authenticate with CRM , you should reference the Auth Helper assembly, write one or two lines of code and possibly show a dialog to collect user information and you are ready to go.

Getting Started with AuthHelper

Using the ctccrm.AuthHelper assembly provided with this book is simple. Before you use it you just reference the ctccrm.AuthHelper.dll to your project. You can use this helper to simplify authentication for applications running on the client and the server.

At the start of your class file that will be using AuthHelper you need to reference the name space for auth helper as you see below.

```
using ctccrm.AuthHelper;
```

The AuthHelper library can work with either the CrmService that is part of the type proxy assembly provided with the SDK or by using a Web Reference to your target CRM servers WSDL. The following two lines show an example of the simplest form of setting up authentication to the server. These two lines show how to use the helper library to get an instance of CrmService as we discussed earlier in this chapter.

```
CrmServiceAuthManager<CrmService, CrmAuthenticationToken> svcMgr =
   new CrmServiceAuthManager<CrmService,CrmAuthenticationToken>();

CrmService service = svcMgr.GetService();
```

Looks much simpler doesn't it? I'm sure now you are saying "that looks too simple." That's the goal. There are other options and ways to use the helper library that we will be discussing as we continue in the chapter.

The CrmServiceAuthManager class is a generic type that wraps up all the logic to deal with interfacing with all the authentication scenarios. It also is capable of detecting that the user is offline and, if allowed, switching the application connection to use the offline API automatically without any intervention required by the calling application.

If you aren't familiar with generic types they allow you to configure at compile time certain types that the class will work with. We use this in our design to accommodate for the fact that we cannot anticipate the name space of the CrmService class when used via the Web reference technique. So when you see <CrmService, CrmAuthenticationToken> after the class name that indicates it's a generic type and those are the types that are being used to configure it. Specifcally this allows us to do things like return a CrmService class that is typed. Without this approach you would typicaly end up replicating a lot of your authentication logic in each application that had a different name space and did a reference to the Web service. The helper classes that you can use from the SDK demonstrate that problem, requiring you to include those in each project rather than referencing a common library.

Specifying Connection Options

You can influence how the CrmServiceAuthManager works by passing a CrmConnectionInfo object to the constructor. This class allows you to provide either hints or specific information on how the CrmServiceAuthManager class should behave.

The following is an example of setting up a CrmConnectionInfo and passing it to the constructor.

```
CrmConnectionInfo connInfo = new CrmConnectionInfo();
connInfo.AllowOfflineUse = true;
connInfo.Server = "http://myserver.com";
connInfo.DeploymentType = CrmDeploymentType.IFD;
CrmServiceAuthManager<CrmService, CrmAuthenticationToken> svcMgr =
    new CrmServiceAuthManager<CrmService,
                              CrmAuthenticationToken>(connInfo);
```

Using the options above we are telling the AuthHelper library that we want to connect using a specific server, and that offline access is ok and we specifically want authentication to occur using the IFD facilitates.

The following are the properties that can be set on the CrmConnectionInfo object.

Property	Description
Server	This provides the host name that will be used for discovery. If not provided the AuthHelper will look into the config file for ctccrm_AuthHelper_Server.
User / Password	This is the user / password information. This is used during authentication. If not provided the library will either pull from config ctccrm_AuthHelper_User / Password or will attempt with Active Directory credentials of the logged in user.
DeploymentType	This indicates the type of deployment. Valid values are ActiveDirectory, IFD, Live , Offline, and Unknown. If Unknown is specified the AuthHelper library will attempt to determine the authorization in use by attempting to connect in the following order – Active Directory, IFD , then Live. Unknown allows the caller to completely leave auth schema determination up to the AuthHelper library.
Organization	Organization name to work with. This is required if there could be multiple for a user unless it is specified in the Configuration file under ctccrm_AuthHelper_Organization. The other option is by specification of the OrgMatchPref property.
OrgMatchPref	This controls how the organization matching will occur, the valid values are MatchExact or MatchFirst.
AllowOfflineUse	This allows you to indicate that you want the API to switch to offfline mode if it detects that has been requested by the user.

Metadata AuthHelper

In addition to working with the CrmService the AuthHelper library can also perform authentication and setup a Metadata Service. Like the CrmService you can either do a Web reference to the MetadataService or use the MetadataService class that is part of the SDK Type Proxy assembly. Unlike the CrmService where you gain the advantage of getting typed entities by doing the Web reference – the MetadataService is the same in either technique. Therefore, we typically recommend using the MetadataService class from the assembly and skip the extra work of adding a Web reference. For the MetadataService the Web reference technique is best left for when doing calls to it from other languages and can't reference the assembly.

The following is a code sample getting a metadata service using the AuthHelper library.

```
MetadataAuthManager<MetadataService, CrmAuthenticationToken> metaMgr =
    new MetadataAuthManager<MetadataService, CrmAuthenticationToken>();

MetadataService svc = metaMgr.GetService();
```

Using Auth Helper Context

Earlier in the chapter we explained how the CrmImpersonator class was provided to handle authentication issues when running on the CRM server. The problem we have with that is it creates a challenge if you're writing code that will work in a number of scenarios such as on-line, offline, and even run within the Visual Studio Debugger. When the CrmImpersonator class was added to the SDK near the end of the CRM 4.0 Beta we looked at how best to integrate that concept into the AuthHelper library and still keep it as simple as possible. To accomplish that goal we created a concept called a Context. The context classes as we will see shortly, wrap around the CrmImpersonator class and only use it when needed. This allows you to write code once and work in all the different runtime environments.

The following is an example of changing our code to use the CrmServiceContext class which implements all the necessary support to work with the CrmImpersonator concept in less code.

```
CrmServiceAuthManager<CrmService, CrmAuthenticationToken> svcMgr =
        new CrmServiceAuthManager<CrmService,
                    CrmAuthenticationToken>(connInfo);

using (CrmServiceContext<CrmService> context =
                    svcMgr.GetServiceContext())
{
    context.Service.Retrieve("contact", m_Guid,
                new  Microsoft.Crm.Sdk.Query.AllColumns());
}
```

Clearly, this is much simpler than the 100+ lines of code from the SDK and it results in your pages being much cleaner. All the hard work is encapsulated into the library so you can reuse it.

As you can see, you still get an instance of CrmServiceAuthManager but then use the GetServiceContext method instead of the GetService method to get your service instance. The GetServiceContext method does all the hard work of detecting if you are offline or online and running on the CRM Server. If you are running on the CRM Server no special configuration is required.

To run from your local machine or on a standalone IIS Web site not hosted in the CRM server process you can enable that support by simply specifying "ctccrm_AuthHelper_UseCrmImpersonator" with a value of false in the configuration option in the Web.config application settings section. You can also force it to false using the CrmImpersonator property on the connection object.

The most important thing to understand about using this approach is you must use the "using" statement to have the correct affect. The key thing that it does is force disposal of the Context and therefore the CrmImpersonator object once you leave that block.

If you were to think about what the CrmImpersonator class has to do to work, it must change the active thread to run as another user. When disposal happens it will return the thread back to the original user. That's why disposal and making sure you use the "using" pattern is critical.

Working with the CRM Attribute Types

When working with data stored in the CRM platform or interacting with the platform Web Service you will be using a set of CRM specific attribute type classes. These classes mirror the data types you selected when you added the attribute to the entity. The reason these exist is to help address issues like how to specify null with the framework data types.

Attribute Type	Description
CrmBoolean	Used to represent the boolean data type.
CrmDateTime	Used to represent Date / Time. This does not directly mirror the .NET data type because it provides support for representing as either a UTC (Coordinated Universal Time) or local time. See the SDK for full details on how CrmDateTime works.
CrmDecimal	Used to represent the decimal data type.

Attribute Type	Description
CrmFloat	Used to represent the double data type.
CrmMoney	Used to represent a money value and uses the .NET decimal type for the data value.
CrmNumber	Used to represent the int data type.
CrmReference	Used to represent an attribute that is a reference to another entity. This allows specification of the entity type and the ID. This is an abstract class and you usually deal with Lookup, Owner and Customer instead.
Customer	Customer inherits from CrmReference but is specifically designed to trace a reference to a contact or a company record.
EntityNameReference	Holds the name of an entity as a string value.
Key	Key contains a Guid value to represent a key on an entity.
Lookup	Used to hold a name and id for another entity. This data type inherits from CrmReference and is like Customer but generic and can be used to reference any CRM entity item.
Owner	Used to indicate the owner of an entity record. Also inherits from CrmReference like Lookup and Customer.
Picklist	Represents the selected picklist value. Contains a name property that is the label for the picklist item and a Value property that is the numeric value for the picklist item.
Status	Used to represent the status of an item. Similar to Picklist and has a name and Value property.
PartyList	Used to store recipient lists. A PartyList is an array of activityparty objects. When working with dynamic entities, you use the DynamicEntityArrayProperty.

Attribute Type	Description
State	Represents the current state of an item, which usually is "Active" or "Inactive". To change an item's state you have to use appropriate SetState method calls. You cannot change the state with an update call.
UniqueIdentifier	Holds a GUID. It's much like a lookup, but does not store the name and type of the referenced item.
String	Stores a string value. This is the only property type using a .NET Framework type (System.String).

Handling Exceptions

When using the Web Service API you must be prepared to properly handle errors that are thrown. One of the most common problems developers have is they simply handle the generic Exception object as you can see in the following example.

```
{
    //call Web service here
}
catch(Exception ex)
{
    LogMessage(ex.Message);
}
```

Upon receiving an error you will typically get the text "An error has occurred please contact your system administrator". This message often results in the developer stomping their foot and saying "but I AM the system administrator". The problem is simple, the call is a Web Service call and what you are getting back is a SoapException object. The SoapException has additional properties you need to interrogate to get more detailed information on what has happened.

One option is to cast the generic Exception object to a SoapException. The following shows an example.

```
SoapException soapEx = ex as SoapException;
```

There are two problems with this approach, first you end up catching more exceptions than you probably need to. As a general approach if you don't need to catch the exception and are not going to add value to the error being thrown then let it bubble up to the caller. The other problem we need to deal with is still checking that soapEx is not null because if the object turned out to not be a SoapException our soapEx variable would be set to null.

The other option which is typically a better approach is to simply catch the SoapException directly as you can see below.

```
try
{
    //call Web service here
}
catch(SoapException ex)
{
    LogMessage(ex.OuterXml);
}
```

Often times the OuterXml will give you enough details to fix the problem that was encountered. If that doesn't do the trick then you might have to resort to turning on a platform trace. We cover more details on how to turn on platform trace in Chapter 25. Platform trace happens on the CRM server and dumps out details as the platform processes your request.

Understanding Dynamic Entities

The DynamicEntity class exists to provide a more generic representation of the platform Entity. This is accomplished by having a collection of properties instead of having them be typed properties on the class. In the following example we contrast the two different techniques for accessing the accountid attribute.

Using the typed object:

```
accountInstance.accountid.Value
```

Using a Dynamic Entity:

```
dynEntity ["accountid"].Value.Value
```

The reason for the Value.Value is because dynEntity ["accountid"].value returns a Property object whose Value property points to the CRM Attribute type which in our case is Key. Key stores the GUID in its Value property. The reason for this extra level of indirection is because in addition to storing the value of the Attribute the Dynamic Entity needs to store information like the name of the attribute that is not necessary when it's just a typed property on the Account class. For each Attribute type there is a corresponding Property class. For example for Key there is a KeyProperty class.

Dynamic Entities provide a lot of flexibility to work with platform data without knowing ahead of time what attributes are on an object. In Chapter 20, we will discuss how to use the platform metadata to generate typed objects that wrap around the Dynamic Entities to provide typed classes. Typed classes provide an improved developer experience because they are typed and also can take advantage of IntelliSense in Visual Studio..

Dynamic Entities should be used heavily by ISVs that are writing a solution that will be configured at runtime. For example, an ISV writing a custom search tool that needs to work with entities that are created after the tool is deployed. They are also what is presented by plug-ins and workflows so if you are implementing either of those in your solution you will be doing some amount of work with Dynamic Entities.

Using Trace to Solve Problems Quicker

One thing you can do that will save you a lot of time when working with Dynamic Entities is to have a trace routine that is able to output the contents and values of the Dynamic Entity instance. By calling this prior to platform operations or when an error occurs from the operation you can review the properties to look for obvious errors. Probably the most common error when working with Dynamic Entities is a typo in the name of an attribute. See Chapter 25 where we discuss this in more detail.

Property Indexer Helper

New to CRM 4.0 is indexer access to the properties on the Dynamic Entity. If you're using the classes by using the Microsoft.Crm.Sdk.dll this is automatic and no effort is required by you. If you are using the Web Services then you need to use a helper class provided with the SDK in order to get the same support. The reason for that is because the WSDL generated does not expose indexers as it's not supported by the standard. To accommodate for that and still give users of the Web Service the same experience Microsoft provides a helper class with the SDK that you can include. This helper class is defined as a partial class of type Dynamic Entity. By placing that in the same assembly where you reference the CRM Web Service you are able to have the same indexed property support. The helper class can be found in the SDK under the folder Server\Helpers\CS\CrmHelpers\DynamicEntityPartialType.cs

In Chapter 3 we discussed the idea of setting up a common project to be the holder of the Web reference to the CrmService. Using this concept, you would also install these helper classes into that project so you only had to do that once.

Property Helper

The indexer support is great but still working with the Dynamic Entity properties can be a little tedious due to the extra steps you need to do. Included in the samples of the book is another helper class that adds helper methods for working with properties on Dynamic Entities. The idea behind this helper class is that using one method you should be able to add or get a value from a Dynamic Entity property with a single line of code. All at the same time not giving up type safety on the types of data we pass. This helper is implemented in CTCDEPropHelper.cs. The class implements a number of static methods that you can call. The following are some of the examples of the methods provided.

Add Property Methods

```
CTCDEPropHelper. AddKeyProperty(entity, "accountid", guidValue)

CTCDePropHelper. AddLookupProperty(entity, "primarycontactid",
 "contact", guidValue)
```

That's just a couple examples of the methods. There are one method for each of the property types.

Get Property Methods

```
CTCDEPropHelper. GetBooleanValue(entity, "crmbook_bitattr", false)
CTCDEPropHelper. GetStringValue(entity, "name","default value")
```

The value add here is the ablity to provide a default value for the property if the property does not exist in the entity property collection.

The Basics Dynamic Entity Style

Create

The following is an example of creating a Dynamic Entity.

```
DynamicEntity de = new DynamicEntity("contact");

StringProperty propFirstName = new StringProperty("firstname", "Dave");
de.Properties.Add(propFirstName);

StringProperty propLastName = new StringProperty("lastname", "Yack");
de.Properties.Add(propLastName);

m_ID = svc.Create(de);

MessageBox.Show("ID = " + m_ID.ToString());
```

Retrieve

The following is an example of retrieving a Dynamic Entity.

```
RetrieveRequest req = new RetrieveRequest();
req.ColumnSet = new AllColumns();
req.ReturnDynamicEntities=true;
TargetRetrieveDynamic target = new TargetRetrieveDynamic();
target.EntityName = "contact";
target.EntityId = m_ID;
req.Target = target;

RetrieveResponse resp =  svc.Execute(req) as RetrieveResponse;

DynamicEntity de = resp.BusinessEntity as DynamicEntity;

Key id = de.Properties["contactid"] as Key;
string firstName = de.Properties["firstname"].ToString();
string lastName = de.Properties["lastname"].ToString();

MessageBox.Show("Contact ID is " + id.Value.ToString()
              + " Name is " + firstName + " " + lastName);
```

One thing to note is you must use the RetrieveRequest via the Execute method instead of just calling Retrieve which does not support returning dynamic entities.

It's important to understand that any property without a value ((null value in the database) is not included in the returned property array on a Dynamic Entity.

Update

```
DynamicEntity de = new DynamicEntity("contact");

Key key = new Key(m_ID);
KeyProperty keyProp = new KeyProperty("contactid", key);
de.Properties.Add(keyProp);

StringProperty propFirstName = new StringProperty("firstname", "John");
de.Properties.Add(propFirstName);

StringProperty propLastName = new StringProperty("lastname", "Smith");
de.Properties.Add(propLastName);

svc.Update(de);
```

Delete

You will notice from the following code that there is no difference in deleting when working with Dynamic Entities.

```
svc.Delete("contact", m_ID);
```

Wrapping up Dynamic Entities

As you can see from the examples Dynamic Entities provide a lot of flexibility to write generic code. While they don't offer the same help as having named properties for each attribute on an entity, they do still enforce type safety. As we continue through the book we will talk about how Dynamic Entities are the preferred entity when working with Plug-in's and Workflows.

Execute Method

The Execute method is the real workhorse call of the API. This method is designed to use a Request/Response call signature. The platform provides more than 200 messages that work with the Execute to perform various platform operations. These operations range from creating a record to executing a workflow.

The CRUD methods we have looked at so far are really just helper calls that make it easier to do those specific operations. Each of those front end calls to the Execute method. In fact each of the calls we performed above could be done using the Execute method but would take a few more lines of code. For example, here's an example of using the Execute method to do a create.

```
contact myContact = new contact();
myContact.firstname = "Dave";
myContact.lastname = "Yack";

CreateRequest request = new CreateRequest();
TargetCreateContact target = new TargetCreateContact();
target.Contact = myContact;
request.Target = target;
CreateResponse resp = svc.Execute(request) as CreateResponse;
```

The Execute method will be used in several of our examples in the next chapter when we start looking at more of the common tasks.

Retrieve Multiple & Query Expressions

Earlier in the chapter we looked at how to retrieve a single record from the platform. When you start wanting to retrieve multiple records or using more criteria than the entity ID you will use the RetrieveMultiple capabilities. The following is a simple example of retrieving multiple records, in this example it will do it using a field name and key value being passed. An example would be to retrieve all the contacts with a specific parent company.

The method call would look like this.

```
RetrieveMultipleBySingleKey("contact","parentaccountid",new Guid("...guid
here"));
```

The method to perform the work looks like the following.

```
protected List<DynamicEntity> RetrieveMultipleBySingleKey(
     string entityName, string keyAttributeName, Guid keyValue)
{
    List<DynamicEntity> list = new  List<DynamicEntity>();

    RetrieveMultipleRequest req = new RetrieveMultipleRequest();
    req.ReturnDynamicEntities = true;

    QueryExpression qe = new QueryExpression();
    qe.ColumnSet = new AllColumns();
    qe.Distinct = false;
    qe.EntityName = entityName;
    FilterExpression exp = new FilterExpression();
    exp.FilterOperator = LogicalOperator.And;
    ConditionExpression cond = new ConditionExpression();
    cond.AttributeName = keyAttributeName;
    object[] valueList = {keyValue};
    cond.Values = valueList;
    cond.Operator = ConditionOperator.Equal;
    exp.Conditions.Add(cond);
    qe.Criteria = exp;

    req.Query = qe;


    RetrieveMultipleResponse resp =
        this.UserService.Execute(req) as RetrieveMultipleResponse;

    BusinessEntityCollection beColl = resp.BusinessEntityCollection;

    foreach (BusinessEntity be in beColl.BusinessEntities)
    {
        list.Add((DynamicEntity)be);
    }

    return list;
}
```

NOTE

req.ReturnDynamicEntities = true; tells the method that we want the data returned as Dynamic Entities. If you wanted the data returned using a typed object instance you would leave that set to the default which is false.

As you probably can tell from the above example, the real interesting part of that code is the QueryExpression class that is used. Using the QueryExpression you can setup simple or complex criteria for what will be retrieved by the method call. Using FilterExpressions and ConditionExpressions you can control the behavior of the QueryExpression and how it works with your criteria.

The ConditionExpression Operator property allows you to indicate traditional operators like Equal, NotEqual, In and many others. In fact the SDK lists about 50 or so that are valid. Many of these are very useful for example OnorBefore or NextMonth. The SDK contains a complete list of the enumeration values – just search on ConditionOperator to find the details. Keep in mind not all work with all data types, some like NextMonth are intended to work specifically with date related fields. Using the wrong operator for the wrong data type will produce an error when you execute the call.

TIP

Build your query incrementally if it is a complex query to avoid trying to figure out what you might have done wrong if an error occurs. By incrementally building, you will be more likely to know what changed and be able to pinpoint the problem quicker.

Ordering Results

You can order the results that are returned by providing one or more OrderExpression instances and setting the Orders property on the QueryExpression. The OrderExpression basically indentifies the attribute name and an order type of ascending or descending. The following is an example of adding a OrderExpression to our query to sort on the date created of the record.

```
OrderExpression orderExp1 = new OrderExpression();
orderExp1.AttributeName = "createdon";
orderExp1.OrderType = OrderType.Ascending;
qe.Orders = {orderExp1};
```

Joining Entities

So far we looked at a simple example of building a QueryExpression to query from a single entity. One of the properties we haven't talked about so far on the QueryExpression object is the LinkEntities property. The LinkEntities property allows you to do joins of the primary entity to other related entities to further qualify your criteria using fields from a related entity.

For example, let's say I want to get a list of role names that a user belongs to. I can't just query the Role entity because that's not able to tell me which role that user belongs to. I can't query only the systemuserroles entity because it doesn't know the name of the actual role just that the user is associated with it.

So what I can do is build a query against the role entity and then use LinkEntities to filter on only the roles that a specific user has.

First, let's retrieve the ID of the current user and setup a standard QueryExpression.

```
//get current user
Lookup user = this.WhoAmI();

//build request for the role names
RetrieveMultipleRequest req = new RetrieveMultipleRequest();
req.ReturnDynamicEntities = true;

QueryExpression qe = new QueryExpression();
string[] colList = { "name" };
qe.ColumnSet = new ColumnSet(colList);
qe.Distinct = false;
qe.EntityName = "role";
```

Our next step is to add a LinkEntity to the collection that will create the join or the link from Role to systemuserroles based on the roleid.

```
LinkEntity link1 = new LinkEntity();
link1.LinkFromEntityName = "role";
link1.LinkFromAttributeName = "roleid";
link1.LinkToEntityName = "systemuserroles";
link1.LinkToAttributeName = "roleid";

qe.LinkEntities.Add(link1);
```

As you can see you are basically creating the link by specifying a from and to entity and attribute pair. Once the link has been created, then you can create conditions that work against the systemuserid that comes from the systemuserroles. So for our example we want to limit the roles returned to those that are for the specific user.

```
ConditionExpression cond = new ConditionExpression();
cond.AttributeName = "systemuserid";
object[] valueList = { user.Value };
cond.Values = valueList;
cond.Operator = ConditionOperator.Equal;
exp.Conditions.Add(cond);

link1.LinkCriteria = exp;
req.Query = qe;
```

One thing to keep in mind is the LinkEntities do not affect the columns of data returned. So just because we joined to the systemuserroles entity doesn't mean we can request to return back columns from that entity as part of our result set.

Fetch

The Fetch method works very similarly to the RetrieveMultiple and QueryExpression. The difference is the QueryExpression is specified as FetchXML which is an XML version of the Query Expression. The other difference is the results from Fetch are returned as a string containing XML instead of Dynamic Entities or typed class objects returned by the Retrieve Multiple.

```
string result = svc.Fetch("<fetch mapping='logical'>"
        + "<entity name='contact'><all-attributes/>"
        + "<filter type='and'><condition attribute='lastname' "
        + " operator='eq' value='Yack'/></filter>"
        + "</entity></fetch>");

MessageBox.Show(result);
```

As you can see in the following image, the output is returned as XML in the form of a ResultSet element that contains one or more <result> elements for each row returned by the query.

```
<resultset morerecords="0" paging-cookie="&lt;cookie page=&quot;1&quot;&gt;&lt;contactid last=&quot;{
/&gt;&lt;/cookie&gt;"><result><customersizecode name="Default Value" formattedvalue="1">1</custome
Yack</yomifullname><ownerid yomi="System Administrator" dsc="0" name="System Administrator" type=
date="12/25/2007" time="12:57 PM">2007-12-25T12:57:38-07:00</modifiedon><fullname>Dave Yack</fulln
formattedvalue="1">1</preferredcontactmethodcode><educationcode name="Default Value" formattedvalu
```

If you have FetchXml and would like to convert it to a QueryExpression you can use the FetchXmlToQueryExpression message to perform the transformation. Then you could use the query with a RetrieveMultiple request to get back Dynamic Entities or typed objects to work with instead of the XML returned by the Fetch call.

MVP Tip: Microsoft CRM MVP David Jennaway adds that FetchXml does support returning attributes from a linked entity, unlike QueryExpression. As a consequence, a FetchXml query that should return attributes from a linked entity cannot be converted to a QueryExpression – the message throws an exception if you try. You can read David's blog at http://mscrmuk.blogspot.com.

Enforcing Validation

One of the new features of the CRM 4.0 when using the 2007 Web service end point is enforcement of validation rules on entity attributes such as max/min length of strings, ranges of numbers, etc.

You might be curious what the error message looks like when this occurs. So I created a custom entity that had two properties, a string and a number (int). On both of these, I set really low limits so it would be easy to force the validation to kick in. I then proceeded to create a dynamic entity that I passed to the CrmService.Create method.

My first test with an invalid string produced a SoapException with the following details:

0x80044331 A validation error occurred. The length of the 'crmbook_stringtest' attribute of the 'crmbook_validationtest' entity exceeded the maximum allowed length of '10'.
Platform

You will notice it even included the length that was allowed. Next, I set out to try with a number. That error is almost as clear but doesn't tell you what the range is.

0x8004432f A validation error occurred. The value of 'crmbook_inttest' on record of type 'crmbook_validationtest' is outside the valid range.
Platform

Keep in mind that this validation only occurs when you use the CRM 4.0 - 2007 end point. If you use the 2006 end point that is designed for backward compatibility with CRM 3.0 applications validation is not enforced.

Wrapping it up

In this chapter, we have touched on the basics of working with the platform Web service to manipulate data. This is fundamental to a number of the future things we will be discussing in the rest of the chapters of the book.

In addition to covering the basics, we also touched on some ways to make working with the services easier. This included a detailed discussion of the AuthHelper that is included in the sample code for use. Even if you don't use it directly it provides a great deal of thought into the concept of a simple to use authentication helper assembly. Our hope is that something like that gets wrapped into the next update to the CRM platform. For now though, use what we provided or use it as an example to create your own.

At this point you should have a clear understanding the basics of using the CrmService, and now we are ready to embark on a more detailed look at ways to use them as well as how it can be used in plug-ins and workflows and other more complex examples.

10

Web Services Common How-To's

This chapter will build on Chapter 9 where we covered all the basics of using the platform web services to access and manipulate data. In this chapter we are going to focus on more specific how tos and explore more complex code samples. We tried to focus on some of the common operations you might do when building a solution on top of the CRM platform.

Instead of just giving you code samples; we have also incorporated many of the examples in this chapter into a class called CrmServiceManager that is a helper class to make it easier for you to invoke the web service calls. By using this approach, we are able to give you a reusable helper class that packages up some of the plumbing necessary to use the web services.

You can either use the CrmServiceManager directly or inherit from it your own CrmServiceManager type class that implements additional common methods. Another approach would be to use it as reference or just pull from it the methods that you find helpful to use in your own class.

There are several benefits to having a centralized class that exposes these types of methods rather than having the code replicated across a number of calling applications. This approach makes bug fixing and enhancements easy, just one place to change the code and it's easy to find all the places your using that method. If you ever need to add more debugging logic again it's located in one place, no need to add it to 10 different places.

Working with CrmServiceManager

This helper class you will find in the ctccrm.PluginCommon class library in the Framework folder. The complete location within the samples is

  $/Framework/PluginCommon/CrmSvc/CrmServiceManager.cs

You can also find an interactive tester that works with the methods in CRMServiceManagerTester. The complete location within the samples is

  $/Framework/CRMServiceManagerTester

WhoAmI

Our first method will get us started simple by returning us the Guid of the current logged on user. You might make this call when you need to find out the ID to set the owner or other lookup field with that value in a CRM record.

The following is an example of setting up to call the method on CrmServiceManager.

```
private void CallWhoami()
{
    using (CrmServiceContext<CTCCRMService> svcContext =
                                    this.GetServiceContext())
    {
        CrmServiceManager mgr =
                new CrmServiceManager((CTCCRMService)svcContext.Service);

        Guid userid = mgr.WhoAmI();
    }
}
```


The following is the implementation of WhoAmI which basically sets up the call and returns the ID.

```
public Guid WhoAmI()
{
    //Create WhoAmIRequest
    WhoAmIRequest userReq = new WhoAmIRequest();

    WhoAmIResponse user = this.m_Service.Execute(userReq)
                                        as WhoAmIResponse;

    return user.UserId;
}
```

Getting a User's Roles

This method retrieves all the roles for the current user.

```
private void CallGetUserRoles()
{
    using (CrmServiceContext<CTCCRMService> svcContext =
                                this.GetServiceContext())
    {
        CrmServiceManager mgr =
                new CrmServiceManager((CTCCRMService)svcContext.Service);

        List<string> roles = mgr.GetUserRoles();
    }
}
```

This method calls the WhoAmI function to find out the user ID and then builds a query to retrieve all the roles for that user. You will notice in the function it's using the Link Entities to do the join query between Roles and SystemUserRoles.

```
public List<string> GetUserRoles()
{
    Lookup user = this.WhoAmI();
    RetrieveMultipleRequest req = new RetrieveMultipleRequest();
    req.ReturnDynamicEntities = true;

    QueryExpression qe = new QueryExpression();
    string[] colList = { "name" };
    qe.ColumnSet = new ColumnSet(colList);
    qe.Distinct = false;
    qe.EntityName = "role";
```

```
//build first link to join the role entity to the systemuserroles
LinkEntity link1 = new LinkEntity();
link1.LinkFromEntityName = "role";
link1.LinkFromAttributeName = "roleid";
link1.LinkToEntityName = "systemuserroles";
link1.LinkToAttributeName = "roleid";

qe.LinkEntities.Add(link1);

FilterExpression exp = new FilterExpression();
exp.FilterOperator = LogicalOperator.And;

//build condition to limit this to the current user
ConditionExpression cond = new ConditionExpression();
cond.AttributeName = "systemuserid";
object[] valueList = { user.Value };
cond.Values = valueList;
cond.Operator = ConditionOperator.Equal;
exp.Conditions.Add(cond);

link1.LinkCriteria = exp;
req.Query = qe;

RetrieveMultipleResponse resp =
        this.m_Service.Execute(req) as RetrieveMultipleResponse;

List<string> roles = new List<string>();

if (resp.BusinessEntityCollection.BusinessEntities != null)
{
    foreach (BusinessEntity be in
        resp.BusinessEntityCollection.BusinessEntities)
    {
        if (CTCDEPropHelper.PropertyExists((
                        DynamicEntity)be, "name"))
            roles.Add(CTCDEPropHelper.GetStringValue((
                        DynamicEntity)be, "name"));
    }
}

return roles;
}
```

Working with File Attachment

Entities that have Notes enabled are able to also have files attached to the notes. You can also attach files to e-mails that you create. CrmServiceManager exposes a couple of methods to make it easier to work with file attachments. The first is AddAttachment that takes care of storing a file and GetAttachments that helps you retrieve attachments.

When attaching a file to an e-mail you create an activitymimeattachment entity record that will store the attachment data. That's a little different than when working with other entities, for them you will create an annotation entity record. Otherwise, working with file attachments is the same for all entities. We shield you from those differences and handle that in the CrmServiceManager methods.

Add Attachment

The following is an example of calling the AddAttachment method. The method takes the file as a file stream along with a title and related entity information. The Guid that is passed is the ID of the related record that we want the attachment related to.

```
private void CallCreateAttachment()
{
    using (CrmServiceContext<CTCCRMService> svcContext =
        this.GetServiceContext())
    {
        FileInfo oFInfo = new FileInfo(txtAttachFile.Text);
        FileStream str = oFInfo.OpenRead();
        byte[] fileData = new byte[str.Length];
        str.Read(fileData, 0, Convert.ToInt32(str.Length));

        CrmServiceManager mgr = new CrmServiceManager(
                        (CTCCRMService)svcContext.Service);
        Guid attachID = mgr.AddAttachment(
            new Guid("C1961A14-D4E6-470C-8D1E-23AE6B1BBB8D"), "email",
            fileData, "filename.docx", "title");
    }
}
```

CRM has good basic support for attaching files to data records. It does not however have sophisticated features for managing files like SharePoint does. If you need more robust features like versioning and check in /out of files you might want to use SharePoint for file management.

The following is the AddAttachment method from CrmServiceManager. This method does the work of creating a dynamic entity to store the file attachment. It decides if it's creating an annotation or an activitymimeattachment based on the entitytype parameter passed. The data from the file stream is base 64 encoded before it is stored as in the body or document body of the data record.

```
public Guid AddAttachment(Guid entityID, string entityType,
            byte[] attachmentData, string fileName, string title)
{
    DynamicEntity de = null;
    string encodedData = System.Convert.ToBase64String(attachmentData);
    if (entityType == "email")
    {
        de = new DynamicEntity("activitymimeattachment");
        CTCDEPropHelper.AddLookupProperty(de, "activityid", entityType,
                                          entityID);
        CTCDEPropHelper.AddStringProperty(de, "body", encodedData);
    }
    else
    {
        de = new DynamicEntity("annotation");
        CTCDEPropHelper.AddLookupProperty(de, "objectid", entityType,
                                          entityID);
        CTCDEPropHelper.AddEntityNameProperty(de, "objecttypecode",
                                          entityType);
        CTCDEPropHelper.AddStringProperty(de, "documentbody",
                                          encodedData);
    }
    CTCDEPropHelper.AddStringProperty(de, "filename", fileName);
    if (fileName.Contains("."))
    {
        string extension = fileName.Substring(
                           fileName.LastIndexOf(".") + 1);
        CTCDEPropHelper.AddStringProperty(de, "mimetype", extension);
    }
    if (title != "")
        CTCDEPropHelper.AddStringProperty(de, "subject", title);
```

```
        Guid attachID = this.m_Service.Create((BusinessEntity)de);
        return attachID;
}
```

Get Attachment

To retrieve the attachments we provided a GetAttachments method that returns a collection of CTCCrmAttachmentInfo objects. The info object simply provides you the details about the attachment and the data. The following is an example of calling the GetAttachments method.

```
private void CallGetAttachment()
{
    using (CrmServiceContext<CTCCRMService> svcContext =
                                    this.GetServiceContext())
    {
        CrmServiceManager mgr = new CrmServiceManager(
                        (CTCCRMService)svcContext.Service);
        List<CTCCrmAttachmentInfo> attachments = mgr.GetAttachments(
            new Guid("C1961A14-D4E6-470C-8D1E-23AE6B1BBB8D"), "email");
    }
}
```

To call the GetAttachments you pass the Guid of the related record and the entity name to the method. The following is the code for the GetAttachments method. I have removed a few parts that we will discuss separately. As you can tell the flow is basically build the query, run the query, build the response collection.

```
public List<CTCCrmAttachmentInfo> GetAttachments(Guid entityID, string
entityType)
{
    List<CTCCrmAttachmentInfo> attachments =
                            new List<CTCCrmAttachmentInfo>();

    RetrieveMultipleRequest req = new RetrieveMultipleRequest();
    req.ReturnDynamicEntities = true;
    QueryExpression qe = new QueryExpression();
    qe.Distinct = false;
    FilterExpression exp = new FilterExpression();
    exp.FilterOperator = LogicalOperator.And;
```

```
    if (entityType == "email")
        //See example for building e-mail query
    else
        //See example for building non-email query

    qe.Criteria = exp;
    req.Query = qe;
    RetrieveMultipleResponse resp = this.m_Service.Execute(req)
                                   as RetrieveMultipleResponse;
    BusinessEntityCollection beColl = resp.BusinessEntityCollection;

    foreach (BusinessEntity be in beColl.BusinessEntities)
    {        //See logic for building CTCCrmAttachmentInfo object  }
    return attachments;
}
```

The following is the code used to build the query if it's an E-mail attachment.

```
string[] colList = { "body", "filename" };
qe.ColumnSet = new ColumnSet(colList);
qe.EntityName = "activitymimeattachment";

ConditionExpression cond = new ConditionExpression();
cond.AttributeName = "activityid";
object[] valueList = { entityID };
cond.Values = valueList;
cond.Operator = ConditionOperator.Equal;
exp.Conditions.Add(cond);
```

The following is the code used to build the query condition if it's not an activity related attachment.

```
string[] colList = { "documentbody", "filename" };
qe.ColumnSet = new ColumnSet(colList);
qe.EntityName = "annotation";

//ObjectID must match
ConditionExpression cond = new ConditionExpression();
cond.AttributeName = "objectid";
object[] valueList = { entityID };
cond.Values = valueList;
```

```
cond.Operator = ConditionOperator.Equal;
exp.Conditions.Add(cond);

//Object Type must match
ConditionExpression condType = new ConditionExpression();
condType.AttributeName = "objecttypecode";
object[] valueListType = { entityType };
condType.Values = valueListType;
condType.Operator = ConditionOperator.Equal;
exp.Conditions.Add(condType);
```

The following is the code to loop through the result entities and build our return collection.

```
foreach (BusinessEntity be in beColl.BusinessEntities)
    {
        DynamicEntity de = be as DynamicEntity;

        CTCCrmAttachmentInfo attachInfo = new CTCCrmAttachmentInfo();

        if (CTCDEPropHelper.PropertyExists(de, "filename"))
            attachInfo.OriginalFileName =
                        CTCDEPropHelper.GetStringValue(de, "filename");

        //if email
        if (CTCDEPropHelper.PropertyExists(de, "body"))
            attachInfo.AttachmentData = System.Convert.FromBase64String(
                        CTCDEPropHelper.GetStringValue(de, "body"));

        //if note
        if (CTCDEPropHelper.PropertyExists(de, "documentbody"))
            attachInfo.AttachmentData = System.Convert.FromBase64String(
                        CTCDEPropHelper.GetStringValue(de, "documentbody"));

        if (attachInfo.AttachmentData != null
                && attachInfo.AttachmentData.Length > 0)
            attachments.Add(attachInfo);
    }
```

List of Saved Queries

Using the client interface users can save advanced finds so they can be re-used in the future. The criteria for these queries are saved as user saved queries. Our next helper method is a method to retrieve a list of these saved queries. The following is an example of calling the GetSavedQueriesList from the CrmServiceManager class.

```
private void CallGetSavedQueries ()
{
    using (CrmServiceContext<CTCCRMService> svcContext =
                                this.GetServiceContext())
    {
        CrmServiceManager mgr =
            new CrmServiceManager((CTCCRMService)svcContext.Service);
        List<Lookup> queries = mgr.GetSavedQueriesList(
            new Guid("C1961A14-D4E6-470C-8D1E-23AE6B1BBB8D"), "account");
    }
}
```

The implementation of this method is pretty simple, it queries against the userquery entity where the owner of the query matches the user we pass. It also filters on an entity name because we are only interested in the saved queries a user has for a specific entity.

The following is the implementation of the GetSavedQueriesList method.

```
public List<Lookup> GetSavedQueriesList(Guid userID, string entityType)
{
    List<Lookup> queries = new List<Lookup>();
    RetrieveMultipleRequest req = new RetrieveMultipleRequest();
    req.ReturnDynamicEntities = true;
    QueryExpression qe = new QueryExpression();
    qe.Distinct = false;
    string[] colList = { "name", "userqueryid" };
    qe.ColumnSet = new ColumnSet(colList);
    qe.EntityName = "userquery";
    FilterExpression exp = new FilterExpression();
    exp.FilterOperator = LogicalOperator.And;
    //UserID must match
    ConditionExpression cond = new ConditionExpression();
    cond.AttributeName = "ownerid";
    object[] valueList = { userID };
    cond.Values = valueList;
    cond.Operator = ConditionOperator.Equal;
    exp.Conditions.Add(cond);
```

```
//Entity Type must match
ConditionExpression condType = new ConditionExpression();
condType.AttributeName = "returnedtypecode";
object[] valueListType = { entityType };
condType.Values = valueListType;
condType.Operator = ConditionOperator.Equal;
exp.Conditions.Add(condType);
qe.Criteria = exp;
req.Query = qe;

RetrieveMultipleResponse resp = this.m_Service.Execute(req)
                            as RetrieveMultipleResponse;=
BusinessEntityCollection beColl = resp.BusinessEntityCollection;
foreach (BusinessEntity be in beColl.BusinessEntities)
{
    DynamicEntity de = be as DynamicEntity;

    Guid queryID = Guid.Empty;
    string queryName = "";
    if (CTCDEPropHelper.PropertyExists(de, "userqueryid"))
        queryID = CTCDEPropHelper.GetKeyValue(de, "userqueryid");
    if (CTCDEPropHelper.PropertyExists(de, "name"))
        queryName = CTCDEPropHelper.GetStringValue(de, "name");
    Lookup query = new Lookup("userquery", queryID);
    query.name = queryName;
    queries.Add(query);
}

return queries;
}
```

Now you could just simply allow the user to pick one of these and use it to pass to Fetch. The other thing you could do with it is convert it to a QueryExpression that could be passed to a RetrieveMultiple call. The following shows an example of the code required to convert from Fetch XML to a QueryExpression.

```
public QueryExpression ConvertFetchXmlToQuery(string fetchXml)
{
    FetchXmlToQueryExpressionRequest req = new
                    FetchXmlToQueryExpressionRequest();

    // Set the Fetch Xml to be converted.
    req.FetchXml = fetchXml;
```

```
    // Execute the request.
    FetchXmlToQueryExpressionResponse resp =
        this.m_Service.Execute(req) as FetchXmlToQueryExpressionResponse;

    if (resp.Query == null)
        return null;

    return resp.Query;
}
```

Import/Export Customizations and Publish

One of the common tasks that you probably have done from the client interface is either import or export customizations. You can also perform these tasks via the API. This can come in real handy if you are trying to automate the installation of customizations to an organization.

Often times if you are adding a new entity to an organization it will be easier to just import the whole entity rather than using the Metadata API.   Using the ImportXml capabilities you are able to create and update the entity including its forms, views and script all with one command.

The following is the ImportCustomizations method that you can find on the helper class. Using it you pass the entities that you are requesting to import and the export xml representing those entities.

```
public void ImportCustomizations(List<string> entities,
                                                string importXml)
{
    //build request for import
    ImportXmlRequest req = new ImportXmlRequest();

    //load customization xml to request
    req.CustomizationXml = importXml;

    //build request parameter xml from the list of entity names
    StringBuilder sb = new StringBuilder();
    sb.Append("<importexportxml><entities>");

    foreach (string entityName in entities)
    {
        sb.Append("<entity>");
        sb.Append(entityName);
        sb.Append("</entity>");
    }
```

```
    sb.Append("</entities><nodes/></importexportxml>");

    req.ParameterXml = sb.ToString();

    ImportXmlResponse resp = this.m_Service.Execute(req)
                                        as ImportXmlResponse;
}
```

In our helper method we use the ImportXml message but there is also an ImportXmlWithProgress message that allows you to get progress updates as the import runs.

The following is an example of calling the ImportCustomizations method – this example assumes that you have either built the exportedCustomizationXml variable from scratch or have previously done an export call to retrieve the values.

```
private void CallImportCustomizations()
{
    using (CrmServiceContext<CTCCRMService> svcContext =
                                this.GetServiceContext())
    {
        CrmServiceManager mgr =
            new CrmServiceManager((CTCCRMService)svcContext.Service);

        List<string> entities = null;
        entities.Add("account");

        mgr.ImportCustomizations(entities, exportedCustomizationXml);
    }
}
```

Exporting Customizations

Exporting of customizations can come in handy for a couple of reasons. First, if you are doing any type of update to the Metadata it's an easy way to take a snap shot of the current values as part of your process. Secondly, it's the best way to grab all the data for an entity including forms, views and scripts. Using the output from this method you can modify contents and then use the import method to re-import the entity back into the system.

Export can provide the caller either a string containing the exported XML for the entities requested or it can give back a byte array of compressed data. The string approach is best used when you plan to manipulate the XML or otherwise use it right away. Using the compressed output you can easily save it to a file with a .zip extension.

In the book code framework folder, one of the projects is a customization backup service. This service takes a list of organizations from the configuration file and then performs an export customizations on each organizations. We use this internally to run backups on a regular basis of our development organizations to take a snap shot at a point in time. Using this approach if a problem occurs we can use the exported customization file to recover without having to resort to database backups. You can find this sample service in the ctccrm_CustomizationBackupService folder.

The following is the ExportCustomizations method from our helper class. This version of the method outputs an xml document for the entities requested.

```
public XmlDocument ExportCustomizations(List<string> entities)
{
    ExportXmlRequest req = new ExportXmlRequest();

    StringBuilder sb = new StringBuilder();
    sb.Append("<importexportxml><entities>");

    foreach (string entityName in entities)
    {
        sb.Append("<entity>");
        sb.Append(entityName);
        sb.Append("</entity>");
    }
    sb.Append("</entities><nodes></nodes><securityroles>"
            + "</securityroles><settings></settings><workflows>"
            + "</workflows></importexportxml>");

    req.ParameterXml = sb.ToString();

    ExportXmlResponse resp = this.m_Service.Execute(req)
                                    as ExportXmlResponse;
    XmlDocument doc = new XmlDocument();
    doc.LoadXml(resp.ExportXml);

    return doc;
}
```

The following is an example of calling the ExportCustomizations method.

```
private void CallExportCustomizations()
{
    using (CrmServiceContext<CTCCRMService> svcContext =
                                    this.GetServiceContext())
    {
        CrmServiceManager mgr =
                new CrmServiceManager((CTCCRMService)svcContext.Service);

        List<string> entities = null;
        entities.Add("account");

        XmlDocument doc = mgr.ExportCustomizations(entities);
        string exportXml = doc.InnerXml;
    }
}
```

Publishing Customizations

One thing that is often overlooked is the fact that changes to forms, views and picklists must be published before they are visible to users. So for example if you were to use the Import method you would follow it up with a PublishCustomizations call. The following is the helper method for doing the Publish.

```
public void PublishCustomizations(List<string> entities)
{
    PublishXmlRequest req = new PublishXmlRequest();

    StringBuilder sb = new StringBuilder();
    sb.Append("<importexportxml><entities>");

    foreach (string entityName in entities)
    {
        sb.Append("<entity>");
        sb.Append(entityName);
        sb.Append("</entity>");
    }

    sb.Append("</entities><nodes/></importexportxml>");

    req.ParameterXml = sb.ToString();

    PublishXmlResponse resp = this.m_Service.Execute(req)
                                    as PublishXmlResponse;
}
```

The following is an example of calling the PublishCustomizations method

```
private void CallPublishCustomizations()
{
    using (CrmServiceContext<CTCCRMService> svcContext =
                                    this.GetServiceContext())
    {
        CrmServiceManager mgr =
                new CrmServiceManager((CTCCRMService)svcContext.Service);

        List<string> entities = null;
        entities.Add("account");

        mgr.PublishCustomizations(entities);
    }
}
```

Many to Many

Many to Many relationships are new to CRM 4.0 and the way you create one between two entities is a little different from how one to many relationships work. The AssociateEntities message is used to add an association between two related items. There must already be an existing many to many relationship defined for this to work.

```
public void AddManyToManyAssociation(string entity1Name, Guid entity1ID,
        string entity2Name, Guid entity2ID, string relationshipName)
{
    Moniker moniker1 = new Moniker();
    moniker1.Name = entity1Name;
    moniker1.Id = entity1ID;

    Moniker moniker2 = new Moniker();
    moniker2.Name = entity2Name;
    moniker2.Id = entity2ID;

    //Issue Associate Request
    AssociateEntitiesRequest req = new AssociateEntitiesRequest();
    req.Moniker1 = moniker1;
    req.Moniker2 = moniker2;
    req.RelationshipName = relationshipName;

    this.m_Service.Execute(req);
}
```

The following is an example of calling the method to add a Many to Many

```
using (CrmServiceContext<CTCCRMService> svcContext =
                this.GetServiceContext())
{
    CrmServiceManager mgr = new
        CrmServiceManager((CTCCRMService)svcContext.Service);

    mgr.AddManyToManyAssociation("account",
        new Guid("6D703417-93B9-DC11-A372-0003FF23671C"),
        "lead", new Guid("FE640394-08F6-DC11-A372-0003FF23671C"),
        "accountleads_association");
}
```

Removing a Many to Many

The other action you might want to take is to remove a many to many association. The following shows the helper method that does the hard work of removing the association.

```
public void RemoveManyToManyAssociation(string entity1Name, Guid
entity1ID, string entity2Name,
                            Guid entity2ID, string
relationshipName)
{
    //Create a Moniker for the first entity
    Moniker moniker1 = new Moniker();
    moniker1.Name = entity1Name;
    moniker1.Id = entity1ID;

    //Create a Moniker for the second entity
    Moniker moniker2 = new Moniker();
    moniker2.Name = entity2Name;
    moniker2.Id = entity2ID;

    //Issue Associate Request
    DisassociateEntitiesRequest req = new DisassociateEntitiesRequest();
    req.Moniker1 = moniker1;
    req.Moniker2 = moniker2;
    req.RelationshipName = relationshipName;

    this.m_Service.Execute(req);

}
```

The following is an example of calling the method to remove a Many to Many

```
CrmServiceManager mgr = new
CrmServiceManager((CTCCRMService)svcContext.Service);

mgr.RemoveManyToManyAssociation("account",
    new Guid("6D703417-93B9-DC11-A372-0003FF23671C"),
    "lead", new Guid("FE640394-08F6-DC11-A372-0003FF23671C"),
    "accountleads_association");
```

Workflows by entity

One of the nice things about the new workflow engine is each workflow that is defined is managed as a CRM entity so you can query it just like any other data in the system. We've used this ability when building custom forms or Outlook/Word integration to allow a user to see a list of possible workflows for an entity. Later in the chapter we will show how you can use the selected workflow information to launch an instance of it to run.

The following is our helper method that builds a custom list of WorkflowInfo for all the workflows related to a specific entity.

```
public List<WorkflowInfo> GetWorkflowRelatedToEntity(string entityName)
{
    List<WorkflowInfo> list = new List<WorkflowInfo>();

    RetrieveMultipleRequest req = new RetrieveMultipleRequest();
    req.ReturnDynamicEntities = true;

    QueryExpression qe = new QueryExpression();
    string[] colList = { "workflowid","name" };
    qe.ColumnSet = new ColumnSet(colList);
    qe.Distinct = false;
    qe.EntityName = "workflow";
    FilterExpression exp = new FilterExpression();
    exp.FilterOperator = LogicalOperator.And;


    /** build query expression conditions - see below **/

    qe.Criteria = exp;
```

```
    req.Query = qe;

    RetrieveMultipleResponse resp = this.m_Service.Execute(req)
                                    as RetrieveMultipleResponse;

    BusinessEntityCollection beColl = resp.BusinessEntityCollection;

    foreach (BusinessEntity be in beColl.BusinessEntities)
    { // builds  list of workflows - see below for code }

    return list;
}
```

The following condition forces our query to match only those workflows that are for the entity requested.

```
//Entity Name must match
ConditionExpression condPrimaryEntity = new ConditionExpression();
condPrimaryEntity.AttributeName = "primaryentity";
object[] valueList = { entityName };
condPrimaryEntity.Values = valueList;
condPrimaryEntity.Operator = ConditionOperator.Equal;
exp.Conditions.Add(condPrimaryEntity);
```

The following condition adds a check to make sure the workflow is configured to be run on demand. Remember, not all workflows make sense to run on demand so you don't want to accidentally let a user call one that is intended to only run when an item is updated or created.

```
//They must be marked as on demand
ConditionExpression condOnDemand = new ConditionExpression();
condOnDemand.AttributeName = "ondemand";
bool isOnDemand = true;
object[] valueList2 = { isOnDemand };
condOnDemand.Values = valueList2;
condOnDemand.Operator = ConditionOperator.Equal;
exp.Conditions.Add(condOnDemand);
```

It's also important to filter out workflows that aren't published. Remember, users can create workflows and only once they are published can we invoke them.

```
//They must be published
ConditionExpression condPublished = new ConditionExpression();
condPublished.AttributeName = "statecode";
int publishedState = (int)WorkflowState.Published;
object[] valueList3 = { publishedState };
condPublished.Values = valueList3;
condPublished.Operator = ConditionOperator.Equal;
exp.Conditions.Add(condPublished);
```

Once our query runs we are going to package up the list in a custom class called WorkflowInfo. The primary reason for this is to make it easier to data bind or otherwise consume in the calling application.

```
foreach (BusinessEntity be in beColl.BusinessEntities)
{
    DynamicEntity de = be as DynamicEntity;
    WorkflowInfo info = new WorkflowInfo();
    info.WorkflowID = CTCDEPropHelper.GetKeyValue(de, "workflowid");
    info.Name = CTCDEPropHelper.GetStringValue(de, "name");
    info.PrimaryEntityName = entityName;
    list.Add(info);
}
```

The following is an example of calling the GetWorkflowRelatedtoEntity method.

```
private void CallGetWorkflow()
{
   CrmServiceAuthManager<CTCCRMService, CrmAuthenticationToken>
          crmSVCMgr = new CrmServiceAuthManager<CTCCRMService,
          CrmAuthenticationToken>();
   CTCCRMService crmSVC = crmSVCMgr.GetService();

   CrmServiceManager crmMgr = new CrmServiceManager(crmSVC);
   List<WorkflowInfo> list =
                crmMgr.GetWorkflowRelatedToEntity("account");
}
```

Launch Workflow from the API

One of the things you might want to do is trigger a workflow to run from the Web Service API. Using this you are able to trigger the workflow without having a platform event. The ExecuteWorkflowRequest and ExecuteWorkflowResponse messages are provided by the API to allow this to happen.

In order to make this happen we must first create an instance of ExecuteWorkflowRequest. This class exposes two public properties to set prior to making the request.

```
public Guid WorkflowId { get; set; }
```

The WorkflowId property indicates which workflow instance you want to invoke. There's a number of ways you could retrieve this ID. The simplest is by double-clicking on the workflow from the list of workflows and grabbing the Guid from the edit page. As you can see below the Guid is highlighted.

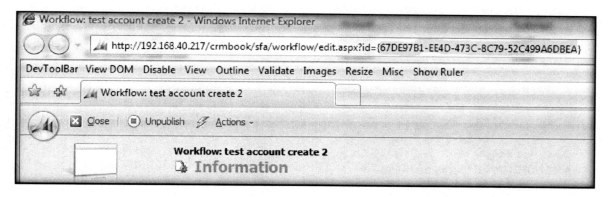

While this works, it's pretty fragile because if you were to try this on different installs the ID for any given workflow would be most likely different. Another way you could accomplish this is by doing some sort of a query using a Retrieve to get the workflow ID. In this scenario you could be more specific on the Name given to the workflow. You still might need to deal with the fact there could be multiple with the same matching name.

```
public Guid EntityId { get; set; }
```

The other public property is EntityID. This property indicates the ID of the primary entity that is being processed. Expect an exception to be thrown by the service.Execute method if you don't provide a value or it can't find the value being passed.

The ExecuteWorkflowResponse is a simple class and only provides one property that you can evaluate and use.

```
public Guid Id { get; set; }
```

This property returns you the ID of System Job (asyncoperation entity instance)that was created to track this request. Using that ID, you could query the System Job to monitor status or perhaps retrieve the workflow log instances associated with the System Job.

Now let's look at a complete example – this example assumes a few things. First, GetService does just that using the magic you use everywhere else. RetreiveFirst simply does a retrieve by a string attribute and gets back a DynamicEntity (simple collection of properties). Finally, I'm assuming a fixed Guid for the EntityID – obviously you would set that as appropriate in your solution.

```
GetService();
DynamicEntity workFlow = RetrieveFirstBySingleString("workflow", "name",
"MyTestWorkflow1");
ExecuteWorkflowRequest req = new ExecuteWorkflowRequest();
Key key = workFlow.Properties["workflowid"] as Key;
req.WorkflowId = key.Value;
req.EntityId = new Guid("957F7F2A-D26F-DC11-97B3-0003FF71B934");
ExecuteWorkflowResponse resp = _service.Execute(req) as
                                      ExecuteWorkflowResponse;
```

TIP

You can also launch a workflow from JavaScript using our helper CRM service javascript class which is discussed in Chapter 6. Using this technique you could have a button on the client interface launch a workflow with a single click of a button.

Wrapping Up

In this chapter we walked through some more detailed examples of using the API to work with the platform. Each of the examples in this chapter is packaged up as part of CrmServiceManager in the book framework. Use these as examples to understand more about how the method calls work. Ideally, you will want to expand on this helper class and add more methods that you find you need to use over and over.

11

Unified Event Framework

One of the major changes in CRM 4.0 was the rearchitecting of how business logic extensions were implemented. In case business logic extensions don't mean anything to you, think of it as ways developers can plug into the platform to provide their own customized processing when things happen. This type of capability is directly related to the flexibility and robustness of the platform and determines not only what developers can do to extend it, but how easy it will be to maintain in the future.

Having extension points to implement custom code into the CRM platform is not new with CRM 4.0. In fact CRM 1.2 and 3.0 had the concept of synchronous extensions that were named callouts and asynchronous support in the form of a proprietary workflow engine. These capabilities have evolved to help shape and form the unified support that is part of the CRM 4.0 platform. Developers leveraged these capabilities to build numerous applications and backward compatibility support was a key part of the thinking as a new unified event model was designed.

In this chapter we will explore the new Unified Event Framework that is part of CRM 4.0 and has taken over for how callouts and Workflow were handled in CRM 3.0.

Why change anything?

If you are new to the platform or just don't care about why things changed and want to get right into the new architecture – go ahead and jump ahead to the next section where we start to explore the new framework. But be warned, the "why" might help you understand the concepts more.

You might be asking why change anything, was the architecture broken in CRM 3.0 and now needs to be re-created? Not at all. Sure you could point out some areas that needed improvement, but the core capabilities of callouts served their need. Most of the changes in CRM 4.0 could be associated with a couple of key areas. First, having two different event models; one for callouts and one for Workflow, was causing problems. Often times the only reason you wrote a callout was because it couldn't be done in workflow because workflow didn't support the Update event. Developers were forced to learn two different models and understand what made both tick.

CRM 3.0's proprietary workflow engine would require a lot of development work just to get it close to where it would have similar capabilities to Windows Workflow Foundation. That's not even talking about how much work it would be to keep up to the ongoing changes. SharePoint is a great example that started leveraging Windows Workflow Foundation. In fact, using Windows Workflow Foundation became a strategic product direction across Microsoft and if CRM did not follow, you would find a big gap in terms of the CRM platform and what other Microsoft products provide in the way of workflow support.

In order to allow the platform to improve its ability to scale out, there needed to be a way to optimize the platform's use of hardware. In CRM 3.0, only one CRM organization could be deployed to a physical application server installation. In CRM 4.0 we are now able to use the same hardware and one deploy of the core CRM platform software to serve multiple organizations. This change is referred to throughout this book as the Multi Tenancy change.

The Multi Tenancy change that happened in CRM 4.0 caused a lot of rethinking across the platform. Multi Tenancy makes it so, unless you want the same workflow / callout deployed to all organizations in the installation, you need to decide a new way to handle registration and deployment of callouts and workflows. In CRM 3.0 these resided on disk in a central folder and the callouts were configured by an XML file on the server. Using that model we could not easily support the Multi-Tenancy concept.

Another spot of weakness was the ability to have callouts still work when a user is disconnected. In CRM 3.0 there was no ability to have callouts execute on the client and most importantly when the client was offline. So for example, if you implemented validation using a callout it would only run when you were connected.

We could go on discussing the pros and cons of the existing model, but it is clear that there were enough challenges that made it obvious to the team it was time to evolve the model into the next generation which we will call the Unified Event Framework. Most important of all, the model that existed in CRM 3.0 was strong enough that we will have backward compatibility support for both callouts and workflow as they upgrade to CRM 4.0.

Back to the basics

Before we dive deep into the new Unified Event Framework let's first discuss what the new model is trying to accomplish. In reality, the whole event framework works around a couple of core concepts, a Platform Operation and a State Change.

A Platform Operation is all the common operations like Create, Delete etc. When one of those is invoked, regardless of how it was invoked, we want the ability to insert our own logic into the processing that happens so that our custom logic is able to influence the outcome of the operation as well as the data being processed by the operation. It's also extremely important that we have consistency in knowing that our custom logic will always be invoked and not bypassed because some internal processing was called instead.

State Changes are a simple cause and effect and they occur when a Platform Operation changes the state of an entity instance in the system. These types of changes can be just as important as a create or delete when you want to be able to connect your own custom logic to the change.

As a result of these happening we want to be able to have our own custom logic invoked. Like in CRM 3.0 we need control over when we get called. This means before the platform operation or after the platform operation occurs. Sometimes, we want our logic to run before the system can continue with its own logic. In these cases we expect support for synchronous call to our custom logic. Other times, our logic is not critical path and running asynchronously is preferred so there's no chance our logic will interfere with the platform operation but will still happen in the back ground.

There are numerous examples of when synchronous execution of custom logic is desired. A common one is to perform more complex validation before an operation occurs and kill or stop the operation if the validation fails. Doing validation asynchronously would be foolish. Imagine that it completes a few milliseconds after the platform operation finishes and you determine that the data was invalid; what good would that do? So synchronous processing is necessary to ensure we can inject critical logic and use it to provide immediate feedback.

Asynchronous execution allows your custom logic to run without interfering and can take the time it needs to complete. In some cases the asynchronous process might wait multiple days for some other event to occur before taking action. On the other hand, the operation might be a simple calculation that finishes in no time at all. Regardless, these types of custom asynchronous logic are invoked after the platform operation occurs. It would not make sense to have them competing for resources and deadlocking with the platform operation if they ran in parallel.

From a developer coding point of view, some of the custom logic might be small routines that are coded in just a few lines of code. While for others we might want to leverage a more visual approach and design them as a workflow. Regardless of the implementation choice we make, we would like the platform to provide us the same ability to hook into the detection of Platform Operations and State Changes.

In addition to having a developer story, more often than not sophisticated users want some ability to do their own "user programming" and extension with their own custom logic. We aren't talking about teaching users to code C#. But we are talking about the ability, through the user interface, to connect into this concept of custom logic related to things that happen in the platform. By allowing the user to have some simple constructs for specification of custom logic they can take control of automating some of their day to day tasks. This capability needs to (and we will see how it does) tie in as part of CRM 4.0 to the Unified Event Framework that is implemented. This gives user-defined custom logic the same standing in the platform as developer created custom logic.

Now that we have established some ideals and some objectives for the Unified Event Framework, let's explore how the CRM 4.0 unified event framework fulfills these.

So How Does CRM 4.0 Handle Events?

CRM 4.0 tackles these objectives head on and implements a progressive event framework that picks up where CRM 3.0 left off. So that we don't confuse you with terminology as we move forward let's get a couple of key points out of the way. First, callouts that existed in CRM 3.0 are now Plug-ins. Secondly, workflow is no longer proprietary to the CRM platform as .NET 3.0 Windows Workflow Foundation replaces the proprietary engine that was in CRM 3.0. Yes, you may have read this before, but it bears repeating. We will explore both of these key items in much greater detail both in the rest of this chapter and the next several chapters that will delve into much greater depths on each topic.

CRM 4.0 unifies the events that it makes available to both plug-ins and workflows in the system. This alone solves one of the major challenges that existed in CRM 3.0 where the workflows were not able to see Update events. This unification of the events is made possible by the concept of an Event Execution Pipeline.

The Event Execution Pipeline (EEP) is responsible for managing the execution of a platform operation. The request/event flows through the EEP when the platform receives the operation request. That request moves through the pipeline invoking one or more steps. The steps are executed based on an execution order that is defined when the step is registered with the platform.

The EEP is currently made up of five stages that break down the actual work that happens as the event flows through the pipeline. The pipeline is not just for custom code, the normal built-in platform logic also runs as part of this execution pipeline. In fact, three of the five stages are reserved for handling the platform processing part of the pipeline.

The following table describes the stages in more detail.

Stage #1

- **Pre-Operation** - This is where custom logic can be registered to execute before the platform operation occurs. Logic that runs in this stage can stop further execution of the pipeline as we will discuss more in the plug-in chapters.   Custom logic that runs in this stage is not part of the platform transaction.

Stage #2

- **Pre-Operation – System** - This stage is reserved as a pre-operation stage for system internal processing. Operations that occur as part of this stage are part of the Platform Transaction. You can't register your own custom logic to run during this stage.

Stage #3

- **Platform Operation** - This is where the real work happens. The request/event that caused us to be in the pipeline is processed here and reflected on the state of the system. This stage is also part of the Platform Transaction. You can't register your own custom logic to run during this stage.

Stage #4

- **Post-Operation-System** -This stage is also reserved as a post-operation stage for system internal processing. Operations that occur as part of this stage are part of the Platform Transaction. You can't register your own custom logic to run during this stage.

Stage #5

- **Post-Operation** -This is where custom logic can be registered to execute. Custom logic in this stage can be either synchronous or asynchronous. Asynchronous logic will be handed off for processing by the Asynchronous Service queue. Custom logic that runs in this stage is not part of the platform transaction.

CRM 4.0 allows plug-ins to be registered as either synchronous or asynchronous steps. All workflows are always registered as asynchronous steps.

As the request/event enters the pipeline it is wrapped by a context object that is made available to each step regardless of whether it's a plug-in or a workflow that is invoked. Using the context the plug-in or workflow can acquire access to information about the platform operation about to or already performed. We will cover this in much greater detail in the following chapters.

Using the pipeline concept the platform is also able to do more complex operations and keep the consistency in those operations. Complex operations sometimes involve actions that could cause nested requests / events to need to be processed. An example of this is the

CompoundCreateRequest. With the pipeline model the platform is able to create child pipelines that process the sub request in the same fashion as the parent or a single pipeline would be processed going through each of the standard stages.

Multi Tenant and the Unified Event Model

The other major change that occurred is how plug-ins and workflows would be registered with the system. Since CRM 4.0 will have the ability to support multiple organizations on a single installation some changes are required. The plug-in or workflow must be registered with each organization. In other words, there will be no sharing of plug-ins or workflow across organizations. The only way each organization would see it is if it is registered directly with each organization. To accomplish that, changes needed to occur to where the assemblies were installed for plug-ins and workflows. Now in CRM 4.0 it supports registration of the assembly so it is stored in the database in addition to on disk. This is also important to allow scaleout of the platform as the system is able to replicate the assembly to any node in the install that is running the plug-in or workflow. We will cover in more detail in the later chapters how this works for both plug-ins and workflow.

Offline Support

In CRM 3.0 there was no support for execution of the callouts when the user was offline. What would happen is when the user connected back up to the CRM server the transactions completed offline would playback, this time going through the host web service which would cause the callouts to be invoked. This causes a number of problems including that you can't use them for validation when the user is offline because the error wouldn't occur until the user connected back to the server. Detecting a problem at that point would not provide for a good user experience. CRM 4.0 still provides for execution of plug-ins and workflows when the user connects back to the host server and plays back their offline work. In addition, CRM 4.0 introduces a new capability to execute custom logic when the user is offline. Currently this is implemented only to allow plug-ins to run offline in the client, but it's possible to think that in the future we might see the ability to have workflow run there as well. This offline support uses a simple event framework and leverages the fact that plug-ins are registered in the database because that allows the platform to download those to the client for execution. Further discussion on offline plug-ins will take place in Chapter 12.

Wrapping it up

In this chapter we have explored the changes to the event framework. Clearly significant changes have occurred to evolve the capabilities that existed in CRM 3.0. We leave this chapter to head to several more where we will dive in deeper on the topics related to both plug-ins and workflows. In each of the following chapters it will help you build on what we discussed in this chapter but more in the context of the specific type of custom logic extension that you can leverage in your solutions.

12

Plug-in Basics

A Plug-in represents custom code called by the platform as part of the Event Execution Pipeline of a platform operation allowing execution of the custom business logic. This capability provides one of the lowest levels of customization that a developer uses to modify the behavior and results of platform operations. This solves one of the more common problems that plague application development platforms of not having enough extension points to provide for custom processing.

Plug-ins participates in the Unified Event Framework that we discussed in Chapter 11. If you are new to the platform that chapter is a great place to start to understand how Plug-ins fit in the overall platform architecture.

Plug-ins can be used by the developer to implement and handle a wide variety of problems encountered in building solutions on the platform. Because plug-ins have the ability to run before a platform operation occurs, they are ideally suited for handling complex validation tasks or calculations that need to occur prior to the saving of data by the platform operation. By handling the post operation event, a plug-in can also consistently get control after a platform operation happens and perform additional processing. This is a great place to put auditing or other lightweight processing. We will discuss some additional scenarios in this chapter and the next, including when to use a plug-in vs. a workflow.

In this chapter, we will explore the basics of building plug-ins using the built-in capabilities. Then in the next chapter, we will look at building on that to build a framework to make it a more repeatable process by packaging up some common plug-in development techniques.

Development vs. Deployment

There are really two parts to using a plug-in with the platform. First is the development where you implement the required interface and code your business logic. That alone though will not cause your plug-in to be invoked or instruct the platform that your plug-in exists. Deployment where you register your plug-in is the second part. Plug-in registration takes care of notifying the platform that your plug-in exists and when it should be invoked. Let's look at a high level summary of the tasks you do during development and deployment.

Development

- Create .NET class that implements IPlugin interface and is configured to run under the .NET 3.0 framework.
- Write the business logic as required by your business requirements. This includes things like validation or creation of other data based on the platform operation taking place.
- Work with Dynamic Entity images of the data passed to you for evaluation.
- Make decisions based on the context passed to your business logic. You can do different logic based on being online/offline, synchronous or asynchronous and of course based on being in a pre or post operation stage.
- Understand that how and when your plug-in will be invoked is determined by deployment registration and not by your code, you can only evaluate context to decide how to re-act.

Deployment

- Use one of the registration tools or the registration API calls that we will be exploring to register your plug-in with the system.
- Identify if the plug-in should be stored in the database, GAC or on disk (often times disk is done for development to allow debugging, more on that later).
- Identify if the mode the plug-in will execute is Synchronous or Asynchronous.
- Identify if the plug-in will be invoked pre or post platform operation.
- Will the plug-in only run only on the server, only on the outlook client offline, or both?
- Identify what Message or event you are interested in e.g Create, Delete, Update etc.
- Identify which entity you are interested in being invoked for e.g Account or Contact.

The separation of responsibility between development time and deployment time provides a great amount of flexibility. This separation can be leveraged to easily create a reusable set of plug-ins that you determine when they are invoked at deployment time. As we progress through the chapter we will explain these concepts in more detail and how they work.

Developing your first plug-in

Plug-ins in CRM 4.0 are simply a .NET class that implements the IPlugin interface. This is a change if you're familiar with Callouts in CRM 3.0 where you inherited from a class provided by the SDK. Using an interface approach gives you more freedom in how you implement your plug-ins but still provide a consistent contract that the platform can use to invoke your plug-in.

Another major change in CRM 4.0 is that plug-ins can be developed in using the .NET 3.0 Framework where in CRM 3.0 use of the .NET 1.1 Framework was required.

Since plug-ins can be registered and stored in the database (we will cover this in more detail later as well as other options) it is ideal to isolate them to their own .NET class library. We will discuss some of the more advanced topics like sharing code later on, but for now let's just assume we are going to build a simple plug-in.

Add Reference to CRM Assemblies

In the new Class Library project you created to store your plug-in code in, you should add a couple of references. These are to the SDK assemblies that we will use during the development of our plug-in. In Chapter 3, we covered more about what capabilities these assemblies provide.

Using the Add Reference dialog from the project browse to the SDK and add a reference to Microsoft.Crm.Sdk.dll and Microsoft.Crm.SdkTypeProxy.dll.

You can reference these files from the SDK install folder, but typically, we like to keep a copy in one folder under our common code – that allows us to keep multiple copies of the SDK around and only update the one in the common folder when we are ready.

Browse to the location that you have placed the assemblies and select the following two.

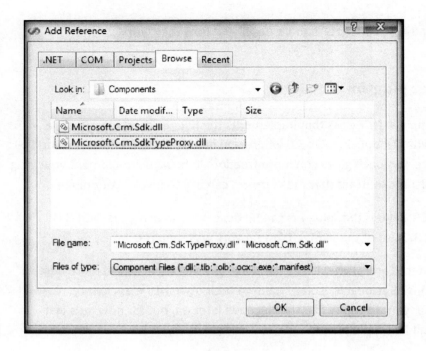

NOTE *On a server these files are registered in the GAC. If you are doing development on the server they can be referenced from there instead of the local file system.*

Adding a Strong Name to the Project

Before we get too far along with building our Plug-in library we should take care of the requirement CRM has that a plug-in class library must be strong named. To accomplish this you should right-click on the project in Solution Explorer and click properties. Select the Signing tab which will show you the following dialog panel – about half way down on the left side is a checkbox "Sign the assembly", check that, and then select "New..." in the dropdown unless you already have a strong name key you plan on using.

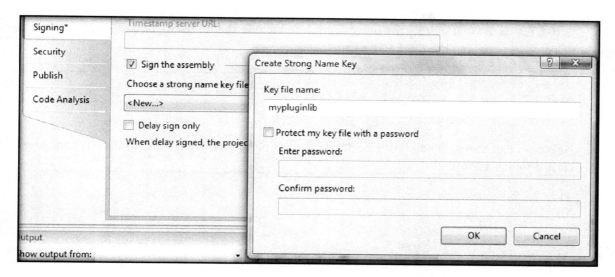

A full discussion on strong name key sharing and other support is beyond what we will cover in this book you can find more details in the MSDN docs on-line.   Once new is selected you will see the Create Strong Name Key dialog appear. Provide a name for the file and unselect the Protect my key checkbox and press the OK button. You have now added a strong name key to the project.

If you are referencing any other libraries they too will need to be strongly named or you will get a compile error.

Adding our Plug-in Class File

The next thing we are going to do is add a Class file that we will create our plug-in code in. For our first "hello world" example let's call the class file ContactPlugin.cs.

While you can store multiple plug-in class files in a single C# or VB.NET file it is not recommended for making the project more understandable. By having a single file for each class file you end up with a cleaner implementation.

In this file we should modify the using section to include the following two using statements that will give us access to the CRM SDK namespaces.

```
using Microsoft.Crm.Sdk;
using Microsoft.Crm.SdkTypeProxy;
```

Next we need to modify our class declaration to implement IPlugin – we do that by changing the class definition from

```
class ContactPlugin
{

}
```

To be

```
public class ContactPlugin : IPlugin
{

}
```

By default when you add the class to your project it's likely it won't have the public modifier. While the class will compile ok, it will not be able to be seen when you try to register it with the CRM platform.

Implement the IPlugin Execute Method

Being a simple interface we could just type in the required method Execute or we could let Visual Studio automation help us out and generate the stub method for us.

To use the Visual Studio automation, mouse over the IPlugin interface name and you should see a little blue bar under the first letter. Shortly after, you should see a dialog asking you which method you would like Visual Studio to use to expand the interface required methods – Implement interface 'IPlugin' or explicitly implement interface 'IPlugin'. For purposes of the CRM Plug-in model either option will work.

Upon selecting the first option Visual Studio will generate the following code for us.

```
public class ContactPlugin : IPlugin
{
        #region IPlugin Members

        public void Execute(IPluginExecutionContext context)
        {
            throw new NotImplementedException();
        }

        #endregion
}
```

As you can see only one method was added by Visual Studio as the IPlugin interface is very simple.

What do we have so far...

At this point our plug-in is valid and would actually register with the CRM Server. It wouldn't get too far because as soon as the CRM Server invokes our Execute method we throw an exception. Before we continue, we will take a break to explore some more concepts of how Context works so you can understand how to access the data in the CRM request that is being processed.

Understanding Plug-in Context

The Execute method, when invoked by the CRM platform, is passed an IPluginExecutionContext object reference. This object is a lifeline for your plug-in to be able to interrogate and react to the type of request that is being processed. Let's start by exploring some of the more simple properties of the object and how they are used.

Who's Calling?

The following first set are properties that identify the origination of the message.

Property	Description
BusinessUnitId	This is the id for the business unit who owns the entity for

	which the platform operation is being executed on.
CallerOrigin	Allows you to determine the origin of the call – for example if the request originated from the offline client – this property would be an instance of the OfflineOrigin class. Other possible values are WebServiceAPiOrigin, AsyncServiceOrigin, and ApplicationOrigin.
InvocationSource	Indicates how a plug-in was invoked. At registration time you can control if you want to be invoked only by a parent pipeline, a child pipeline or both. Tthis property allows you to determine which you are being invoked from.
OrganizationId	The organization ID that initiated this request and owns the entity that caused the plug-in to be invoked.
OrganizationName	The organization name – this can be helpful to save you from having to retrieve it.
ParentContext	This is set when you are executing as the child - you can have access to the IPluginContext of the parent plug-in.
UserId	This is the id for the user who caused the plug-in to be invoked.

Where are we in the pipeline?

The following subset of properties from the Context represent those that tell you information about where in the Execution Pipeline you are being invoked and if you are on or offline.

Property	Description
Mode	Indicates if the message is being processed in Synchronous (Value = 0) or Asynchronous (Value = 1) mode. This could be used if your plug-in supports being run in either mode but you need to alter your processing. For example, if running in Async mode throwing an exception to alert a user would not make sense.
Stage	Indicates the stage of processing. See Chapter 11 for a full discussion of Stage. Values for our plug-ins will be Before Operation (pre) or After Operation (post). Similar to how you might use Mode; this can be used to handle processing different. It's also possible the same plug-in be registered to be invoked before/after the operation and do different processing each time.
IsExecutingInOfflineMode	This property is important when you are doing offline plug-in development because it allows you to detect what mode you are running in. You might use this to conditionally do logic only when offline or only when your plug-in runs online. For example if you were integrating with SharePoint and wanted to create a document workspace but only do it if you are running on-line you could check this flag and conditionally perform the operation.

Execution of your plug-in is completely controlled by how it is registered with the system. Because the interface is generic, while not desirable, it is certainly possible to register a post operation plug-in expecting to work with an Account entity as a pre-operation plug-in connected to the Contact Entity. In this case the most likely outcome is an error. The same is true about being registered for online/offline and synchronous vs. asynchronous. Therefore, it's important that the plug-in confirms any assumptions it makes on where and on what it is running.

The context exposes the above properties to let you know more about how you were invoked so you could do checks if you want to make sure you are working in the desired mode or stage.

It's possible to write a single plug-in that is invoked both at pre-operation and post-operation time performing different logic. Often times this might be a better example to create two separate plug-ins; each having their own logic.

Knowing if your plug-in is running in offline mode can be very helpful because there's times where certain logic is only useful if you're connected. A common example is if you have a plug-in that does an action like create a SharePoint Document Workspace, attempting to do so while working offline is likely to fail. In this example, I say likely because it's possible to be offline in the client, but the user could still have network access to the SharePoint server Using the IsExecutingInOfflineMode we could detect that and avoid invoking that logic. Then when the user re-connects, assuming that plug-in is configured to work on the server as well, the logic would be invoked and the workspace would be created. Another example of this might be avoiding a call to an external Web Service to obtain GEO-coding or other information. If the user is offline that could be deferred till the plug-in ran on the server. You could also use the IsExecutingInOfflineMode to have default logic that runs when your offline and when on-line callout to a web-service for more real time data.

What's the request for?

The following properties help you understand "what" you are processing. These fields are not very useful if you only will be registered for one type of message or entity, but if you're writing a multi-purpose plug-in these can be interrogated to figure out what you're dealing with.

Property	Description
MessageName	The MessageName property contains the type of message that is being processed e.g Create, Update , Assign etc. A class with static constants representing the standard MessageNames can be found in the Microsoft.Crm.Sdk assembly and also in the following helper class SDK\Server\Helpers\CS\CrmHelpers\enums.cs .
PrimaryEntityName	This represents the name of the entity that triggered the event/request. The primary reason you would use this is if your plug-in supports being registered on a number of entities and you vary your processing based on entity name.

Property	Description
SecondaryEntityName	Name of the secondary entity involved in the request.

Knock, Knock – Who's There?

While you might have great intentions of knowing who will be calling your plug-in, the reality is it will be called by the platform anytime an event occurs that is registered to trigger your plug-in. In a typical case the plug-in would only be called for a specific operation on a specific entity in the system. If the plug-in could be called by events on multiple entities you might want to check the PrimaryEntityName property to make sure the plug-in is being invoked for an entity that you are able to process. The following shows an example of checking that context property.

```
If (context.PrimaryEntityName == "crmbook_property")
{
    //do stuff
}
```

Accessing the data for the request

The following properties in the context present you the data for the request being processed. The type of each of these properties are a PropertyBag object. The PropertyBag is simply a generic collection.

Property	Description
InputParameters	Represents the data that was passed along with the request to the platform. Currently the two keys we care about are "Target" and "OptionalParameters". The Target property will be passed as a DynamicEntity and represents the image of the data passed.

Property	Description
OutputParameters	The OutputParameters is populated by the platform operation and only contains valid data during the After Operation stage. This will contain the properties of the response message. The most common property returned is an "id" entry that will represent the Guid. In that example, it works exactly the same way the Request will produce a Response object with an id property. You would use this value to do subsequent processing that you need the entity Id value to be able to relate data.
SharedVariables	SharedVariables can be used to hand off data between plug-ins within the execution pipeline. In other words, a Pre operation plug-in could store something in this collection so that a Post operation plug-in can evaluate and act on it.
PreEntityImages	These properties will only contain data if you request it during registration and are intended to give you a "before" image of data. Later in this chapter we will discuss in more details how pre/post entity images work.
PostEntityImages	Contains an image of data as it existed after the request. You must indicate at plug-in registration time if you want to receive post entity images.

The ParameterName class can be helpful in working with the above collections as it exposes string values that can be used instead of hard coded strings in your code.

Context InputParameters Example

Now that we have explored some of the properties , let's take a look at an example of using the context passed to access the DynamicEntity that was passed as target to the CRM platform operation being performed.

```
If (context.InputParameters.Properties.Contains("Target"))
{
    DynamicEntity entity = context.InputParameters.Properties["Target"]
as DynamicEntity;
    If (entity != null)
    {
      // do stuff with entity here....
    }
}
```

In this example we check to see if we were passed a target, and if that target is a DynamicEntity. In the next chapter we will wrap this up into a helper property on our plug-in base class to make it less code each time.

Accessing the Properties

Now that you have the entity from the InputParameters collection you can manipulate it just like we discussed in Chapter 9 where we covered Dynamic Entity basics. For a refresher if we wanted to get a property value from the Dynamic Entity the code would look like the following:

```
CrmBoolean myValue = entity.Properties["crmbook_newcustomer"] as
CrmBoolean;
```

Or if you are using the helper class it would look like the following.

```
CTCDEPropHelper. GetBooleanValue(entity, "crmbook_newcustomer", false);
```

What Properties Are Provided?

It's important to understand that not all properties that exist in the data model for a given entity will be passed as part of the InputParameter Target Dynamic Entity properties. Only those that were passed as part of the request to the CRM platform operation will be included and accessible from the Dynamic Entity that is represented by Target. In the case of where the request originated from the web client or the client UI, the request will only contain those properties that were on the form and were modified by the user or their treat as dirty flag was set. If you need other attributes from the entity, you will need to use a separate retrieve request to get the data or register pre or post entity images on your plug-in step as we will see later on in the chapter.

If the processing you are performing depends on all possible properties to be available for a given entity you will need to take steps to register a entity pre or post image with the properties you need or to retreive the full set of properties by doing a retreive against the CRM data store.

Context SharedVariables

The SharedVariables property allows plug-ins to share data with each other. To understand this, you need to think about how the execution pipeline works, you start at the top and then run the plug-ins from top to bottom. That means that a plug-in higher in the pipeline could stuff data into the SharedVariables propertybag (collection) so that a plug-in later in the pipeline could retrieve it and act on it. When you register a plug-in a rank value is set and that is used by the platform in addition to the stage to determine the order of execution. The folowing image illustrates four separate plug-ins (A-D) and the fact that shared variables are available to each of them as it passes through the pipeline.

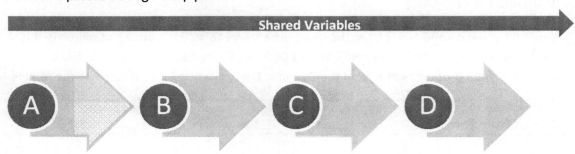

Using this property you could allow plug-ins to build on top of each other's results. A pre-operation plug-in could do some work and place it in SharedVariables so that a post operation plug-in could pick it up and finish the processing.

We used this technique in our Trace plug-in that determines if trace is enabled for the request, and if it is an object is placed in the SharedVariables. Inside the object is an identifier so that we can correlate all the traces from the plug-ins in that pipeline.

One thing to keep in mind when you're using SharedVariables is you want to be careful not to create too much dependencies amongst plug-ins. Ideally if they are sharing data make sure they are as loosley coupled as possible. If they depend on specific format of the data structure you need to make sure when you do updates they deploy at the same time.

Another thing to think about is how SharedVariables work when one of the plug-ins is configured to run asyncrounously. In that case, the asyncronous plug-in gets a "copy" of the

SharedVariables at the point in time it is queued up for execution. That means that you should not depend on being able to see any changes produced from an asyncronous plug-in by a plug-in that has a higher rank value and will run after.

Everything that is put in the SharedVariables property bag will be serialized. The PropertyBag also restricts the allowable types to known SDK types and .NET primitives. Other custom types should be avoided.

Avoiding Deadlocks using Web Service Calls

The following properties are provided to a plug-in to aid in the detection of deadlocks and re-cursive requests that would cause a loop.

Property	Description
CorrelationId	Id used for tracking and making sure you don't loop during plug-in execution – typically only used when making direct web service requests.
CorrelationUpdatedTime	Works in conjunction with the correlationId to allow the platform to perform loop detection. (Other than building a CorrelationTokenValue you probably won't directly use this.)
Depth	This tracks how deep you are in the plug-in call stack as you make other calls that in turn invoke other plug-ins, it's possible to re-enter your own plug-in. In that case, this value will be incremented until the limit of 8 is reached and then an exception will be thrown by the system. If you are having problems with this, consider checking its value prior to 8 and dumping out any useful information to track down the problem.

These properties need to be used when you are going to do calls to a CRM Service that was acquired via a separate web reference added to the project or if you manually create an instance of the CrmService.

If you use the CreateCrmService method on the context to get an instance of the CrmService then you don't need to set the CorrelationTokenValue property because it has already been set for you by the system.

By setting the CorrelationTokenValue property on the web service, you enable any calls that are made to that web service to have information on the current depth and correlation information. Without this, subsequent calls would not be able to detect dead lock problems so it is important to make sure to pass on the values.

It's important to remember that when you invoke other platform calls from inside the Execute method your request can also trigger the calling of other plug-ins or your same plug-in if the operation matches a registered event.

As a simple example, imagine an Update Account request was made, it caused invoking your plug-in. In your plug-in you did another Update Account using a web service call from inside the Execute method scope. That call would also invoke your plug-in. Assuming the CorrelationTokenValue wasn't set, the system would allow that to happen indefinitely causing a terrible loop. By setting the property, even though you have likely changed process address spaces in the course of the transaction, the system would still be able to determine it was part of the same request causing a deep recursive loop and terminate the request.

The following is an example of how to set the CorrelationTokenValue from the context of the plug-in.

```
myWS.CorrelationTokenValue =
        new CorrelationToken(context.CorrelationId, context.Depth,
                        context.CorrelationUpdatedTime);
```

If your CRMService instance came from calling CreateCrmService this is not necessary because the plug-in infrastructure takes care of this for you.

Wrapping up Plug-in Context

That pretty much covers the context that you are passed. As you can see there's a lot of information that you can evaluate and use to control the plug-in processing. In the following code example we put together a few of the concepts we just discussed with regard to context.

```
public class ContactPlugin : IPlugin
{
    #region IPlugin Members

    public void Execute(IPluginExecutionContext context)
    {
        If (context.PrimaryEntityName == "crmbook_property")
        {
            If (context.InputParameters.Properties.Contains("Target"))
            {
                DynamicEntity entity =
                        context.InputParameters.Properties["Target"]
                        as DynamicEntity;
                If (entity != null)
                {
                    // do stuff with entity here….
                }
            }
        }
    }

    #endregion
}
```

In the example above, we simply check to see if our entity is crmbook_property and if a Target was passed as input parameter. If so we get a reference to the Target bag entry and cast it as a Dynamic Entity. Obviously, in a real plug-in we would then do other processing but this shows a basic example combining some of the concepts we have been discussing.

Now that we understand how to use the plug-in context we can move on to doing something with the data that we were passed.

Using the CRM Web Service API from a Plug-in

Using the CRM Web Service to make additional calls from the plug-in is an extremely common thing to do. For example, maybe you want to look up some additional CRM data to validate that the Create request that is being processed should be allowed to proceed. Or perhaps you want to update a parent record with a total of all children records of a certain type. All of these are examples where you would want to use the web service API from within the plug-in execute method.

You have two choices for how to get an instance of the Web Service API from within your plug-in. First, you can use the CreateCrmService method that can be called from the Context object passed to your Execute method. Using this technique saves some time because discovery and url resolution to the CRM Server is taken care of for you by the plug-in infrastructure that called your plug-in in the first place.

The following is the method signature for the CreateCrmService.

```
ICrmService CreateCrmService(bool useCurrentUserId);
```

The following is an example of how to call the CreateCrmService method and indicate you want to impersonate the current user that caused the plug-in to be invoked.
```
ICrmService service =  context.CreateCrmService(true);
```

There's a similar method you can call on the context to create an instance of the Metadata Service API. As you can see below it has a similar method signature as the CRMService.

```
IMetadataService CreateMetadataService(bool useCurrentUserId);
```

Using the CRMService that is returned by calling context.CreateCrmService you get back a generic Plain Jane web service API. Meaning that if you have added any custom entities, the web service WSDL and therefore the class you will be using won't recognize those custom entities. That doesn't mean you can't work with them via this Plain Jane version of the web service API. It just means that you will be working with them exclusively with DynamicEntities and via the Execute style calls. This approach is the recommended approach for ISVs and other developers that need some level of generic access to install in an unknown customization environment. It also is a preferred by many because they don't have to worry about constantly updating their web references.

Alternatively, plug-in developers can add a Web Service reference to their project and choose to make calls to the Web Service API directly. In this case the class for the proxy would be customized based on the web reference that was added. This approach would allow you to work with the typed entities that exist in the CRM Server that the web reference was added from. As those entities change it would be necessary to update this web reference and its associated proxy class to pick up the change in interface. This approach typically isn't as good for ISVs because often times they don't know what entities will be in the installed system. For internal, corporate-type developers this offers a chance to leverage the API that is exposed by the dynamic web service API and take advantage of its typed instances of objects.

For an example of how to add the Web Reference to the API to your project see Chapter 3 where we discuss this in detail along with some options and an example.

If you use the web service via a custom web reference and not by calling CreateCrmService on the context you must ensure you set the correlation properties as we discussed previously in this chapter when we were talking about Context properties.

MVP Tip: Microsoft CRM MVP Marco Amoedo adds that CreateCrmService works much faster as instantiate your own CRM Service proxy as the actual object is cached by the platform, it's the same that happens when you are using the CRM Service on your custom code and the first call that uses the proxy takes longer than next ones. So, if there is no reason to use your own generated endpoint and you can live with Dynamic entities from this method then it's the most recommend as it improves performance and takes care of the setup of all the additional parameters like the correlation id.

Marco also added that the CreateCrmService and CreateMetadataService method have a bug that causes an "HTTP:401 Unauthorized error" when using the proxy returned if your organization friendly name has spaces. There is a hotfix available for download to solve this issue, and it will probably be included on a future Update Rollup. http://support.microsoft.com/kb/948746/en-us. You can read Marco's blog at http://marcoamoedo.com.

Passing Configuration Information to Plug-ins

Often times you may need to get some type of configuration information to your plug-in to control its runtime behaviors. For example, you might need to pass a Url to another service or modify parameters on calculations, specify different number of days for a delay, or any other type of configuration information.

You might be thinking, oh I will just use a configuration file. While that might work well for a standard server application, or event a client application it doesn't fit well with the plug-in model, since the same plug-in can be registered to run on multiple servers, multiple clients, or even a combination of both client and server. That makes a file based configuration much less practical. Instead, a registration based approach is used to set the configuration information. That way it is stored once in the organization database along with the rest of the plug-in configuration data and is simply passed to your plug-in class at runtime.
This type of configuration information can very well be different on different installations of your plug-ins. A good example of that is the differences between test and production. Many times in test for example you might want to modify parameters to help facilitate testing.

To support this, the platform plug-in framework allows you to specify two types of configuration information at the time you register your plug-in. The first type is made available to plug-ins invoked both on the server and in the outlook client. The second type is more secure and is only passed to the plug-in when it executes on the server. The secure configuration allows you to keep the information from being distributed to client machines that might be less secure.

In order to implement a plug-in that accepts configuration information you need to make a change to your plug-in class constructor signature as well as the plug-in registration information. A new constructor to your plug-in needs to be added that will string two parameters for the configuration information. The following is an example of the revised plug-in constructor.

```
public class ContactPlugin : IPlugin
{
    public ContactPlugin (string normalConfig, string secureConfig)
    {
    }
    #region IPlugin Members
    public void Execute(IPluginExecutionContext context)
    {
        //do normal stuff here
    }
    #endregion
}
```

The main change to our plug-in example above is we have provided a constructor that expects normalConfig and secureConfig. Keep in mind since a plug-in can be used over and over again to process multiple requests it's necessary for you to retain a copy of these values for reference later when your Execute method is called.

NOTE

In Chapter 11 where we built our re-usable plug-in framework we will also be exploring how to pass more complex configuration data to your plug-ins and creating a re-usable configuration approach.

That takes care of the code change. Next we need to make a small change to how we register our plug-in to provide the configuration data to pass as part of these two parameters. We will be discussing basic registration a little later in this chapter, and then again in Chapter 24 where we discuss packaging your solution in more detail. In the mean time, let's take a quick peek at a couple of the registration details that are applicable to configuration data.

The first thing to understand is the basic "configuration" property that is on the sdkmessageprocessingstep class. This class is used during registration of our plug-in to provide basic information about our plug-in. The "configuration" property is a string property that you can store data in that you want passed to the normalConfig parameter . This configuration data can be used to pass configuration information to offline plug-ins that will run on the client.

The secureConfig parameter is setup and stored a little different during registration. On the sdkmessageprocessingstep class is a property sdkmessageprocessingstepsecureconfigid. This property will be set to the unique id assigned when you create a sdkmessageprocessingstepsecureconfig entity instance. The sdkmessageprocessingstepsecureconfig entity is setup specifically for storing the secure configuration information. By secure, it really means that it will not allow it to be downloaded to a client machine for use by an off-line plug-in.

That covers the basics of being able to pass configuration information to your plug-ins. In subsequent chapters, we will be covering ways to store more structured data as well as how to do this as part of your plug-in installation.

Registering our Plug-in

At this point we are going to look at how to register our plug-in so it will be invoked by the platform. We aren't concerned with all the registration options because we will be discussing that in more detail in the deployment chapter. Here we are simply interested in deploying our plug-in so that we can test it with our development or test server. In this example we are deploying to a single organization.

The following shows our example xml that is passed to the Plug-in developer helper utility and will register our plug-in with the platform.

```
<Step
     CustomConfiguration = ""
     Description = "Simple Plugin For Contact"
     FilteringAttributes = ""
     ImpersonatingUserId = ""
     InvocationSource = "0"
     MessageName = "Update"
     Mode = "0"
     PluginTypeFriendlyName = "MyPlugin-Update"
     PluginTypeName = "MyNameSpace.ContactPlugin"
     PrimaryEntityName = "contact"
     SecondaryEntityName = ""
     Stage = "50"
     SupportedDeployment = "0" >
</Step>
```

See a more complete discussion of registering plyug-ins in Chapter 24.

Using Pre/Post Images

When you start coding to the new plug-in model one of the things you might want to do is access the pre/post images. When the plug-ins execute method is invoked at the appropriate time in the platform operation pipeline you will be passed a context object that will allow you to get access to information about the current message being processed. It's pretty common for example on an update to access the InputParameters property of the context object to access the Target image that is placed inside the Input Parameters collection.

Once you get that down, typically you will start looking for Pre/Post operation images. The PreImage is very useful if you're plug-in is invoked as a post operation plug-in and you want to know what the value of an attribute was before. On the context object is a PreEntityImages and

PostEntityImages property that similar to the InputParameters is a collection of properties being passed in.

By default when you register a plug-in the Pre/Post collections do not contain any images. When you register a plug-in you must include images you want passed. There are a couple of ways to accomplish that either using the tool with the SDK or via the API directly.

One thing to point out is there are two tools that are currently in the SDK – a Plug-in Registration tool and a Plug-in Developer tool. The plug-in registration tool is intended to be an interactive tool for developers and requires you to manually input the plug-in info each time. This tool originated in CTP2.

New to CTP3 is the Plug-in developer tool. This tool is driven by an xml file that describes the plug-in assembly as a "solution" and that solution has one or more steps that will be registered. This tool is intended to make life easier especially when you're registering your plug-in over and over.

MVP Tip: Microsfot CRM MVP Marco Amoedo adds that registering images can be done easily with the latest version released of the plugin registration tool (v2). This will allow you to instruct the platform to pass a image of the entity before (pre-image) or after (post-entity) the platform operation with the possibility of especify the attributes that you want. Using this images is recommended instead of retrieving the data using the Web Services as it is a cheaper operation. You can read Marco's blog at http://marcoamoedo.com.

The following is an example of a step in the registration file that indentifies your plug-in and hooks it up to the Update message.

```
<Step
        CustomConfiguration = ""
        Description = "Simple Plugin"
        FilteringAttributes = "opportunityproductid,opportunityid"
        ImpersonatingUserId = ""
        InvocationSource = "0"
        MessageName = "Update"
        Mode = "0"
        PluginTypeFriendlyName = "MyPlugin-Update"
        PluginTypeName = "MyNameSpace.MyPlugin"
        PrimaryEntityName = "opportunityproduct"
        SecondaryEntityName = ""
        Stage = "50"
        SupportedDeployment = "0" >
        <Images>
                <Image
```

```
                    EntityAlias = "PreImage"
                    ImageType="0"
                    MessagePropertyName="Target"
                    Attributes ="opportunityproductid,opportunityid">
            </Image>
        </Images>
</Step>
```

Notice in the XML <Images> tag we specify that we want to be passed a PreImage and what attributes we want to be passed. The developer tool will take care of registering that and when invoked we will be passed the PreImage as part of the PreEntityImages collection.

The other way you can indicate the type of images you want is via the API directly. That's really what's happening inside the Plug-in Developer tool, it just does it based on what you put in the XML. For now, we won't cover that. If you need more info on this just take a wander though the Solution.cs file that is used by the Plug-in Developer tool.

Understanding the Life of a 4.0 Plug-in

In designing and coding plug-ins it's important to understand the life cycle to avoid problems. The first thing you need to know is that your plug-in is completely at the mercy of the platform as it manages instancing of your class to service a request. It will decide when it's appropriate to create a new instance or re-use an existing one. Specific details on those decisions are not available right now but knowing that an instance of a plug-in can be re-used for processing multiple requests is very important to your design and implementation of the plug-in code. You need to ensure that you design your plug-in to be stateless so that the class can handle multiple requests.

Using the following overly simplified plug-in example let's explore some ways that you can get into trouble.

```
public class SimplePlugIn : IPlugin
{
    public void Execute ()
    {    // Do real work here…    }
}
```

Using Class Instance Variables

In this scenario you might have a counter or some other value that you want to share with other functions in the class that might be called by the Execute method. The following shows an example of using a class instance variable to store a working value.

```
public class SimplePlugIn : IPlugin
{
      private int _myWorkingValue = 0;
      public void Execute ()
      {
          DoStuff();
          Do more real work here...
      }
      private void DoStuff()
      {
          __myWorkingValue ++;

      }
}
```

The problem you can encounter here is the fact that _ myWorkingValue is only initialized the first time when the class is first instanced. If the class instance is re-used by the system, the value will still be as it was from the last request. Initialization must be done as part of the Execute method to ensure the values are cleared each time.

Using Class Constructor for Initialization

In this scenario we are using the class constructor to initialize the value or other items and intend for them to be reset each time.

```
public class SimplePlugIn : IPlugin
{
      private int _myWorkingValue;

      public SimplePlugIn()
      {
          _myWorkingValue = 0;
      }
```

```
    public void Execute ()
    {
            DoStuff();
            Do more real work here...
    }
    private void DoStuff()
    {
            __myWorkingValue ++;

    }
}
```

The problem with this is the same as the previous Class Instance Variable in that the constructor is only called the first time the class is used by the system. Initialization must be done as part of the Execute method to ensure the values are cleared each time.

Using Class Static Variable

In this scenario we define a class static variable that we want to keep track of how many times the plug-in was invoked.

```
public class SimplePlugIn : IPlugin
{
      private static int _myCountInvoked;
      public void Execute ()
      {
            _myCountInvoked++;
            Do more real work here...

      }
}
```

There are a couple of problems with this approach. First, it's possible there are multiple instances of this class running in different threads. In that event we need to provide some thread safety during our update to prevent having problems that are inconsistent and very hard to track down. Second, if we are relying on this count to be accurate we would be wrong since it's possible to have multiple processes running the plug-in. This can occur under a couple of deployment models of the platform such as a web farm, or running the asynchronous service on multiple back end servers. If you needed to solve that type of problem you would need to store the value in a central place externalized from the plug-in.

So the bottom line is that best practice for plug-in development is to minimize, if not eliminate, anything that requires your plug-in to maintain state. If you do need to maintain some type of state make sure you are very aware of possible issues that could arise. If for caching reasons or other performance needs you do leverage one time initializations for a class or an instance make sure you take steps to prevent threading issues or other variable reuse problems.

Plug-in Code Reviews

Plug-ins offer a lot of power in being able to hook into platform requests. As the saying goes, with power comes responsibility. This is certainly true in the case of plug-ins because when you introduce errors if you're lucky they will be obvious because the user received an error message. The challenging problems are the ones introduced by lengthy processing or that only happen sporadically. It is also important to know that plug-in code runs as trusted code and has access to greater resources than a normal user of the system would have. The full extent of that access is really up to the administrator that installed and configured the CRM server software and the entitlements granted to the user that plug-ins run under. Ideally, least privilege concepts should be exercised with plug-ins by ensuring the user that CRM uses to invoke plug-ins don't have unnecessary access to resources.

Some proactive planning can often times help avert these problems from happening. Code reviews offer a great way to accomplish a couple of things. First, you can spot problems that the original developer did not see and catch. Secondly, it's a great way for developers to learn new ideas and share techniques with each other.

In the next chapter where we present a plug-in framework we push the concept of tracing heavily because it's a technique that can be utilized to track down problems even in production. We also encourage use of the test harness to be able to simulate plug-in execution outside the platform environment. Both of these techniques should be used in addition to some form of a code review process to help ensure the plug-in code is ready for prime time.

One thing you might consider is developing a plug-in check list that you use as part of your review. Often times in a review it's too easy to get side tracked on a specific issue and not accomplish the goals of the review.

Here are a few items to get you started

- How is the CRM Web Service Used, and is it proper deadlock detection done?
- Is error handling well done so that the user won't see "object null reference messages"?
- Is there too much code stuffed in the Execute method and not well organized?
- Is the plug-in code stateless or will running multiple request cause problems?
- If it is a synchronous plug-in, does it need to be?
- Are provisions in place for handling problems in production?

Wrapping it up

In this chapter we walked through the basics of building plug-ins. By now you should be starting to see how powerful plug-ins can be as part of your solution. They allow you to extend the core platform operations for extra processing like validation, calculation and even some forms of automation.

Since plug-ins can now happen either synchronously or asynchronously you have another option to still be integrated as part of the platform operation, but not necessarily make the user wait for your processing to complete. In the workflow chapters we will continue this discussion comparing and contrasting the use of asynchronous plug-ins compared to leveraging the workflow capabilities which also are asynchronously processed by the platform.

In the next couple of chapters we will explore a framework for building plug-ins more efficiently as well as some common examples of plug-ins.

13

Plug-in Developer Framework

This chapter will build on what we learned in Chapter 12 about building basic plug-ins. Plug-in development can be very simple. They are really just a class that implements a single Execute method. But they can also be very complex when you think about how they fit into the overall architecture of the platform.

In the prior chapter, we discussed only the out of the box capabilities that exist to support plug-in development. In this chapter, we are going to look at some ideas for building a reusable framework to make building plug-ins more consistent and easier to manage.

The approach we discuss in this chapter is just one approach, and there is no single right answer to how this could be accomplished. So use the example in this chapter as a way to get to understand plug-ins a little better as we will address some basic topics as well as some that are more advanced and you might not have thought of yet.

We will start out talking about base classes and how to inherit your plug-ins from a consistent base class, and we will end with discussing data caching strategies for lookup data that is used over and over again in your plug-ins and how to optimize and make that more friendly for the repetitive calls.

We will also discuss in this chapter how we can do testing of our plug-in outside the CRM platform without registering the plug-in with the system. To accomplish this we will dive deeper into how the plug-in works to attempt to simulate that environment with a test harness.

Finally, we will look at how Tracing support can be integrated into your plug-in framework so that when your plug-in is running in production you have something other than the debugger to rely on to determine what went wrong to cause your plug-in to throw unexpected errors.

Referencing PluginCommon

The first thing we should get out of the way is adding a reference to our PluginCommon assembly. This assembly and the code is included in the book sample code and contains common code for plug-ins as well as general CRM development.

In order to use this assembly we need to add a reference to our project to the ctccrm.plugincommon assembly as you can see in the following image.

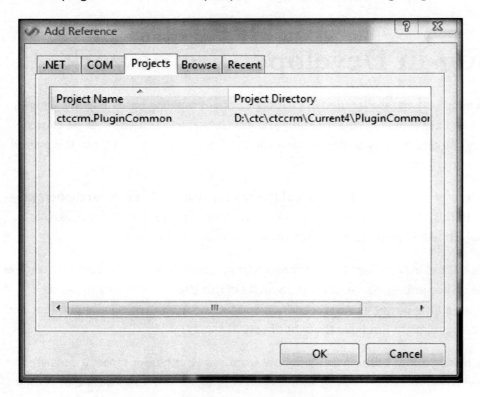

If you haven't included the ctccrm_plugincommon project in your solution you can also accomplish this by doing a browse and referencing the assembly.

Setup the Namespace References

```
using ctccrm.PluginCommon.BaseClasses;
```

```
using Microsoft.Crm.Sdk.Query;
using Microsoft.Crm.Sdk;
```

Why a Base Class

When you look at the new interfaced based plug-in model that is provided as part of the platform it makes a lot of sense that they just stuck with a single simple interface. By having one method, it is so simple to implement, and by not using a base class of their own they leave it up to you to implement this interface in whatever class you want.

That said, one of the things we realized after implementing a few plug-ins there were some common themes we saw emerging that we had to do over and over again in each plug-in. So that lead us to build a common plug-in class library that would have some common code we could use time and time again when building plug-ins.

At the heart of this common code is a new base class that we plan to inherit all of our plug-ins we build from. The following is the class signature for our base plug-in class.

```
public partial class CTCPluginBase : IPlugin
{

}
```

You probaby notice two things right away. First it is defined as a partial class. That really is for internal implementation purposes because we wanted to be able to split its implentation across a couple of logical files that would implement key parts of our base class.

The second thing you will notice is that we implement the IPlugin interface. This is done for a few reasons. The most important is we plan to implement some common error handling and tracing support that all our plug-ins will use. We will accomplish that by intercepting the call to Execute allowing us to do our own error handling and tracing prior and after calling our actual plug-in code. Don't worry we will explain more and show examples as we continue forward in describing the framework.

If we were to look at one of our plug-ins that uses the base class their defintion would change from:

```
public class MyPlugin : IPlugin
```

```
{
}
```

to look like the following:

```
public class MyPlugin : CTCPluginBase
{
}
```

Because our base class implements IPlugin and also implements the Execute method we don't need to implement directly the IPlugin interface in our class.

Expanding on Execute Method

The out of the box interface for plug-ins provides the one entry point via the Execute method. We have already explained that we intend to hijack that in our base class to provide some common services. By doing that we needed to figure out would we just have the real plug-in we were calling override the Execute method again or would we come up with another set of methods that would be called to process the request by our base plug-in logic?

After much debate we decided on an approach that would implement two methods HandleBeforeOp and HandleAfterOp. If they sound familiar they are modeled after the stages that our plug-in can be invoked by the platform to perform work. This is a great example of where you could choose to implement your own methods. For example instead of our two, you could choose to do a single HandleExecute method, or for that matter break it up into more methods by having them tied more to the Message being processed in addition to the stage. Regardless, for our sample implementation we are discussing in the book we used the two methods described above.

What this means is since your plug-in code that inherits from our base class you don't need to check if your code is being called before or after the operation because you explicitly determine that by overriding either the HandleBeforeOp, the HandleAfterOp or both if you want to be invoked in both places.

In practice what we found was most plug-ins handle one or the other, and make certain assumptions on their processing based on that. By separating them out, that made it one less check that had to be done in each plug-in implementation.

If you were to peer inside the code of our base class Execute method you would see code similar to the following doing the check for the stage and calling the appropriate method.

```
//check if this is before main op and call the HandleBeforeOp method
if (context.Stage ==
MessageProcessingStage.BeforeMainOperationOutsideTransaction)
{
    HandleBeforeOp();
}

//check if this is after main op and call the HandleAfterOp method
if (context.Stage ==
MessageProcessingStage.AfterMainOperationOutsideTransaction)
{
    HandleAfterOp();
}
```

The code above has been simplified for readability, but you get the idea of how we do the check of where we are and what method to invoke.

In addition to the two above methods, we also have some more specific methods you can override so you do not have to check to see if you're in a Delete message for example. The following are the methods that can be overridden that are more specific.

Method	Description
HandleBeforeOpCreate	Called before platform operation only for Create.
HandleBeforeOpUpdate	Called before platform operation only for Update.
HandleBeforeOpDelete	Called before platform operation only for Delete.
HandleAfterOpCreate	Called after platform operation only for Create.
Method	Description
HandleAfterOpUpdate	Called after platform operation only for Update.
HandleAfterOpDelete	Called after platform operation only for Delete.

Using these methods is easy. Simply override them and implement your code. Using this approach there is no need to explicitly check that your called because of a Create, Delete or Update request. The following is a simple example of using the methods.

```
public override void HandleAfterOpCreate()
{
    List<DBSPParm> parms = new List<DBSPParm>();
    string sqlInsert = BuildInsert(GetConfigValue("SQLTable",
                                    ""),parms);
    execCmdInsert(sqlInsert, parms.ToArray());
}
```

Using Context

Another issue we had to address was how we wanted to handle the Context that normally is passed to the class via the Execute method. What we found was often you needed this in other functions in the class and often ended up passing this all over the place as a parameter. To make the Context more readily available and not clutter up parameters we have exposed a class property named Context.

This allows access using the following syntax.

```
this.Context.InputParameters[...]...
```

You could easily also pass this on the HandleAfterOp/BeforeOp methods if you wanted. That would just be an implementation choice of how you handle it. Regardless of how, the Context is important to make available for use though out your plug-in code.

NOTE

It's important to keep in mind that due to re-use of instances of a plug-in the Context property in our implementation is only valid from the time the Execute method is called by the system until it completes. You should not retain a reference to the Context in another class variable for reuse later.

Simplification of InputParameters

The next pattern we saw was we kept spending time trying to get the Target Dynamic Entity out of the InputParameters. To simplify this, we added a property to the base called InputTargetDE that will either be null if the Target is not a Dynamic Entity or will have a valid value. Remember Create and Update pass a target property as a Dynamic Entity. The following is a brief example of using the property.

```
if (CTCDEPropHelper.PropertyExists(this.InputTargetDE,
                            "opportunityproductid"))
{
    oppProductID = CTCDEPropHelper.GetKeyValue(this.InputTargetDE,
                            "opportunityproductid");
}
```

In addition to receiving a Dynamic Entity as the Target key in the InputParameters collection you can also receive a Moniker. If you're not familiar with a Moniker, it basically contains the entity name plus the entity ID value. It is used to identify a unique occurrence of a CRM entity data record. Plug-ins receive this as the input parameter when they are called to handle Retrieve, Merge and Delete operations.

A helper property exists on the base class for this as well. The InputTargetMoniker property is null if the Moniker is not the Target key. The following is an example of code using the property.

```
List<DynamicEntity> oppProds =
        this.RetrieveMultipleBySingleKey("opportunityproduct",
                            "opportunityproductid",
                        this.InputTargetMoniker.Id);
```

If you write plug-ins that deal with the Merge operation in addition to passing a Moniker as the Target property it needs to also indicate the other ID that will be involved in the Merge operation. That is accomplished by passing in a SubordinateId key in the InputParameters. This key comes in as a Guid object. You can access this via the helper property this.InputTargetSubordinateId

There are other keys that you might encounter when using plug-ins for various operations. The ones we have added to our base class represent the more common ones. A good way to get your head around what might be passed in is to remember that the Input Parameters closely follow what you specify on the Request class when the platform operation is requested.

Working with OutputParameters

If your plug-in is a post operation plug-in the most common thing that you will want to find out is the Guid that was assigned if the operation invoked was a create. As we discussed in the prior chapter the Output Parameters collection stores the id that would be in the Response sent back to the caller of the operation. To make retrieving the ID value easier, we have added an OutputID property to the base class. So in your plug-in code you can check and access the output id using the following syntax.

```
If (this.OutputID != Guid.Empty)
{
    / /do other logic that requires the OutputID Guid
}
```

Using CrmService

We talked in the prior chapter about the two options for utilizing the CRM Web Service from a plug-in. Now we are going to expand on how you can use the implementation that comes back from the CreateCrmService method on the Context.

To ensure that we can provide tracing support before and after all platform operations and so that we can run as part of a standalone plug-in test harness outside the platform we are going to have to make some changes in how we get the CrmService. We have exposed two properties from the base class; UserService and SystemService, that expose access to the CRM web service going through a custom proxy class that works with tracing and the test harness. The following is an example of using the helper properties.

```
this.UserService.Execute(…..)
```

By making sure that all our web service calls from the plug-in are done via the property we will ensure we get consistent trace data both in the test harness and when deployed on the CRM Server.

Keep reading if you want to understand more about why and how we implemented those properties. For the less curious you can proceed to the next section Plug-in Trace Support.

Let's explore what we need to do in our base plug-in. If you recall one of our key goals was to use our common plug-in framework to make our plug-ins more supportable in production. We also wanted to make it so it was capable of running in a standalone test harness. To aid in that we decided we wanted to be able to inject trace calls before and after calls to the Web Service API. We have found that is a great way to track down errors that are returned from the service calls. We could simply have a "development rule" that developers always put in trace statements before and after the calls to the web service. Sure, that might work, but more than likely the developers would not consistently implement the tracing and it would provide less value.

To make it easier on the developer we needed to tackle the problem in a different way. Our approach is we are going to wrap a class around the actual CRMService class it will be a pass through to the real CRMService class but will take care of doing the appropriate trace calls. This concept is also important later on when we rig up our test harness. To allow our plug-in to run standalone outside the CRM Server our test harness will have to simulate part of the runtime environment which includes providing an IPluginExecutionContext implementation as well as ensuring our implementation provides a CreateCrmService method that works.

If you look at the definition of the CreateCrmService method it returns an object instance that must be cast to a CRMService. Unfortunately the CRM Team did not have time to implement that to return an ICrmService interface that could have a custom implementation if needed. So in the SDK it recommends casting it as follows.

```
CrmService myService = (CrmService) context.CreateCrmService(true);
```

The problem with this code is if it ever returned something other than a CrmService object the code would break. This leaves no room for working transparently with a testing harness so we're going to have to make some changes.

Our first step was to create our own Interface that represented all the methods and properties that are exposed by the real CRMService. The following ICRMService Proxy interface provides that capability.

```
public interface ICRMServiceProxy
    {
        Guid Create(Microsoft.Crm.Sdk.BusinessEntity entity);

        void Delete(string entityName, Guid id);
```

```
     string Fetch(string fetchXml);

     BusinessEntity Retrieve(string entityName, Guid id,
                      ColumnSetBase columnSet);

     BusinessEntityCollection RetrieveMultiple(QueryBase query);

     void Update(Microsoft.Crm.Sdk.BusinessEntity entity);

     Response Execute(Microsoft.Crm.SdkTypeProxy.Request Request);
 }
```

The next thing we need to do is to create our proxy class. This class will be simple; it will take a CrmService on the constructor and internally proxy requests to the real CRMService after performing the appropriate tracing.

If you looked inside the workings of the UserService property it calls the normal CreateCrmService method from the context and then does a check if it needs to wrap the proxy around the object returned. The following is a subset of the logic in the UserService property.

```
ICrmService service =  this.Context.CreateCrmService(true);

if (service is ICRMServiceProxy)
    m_UserService = service as ICRMServiceProxy;
else
    m_UserService = new CTCCRMService(service);
```

That's the magic behind the CRM service and hopefully as we get into the testing harness discusion we can explain more about how this new interface will benefit us.

Plug-in Trace Support

Using the debugger to work through the kinks in your plug-in is great while you're in development. Once you are deployed to your QA server or production servers how often do the people responsible for those environments like you connecting a debugger up to the live application. That conversation normally ends with someone saying "You want to do what?" A better approach is to tackle the problem head on and build into your plug-in support for dealing with problems in a live environment.

As a platform, CRM has a platform level trace implemented throughout. Often times this is requested by support staff to be able to assist you in determining problems. In fact, you will find it a great way to save time for yourself if you get comfortable reading a platform trace. Often times a call to support or a few hours of scratching the head can be solved with a quick look at the platform trace output. The platform trace, while powerful, it is not ideal for broad use because when it is on, it's on for all users. In Chapter 25, we will discuss in detail how to use the platform trace.

In this section we are going to talk about plug-in level tracing from your own plug-in. The goal is to get context information relevant to your business logic customization so you can quickly resolve problems. We want to be a lot more surgically precise than the platform trace is, in fact we want to be able to isolate a single user and produce trace output that we can analyze.

Our solution is going to consist of three parts. First, in our code we need a set of methods that we can call to easily output data. Second, we need a way to tell our plug-in that it should be producing the trace. Finally, we need our plug-in common code to help out and do as much to help as possible so our plug-in doesn't have to do repetitive implantation of tracing infrastructure.

Adding Trace Calls

Let's first talk about adding trace calls to our plug-in. To make it simple we have exposed a helper property from our plug-in base class called CTCTrace. Using this property and the methods it makes available you can easily output trace messages. For a simple example if you wanted to trace out an exception you would do the following.

```
try
{
//do stuff here
}
catch(Exception ex)
{
    this.CTCTrace.Write(ex);
}
```

Methods of CTCTrace

The CTCTrace property exposes a number of methods that can be called by your plug-in to output information to the trace. Each of these performs no output if the trace is not enabled for the user causing the invocation of the plug-in.

Method	Description
Write(Exception e)	Write out the exception, no message.
Write(Exception e, string message)	Write out the exception along with a message.
Write(string sCategory, DataSet dsTraceInput)	Categorize the trace entry and trace a dataset's contents.
Write(string sCategory, DataTable dtTraceInput)	Categorize the trace entry and trace a datatable's contents.
Write(string sCategory, DynamicEntity oData)	Categorize the trace entry and trace a Dynamic Entities contents.
WriteXml(string sCategory, string sMessage, string sXml)	Categorize the trace entry and out a message and some xml content.
Write(string sCategory, string sFormatString, params object[] oDataArray)	Categorize the trace entry and out a message and using a format string.
WriteObject(string sCategory, object oData)	Categorize the trace entry and trace the public properties on an object.
WriteObjectVertical(string sCategory, object oData)	Similar to WriteObject but it writes the properties vertically instead of horizontally in the trace output.

These same methods can also be accessed using the class CTCTraceContext . This class exposes the same methods as static methods. Typically the reason you would use this class instead of the CTCTrace property would be if you're trying to output trace data from another class called by your plug-in that doesn't have direct access to the CTCTrace property.

Turning Trace On/Off at Runtime

One of the major goals we had for adding trace support to our plug-in infrastructure was to do it in a way that it could be used in a live production system. To make that viable, we had to devise a way that we had the flexibility to configure the trace on a user by user basis and even then be able to be picky about what gets traced.

To accomplish this we decided we would create a custom entity that would identify what we wanted to trace and other options that we wanted to provide. In order to be able to use the trace you must import in the ctccrm_Traceconfig custom entity that we will be using in the following examples to configure trace. You can find this in the sample code in the following folder $BookCode/Framework/CRMEntities.

Once imported you should go to System -> Customizations and pull up the custom entity and check that you would like it to show up on the Settings page. By default there's no need to modify security to grant access to the custom entity as long as only system administrators need access. If you want to make it visible to other users, maybe the developer working on the problem, you need to grant them that access through a security role.

Step 1 – The first step in turning on trace is to create a new Trace Config entry. The following is an example of the custom form general tab for the trace config.

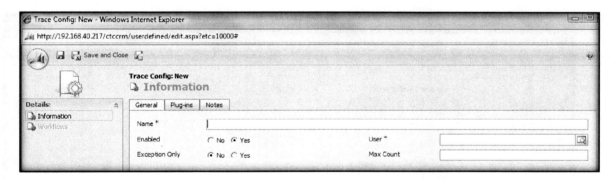

You must provide a Name and the User prior to saving the trace config. The name is a user defined name that will help you remember why you turned on trace. For example, "Trace for user John Smith". You will then use the user lookup to select a user to enable trace for. The following table explains the other fields on the form that you can modify.

Field	Description
Enabled	Yes or No indicates if this trace config is active. You can use this to temporarily turn off trace without having to delete the trace config entry.
Exception Only	Means that a trace output will only be saved by a plug-in if the plug-in encounters and throws an unhandled exception that is caught by the common plug-in base class. This is a way to reduce the amount of trace produced where the error is an unhandled exception but only occurs occasionally.
Max Count	Max count allows you to limit the number of trace outputs that will be captured for this particular trace config. This is useful if you have a high volume of activity and you only want to capture a handful of trace outputs to look at.

Step 2 - The second tab is a plug-in specific tab allowing you to configure options that are specifically related to plug-ins.

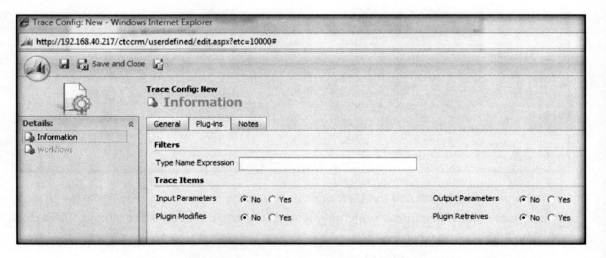

Field	Description
Type Name Expression	This allows you to refine the trace to a specific plug-in pattern using regular expression. Don't worry if you're not familiar with regular expressions, you can just specify an exact match. The regular expression would just let you do more generic matching so you could turn trace on for multiple plug-ins with one pattern. By leaving blank no filtering will be done and all plug-in types will qualify.
Input Parameters	Turns on automatic tracing of what is passed via the InputParameters.
Output Parameters	Turns on automatic tracing of what is passed via the OutputParameters property.
SharedVariables	Allows for tracing of shared variables.
Plug-in Modifies	If the plug-in uses CRMService created using the Context call then it will trace any calls to modify related calls to the API.
Plug-in Retrieves	Same as modifies only this is for the retrieve of data.

The ability to trace the Input and Output parameters represents a great way to understand what is being passed into your plug-in. In fact when I was doing a lot of the initial writing for this book, that was one of the few ways to figure out what was going on and what was being passed around. Now, the combination between the book contents and the SDK can help you understand more about the internals and how things work.

Tracing the calls to the CRM Service is also valuable when you are getting errors back that don't provide enough specifics to know what the problem is. For example if you get "Unspecified Error Occurred" one of the first things I do is try to verify what was passed into the web service API call. Often times an invalid parameter can cause problems and seeing it in trace output is easy to spot and fix.

Viewing the Trace

No need to break out remote desktop and log into the CRM server to view the trace. Trace data is output as a note on the Trace Config custom entity. This solves a few different problems that can occur with the typical trace to a file solution. For example, if you have the platform running on a web farm, which server do you login to to get the trace? It's also always difficult to take a log file from a secure server and get it sent to a developer or someone outside the network administration group on a production server. This way, through the CRM interface you can manage access to the trace output. In fact you could even share the trace config record with a support person and allow them to just view it via CRM. The following shows what you will see when you look at the notes tab after a trace has been captured.

NOTE

On some systems when you click on the trace file it might not open correctly. When this happens the trace file will open in the small window of the open file dialog making it almost impossible to read. A work around is to use ctrl-N and then force it to re-open the file.

Caching Lookup Data

Another area that you might run into is related to the fact that a plug-in instance is re-used to process multiple platform requests. If you have any data that is stored in CRM and used over and over or needed as lookup data then you have two choices. First, you could simply reload this data for each plug-in request. Clearly this approach is not ideal as it would lead to the ongoing performance hit each time you had to fetch the data. Another approach is to do your own caching of the data – so you load it up once and then share it across all instances of your class. The problem with that is if you have more than one place where you need that capability you will be replicating the logic in multiple places.

To make life easier we decided we wanted to implement some basic caching support into our plug-in base class. That way all plug-in instances running can use it if they have the need and we can also more easily expand it in the future.

It's important to note that depending on how your plug-in is configured to execute or if your deployment consists of multiple servers you may find that there are multiple "processes" that have created one or more instances of your plug-in to run it. In that case each "process" will obtain its own copy of the cached data and each will manage their own expiration.

Initially, there will only be supporting caching of CRM data, however, it could easily be extended to cache other data perhaps data that you retrieve from an external web service. We will be configuring the data to be cached by registering a CRM Query Expression and an expiration time. Using that information the base class will be able to manage the cached data and as needed call to the CRM platform to request a refresh of the data using the provided query expression.

We have provided a few methods that you will be able to call to register and get data back from the cache.

Base Class Cache Methods

The following methods are part of the base class and help manage the lookup data so the plug-in developer does not have to constantly deal with locking, threading, reloading and other issues related to a shared data cache.

Method	Description
RegisterDataCacheSets	This method you actually don't call but you override and it's called once by the plug-in base class to allow you a central spot to be able to call one or more RegisterCacheQuery calls.
RegisterCacheQuery	This method is called to register a set of cache data that you want to store. Currently it only supports caching of CRM data, but could be extended to support other types. You will pass a CRM QueryExpression to identify what data that should be cached along with the attribute used as the key.
GetCacheItemDynEntity	This method is used to retrieve a dynamic entity instance from the cache by passing the cache name and a cache key.

Registering Cache Sets

While technically you could call the RegisterCacheQuery method from anywhere and it would only register the first time, we have provided the RegisterDataCacheSets override to make your code cleaner. By overriding this method the base class will make sure to only call it once per plug-in instance. The following shows adding the override method to our plug-in class.

```
public override void RegisterDataCacheSets(IPluginExecutionContext
context)
{
   // register calls here...
}
```

The next thing we need to do is build our Query Expression that we will pass to the individual RegisterCacheQuery calls. This is just a standard platform Query Expression just like you would pass to a Retrieve Multipe directly.

The following is an example of building the query expression and calling the RegisterCacheQuery.

```
public override void RegisterDataCacheSets(IPluginExecutionContext
context)
        {
            QueryExpression qe = new QueryExpression();
            qe.ColumnSet = new AllColumns();
            qe.Distinct = false;
            qe.EntityName = "product";
            FilterExpression exp = new FilterExpression();
            exp.FilterOperator = LogicalOperator.Or;

            ConditionExpression cond1 = new ConditionExpression();
            cond1.AttributeName = "name";
            object[] valueList1 = { "ABC" };
            cond1.Values = valueList1;
            cond1.Operator = ConditionOperator.Contains;
            exp.Conditions.Add(cond1);

            qe.Criteria = exp;
            this.RegisterCacheQuery(context, "ProductCache",
                    qe, "productid", new TimeSpan(1, 0, 0));
        }
```

In the above code we build a Query Expression that indicates we want to retrieve all columns from the product entity. We provide a filter expression to limit the rows returned to only those that contain "ABC" in the name attribute. This is just for example purpose. You could build any query expression that could be passed to a RetrieveMultiple request and it would work with caching.

Once we built the query expression we call the RegisterCacheQuery method. We pass "ProductCache" as our cache set name. We will use that name to refer to this set of data when we want to retrieve it later. This name must be unique across all cache sets that are registered for the plug-in. If we try to register multiple cache sets with the same name the subsequent registration requests will just be ignored. The "productid" that is passed indicates what attribute we intend to use as the key for our lookup purpose. In the future it would be possible to provide multiple keys or more flexibility but for simplification purposes we are only supporting a single key at this time. The final parameter which is a TimeSpan indicates how long we want to cache the data before the cache will expire. Upon expiration the plug-in base will attempt on next access of the cache to refresh the cache data. If the request is successful the new cache data is used. If the request fails for some reason, the older data will be used and the reload will be retried.

In the RegisterDataCacheSets method you could make multiple calls to RegisterCacheQuery to register different cache sets you intend to use in your plug-in.

Retrieving Data from the Cache Set

The common code in the plug-in base will take care of doing the actual retrieve of the data and storing it in the cache based on the registration information. To use the data that has been cached you can simply call the GetCacheItemDynEntity method. The following shows an example of getting that data.

```
DynamicEntity productEntity =
                this.GetCacheItemDynEntity(this.Context,
                        "ProductCache", "productidhere");
```

We pass to the method the cache set name and the key, and we get back a Dynamic Entity. If the key can't be found in the cache, then a null will be returned.

Plug-in Test Harness

One of the challenging things with plug-in development is the fact you can't simply hit F5 and debug your plug-in. You must first deploy and register it with the target CRM server and then run a debugger either locally on the server or attach using Visual Studio Remote Debugging capabilities. As you probably noticed in Chapter 3 where we talked about the development environment, I'm not a big fan of having to run Windows Server on your local machine just to be able to debug. During initial plug-in development this process of deploy, register and test can become very cumbersome not to mention tiresome to do over and over again. As we started thinking about the problem we realized the IPlugin interface is pretty simple and it wouldn't be that hard to mock or imitate some of the CRM server capabilities to allow a plug-in to be tested stand alone. To accomplish this we set out to build a test harness that would just be a simple application designed to invoke our plug-ins.

The goal of the plug-in test harness was to allow us to run our plug-ins from a developer machine without needing to have CRM installed. We also wanted to not require the plug-in to be registered to run a test. We also needed to allow the user to specify what stage and what message the plug-in was being invoked for. The other challenge was plug-ins often depend on having access to the data that was passed in the request. This could be a dynamic entity representing a record being created or a Moniker for a record being retrieved or deleted. To accommodate for this we allowed our test harness to retrieve and pass the data as if it was part of a real request.

You can find the plug-in test harness in the book code in the following folder $BookCode/Framework/CTCPluginTester

Connecting to CRM

The first thing you need to do is connect to CRM. To do this click on the button marked "…" next to the server input area and it will launch the standard connect dialog from our AuthHelper assembly as you can see below

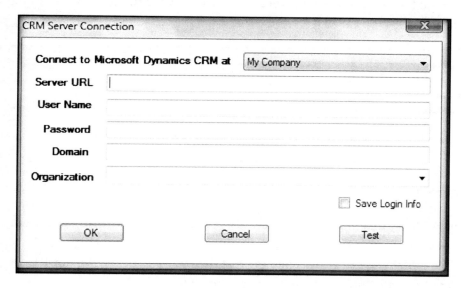

I typically will click the save login info so that next time I don't have to fill out this dialog. Once you are done with the connection information click the connect button.

Since the tester uses the book Framework code including the AuthHelper assembly it's possible if you are running Outlook on your development machine that you can connect and do testing to the local CRM web services in offline mode!

Load the Assembly

Next step is to locate and load the assembly that contains the plug-in that we are going to test. Click the "..." on the assembly input line and it will show a standard file open dialog allowing you to locate and select the assembly containing the plug-in. Once selected, click the Load button and this will load the assembly and detect what classes in the assembly implement IPlugin using reflection.

Setup for Invoking

After loading the plug-in assembly you should choose the plug-in you want to test from the drop down list of plug-ins. This list will show any class in the assembly that implements IPlugin so if your class doesn't show on the list confirm that it implements that interface.

You should also select the Stage and the Event Type. These will be used to setup the call to the plug-in to simulate how it would be called if it were called from the real CRM server.

At this point, you could click the invoke button if you don't want to setup any other configuration.

Specify a Target or Pre-Image

Because your plug-in will likely depend on having data that CRM would provide for the current request we provide two tabs to help by allowing you to specify Target and Pre-Image data. Using these tabs on the tester you can either build the test data by hand or use the Retrieve button to pull test data from the CRM server you are connected to.

The data specified on the data grid for these two tabs is then packaged up and passed along as part of the context data for the plug-in that is being tested. To allow it to be more realistic you can retrieve data from an existing CRM record and then modify the values for your testing. You can also remove values from the grid to simulate them not being provide on the request. For example, if simulating a Create request only the fields that a user fills out on the form in the client interface are passed as part of the Target. So to simulate that you would retrieve an existing CRM record and then delete the rows for the fields you want to not be present.

The following is an example of the Target tab and pulling data for an existing contact record.

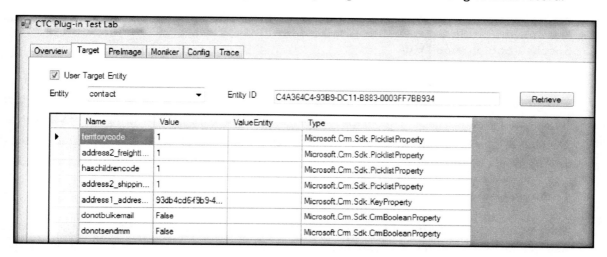

The easiest way to get the Entity Id for an existing record is to open the record in the client interface then press ctrl-N. That will launch the form where you can easily copy the ID from the URL as you can see in the following image.

Specify a Moniker

Some messages like Retrieve and Delete expect to have a Moniker passed in to indicate the name of the entity and the entity ID. Using the Moniker tab you can select an entity and provide the entity ID that will be passed.

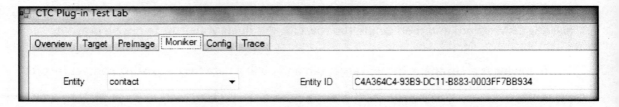

Specify Configuration Data

The other thing you might need to be able to test your plug-in is to have the configuration data passed to it. By convention in our plug-in framework we have chosen to use XML as the format for our configuration data. That made it easy for us to parse it from the string passed and give the plug-in easy access to the values. Using the Config tab you can specify both normal config as well as secure config XML values.

Common Uses

The test harness covers a number of common use test cases like plug-ins that deal with create or delete type requests. In the current implementation there's no support for some of the more advanced scenarios like child pipelines or compound operations. The test harness could easily be enhanced to handle those if that was needed for your solution.

Wrapping it up

In this chapter we presented a framework that you could build your plug-ins with. The goal of the framework is to look for common things you do over and over and package them up into re-usable concepts. Additionally, we looked for opportunities to add tracing support to make your plug-ins more supportable. Finally, using the debugging framework we took aim at how you could test your plug-ins outside the CRM platform.

The concepts presented in this chapter are just ideas. In some cases you might be able to take our sample code and use it as your base classes and use the same model for your development. In other cases, use them as examples to help you understand more about how plug-ins work. In the process of putting these concepts together we did a lot of digging around and have tried to present you some of what we found during that digging. Our goal was to not just give you some sample code, but explain the hows and whys behind the choices made during the chapter to implement the framework.

Combine these concepts with our examples in the next chapter and the plug-in basics we covered in the prior chapter and develop some of your own best practices. The important thing is to have consistency where possible as it makes your plug-ins more supportable in the long run.

14

Plug-in How-To's

In the prior two chapters we explored plug-in development basics and how to package it up into a reusable framework. In both chapters, we focused on the mechanics of how plug-ins work and building a deeper understanding of the inner workings.

This chapter will build on what you learned in those chapters by building some actual utility type plug-ins that can have general purpose use. By general purpose use, these plug-ins won't implement logic that is specific to one project or product.

The goal here is to start putting together some of the pieces and infrastructure that has been discussed in the last two chapters. The following is an overview of the plug-ins that we will be discussing in this chapter.

- Trace Plug-in – This plug-in will demonstrate using the SharedVariables and is used to allow our tracing to minimize overhead when performing its runtime check.
- Data History Plug-in – This plug-in is very handy because it tracks changes to entities and stores a before and after delta of the values that changed. It's configurable too via the plug-in configuration.
- Send To SQL Plug-in – This allows for synchronization of CRM data to a target SQL table and allows for it to mirror the data in the CRM entity.
- Data Rollup Plug-in – This plug-in works on related entities to allow rolling up values from a child entity to a parent using expressions and other basic calculations. The plug-in is configured using a system entity that provides what should be rolled up by the plug-in.

Each of these plug-ins is built on top of or works in conjunction with the plug-in framework we covered in the previous chapter. As we explain each in greater detail we will be highlighting techniques employed to handle each of the different problems.

The source code for each of these is included in the book sample as part of the ctccrm.PluginCommon assembly. You can download the code from the book web site http://www.thecrmbook.com.

Trace Plug-in

One of the features of the plug-in framework shown in this book is it has the ability to do per user tracing of plug-in and workflow operations. This can come in real handy when you're in production and need to turn on tracing for a single user. The following are some of the design goals and concepts demonstrated.

- Allow the capture of trace output from workflows and plug-ins that are built using the framework code in the book.
- Use a custom entity to configure if trace should be enabled for a user and to store the output of the trace as note attachments.
- Allow trace to be turned on by an administrator without touching the user's computer.
- Minimize overhead of plug-in execution – where possible only check if user level trace is enabled on events where it has been indicated - we will accomplish that using a plug-in.
- If there are multiple plug-ins for an event – don't require each of them to retrieve the trace configuration settings – use shared variables to make it available to all plug-ins.

ctccrm_traceconfig Entity

Our first step is to create a custom entity that will allow us to configure which user we want to enable trace for and what options should be applied. We covered this entity and its attributes in detail in Chapter 13 so we won't be repeating that here.

CTCTracePlugin

Our next step is to create a plug-in that will check to see if a ctccrm_traceconfig exists for the user that is executing the plug-in. When a ctccrm_traceconfig is found for the user it is stored in SharedVariables. If you recall from our previous discussion on the plug-in basics in Chapter 12, SharedVariables are available to all plug-ins and workflows that are part of the execution pipeline of the message. So that means once this plug-in runs and places an item in SharedVariables any plug-in or workflow that runs after will be able to see the same data.

The reason we do this is to help minimize overhead. Often times plug-ins can do very simple operations and you wouldn't want to incur overhead during times that you aren't having any problems. Using this design we have flexibility to register this plug-in for all message events in the system or for specific entity / message event combinations.

The code for CTCTracePlugin is part of the ctccrm.plugincommon assembly and you can find the code in the framework folder of the samples $/Framework/PluginCommon/Trace/CTCTracePlugin.cs

```
public void Execute(IPluginExecutionContext context)
{
CTCTraceContext.TraceMode = CTCTraceContext.enumTraceMode.AutoOutput;
CTCTraceContext.Write(this.ToString(), "Starting");
DynamicEntity traceConfig = null;
try
{
    CTCTraceContext.Write(this.ToString(), "about to call retreive");
    traceConfig = RetrieveByUserID(context, context.UserId);

    if (traceConfig == null)
    {
        CTCTraceContext.Write(this.ToString(),
                "Ending- did not find config ");
        return;
    }
}
catch (Exception ex)
{
    CTCTraceContext.Write(ex);
    CTCTraceContext.SaveToFile(@"c:\temp\trace.htm");
}

context.SharedVariables.Properties.Add(
    new PropertyBagEntry("ctccrm_traceconfig",traceConfig));

CTCTraceContext.Write(this.ToString(), "about to trace out config");
CTCTraceContext.Write(this.ToString(), traceConfig);
}
```

As you can see the plug-in code is pretty simple. The UserID is retrieved from the IPluginExecutionContext that is passed to our plug-in. Using that UserID we query ctccrm_traceconfig to look for a matching entry. If we find a matching Trace Config for the user we get it back as a Dynamic Entity.

The following is the query we are using to retrieve the config for the user.

```
protected DynamicEntity RetrieveByUserID(
        IPluginExecutionContext context,Guid userID)
{
    ICrmService service = context.CreateCrmService(false);
    List<DynamicEntity> list = new List<DynamicEntity>();
    RetrieveMultipleRequest req = new RetrieveMultipleRequest();
    req.ReturnDynamicEntities = true;
    QueryExpression qe = new QueryExpression();
    qe.ColumnSet = new AllColumns();
    qe.EntityName = "ctccrm_traceconfig";
    FilterExpression exp = new FilterExpression();
    exp.FilterOperator = LogicalOperator.And;
    ConditionExpression cond = new ConditionExpression();
    cond.AttributeName = "ctccrm_userid";
    object[] valueList = { userID };
    cond.Values = valueList;
    cond.Operator = ConditionOperator.Equal;
    exp.Conditions.Add(cond);
    qe.Criteria = exp;
    req.Query = qe;
    RetrieveMultipleResponse resp =
            service.Execute(req) as RetrieveMultipleResponse;

    BusinessEntityCollection beColl = resp.BusinessEntityCollection;
    foreach (BusinessEntity be in beColl.BusinessEntities)
            list.Add((DynamicEntity)be);
    if (list.Count > 0)
        return list[0];
    else
        return null;
}
```

One thing to note is currently the plug-in doesn't support having multiple Trace Config entries for a single user – only the first one retrieved will be used. It would easily be possible to make that selection more flexible.

You might also notice that this plug-in isn't using the plug-in framework . That was by design to keep this plug-in as simple as possible. We want to be sure we don't create a circular dependency since our plug-in base class relies on checking output from this plug-in seemed best to keep them separate.

Checking SharedVariables

Now that the plug-in is retrieving the Trace Config data we need to modify our base class in the plug-in framework to check to see if trace is configured. Our plug-in base class can be found in the samples folder $Framework/PluginCommon/BaseClasses/CTCPluginBase.cs

The following is a snippet of code from the base class where we are checking SharedVariables to see if trace should be enabled for this specific request.

```
private void CheckAndEnableTrace()
{
    //if no trace config we are done
    if (!m_Context.SharedVariables.Contains("ctccrm_traceconfig"))
        return;

    DynamicEntity config =
        m_Context.SharedVariables["ctccrm_traceconfig"] as DynamicEntity;

    CTCTraceContext.Write(this.ToString(), config);

    //if trace not enabled we are done
    if (!CTCDEPropHelper.GetBooleanValue(config,
                    "ctccrm_enabled", false))
        return;

    //check if plugin input param trace is enabled
    m_TraceInputParams = CTCDEPropHelper.GetBooleanValue(config,
                    "ctccrm_plugininputparameters", false);

    CTCTraceContext.TraceMode =
            CTCTraceContext.enumTraceMode.AutoOutput;


}
```

Wrapping up Trace Plug-in

In this example we looked at how you can easily have plug-ins use SharedVariables to pass data along to other plug-ins in the pipeline. Using this plug-in in combination with the base class that can detect and output the trace on a per –user basis will make it a lot easier for you to track down problems once you get onto the real production server where Visual Studio isn't there to simply run the debugger.

Data History Plug-in

Our next plug-in example is the Data History plug-in which will help you track changes to entities. This type of capability can come in handy when you simply want to keep track of changes but can also be useful where you have data auditing requirements. The following are some of our design goals and concepts demonstrated for the Data History plug-in

- Have the ability to create a history record after a change occurs to a monitored entity
- Have the ability to configure which fields will be stored as part of the history
- Allow execution to happen without drawing attention to the user
- Allow storage in a single custom entity by default but allow each configuration to specify their own custom entity to store the data

ctccrm_datahistory Entity

By default the plug-in we are building is designed to work with the ctccrm_datahistory entity. This can be configured via the plug-in registration configuration. If you want to have a separate data history entity for each entity you are tracking changes on just clone this using the Attribute Replicator tool (See Chapter 8) or manually create the copies. Each of them however, must have the same fields as you see below.

The following are the required attributes for the data history entity.

Attribute	Description
ctccrm_fieldlistpreview	This will hold a comma separate list of what changed.
ctccrm_changedetails	This will contain a detail of what changed including a before and after representation of the data.

In addition to these the standard attributes exist that are created on every custom entity. It's not necessary to have notes or tasks on this entity.

ctccrm_datahistory Relationship

Another key part of storing the data for the history is to be able to record what record this change occurred on. To accomplish that we will depend on a relationship from Data History to the entity that was changed. This is always a N:1 relationship where we relate one data history to the corresponding entity row that was changed. This allows us to also show the data history for a specific entity in the left nav during edit.

If you are using ctccrm_datahistory it is possible to create multiple relationships from it to other entities in the system. You can also create your own entity to store the history and then you would not share it.

As part of the standard relationships created by the system for custom entities the Owner will be a reference to the system user that made the modification.

CTCDataHistoryPlugin

Now that we have a place to store our data history – let's walk through our implementation.

The full code for CTCDataHistoryPlugin is part of the ctccrm.PluginCommon assembly and you can find the code in the framework folder of the samples $/Framework/PluginCommon/Plugins/CTCDataHistoryPlugin.cs

For this plug-in we are going to inherit from our base class CTCPluginBase. As you can see in the following example we inherit from CTCPluginBase and also provide two constructors.

The reason we are implementing both of these constructors is related to the support CRM provides for passing configuration settings to a plug-in. If it detects a constructor that has two string parameters it will pass config and secureconfig to the plug-in. Since we aren't going to process the config directly, we just simply pass that along to our constructor in the base class. We will discuss more on how to use the config data via the base class methods later in the chapter.

```
public class CTCDataHistoryPlugin : CTCPluginBase
{
    public CTCDataHistoryPlugin()
        : base()
```

```
    {
    }

    public CTCDataHistoryPlugin(string config, string secureConfig)
        : base(config, secureConfig)
    {
    }
}
```

Next, we are going to override the HandleAfterOp method of our base class. If you recall from the previous chapter I discussed all the Handle methods and how they take care of the work of checking to make sure the plug-in code is called at the right time. HandleAfterOp will be called after the platform operation occurs and for all platform operations.

From the 50,000 foot perspective here's what the flow of our plug-in does

- Validate that we were passed enough data to keep going.
- Setup an ADO.NET DataTable to hold the field change history.
- Loop through each property passed and update the DataTable.
- Using the DataTable to build out two strings; one with a field summary and one with the detail.
- Create the history record based on the configured data history entity.

```
public override void HandleAfterOp()
{
    if (!IsValidRequest())
        return;

    DataTable dt = SetupDataTable();

    foreach (Property PreProp in this.TargetPreImage.Properties)
        AddRowForProperty(dt, PreProp);

    if (dt.Rows.Count < 1)
    {
        this.CTCTrace.Write(this.ToString(), "No auditted fields ");
        return;
    }

    StringBuilder sbFields = new StringBuilder();
    StringBuilder sbChanges = new StringBuilder();

    BuildChangeHistory(dt, sbFields, sbChanges);
```

```
    string keyName = InputTargetDE.Name + "id";
    Guid keyValue = Guid.Empty;

    keyValue = CTCDEPropHelper.GetKeyValue(InputTargetDE, keyName);
    CTCTrace.Write(this.ToString(), " Key Value= " +
                                    keyValue.ToString());

    CreateDataHistory(sbFields, sbChanges, keyName, keyValue);
}
```

Now let's walk through each of these areas in more details and see how it works.

Our first method we are going to look at is the IsValidRequest method. The key take away from this method is the fact that you need to be defensive when building your plug-ins to ensure that you are invoked with the proper parameters. This is important because CRM provides you the flexibility to register a plug-in for multiple events. Because of that, it doesn't try to validate when you register your plug-in that the configuration registered is appropriate for what your plug-in expects for operation.

```
private bool IsValidRequest()
{
    if (this.TargetPreImage == null)
    {
        this.CTCTrace.Write(this.ToString(),
            "No Target PreImage DE Found ");
        return false;
    }
    if (this.InputTargetDE == null)
    {
        this.CTCTrace.Write(this.ToString(),
            "No Input Target DE Found ");
        return false;
    }
    string keyName = InputTargetDE.Name + "id";
    Guid keyValue = Guid.Empty;
    if (!CTCDEPropHelper.PropertyExists(InputTargetDE, keyName))
    {
        this.CTCTrace.Write(this.ToString(),
            "No key ID was found, ");
        return false;
    }
  return true;
}
```

The SetupDataTable method isn't all that interesting, it just adds the columns to an ADO.NET DataTable that we will use to populate in a later method.

```
private static DataTable SetupDataTable()
{
    DataTable dt = new DataTable();
    dt.Columns.Add("PropertyName");
    dt.Columns.Add("StartValue");
    dt.Columns.Add("EndValue");
    return dt;
}
```

The next thing we do is loop through all the properties on the Pre-Image. The TargetPreImage property is a Dynamic Entity object that contains the value of all the entity properties prior to the operation. The properties it will contain is set based on what is configured at the time of registration. When you register this plug-in you specify that you want a pre-image and which specific fields should be passed. In the plug-in this is used to determine which fields we care about changes for.

In the AddRowForProperty method we will look to see if the matching property was provided as part of the request . CRM doesn't pass all properties all the time on the request. For example, if you only updated a single field on the form only that field plus the key would be provided.

```
private void AddRowForProperty(DataTable dt, Property PreProp)
{
    string propName = PreProp.Name;
    string startValue = CTCDEPropHelper.GetPropertyValue(PreProp);

    foreach (Property PostProp in this.InputTargetDE.Properties)
    {
        if (propName == PostProp.Name)
        {
            string endValue =
                    CTCDEPropHelper.GetUserReadableValue(PostProp);

            if (startValue != endValue)
            {
                DataRow oRow = dt.NewRow();
                oRow["PropertyName"] = propName;
                oRow["StartValue"] = startValue;
                oRow["EndValue"] = endValue;

                dt.Rows.Add(oRow);
```

```
                    }
                break;
            }
        }
}
```

Before we jump to our next method, let's take a quick look at a helper function GetUserReadableValue from the CTCDEPropHelper class. CTCDEPropHelper class is just a bunch of utility methods to try to help make it easier to work with Dynamic Entities.

You probably noticed that when we were working with Property objects which is the parent class for each of the Dynamic Entity Property types. For example, they are really StringProperty or whatever type of property but are easier to work with by using their parent class. The purpose of the GetUserReadableValue method is to take a generic property and give back a string representation of the property based on the type.

```
public static string GetUserReadableValue(Property prop)
{
    return GetPropertyValue(prop, true);
}
```

Ok, so the actual method that does all the work is GetPropertyValue. GetUserReadableValue is just a short cut to tell the GetPropertyValue method that we want a user readable value. What that does is cause things like a Lookup field to give back the name instead of a Guid value.

As you can see in the following example, each of the property types can be a little different.

```
public static string GetPropertyValue(Property prop, bool UserReadable)
{
    switch (prop.GetType().ToString())
    {
        case "Microsoft.Crm.Sdk.StringProperty":
            return ((Microsoft.Crm.Sdk.StringProperty)prop).Value;
        case "Microsoft.Crm.Sdk.CrmMoneyProperty":
            return ((CrmMoneyProperty)prop).Value.Value.ToString();
        case "Microsoft.Crm.Sdk.PicklistProperty":
            if (UserReadable)
                return ((PicklistProperty)prop).Value.name;
            return ((PicklistProperty)prop).Value.Value.ToString();
        case "Microsoft.Crm.Sdk.LookupProperty":
```

```
        if (UserReadable)
            return ((LookupProperty)prop).Value.name;
        return ((LookupProperty)prop).Value.Value.ToString();

    ...Some code omitted for readability....
    }

    return "";
}
```

You might notice the source for BuildChangeHistory isn't printed , but you can view it in the samples. The reason is simple it's more generic .Net formatting logic.

At this point, we have built our change data into two strings; one that is a preview and one that is the details. Now it's time to build a dynamic Entity and call the create method. You will notice we are calling GetConfigValue in a few places that retrieves configuration information that was set at the time the plug-in step was registered.

```
private Guid CreateDataHistory(StringBuilder sbFields,
            StringBuilder sbChanges, string keyName, Guid keyValue)
{
    DynamicEntity de = new DynamicEntity(
                GetConfigValue("Entity", "ctccrm_datahistory"));
    CTCDEPropHelper.AddStringProperty(de,
                "ctccrm_fieldlistpreview", sbFields.ToString());
    CTCDEPropHelper.AddStringProperty(de,
                "ctccrm_changedetails", sbChanges.ToString());
    if (keyValue != Guid.Empty)
    {
        CTCDEPropHelper.AddLookupProperty(de,
                GetConfigValue("RegardingAttribute",
                "ctccrm_" + keyName), InputTargetDE.Name, keyValue);
    }
    else
    {
        CTCTrace.Write(this.ToString(),
                "Not adding regarding attribute");
    }

    this.SystemService.Create((BusinessEntity)de);
    return keyValue;
}
```

Workflow vs. Plug-in

One question you might be asking is why not just use a workflow to accomplish this? I have seen samples that do that. Technically, there's no reason you couldn't do something similar with workflow but it would be slightly different.

First, let's look at it from a workflow you created with the user interface workflow editor. In that scenario, there's no way to have a generic entity e.g crmbook_datahistory that you used for storing changes from multiple entities. Also, from the workflow editor, it doesn't give you any ability to concatenate strings or otherwise combine things together so your change history would have to be assignment of properties in the input to the output. In fact, if using the workflow web editor each property would have to be specific to the type you are trying to save because the workflow editor won't let you assign unlike types. The biggest challenge you would have is you don't really have access to the pre-image of the data. So the way I have seen this accomplished with workflow really is just storing a duplicate of the data at that point in time which technically becomes history once the data has been updated again. Finally, using this approach you would have to create workflow for each specific entity you want to track changes on. There's no ability to create a generic Data History workflow using the user interface workflow editor.

The other way you could accomplish this would be to create a custom workflow activity e.g DataHistoryActivity, that you would register and then reference from a user interface workflow. Using this approach you would still create a workflow for each entity that you wanted to track changes. You would have more flexibility as to where to store the history data like we do in the plug-in approach because ultimately the custom activity is just code like the plug-in.

Using a plug-in you gain the ability to have a little more control over when the plug-in runs and if your user knows it ran. For example, you might have a requirement to do auditing in a synchronous or pre-operation fashion. That can only be accomplished using the plug-in approach. In cases where you don't want the users to see the workflows running to create the audit/history plug-ins happen behind the scenes and really unless they cause an error the use would never know it existed. Plug-ins are a little less configurable on the fly than a workflow is since using the workflow approach it could be configured using the web editor. I'm not sure how big of a deal that is because most the time this type of system feature is not changed often once established for an entity.

The bottom line from my perspective is if you don't have the ability to do a plug-in then workflow is a good approach otherwise use a plug-in.

MVP Tip: Microsoft CRM MVP Marco Amoedo adds that the decision about when to use workflows and when to use plug-ins can be confusing in Microsoft Dynamics CRM v4.0. Some of the improvements, like the asynchronous plug-ins and the on update workflows had made more difficult to determine which technique we should apply to fulfill a requirement. But the main rule, as it happens in this audit case, is normally to analyze what you want to achieve in your particular requirement and then choose the technique that best fits. For example, if your audit trail need is limited to a few entities (and this is not likely to change), and you are happy with just having a record of changes of data but not to store the previous value on the same record then workflows are fine. Otherwise you should start to look to plug-in. A good example of this type of workflow can be found on the Microsoft Dynamics CRM Team blog.

In general, using the trick of thinking in workflows as a way of mapping business processes (such an approval process, sales process, escalation process, etc) and in plug-ins as a way to enforce or add some business rules and logic to the platform, like complex validations, advanced data auditing, integration with other systems, etc; would help you to start the evaluation of which technique fits best for your requirement. However, this is not a fixed rule and you always should check the pros and cons for your own situation. You can read Marco's blog at http://marcoamoedo.com

Wrapping up Data History Plug-in

The Data History plug-in shows an example of using a number of the plug-in capabilities including pre/post images and configuration settings. By using configuration you can alter how this plug-in works allowing it to be configured for your particular use. At runtime you can decide if you want to put all history in a single entity or have multiple for each entity you are tracking history on. Configuration being done at registration time makes this less of a on and off type thing and when combined with the ability to just happen behind the scenes this becomes almost like it's a built-in feature of a system.

Send To SQL Plug-in

The SendToSQL Plug-in is a simple example of using the plug-in capabilities of the platform to push data to another system. In this example, we will use SQL Server as the target but this could be done with an ERP system or any other external system that exposes an API.

Similar to the Data History plug-in we are going to use the configuration data provided at the time the plug-in step is registered to control what the plug-in will be doing. The following shows inheriting from CTCPluginBase and implementing the two constructors to ensure that the platform provides the configuration settings to the plug-in when it's instantiated.

```
public class CTCSendToSQLPlugin : CTCPluginBase
{
    public CTCSendToSQLPlugin()
        : base()
    {
    }

    public CTCSendToSQLPlugin(string config, string secureConfig)
        : base(config, secureConfig)
    {
    }
}
```

In this example we will be implementing a method for each operation that can modify the data. Rather than having to write custom code to check the plug-in context to see what event we are being invoked for we have instead elected to use more specific methods. If you recall in our Data History example we just used the HandleAfterOp method which would be called for each message. That worked ok because we really didn't have different logic that we wanted to perform based on if it's a create, update or delete event/message.

TIP

You can create your own base class that inherits from CTCPluginBase and add some of your own common functionality. Using this approach you can promote consistency across the different plug-ins that you build.

In our case here we have different logic so it makes more sense to override the more specific methods. As you can see in the following code example we have overridden HandleAfterOpCreate. This method will only be called when our plug-in is invoked during the post operation phase and only if the message being processed is a create. In chapter 13, we gave you a list of all the specific override methods our CTCBasePlugin exposes.

```
public override void HandleAfterOpCreate()
```

```
{
    List<DBSPParm> parms = new List<DBSPParm>();
    string sqlInsert = BuildInsert(
            GetConfigValue("SQLTable", ""),parms);
    execCmdInsert(sqlInsert, parms.ToArray());


}
```

Our processing in the HandleAfterOpCreate method is pretty straight forward. Our goal is to build a list of parameters to be passed to a SQL insert command. The build Insert method which we will look at later in the chapter simply takes a table name that it retrieves from the configuration settings. It then builds an insert based on the contents of the InputTargetDE property that we expose in the base class and contains the data items that were passed to the platform by the requester of the create.

The following is a similar example of the Update to show you how you can handle the different message types using the override methods as well as vary what processing is actually done.

```
public override void HandleAfterOpUpdate()
{
    List<DBSPParm> parms = new List<DBSPParm>();
    string sqlUpdate = BuildUpdate(
                GetConfigValue("SQLTable", ""), parms);
    execCmdModify(sqlUpdate, parms.ToArray());
}
```

A similar method to the above two exists for delete however is not shown to conserve print space.

The following method helps us build the insert SQL, it basically loops through all the properties in the InputTargetDE and gets a value as an object. The reason for this is it needs to be able to hand it off to SQL in the correct type (e.g . double as a double)

```
private string BuildInsert(string tableName,List<DBSPParm> parms)
{
    StringBuilder sb = new StringBuilder();
    StringBuilder sbValues = new StringBuilder();
    sb.AppendFormat("insert into {0} (", tableName);
    bool firstTime = true;
    foreach (Property PreProp in this.InputTargetDE.Properties)
    {
        string propName = PreProp.Name;
        object startValue =
                CTCDEPropHelper.GetPropertyValueAsObject(PreProp);
        if (!firstTime)
        {
            sb.Append(",");
            sbValues.Append(",");
        }
        else
            firstTime = false;

        sb.AppendFormat("{0}", propName);
        sbValues.AppendFormat("@{0}", propName);
        DBSPParm parm = new DBSPParm("@" + propName, startValue);
        parms.Add(parm);

    }

    sb.AppendFormat(") values({0})", sbValues.ToString());

    return sb.ToString();

}
```

One key area to note is around handling of the more complex property types. In the above example we don't really accommodate for multi value property types. A good example of one of those is a Lookup Property. A Lookup Property has three items that are really values from the perspective of what we are trying to accomplish. First, you have the Entity Name that represents the type of entity it is a lookup for. Second is the Entity ID. Finally the name that is the readable version. You would need to expand and handle those as well if you wanted to have the full data stored.

The following is just standard ADO.NET insert logic used to execute the SQL statement that was built.

```
private void execCmdInsert(string sCmd, DBSPParm[] oParms)
{
    SqlConnection dbCon = GetConnection();

    try
    {
        SqlCommand dbCmd = new SqlCommand(sCmd, dbCon);
        dbCmd.CommandType = CommandType.Text;
        if (oParms != null)
            foreach (DBSPParm oWorkParm in oParms)
                oWorkParm.AddToDBCommand(ref dbCmd);

        dbCmd.ExecuteNonQuery();

    }
    catch (Exception e)
    {
        TraceSQLParms(sCmd, oParms);
        CloseConnection(dbCon);
        HandleSQLException(e);
        throw new Exception("execCmdInsert - " +
                      sCmd + " - " + e.Message, e);
    }
    finally
    {
        CloseConnection(dbCon);
    }
}
```

Wrapping Up SendToSQL Plug-in

In this example we highlighted using a plug-in for the purpose of sending data to another data repository or an external system. While the version implemented in this chapter is rather simple, it does highlight what you can accomplish.

MVP Tip: Microsoft CRM MVP Marco Amoedo adds when it comes to integration to other systems, or just storing data on other places using plug-ins it's good to keep queuing technologies in mind because they can be very useful if you have failover requirements. For example, to make a bespoke integration with another system you can generate MSMQ messages (a queuing technology from Microsoft that is available on most of the Windows OS, including Windows mobile) to notify the create/update to the other system and have a service processing the message queue to consolidate this data operations on the integrated system. This will provide to your plug-ins all the benefits derived of using queuing technologies, like avoid the loss of sync if the other system is down since all the data operations notifications would be queued waiting a nothing will be lost. You can read Marco's blog at http://marcoamoedo.com.

Data Rollup Plug-in

Our next example is a Data Rollup Plug-in. The goal of this plug-in is to take values of children that were updated and post the values to a parent record. Typically this is where there are multiple records but it is possible to do this where there's a 1:1 relationship. Before we jump into the code let's go over some of our design goals and concepts we will handle in this plug-in.

- Allow for zero to many fields to be rolled up from a child entity to a parent entity.
- Allow each parent to have multiple rollups defined for its children.
- Where possible retrieve all children rows and use them for multiple calculations.
- Allow use of an ADO.NET style expression to calculate or determine the value stored.
- Allow indication of a separate field on the child as source and the target field on the parent.
- Allow use of an ADO.NET style filter to limit which children will qualify for inclusion in the calculation.
- Allow configuration of which fields get rolled up via a custom entity so they can be modified via the user interface.

ctccrm_rollup Custom Entity

The following is an example of the custom entity we are going to use to store the configuration.

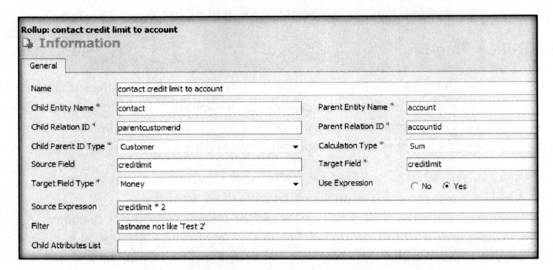

The following are the required attributes for the data history entity.

Attribute	Description
ctccrm_calculationtype	The type of calculation to use for the rollup. Choices are Sum, Average, Minimum, and Maximum.
ctccrm_childattributelist	Comma separated list of attributes needed for the rollup. This included attributes needed for the filter and the expression.
ctccrm_childentityname	Name of the child entity.
ctccrm_childrelationattributename	Name of the attribute on the child entity that holds the ID for the relationship to the parent.
ctccrm_filter	ADO.NET filter expression for limiting the child rows used in the rollup.
ctccrm_parentattributeidname	Name of the attribute on the Parent entity that holds the ID for the relationship.

Attribute	Description
ctccrm_parententityname	Name of the Parent entity.
ctccrm_relationattributeidtype	The type of the attribute on the child that relates to the parent.
ctccrm_sourceexpression	The expression used on the data to get the source value for the calculation.
ctccrm_sourcefield	Attribute on the child used for the calculation.
ctccrm_targetfield	Attribute on the parent to store the result of the rollup.
ctccrm_useexpression	Indicates an expression should be used to determine the value instead of a calculation.

The above allow for a basic functioning rollup plug-in and sets up the ability to extend the concept to handle specific application needs you encounter.

CTCRollupPlugin

The code for CTCRollupPlugin is part of the ctccrm.PluginCommon assembly and you can find the code in the framework folder of the samples $/Framework/PluginCommon/Plugins/CTCRollupPlugin.cs.

Like our other plug-ins CTCRollupPlugin will take advantage of the CTCPluginbase base class.

```
public class CTCRollupPlugin : CTCPluginBase
{
}
```

Unlike a couple of the other examples, this plug-in doesn't rely on the plug-in configuration. It uses a custom entity to store the data that is used to configure its operation.

To make our plug-in more efficient we are going to use the cache feature we discussed in Chapter 13. Caching is built in to our CTCPluginbase class. To use the cache we must override the RegisterDataCacheSets method which is called once the first time the plug-in is executed in a process.

In the RegisterDataCacheSets method we can register one or more Cache Queries. A Cache Query is simply a QueryExpression just like we would use with a RetreieveMultiple call. The advantage of using this approach is we let the common cache code manage when to use the query to fetch the data. This approach also allows one copy of the data to be shared with multiple plug-in instances as well as multiple calls to the same plug-in. You will notice in the following example that a TimeSpan is passed to control expiration. When the time passes it will attempt to re-execute the query and reload the cache with any special code in our rollup plug-in.

The following is the registration of the query against the ctccrm_rollup entity to pull all of the rollup configurations.

```
public override void RegisterDataCacheSets(IPluginExecutionContext
context)
{
    QueryExpression qe = new QueryExpression();
    qe.ColumnSet = new AllColumns();
    qe.Distinct = false;
    qe.EntityName = "ctccrm_rollup";
    FilterExpression exp = new FilterExpression();
    exp.FilterOperator = LogicalOperator.And;
    qe.Criteria = exp;
    this.RegisterCacheQuery(context, "ctccrm_rollup",
            qe, "ctccrm_rollupid", new TimeSpan(1, 0, 0));
}
```

Our next step is to override the HandleAfterOp method. We use the after operation because it gives us the most flexibility. For example, just using configuration of the plug-in step registration we can determine if our plug-in will run asynchronous or synchronous.

The processing in our handle method is pretty simple as most of the real work is done in the sub methods. After checking to see if we are passed a valid Input Target we then proceed to call GetRollups to retrieve the rollup configurations from cache. After that if there were not any rollups configured we exit the plug-in. Finally, we call ProcessRollups which will do all the hard work and we will look at later in the chapter.

```
public override void HandleAfterOp()
{
    if (this.InputTargetDE == null)
    {
        this.CTCTrace.Write(this.ToString(),
            "No Input Target DE Found ");
        return;
    }

    List<DynamicEntity> rollups = GetRollups(this.InputTargetDE.Name);

    if (rollups == null || rollups.Count < 1)
    {
        this.CTCTrace.Write(this.ToString(),
            "No rollups found for entity");
        return;
    }

    ProcessRollups(rollups);

}
```

TIP

Not shown in this plug-in is more aggressive validation to ensure that we are called at the right time and for an expected entity. You might want to consider adding more validation depending on where your plug-in will be used and the sophistication of the admin that is doing the configuration.

The GetRollups methods job is to request the currently cached ctccrm_rollup entities from the Cache. To accomplish that we call the this.GetCacheItemsDynEntity method and pass the name we used when we registered our cache query "ctccrm_rollup". The caching routines will attempt to locate and if necessary invoke our cache query to retrieve the items. Once we get the data from cache manager we simply filter it based on the child entity that was passed as the childType parameter. Finally, we sort the rollup items found based on parent entity and the child attribute names to allow for similar items to be processed at the same time.

```
private List<DynamicEntity> GetRollups(string childType)
{
    List<DynamicEntity> list = new List<DynamicEntity>();

    List<DynamicEntity> cacheList =
        this.GetCacheItemsDynEntity(this.Context, "ctccrm_rollup");

    foreach (DynamicEntity de in cacheList)
    {
        if (String.Compare(CTCDEPropHelper.GetStringValue(de,
                "ctccrm_childentityname"), childType, true) == 0)
            list.Add(de);
    }

    list.Sort(CompareRollup);

    return list;
}
```

The ProcessRollups method basically walks thru each rollup that was found to match the record being processed. For each found, it will call RetreiveParentandChild and then call ProcessSingleRollup that will actually do the calculations and update the parent record.

```
private void ProcessRollups(List<DynamicEntity> rollups)
{
    string lastParentType = "";
    string lastChildRelationID = "";
    DynamicEntity parent = null;
    List<DynamicEntity> children = new List<DynamicEntity>();

    foreach (DynamicEntity de in rollups)
    {
        RetrieveParentAndChildren(ref lastParentType,
            ref lastChildRelationID, ref parent, ref children, de);

        if (parent == null)
            continue;

        ProcessSingleRollup(de, parent, children);
    }
}
```

The RetrieveParentandChildren method is responsible for determining what data needs to be retrieved to do the rollup. The parameter named "de" contains the ctccrm_rollup and is used to determine what data is needed. We use two query helper methods RetrieveFirstBySingleKey and RetrieveMultipleBySingleKey that are part of our base plug-in class to make doing basic queries easier.

```
private void RetrieveParentAndChildren(ref string lastParentType,
        ref string lastChildRelationID, ref DynamicEntity parent,
        ref List<DynamicEntity> children, DynamicEntity de)
{
    string currentParentType =
            CTCDEPropHelper.GetStringValue(de,
"ctccrm_parententityname");
    string currentChildRelationID =
            CTCDEPropHelper.GetStringValue(de,
"ctccrm_childrelationattributeidname");
    int childRelationIdType =
            CTCDEPropHelper.GetPicklistValue(de,
"ctccrm_relationattributeidtype", 0);
    string childType =
            CTCDEPropHelper.GetStringValue(de, "ctccrm_childentityname");
    string parentAttributeIdName =
            CTCDEPropHelper.GetStringValue(de,
                    "ctccrm_parentattributeidname");

    if (lastParentType != currentParentType ||
        lastChildRelationID != currentChildRelationID)
    {
        Guid parentID = Guid.Empty;
        if (CTCDEPropHelper.PropertyExists(this.InputTargetDE,
                        currentChildRelationID))
        {
            parentID = GetParentIDFromDE(currentChildRelationID,
                        childRelationIdType, parentID);
        }

        parent = this.RetrieveFirstBySingleKey(currentParentType,
                    parentAttributeIdName, parentID);

        children = this.RetrieveMultipleBySingleKey(childType,
                    currentChildRelationID, parentID);
    }

    lastParentType = currentParentType;
    lastChildRelationID = currentChildRelationID;
}
```

One thing you might notice is the GetParentIDFromDE method. Since the parent ID can be of different data types in the child record we need to check what type the key is and get the appropriate value. Lookups, OwnerID and CustomerID are the ones we support.

```
private Guid GetParentIDFromDE(string currentChildRelationID,
                        int childRelationIdType, Guid parentID)
{
    if (childRelationIdType == (int)enumRelationType.Lookup)
        parentID = CTCDEPropHelper.GetLookupValue(
              this.InputTargetDE, currentChildRelationID);
    else if (childRelationIdType == (int)enumRelationType.Owner)
        parentID = CTCDEPropHelper.GetOwnerValue(
              this.InputTargetDE, currentChildRelationID);
    else if (childRelationIdType == (int)enumRelationType.Customer)
        parentID = CTCDEPropHelper.GetCustomerValue(
              this.InputTargetDE, currentChildRelationID);
    return parentID;
}
```

Now that we have the parent and all the children, we are going to use a DataView so we can leverage its expression capability. Since our children are currently in Dynamic Entity objects we will need to convert the fields we care about that will be done in the BuildViewForRollup method. Once we have done that we can calculate the result value in CalculateValueFromView. Our final step is to call the UpdateParentWithResult method to post the result value back to the parent entity.

```
private void ProcessSingleRollup(DynamicEntity rollup,
        DynamicEntity parent, List<DynamicEntity> children)
{
    string sourceField =
        CTCDEPropHelper.GetStringValue(rollup, "ctccrm_sourcefield");
    string targetField =
        CTCDEPropHelper.GetStringValue(rollup, "ctccrm_targetfield");
    int calculationType =
        CTCDEPropHelper.GetPicklistValue(rollup,
"ctccrm_calculationtype", 0);
    int targetFieldType =
        CTCDEPropHelper.GetPicklistValue(rollup,
"ctccrm_targetfieldtype", 0);
    bool useExpression =
        CTCDEPropHelper.GetBooleanValue(rollup, "ctccrm_useexpression",
false);

    DataView dv = BuildViewForRollup(rollup, children, sourceField);
```

```
    double result = 0.0;
    string column = sourceField;
    if (useExpression)
        column = "ExpressionValue";

    result = CalculateValueFromView(calculationType, dv, result,
column);

    UpdateParentWithResult(parent, targetField, targetFieldType,
result);
}
```

The following is an abbreviated example of the BuildViewRollup. The GetChildrenDT method is called to get a DataTable and then we create a DataView of that using the rollup configuration options.

```
private DataView BuildViewForRollup(DynamicEntity rollup,
            List<DynamicEntity> children, string sourceField)
{

...Some processing omitted to save space...

    DataTable dtChildren = GetChildrenDT(children,
            sourceField, sourceExpression, otherAttributes);

    DataView dv = new DataView(dtChildren,
            filter, "", DataViewRowState.CurrentRows);
    return dv;
}
```

The GetChildrenDT method uses a helper method on the CTCDataTableHelper class that converts a Dynamic Entity to an ADO.NET DataTable. You will notice it also accepts which attributes should be copied. This method also handles creating the expression field if one was specified on the ctccrm_config.

```
private DataTable GetChildrenDT(List<DynamicEntity> children,
   string sourceField, string sourceExpression, string[] otherAttributes)
{
    if (otherAttributes != null)
    {
        List<string> s = new List<string>(otherAttributes);
```

```
            if (!s.Contains(sourceField))
            {
                s.Add(sourceField);
                otherAttributes = s.ToArray();
            }
        }
        DataTable dt = new DataTable();
        foreach (DynamicEntity entity in children)
            CTCDataTableHelper.ConvertToDataTable(dt, entity,
                                                  otherAttributes);

        if (sourceExpression != "")
            dt.Columns.Add("ExpressionValue",
                    Type.GetType("System.Double"), sourceExpression);

        return dt;
    }
```

The Calculate method basically determines which type of calculation should be performed and calls the correct method.

```
private double CalculateValueFromView(int calculationType,
        DataView dv, double result, string column)
{
    if (calculationType == (int)enumCalcType.Sum)
        result = GetSum(dv, column);
    else if (calculationType == (int)enumCalcType.Average)
        result = GetAverage(dv, column);
    else if (calculationType == (int)enumCalcType.Min)
        result = GetMin(dv, column);
    else if (calculationType == (int)enumCalcType.Max)
        result = GetMax(dv, column);
    return result;
}
```

Finally, the UpdateParentWithResult method will add the result field to the Parent dynamic entity and then call the update method.

```
private void UpdateParentWithResult(DynamicEntity parent,
        string targetField, int targetFieldType, double result)
```

```
{
    if (targetFieldType == (int)enumTargetFieldType.Decimal)
        CTCDEPropHelper.AddDecimalProperty(parent,
                targetField, Convert.ToDecimal(result));
    else if (targetFieldType == (int)enumTargetFieldType.Float)
        CTCDEPropHelper.AddFloatProperty(parent, targetField, result);
    else if (targetFieldType == (int)enumTargetFieldType.Integer)
        CTCDEPropHelper.AddNumberProperty(parent,
            targetField, Convert.ToInt32(Math.Round(result, 0)));
    else if (targetFieldType == (int)enumTargetFieldType.Money)
        CTCDEPropHelper.AddMoneyProperty(parent,
                targetField, Convert.ToDecimal(result));

    this.SystemService.Update((BusinessEntity)parent);
}
```

Wrapping up CTCRollupPlugin

As you can probably tell, this plug-in took a little bit of code and can easily handle several different business problems that you might encounter. More importantly it demonstrates use of some of the different techniques like caching and using a custom entity to drive the plug-in operation.

Wrapping it up

In this chapter we have looked at a few different examples of building plug-ins. In the process we tried to show some examples of using some of the capabilities of the plug-in framework that ships with the book.   These examples are provided to get you started thinking about some of your own ideas. We also hope that these might help solve some problems you encounter in your solutions.

15

Workflow Re-Energized

Microsoft CRM 3.0 provided a workflow engine that could be used by developers and system administrators to implement simple business process automation ("BPA"). The workflow engine in CRM 3.0 was implemented as a proprietary workflow engine. In fact, to create and manage the workflows, you had to remote into the CRM web server and run a CRM 3.0 proprietary Windows application that was used to define the flow. The proprietary engine had many limitations such as not being able to trigger a workflow on an update event. Developers also had to use CRM specific system knowledge to create custom workflows. We will compare and contrast more of the differences later, but for now let's just say it wasn't a great story.

Microsoft completely re-energizes workflow in CRM 4.0 by not only replacing the workflow engine but by re-architecting how workflow is plumbed to integrate with the platform. The first big change was dropping the proprietary workflow engine and replacing it with Microsoft's flagship workflow engine Windows Workflow Foundation. This is a major improvement and allows CRM to start to benefit from the significant investments that Microsoft has made in Windows Workflow Foundation. You can now learn workflow as a developer skill and use it on more than one Microsoft product. Other products such as Speech Server and SharePoint to name a couple also use Windows Workflow Foundation as their workflow engine. If you already have done some Windows Workflow Foundation development, then all you will be learning is how it is integrated and works within CRM.

While this change is a major one for developers, Microsoft also exposes for the first time the ability for users to create their own workflows using the normal client interfaces. In fact, these custom user defined workflows can also reference and include custom workflow activities that developers build to further extend the platform. The ability for users to easily include custom workflow activities is done using the same techniques the user uses when building a workflow with the standard built-in workflow activities.

In the rest of this chapter we are going to set the stage for our next several chapters where we discuss workflow. Each subsequent chapter will be diving deeper into the platforms workflow capabilities.

Understanding Business Process Automation

Like many things, if you asked ten people what business process automation (BPA) is you would probably get several different answers. But each would have the theme that they automate some aspect of a process with the intent of making the business more efficient or increasing the velocity in which a business can operate. BPA kicks in after data has been input or captured because only then can it be acted on by an automated process. Without data there isn't a lot of automation that can happen.

Business process automation is the act of giving the system instructions that it can carry out to automate what would otherwise be a manual step or steps. To make this more tangible, imagine you call a realtor and say you're interested in selling your house. The realtor spends 10-20 minutes with you and finds out all about your house and gives you a proposal. At this point you review the information and plan to get back to it next week. The realtor, being a busy person, forgets about you. Big problem for them, they just lost an opportunity. What if they could invoke a "New Seller Prospect" automation that 3 days after first contact sends a couple of interesting tidbits about how they work to you, and then 5 days later schedules a follow-up call to see if you're still interested. That's an example of BPA and also an example of something a simple workflow could facilitate.

It's easy when talking about CRM to jump to a sales related example, but Workflow can automate many back office tasks as well. For example, I travel a lot and keeping track of the details of my trips seemed like a perfect fit for a custom entity named Business Trip. Workflow comes into the picture because there are several tasks that have to happen before and after the event. Workflow can be used to automate the creation of those tasks. That workflow can then be reused for each trip. That's a simple example that has nothing to do with a sales process and we will look at more complex examples in the upcoming chapters.

As we explore the use of Workflow / BPA in the Microsoft CRM 4.0 release you will be able to implement simple and complex business process automations that will deliver sustainable value back to your client or organization.

Looking back at CRM 3.0

Microsoft CRM 3.0 implemented a proprietary workflow engine that was only exposed for administrators to define workflows. In fact, for an administrator to manage the workflows, they had to remote into the CRM web server and run a CRM 3.0 proprietary Windows application that was used to define the flow. This same Windows application provided monitoring of the workflow (if you could call it that).

The workflows in CRM 3.0 were triggered by a few basic entity events. For example if a Contact was created you could cause this workflow to run. However, key events such as update were not available to trigger the start of a workflow. This kept workflow from being a viable solution for many problems that needed to detect and respond to the update event. In these cases users were required to implement callouts that ran in line with the update or save of the form by the user. While this solution worked, often it caused the save or update process to run longer than necessary for the user. That approach also did not have much in the way of ability to do real "workflow" as the callout must finish so the control of the form could be returned to the user.

The scariest thing was trying to find someone that was a "Workflow Guru". This wasn't like finding a C# developer. You needed someone that had done specific work on Microsoft CRM 3.0. Going forward in CRM 4.0 having it based on Windows Workflow Foundation we will see a much more extensive set of resources and people to help out that have basic training on workflow and just need to learn the CRM specifics.

CRM 3.0 workflow ran on the CRM web server. This created a scale out problem if you wanted to run in a cluster or move workflow to its own workflow cluster. It simply wasn't designed for that. This meant that you ended up designating a single CRM web server to run the workflow process.

As we look into more about how this changes in 4.0 you will more fully understand the magnitude of this change and how CRM 4.0 brings an enterprise scale workflow solution to the table that will have much broader support.

Workflow in CRM 4.0

Microsoft CRM 4.0 has dumped the proprietary implementation of workflow in favor of leveraging Windows Workflow Foundation. This game changer gives a number of opportunities for user and developers to create some interesting solutions. Often times not even requiring custom code but simply done using the workflow editor in the client interface.

Let's walk through what this means from a high level perspective then in subsequent chapters we can drill down to more detail. The CRM team has used many of the extensibility points of Windows Workflow Foundation to integrate it with the CRM platform. From a users point of view they see the concept of workflow but will never see it labeled as Windows Workflow Foundation. Users will however be able to now create their own workflows, if security permits using a pretty straight forward workflow editor from within the client interface. I will walk you through how all that works in Chapter 16 but you can look at the following image to see an example of the workflow editor.

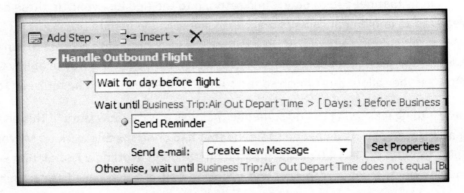

In addition to being able to define workflows, users are able to run them on demand if they are configured for that type of execution. Users are also able to view the progress of workflows from each entity by navigating to the workflow link available on each entity. There they will be able to see the progress and if any workflow is executing and if so what step of the workflow it's in. Compare this level of user visibility with what CRM 3.0 had and you can immediately see that this is a huge improvement to how CRM 3.0 worked.

The execution of workflows has been greatly improved as well. System Administrators and those responsible for capacity planning and keeping things running will greatly appreciate the new runtime architecture. The execution of workflows can now run on multiple servers allowing a much greater scaling story than CRM 3.0 had. CRM 3.0 was limited to running the workflow processes on a single node. Administrators can also use the client interface to monitor overall execution of workflows in the system. This includes the ability when required to cancel or terminate a running workflow.

For developers, the story is even better because in addition to being able to use the client interface to define workflows, we can build custom workflow activities. These custom activities, as we will see in Chapter 18, can be simple single task activities or complex composite activities that do a large amount of processing. For each custom activity we can register with CRM so that users can add them as part of their larger workflows. These activities are built using Visual Studio and the Workflow Designer using standard workflow development skills.

Probably the most compelling thing for me about CRM moving to use Windows Workflow Foundation is the continued investment from Microsoft to keep improving and building more capabilities into the engine. This should allow the CRM team to be faster at releasing improvements to the workflow engine.

Can we automate XYZ?

Once you're up and running on CRM your end users will likely start asking questions like "Can we send out an e-mail 3 days after I create a new contact?" Your job then becomes to figure out the best way to do that. Probably the simplest thing you can do at this point is determine if it's something that can be done by an End User Workflow and they could just do the setup. The important thing with End Users getting involved in definition of workflows is to make sure they have enough training on how the concept works so they don't get into trouble. One strategy here is to have a set of defined business analysts in the organization that do the creation of the workflows that are simply used by the larger end user audience. Using that approach you limit the number of people needing understanding of how end user work flow definition works. Workflow Templates can also help by providing a basic layout for a workflow where someone only needs to make minor changes to personalize it.

I think one of your biggest goals at this point is to try to determine if what is being asked is really part of a more complex or larger workflow strategy that should be flushed out so you don't end up with 100's of workflows where one solid "Sales Process" flow would have been best. To accomplish that you need to dig more out about what the user wants and how they see it working.

Key End User Questions

The following list shows some common questions you might want to ask the end user and the associated reasons why to ask. These aren't a complete set of questions, but more some to give you ideas on how to pry away critical information from your end user earlier in the process.

- Who prepares that today?
- What happens if they don't remember to do it?
- How do you track those items today?
- How do you determine which person the item gets assigned to?
- Do you send out any e-mail notifications when that happens?
- If you were to start over today, how would you change the process?
- Are there any steps you find you do over and over?
- How do you know when the process is completed?

Like I said these are intended to just get you thinking about the questions to ask. You will notice none of these say "Lead" or "Account" or anything specific the real questions you ask you need to always tailor to make sense to your user. You need to speak with them in their language so they feel comfortable talking with you. If you are working with a subject area you aren't familiar with take time to learn about it before approaching the users for details. Often times once you have a basic understanding users will be more than happy to spend a few minutes filling you in on how things work if you show interest .

Remember, the goal here is to get them thinking outside their box.

© 2002 by Randy Glasbergen.
www.glasbergen.com

"What some people fail to grasp, Larry, is the difference between 'thinking outside of the box' and just being a weirdo."

Explaining workflow to a user

Taking the time to educate your end users on the basics of workflow in CRM could be useful so they understand a little more about the capabilities. I'm not talking about digging into Windows Workflow Foundation or detailing out the execution pipeline of a CRM web service request. I'm talking about from a high level. You need to adopt and be able to talk to users with vocabulary that will not confuse them. For example, to a CRM user an Activity is a entity in the system that represents a Task, Email, Phone Call etc. To a workflow developer, an activity is a step within a workflow. To avoid confusion you should be prepared to talk to users about "Steps" in workflows because that is less likely to confuse them and consistent with the client interface where they will see Steps as part of the workflow. Think like a user not a database.

Users also aren't interested in the nuts and bolts of how you build a custom workflow activity. But explaining to them that you can build a custom step that they could then use and it could do everything including their dishes would be helpful. You might be surprised with some of the ideas your users will think of if you can articulate the capabilities of the platforms from a business value point of view.

Extracting the real requirements

Speaking of those crazy ideas that business users might come up with, what better place to start than a discussion about extracting real requirements. When talking with your users about automation, sometimes you need to listen very carefully to what they are suggesting. Make sure you don't cut them off because they aren't talking about automation in terms of how workflow works. It's ok to let them share their ideas, then bring them back around to something that will work with the platform workflow capabilities. While you are listening, look for opportunities to ask questions like "if we could do this would that help?". That's a great way to educate your users on what capabilities exist and you might find a few places where some simple automation can save your users a ton of time. Keep in mind that most users are good at telling you what they do today, not what they would like done or what could be done that would accomplish the same thing. Often times they think there's only one way (their way) to accomplish a task and suggesting early on there are others can do nothing good to help you understand the real problem you're trying to automate.

Don't be surprised if your users can't say I want x, y and z automated. Often times they don't even realize that they are wasting hours or even worse forgetting to do something that an automated process would never fail at. Sometimes these types of savings can be discovered by asking if you can simply spend some time with the user observing how they work so you can better understand their day to day processes. Once you have done that then you should be in a position to make some suggestions on process improvements that you could automate using the CRM workflow capabilities.

Requirements and Design

The simplest business process automation clearly doesn't need a lengthy analysis and design phase prior to putting in a rule that creates a new task every time a new opportunity entity is created. That said, new installations or solutions that are being built that will have extensive customizations should give considerations to a workflow strategy.

During that analysis you should evaluate the requirements for security and how you want to handle organization and authoring of workflows in the organization and associated business units. For example, will you allow all users to create simple workflows or limit it to certain people in an organization? Even the simplest things can cause problems, imagine if you created an "Add Task" workflow that triggered when a contact was created and Joe Smith also created a workflow called "Add Task" and shares it with you. Now you have two "Add Tasks" workflows on your list! While simple and not a big issue it's annoying and avoidable with a little bit of up front strategy.

If you are working on an internal system that is only used by your company being a little looser on the thought process is probably ok. If you're an ISV on the other hand building a product to sell and deploy multiple times it would be in your best interest to invest more in a workflow strategy. There are lots of opportunities for ISVs to package up some reusable workflows and custom workflow activities that their customers can use and customize for their particular implementation needs.

Some up front planning can also result in a better performing system. For example, just because you can use workflow to send a Happy Birthday e-mail when the person's birthday arrives doesn't mean that's the best implementation for all size deployments. What I mean is if you have 3 million contacts and have 3 million workflows sitting around waiting for a birthday might not be as efficient as a nightly query that only runs a workflow on people having a birthday that day. Depending on the type of solution you might develop some of your own workflow best practices and patterns that you use. Like most architecture decisions the more solid they are up front the easier it is to evolve your solution as your users' needs change.

Capturing requirements can be as simple as a Word document, a picture of a white board process flow or more complex like a well documented VISIO flow chart. The white board is my personal favorite for early discussions of workflow flow because it's so easy to move things around and accommodate those "Ah" moments when you keep discovering more about how the real business process works.

Workflow or Plug-in

In Chapter 11 we covered the new unified event architecture. In that discussion we explored how both plug-ins and workflows hook into the event model in similar ways. Both give us the capability to have custom logic happen based on an event that occurs in the system like a record being created or updated. As you start designing your solution you will need to make some decisions on when to use workflow and when to use plug-ins. Both have some unique characteristics that can be leveraged and when possible choosing the one that best matches your needs is ideal.

The first thing to consider is if your processing needs to happen before the event occurs. For example if you want to set some default values before a new record is created. In that case plug-ins are the only extensibility point that allow you to react to the create event occurring and modify the data before it is saved to the database. Workflows can only run asynchronously and therefore only occur after the platform operation happens. In this case that would be after the record was saved, so it wouldn't help us accomplish our customization.

Another area to think about is visibility to the user that something has occurred. Workflows can be seen by users so they are very visible. There's no real good way to hide that they exist or ran. Plug-ins on the other hand can run silently showing no traces to the user. For things like auditing where it just needs to happen plug-ins are better suited. On the other hand, where you have a long running task that needs to happen workflow can make it easier for users to check on progress and know that something is happening.

Access to data is another important thing to consider. Workflows run on the context of the user that owns the workflow so that means that they only have access to update or read data that that user can. Plug-ins on the other hand can be triggered by any user but run in the context of the system user and can access all data and impersonate any user. This means that for plug-ins they always will run regardless of the user access they are strictly tied to firing based on the event and there is no scope that controls them like workflows.

Plug-ins have the ability to run synchronous or asynchronous compared to workflows that always run asynchronously. Using a synchronous plug-in is ideal where the task needs to be completed before the user regains control. Workflows are more of a fire and forget and can happen at anytime depending on the load on the system.

Workflows can be configured to be run on demand for one or more records by users. Plug-ins on the other hand can only run in reaction to a platform event that occurred. Using workflows in this method gives users more control over determining when workflows will be configured. That means a user can run workflows like they would run a macro to accomplish certain tasks based on decision factors only they know about. For example, I might run workflow XYZ when I have a certain type of business trip. Using a plug-in there isn't a way to configure that type of user controlled flexibly.

That's just a sampling of some of the considerations. I'm sure there are several more that we could brainstorm and list out. The point is, give some thought to which technique would best fit what you're trying to accomplish.

Wrapping Up

In this chapter, we set the stage for an exciting exploration of the workflow capabilities of CRM 4.0. Of all the enhancements that were in this release, workflow moving to Windows Workflow Foundation is by far my favorite. I think it adds the most value to the platform because of the many ways that not only developers, but users, can now customize the platform. So far we have just touched on some of the features this new version supports. In each of the following chapters we will cover each of the following areas in much greater detail.

- **Chapter 16 - Workflow User Interface** - In this chapter we will be walking through the capabilities of the workflow engine from a user's perspective.
- **Chapter 17 - Workflow Basics** - In this chapter we will be diving into how Windows Workflow Foundation works and how its extensibility features were used to glue it into the platform.
- **Chapter 18 -Custom Workflow Activities** - In this chapter we dig into the details on how you develop custom activities
- **Chapter 19 - Workflow Developer Framework** - In this chapter we look at some reusable code that comes with the book as well as a test harness to allow you to test your custom activities without deploying them to CRM each time.
- **Chapter 20 - Workflow Code Generation** - Using the platform metadata we generate typed activities for entities defined to CRM. The generated activities provide for retrieval and create/update of data using a typed entity.
- **Chapter 21 - Workflow How To's** - In this chapter we look at some fuller examples of things you can do with both the user defined workflows and custom workflow activities.

16

Workflow User Interface

Today's business users want more empowerment and control over the work they do, they also want simplicity, and they want as much automated as possible. That combination is tough to provide and does not even begin to describe the diversity of the skills of the users that will be accessing solutions built on the platform. Add on to that the need to put in place a way to expose custom workflow assets built by developers to users in a friendly way. That is the challenge the product team had in front them when building the user experience portion of the workflow capabilities.

CRM 3.0 exposed workflow to users but only in a way that they could execute pre-defined workflows. Administrators who had access to the CRM server, logged into the server to create the actual workflow definition. This drastically limited the ability for business analysts or power users to be involved in the creation of the workflows. Now in CRM 4.0 not only can you invoke workflows on demand, authorized users can define their own flows as well as monitor the progress of workflows that have run, are running or are pending execution.

In this chapter, we will explore the user experience enough so that as a developer you understand how you can leverage it in your solution. It's important to understand what you can do with the out of box capabilities as well as how you can extend it. Using custom code workflow activities you will see how you can expose custom business or product logic that can be leveraged by power users to build their workflows.

What Workflows are Configured?

Users that have appropriate security configured are able to see workflows from the Settings - > Workflow menu option. This is also where users are able to create new workflows. Workflows are stored as a system entity, and therefore allow standard features like advanced find and standard security. The list shown will be filtered based on the user's access security allowing them only to view the subset of workflows they have access to. If you have a large number of workflows you can use advanced find to reduce the list to what you want to see.

The default view for workflows does not show workflow templates – they are available as a separate view.

Draft or Published

When you create a new workflow it initially starts out in draft mode. While the workflow is in draft mode it is not active to execute either by an event trigger or on demand. This allows the user to keep modifying and saving the workflow without worry that it might be executed by accident before completed. Once you have completed setup of the workflow you will then "publish" the workflow. Under the covers the platform at that point will generate the necessary Windows Workflow XAML (Extensible Application Markup Language) to allow your workflow to run. Once published, you will no longer be able to make changes to the workflow without "un-publishing" it. Keep in mind if you un-published a workflow to make changes, during that time it will not be executing for any events that occur.

It is possible that if you are using custom activities that you may encounter errors during the publish process due to assembly reference issues related to the custom component. It's recommended that on a system using custom activities you create test workflows using your custom activities to ensure they will publish correctly for users.

Workflow or Workflow Template

When you chose to create a new workflow, you are prompted with a dialog similar to the one below that asks if you want to create a blank workflow or start from a workflow template. A blank workflow will be just that, a clean slate for you to start from scratch. A template on the other hand is designed to be a starting point for building your workflow. It will contain one or more pre-completed steps and then allows you to make final modifications to it.

Templates will be handy to build users some examples of common things they might want to automate but allowing the user to do the final customization. During final customizations they could remove steps or provide defaults for the steps in the workflow.

When you select that you want to start from a template the list will show the available templates to choose from. When you select one of the templates it will pre-fill the workflow editor page with the steps from the template and then allow you to continue modification.

You must be on-line to be able to define new workflows using the user interface.

The following is an example of the dialog used for creating a new workflow – notice the list of templates that shows if you select create from a template.

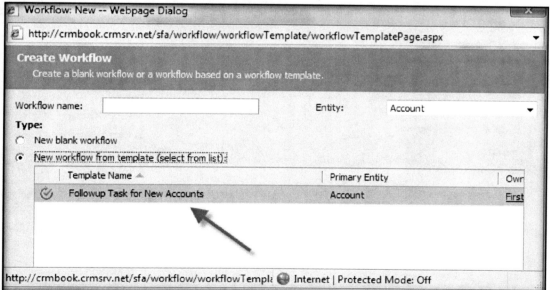

Workflow templates must be published before they will show on the template list.

Understanding Triggering Events

Workflows start because of a triggering event that they are configured to response to. A triggering event can be as simple as manual user request, or automatically in response to a record creation. Using the workflow properties, you can modify these triggering events at any point as long as the workflow is not in a published state. This means you do not have to decide at creation if you will ever have a need for a workflow to run on demand by a user.

The triggering options apply to the Primary Entity of the workflow. The Primary Entity is the entity you selected on the prior page that the workflow will process against. This doesn't mean that you can't have you workflow evaluate and modify or create other entities, but the primary entity will be the one who will trigger execution.

The following image shows the workflow properties page that you will use to configure the triggering options.

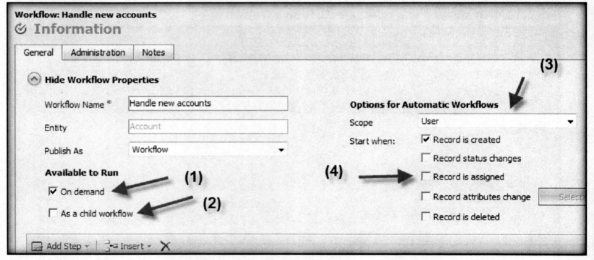

1. **On demand** – indicates you want the user to be able to invoke this workflow on demand by selecting it from a list. On each list of entity records if there are any published workflows configured to run on demand it will show a button to allow the user to see a list of workflows and select them to run against one or more records in the grid.

2. **As a child workflow** – This indicates that the workflow you are building should be available to be started from another workflow. An example of this might be a workflow that is designed to handle specific types of accounts and is launched by the Handle New Account workflow so the main workflow can be simplified and not overly complex.

3. **Scope** - This allows you control what records that the workflow will process against. This works in combination with the owning user's security to determine records that will qualify for processing. The following are the valid settings for scope:
   a. **User** - By specifying user scope, only those records that have the same owner as the workflow will trigger this workflow.
   b. **Business Unit** – The workflow will be triggered by a record owned by any user in the same business unit as the workflow owner.
   c. **Parent/Child Business Unit** – Same as business unit but will include records owned by any child business unit.
   d. **Organization** – Will trigger on all records owned by a user.

4. **Start When** – This identifies specific data related events that will trigger the workflow to run. Record is assigned option essentially tracks when the ownerid property on the record has changed.

Selecting Changed Attributes

If you choose to have the workflow triggered by update of attributes – you must specify which attributes will cause the trigger otherwise it will not have any effect. Once you select that option, you must click on the Select Attributes button to make your choices.

The following shows an example of the selection list.

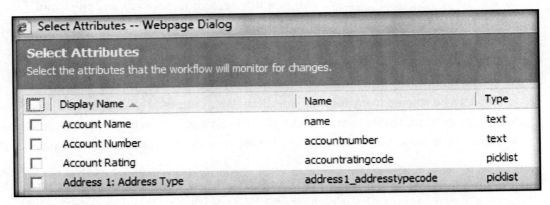

Choose only the attributes that you are interested in having trigger your process. While selecting all would be easy, it will increase overhead due to unnecessary triggering of your flow.

If you had selected Record Assigned on the prior page, you will notice that the ownerid attribute is pre-selected on this list. In fact, if you remove that selection you will turn off the Record as Assigned option.

Building the Workflow Logic

The process for building a workflow is the same regardless of whether you are building a workflow or a workflow template. The process is straight forward. You add one or more steps to the workflow. These steps together make up the business rules that are implemented when the workflow executes.

If you are familiar with Windows Workflow Foundation, a step in the CRM client is basically an Activity in the Windows Workflow Foundation vocabulary. The problem with calling them activities is CRM users typically associate the word activity with a CRM data Activity such as an e-mail, FAX, etc. So as developers you will need to be able to understand both concepts.

We will be discussing Windows Workflow Foundation concepts in more detail in a future chapter if you haven't used it yet.

The following is an example of the out of the box Steps that are available to be added to a workflow. You will notice that the list is broken up into three distinct sections. The first two are reserved for Microsoft and are related to "flow control". By "Flow Control" they are responsible for controlling the flow of the logic and not the end actions like a Send E-mail. The final section are the "End Actions", these are steps like Send E-Mail, Assign Record etc. We will be discussing each of these in more detail later in the chapter as well as how to get your own items to show on the third section list.

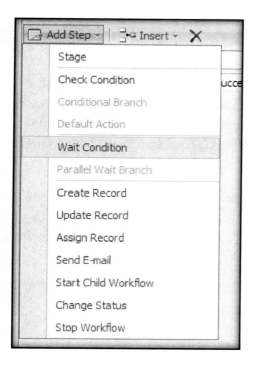

In addition to being able to add a step, you can also use the Insert Before Step and Insert After Step to add an item to an existing flow at a specific spot.

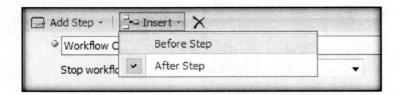

Each of the Steps in your workflow will allow you to specify a description. This description allows you to describe in business terms what the step is trying to accomplish. This description is visible during execution when you view a workflow's progress. So providing useful descriptions can be very helpful. The description is also stored in the WorkflowLog record that is created for each step in the workflow – that could also be used for reporting or audit purposes if they had a consistent pattern.

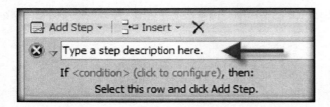

Each of the steps can have additional configuration details that need to be provided. In the above example where we added a Check Condition step; it wants us to configure the "condition" that it will use to determine if it should run additional steps. Each step that shows up on the Step menu provides details on what configurable properties it provides. The CRM Workflow Designer then presents those options to the user.

In the case of the Check Condition step, when you click on the configure link you would see the following dialog show and you could provide a series of "clauses" that will be evaluated to determine if the condition is true. In this example, the "clause" is built using a metaphor similar to how you would build advanced finds.

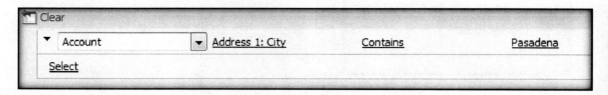

In addition to how advanced find works where you can provide static data, the "clauses" can also bind to other workflow related data such as data from the entity that triggered the workflow to run. This capability comes in handy not only in Check Condition steps but when you are using other steps like the Create or Send E-Mail steps. It is also possible as we will discuss later to build your own Steps that will expose options that you too can leverage the dynamic binding capability.

Steps can be Containers

It is also possible that steps can act as containers for other steps. The Condition Check step we have been using in the last example demonstrates just that. If the condition is true, then one or more steps should be executed. The following image shows the Condition Check step with a Send E-mail step configured to run if the condition is true.

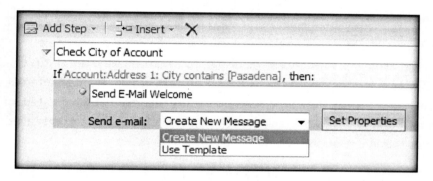

To continue our contrast with the Windows Workflow Foundation vocabulary, in some ways you can think of this capability being similar to a composite activity in Windows Workflow Foundation.

Exploring the Steps

Now that we have taken a look at how the basic mechanics work, let's take a look at how each of the steps work.

Stage Step

The stage step acts as a simple container that will contain one or more other steps. The Stage step provides no behaviors or changes to the workflow results other than its name is used for tracking and reporting. The following is an example of a workflow with two stages.

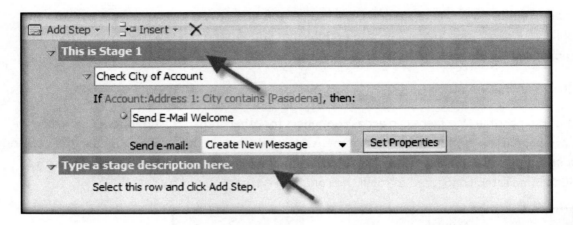

As each of the arrows indicates, there is an area that you can name the stage or provide a meaningful description. The name you indicate will be displayed when you view the status of your workflow either via System Jobs or the Workflow job list on each entity. From an internal point of view this name is also stored on the AsyncOperation entity records that are created for each stage in the workflow in the WorkflowStageName column. There is a built-in report called the Sales Pipeline that uses this information.

The Stage step should be used to group your workflow activities into meaningful chunks of work. By doing this, the workflow becomes easier to understand and maintain.

The Stage Step expands the "Sales Process" concept that existed in CRM 3.0 that allowed for a single staged workflow. Now in CRM 4.0 all entities that are workflow eligible are able to work with Staged workflows and can support multiples of them running in parallel at the same time.

While the original concept was for simple tracking of the sales process as it progressed through the various sales steps, with the new capabilities this concept has greater potential uses.

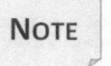

If you add a stage to a workflow after there is already one or more steps, the system will add the initial steps as part of the first stage of the workflow.

Check Condition Step

Check Condition translates for developers the same as an if/then statement. Using its options you will specify a specific condition that will be evaluated and the steps to be run if the condition is true. The conditions consist of one or more evaluations against the data of the primary entity or its related entities. Each evaluation or expression listed in the condition are required to all match so the condition items are basically "and" together to constitute the full evaluation that will be done to consider this condition to be true or false. The following shows an example of a check to see if the account is located in Colorado and the United States.

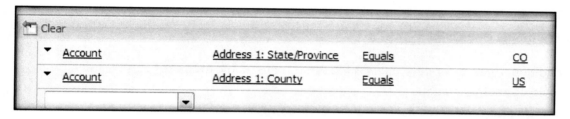

In the above example if both of those evaluations are not true the condition will be set to false and the actions of the "Then" will not be performed.

Conditions can be nested which allows the "Then" option to contain other check conditions. The following example shows a nested check condition.

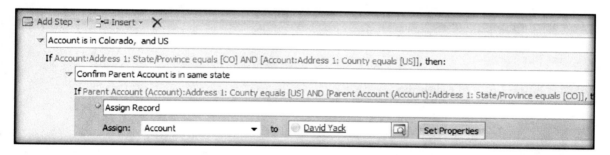

When you're building your evaluations of the data you can also use data that is contained in the entity or related entities that triggered the workflow. In our above example, we could further qualify that we only want to do the assign if the owner of the account is different than the related parent account. This would allow us to ensure we always have the same person handling all related accounts. To accomplish this we add a check of the parent owner. When it comes time to set the value we compare to we use the Form Assistant Dynamic Values capability to select the owner of the account entity for the value. This will cause a highlighted expression to be placed into the value text box as you can see in the following image.

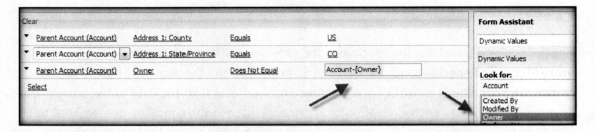

The list of values that you will see in the Form Assistant will be filtered by the data type that you are trying to set. For example, you would only see date fields if the attribute you are evaluating is a date field.

Conditional Branch Step

Conditional Branch for developers is the same as specifying the "else" part of the "if" and providing another condition.

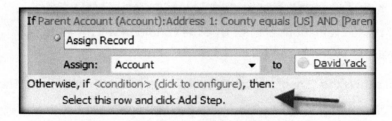

If account is in Colorado

  Do this

Else if account is in California

  Do this

The Conditional Branch can only be used if you select in the editor a Condition Check Step or another Conditional Branch step. If you are not currently selected on one of those the option to add it will be grayed out (disabled) on the list.

Default Action Step

The Default Action step is the developer equivalent of the final "Else". It allows you to specify one or more steps / activities that will execute when the Condition Check and all Conditional

Branches failed to evaluate to true. The following is an example of what it looks like on the editor.

Otherwise:
   Select this row and click Add Step.

You can only have one default action inside a Check Condition. The option to add the Default Action will not be active unless you currently have selected either the Check Condition or one of the associated Conditional Branch steps and also do not already have a Default Action setup.

Wait Condition / Parallel Wait Branch Steps

The Wait Condition Step allows you to indicate one or more data conditions that need to occur before the workflow will continue. The following is an example of sending an e-mail to notify users and then waiting for one of them to assign record.

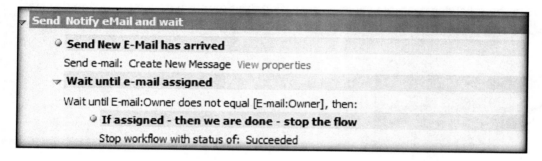

Send Notify eMail and wait
   ○ **Send New E-Mail has arrived**
   Send e-mail: Create New Message View properties
   ▽ **Wait until e-mail assigned**
   Wait until E-mail:Owner does not equal [E-mail:Owner], then:
      ○ **If assigned - then we are done - stop the flow**
      Stop workflow with status of: Succeeded

In the above example once the wait condition is satisfied we stop the workflow using the Stop Workflow step.

The problem with this scenario is what happens if nobody responds to the e-mail and assigns the record. In that case this workflow would run forever (or at least it will seem like forever!) waiting for someone to assign it.

The Parallel Wait Branch step helps with this allowing you to add another condition that will cause the workflow to continue. This additional step could be another data check or a check based on time. For example, we could want to say, wait until assigned or 1 day has passed. You can also use output from prior steps, see Chapter 21 where we give some custom activities to calculate dates. Using them in conjunction with a wait could allow you to do things like wait till next Wednesday or when some other event occurs.

When setting the condition on the Wait Condition or the Parallel Wait Branch steps you can indicate you want to do a timeout by selecting Workflow in the first column when building the condition. The following shows how to indicate you want a Timeout condition.

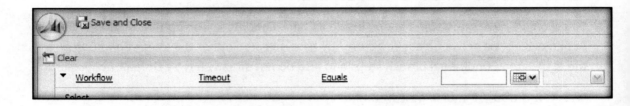

The "Workflow" option is all the way at the bottom of the first drop down under Local Values.

Using the Form Assistant we can help to calculate a variable date based on the data in the record. In the following example, we are calculating the timeout date based on one day after the record was created.

Now looking at our workflow – we would have added a "Timeout" that will assign the record and notify the user of the assignment if nobody responds one day after the initial created on date.

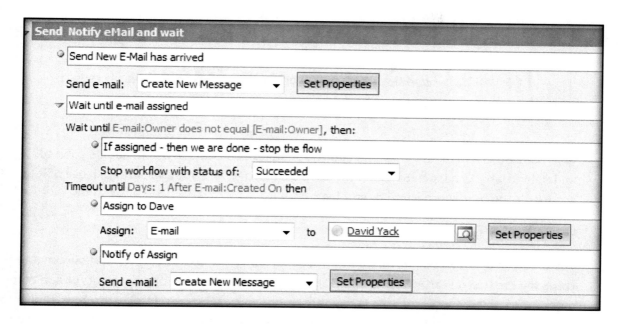

Now that you understand the capability, let's look under the covers at what is happening in the system as a result of your wait conditions.

For each wait, the platform will insert a row into the WorkflowWaitSubscriptionBase table that will track the wait condition. This is important to understand because if you create a large number of workflows that have a large number of wait conditions it might impact performance.

In the future, when the related entity is updated, regardless of the attributes changed, the platform will modify the IsModified flag on that wait subscription. It will also modify the pending AsyncOperation to indicate that something has been modified. The platform will then "wake" the workflow long enough to determine if there is any work to be done as a result of the changed attributes.

Since there is some expense associated with using the wait condition you might want to ensure you are using the best technique for what you are trying to accomplish.

For example, you simply want a workflow to run whenever it's someone's birthday. It might be more efficient to have a query that runs once a day and fire off workflows only for those whose birthday is today rather than having 50,000 workflows with wait conditions waiting for a birthday to occur.

TIP

You should use extreme caution while adding wait steps inside workflows that trigger on update events as it can easily cause a loop condition.

Wait condition is extremely powerful and you shouldn't be afraid to use it, but it's good to understand what is happening under the covers and make sure you evaluate each use of it to ensure it's the best approach to the problem.

Create Record Steps

The Create step allows you to create other records during the course of the workflow running. Using the Create you can easily do things like create follow-up tasks, appointments or audit type data. To set the properties on the new entity record you will be presented with a form similar to what you would get creating that new entity via the normal user interface. Using this form you can hard code items to specific values or use the Form Assistant to add Dynamic Values as we have seen with other steps earlier in the chapter.

The following is an example of using the Create step to create a task.

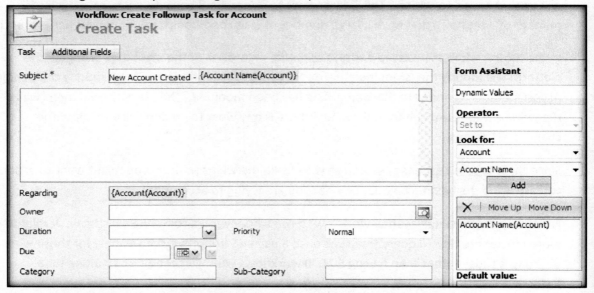

As you add more workflow steps after the create you will see create step and its related properties available in the local variables window.

Using this, you could in a subsequent step use the reference to update the same created entity as the workflow progresses.

Any attributes that is valid for display in a form but are not allocated to a form will show on the Additional Fields tab in the editor. This allows you to still manipulate fields that are not exposed to the user on the normal input forms.

The Create step is very powerful since you can create most of the entity record types including all custom entities. The properties of the created records can also be used in conditions and actions in subsequent steps. This allows for modeling many end to end business processes like "lead to cash" or even more generic internal processes like helping to orchestrate a business trip.

Update Record Step

The Update Record step can be used to update the primary entity record that triggered the workflow or any related entity record. Related entities are those that have N:1 relationships to the primary entity. For example, on account you could update the parent account. In addition, any entities that were created as a result of a Create Record step will also be available to update.

Setting values will be similar to how we saw previously in the Create Record step using a mock-up of the input form. Additionally, you can append text values and add to numeric values, as well as clear values from most fields.

Assign Record Step

The Assign Record allows you to change the ownerid attribute on the entity. You can choose to set this to a specific user account, or use the Set Properties option to bring up a form that allows Dynamic Values. Using the Dynamic Values you can assign to owners of any of the related entities that have an owner property. For example, you could assign an account to the same owner as its parent account.

You can also use the Assign Record step to assign activities to a queue. In that scenario the owner of the record would not change.

The Assign Record step allows you to assign the owner on specific related entities and records created previously in the workflow using the Create Record step.

Send E-mail Step

The Send E-Mail step allows you to tailor an e-mail and prepare it for being sent. You can choose from using a template either global or specifically related to the entity type chosen. When you select a template you are limited on what items you can modify to simply the To, From, CC and BCC properties. The rest of the values will come from the e-mail template. Keep in mind that the template can also do substitution of values, but you won't be able to further customize it while working with the workflow editor.

If you choose to not use a template you will be presented with a similar input form as you normally see in the user interface and will be able to completely tailor the contents as well as who it's going to and who it's from.

Once this step completes, the e-mail is sent, there is no separate action required to send the e-mail.

Start Child Workflow Step

The Start Child Workflow is a powerful step because it allows you to start another workflow to do further processing. You can chose to start a child workflow for any of the workflows that are marked for use as a child workflow. When you configure the step, you specify which entity will be the primary entity for the child workflow. The primary entity could be set to the primary entity of its parent workflow or any other related entity.

One way you can use this capability is to centralize some logic that needs to be called by multiple workflows. This would avoid redundancy in each of the calling workflows. This can also be used to simplify workflows if they get too complex to manage. Keep in mind that child workflows run asynchronous to the parent workflow.

You can use the Start Child Workflow to re-start your same workflow to cause it to run in a loop. This pattern allows you to simulate how a Stateful workflow might work.

Child workflows execute in the security context of the workflow owner of the calling (workflow that started it) workflow which might be different than the owner of the called workflow. If the called workflow assumes a security context of the owner its possible it might attempt to do actions or access data that the caller does not have access to and would cause the workflow to not work correctly.

Starting child workflows can also be used to restart the same workflow to allow it to reoccur multiple times. In Chapter 21 we also discuss the concept of using a workflow scheduler to accomplish the same thing.

Change Status Step

The Change Status step is very simply a way to change the status code value of a particular entity. You can modify the status code of the primary entity that triggered the workflow or its related entities. The workflow editor will prompt you for what the valid status values are and you will set a specific status.

Stop Workflow Step

The Stop Workflow step can be used to exit a workflow early. Using this you can do a check early on in the process to determine if you need to continue processing and stop. Otherwise you might end up with a complex series of check conditions that is hard to read and troubleshoot.

Additionally, using this activity you can set a completion state of either success or canceled.

Custom Steps

In addition to the steps we have discussed so far, developers can build custom workflow steps that are registered with the platform and will show on the menu. When the developer creates the activity they indicate what category and name of the step should show in the workflow editor interface. The developer can also attribute the custom code so that the workflow editor knows what properties the user should be allowed to configure.

These custom activities look just like the built-in activities but provide a powerful way to extend and customize the workflow editor. We will be discussing these custom activities in detail in Chapter 18.

Digging Deeper

Once the workflow has steps defined and the user saves the edit session the workflow and its steps are saved to the Workflow entity (WorkflowBase in the database). The Workflow is one of the system entities that are available for use via the API. In fact you can actually create workflows using Create calls and a subsequent call to publish it. The key columns on the Workflow Entity are the Activities and the Rules property. The Activities property contains a XAML version of the workflow you created using the workflow editor. In fact, the markup would be very similar to if you had used Visual Studio create the workflow.

```
<ns0:CrmWorkflow x:Name="Step_0" Context="{x:Null}" xmlns:ns1="clr-namespace:Microsoft.Crm.W
    PublicKeyToken=31bf3856ad364e35" xmlns="http://schemas.microsoft.com/winfx/2006/xam
    namespace:Microsoft.Crm.Workflow;Assembly=Microsoft.Crm.Sdk, Version=4.0.0.0, Culture=
    <ns1:StageActivity x:Name="StageStep1_stage" StageName="Determine if SouthColorado.NET">
        <ns1:StepActivity x:Name="ConditionStep2_step" Description="Check if queue" StepName="Step_
            <IfElseActivity x:Name="ConditionStep2_ifElseActivity">
                <IfElseBranchActivity x:Name="ConditionBranchStep3_ifElseBranchActivity">
                    <IfElseBranchActivity.Condition>
                        <RuleConditionReference ConditionName="ConditionBranchStep3_conditionExpressionNa
                    </IfElseBranchActivity.Condition>
                    <ns1:StepActivity x:Name="StopWorkflowStep4_step" Description="We are done - not for :
                        <ns1:StopWorkflowActivity Message="{x:Null}" Status="Succeeded" x:Name="StopWorkfl
                    </ns1:StepActivity>
                </IfElseBranchActivity>
            </IfElseActivity>
        </ns1:StepActivity>
    </ns1:StageActivity>
    <ns1:StageActivity x:Name="StageStep5_stage" StageName="Send Notify eMail and wait">
        <ns1:StepActivity x:Name="SendEmailStep6_step" Description="Send New E-Mail has arrived" S
            <PolicyActivity x:Name="SendEmailStep6_policy">
                <PolicyActivity.RuleSetReference>
                    <RuleSetReference RuleSetName="SendEmailStep6_ruleSet" />
```

You will notice in the above image that it references rule sets. These are references to the XML that is stored in the Rules property/column. The rules extract out conditional type compares and assigns from the workflow markup.

We will continue to dive deeper into this as we proceed to discuss workflow in the rest of the chapters.

Workflow Security Context

Workflows run in the context of the owner of the workflow. So a workflow that is owned by a user with the role of system administrator will have broad access. On the other hand, a user that owns a workflow with just minimal privileges will have the same when their workflow runs. This affects a few things such as what data will trigger the workflow to run. That is determined based on a combination of Workflow Scope as we discussed earlier and the ability for the user who owns a workflow to see the data in question. The workflow owner's security also matters when that workflow is going to update or create new records. The owner must have the privileges necessary to complete those operations as if they did them manually through the user interface.

A particular place to pay attention is when a workflow creates a record, as a result of another user performing an action. In this case the owner id by default of that new record will be the owner of the workflow not the user that triggered the workflow to run. It's possible that the workflow could modify or assign the new record to the user that triggered the workflow to run as long as the workflow owner had assign privileges for the record in question.

One exception to the above is when a workflow is run "on demand" in that case it runs in the security context of the user clicking on "Run Workflow" who might be different than the owner of the workflow. That should be considered if special privileges are required for any action inside workflows made available on demand.

Workflow and Entity Deletion

One situation you might run into is if you have published workflows and need to delete an entity for some reason. The most common reason for this is you find a problem with the entity definition and need to re-create the entity. Prior to being able to delete the entity the platform will require that you delete all workflows that target the entity that will be deleted. Un-publishing the workflow is not enough to get around this error, the workflow must be deleted and any active running workflows canceled.

It is possible however, to export the workflow, delete it and then re-import it back into the system after the entity is re-created.

When deleting an entity it is recommended to complete or cancel any running workflow instances before the entity is deleted..

Monitoring Workflow Execution

Once workflows have been built, configured and published, the next thing you typically want to do is see if it is working. In CRM 3.0 this required logging into the CRM server and looking at the workflow monitor to see what has run, is running or possibly encountered problems. Now in CRM 4.0 you have a few options for how to handle monitoring workflow. First, is from inside the actual workflow definition, the "Workflows" tab on the left will show you a list of the workflows that were instantiated regardless of the specific entity instance it was executed against. The other way you can see workflow status is by looking at a related entity and it too will have a "Workflows" menu item on the left. In this case, however, you will see all the workflows that have run against that particular entity instance.

 In CRM 4.0 workflows execute on the server, so when the user is off-line the triggers on workflows won't happen until their transactions playback once they connect to the server.

Wrapping it up

In this chapter we have looked at CRM 4.0 workflow from the user experience point of view. This is important to us as developers because it helps us understand what the users can do. It also gives us insight into how we might want to build custom steps that can be leveraged by users to build workflows directly in the platform workflow designer.

In some cases, we have explored deeper details of what happens behind the scenes. As a developer, architect or consultant you will often be asked for suggestions on how to use these capabilities. Knowing more about what happens allows you to give better advice when asked.

In the following chapters we will be leveraging what you learned in this chapter to build custom steps that will be deployed and available for users to build workflows from inside the CRM interface.

17

Windows Workflow Basics

In this chapter we are going to explore some of the basics related to Windows Workflow Foundation, which CRM 4.0 leverages as the workflow runtime. Windows Workflow Foundation is a programming model, engine and a set of tools for quickly building workflow applications. It was built with the idea that it could be included as part of the infrastructure of a larger application. In addition to being used as part of the CRM platform, you will also encounter it in other Microsoft products such as BizTalk, SharePoint, Speech Server and other Dynamics branded products. By design each product will use more or less of the workflow capabilities as required for accomplishing the product goals.

The primary goal of workflow is to abstract and provide a consistent programming and execution model for adding workflow within line of business applications. At the lowest level this goal is achieved by having a common workflow runtime engine that is used in all the products. The runtime itself is extensible to allow it to adjust to work in the target hosting application. This is accomplished by allowing many of the runtime services to be overridden with custom implementations by the integrated application. A great example of this is state management that handles storing of the asynchronous state during the execution of a workflow. By default, workflow (WF) provides some implementations of a State Service; however applications like CRM will implement a custom service provider to allow it to store state within the CRM database. Another example of this is regarding tracking of the process. In some applications no tracking is required to monitor the process steps of a workflow. However, many applications like CRM need the ability to externalize tracking to users so workflow provides a service interface for that as well. CRM leverages the tracking service capabilities to provide the real time status inside the CRM user interface allowing rich information about what step/stage a workflow is current executing. This means that users with the correct permissions set can monitor their own workflows and cut down on the requests that the administrator may get for this.

From a developer point of view workflow provides a consistent developer experience with other .NET technologies such as ASP.NET, WCF etc. There is a core set of libraries that developers will reference that include the System.Workflow namespace and allow developers to build custom workflows and workflow activities to be executed by the workflow runtime engine. To make workflow easier to build, workflow provides an integrated designer that runs inside of Visual Studio. Using the workflow designer a developer can drag and drop workflow activities on the designer surface and connect them together to build a more complete workflow. The activities the developer uses can be from the built-in set, from CRM provided activities or even custom activities the developer or another 3rd party provides.

In its simplest form a workflow is just a set of activities that describe a business process. In fact, to make it even simpler, a workflow is really just an activity that contains a set of activities. Reflecting on that statement, basically a workflow itself is just the top level activity that acts as the container for other activities. Inside the workflow it is also possible for an activity to contain other activities – that would be called a composite activity.

In Windows Workflow Foundation there are two fundamental types of workflows supported. The first is Sequential Workflows; these types of workflows start at the top and execute each activity in a sequence until it reaches the end of the workflow. The other type is a State Workflow which allows one or more activities to be executed each time the workflow changes state. State workflows allow for jumping to different parts of the overall workflow based on the state changes. For the rest of this book we will only be discussing Sequential Workflows since that is what CRM provides support for currently.

Hosting Windows Workflow Runtime

When using workflow as part of CRM, a lot of the work has been done for you by the CRM product team but I think it's a good idea for you to have a basic understanding of what is happening for you. Often times we can take for granted the amount of work involved in completely integrating workflow or similar technologies. I think that's caused by how simple it is to do the basics necessary to run workflow. For example, the following creates an instance of the workflow runtime and starts a workflow.

```
WorkflowRuntime wfRuntime = new WorkflowRuntime();

WorkflowInstance instance =
            wfRuntime.CreateWorkflow(typeof(MyActivity),parms);

Instance.Start();
```

Looking at those three lines it's easy to think "what's the big deal" with CRM hosting the runtime for you? In reality implementing a fully integrated workflow service is not easy. There's a lot of additional plumbing that has to happen. Let's walk through some of that from a hosting point of view to give you a better understanding.

The first thing to discuss is the process that actually hosts the runtime. while it's true you could just host it in a console application that wouldn't work well in production! CRM hosts the workflow process inside the CRM Asynchronous Service, implemented as a Windows service. One instance of the CRM Asynchronous service is active on each server that was installed with the server role. The Asynchronous service is responsible for execution of long running operations. In addition to workflow related processing, this service is also responsible for asynchronous plug-in execution, bulk mail, bulk import and campaign activity propagation. That Asynchronous service hosts the runtime for workflow that is used to fulfill workflow request for all organizations that are part of the deployment.

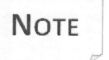

NOTE

There is not a separate asynchronous service running for each organization in a multiple tenant deployment. The single service handles all the organizations. You can however, have multiple asynchronous services by having multiple servers configured to run that role.

The following image helps to illustrate how the Asynchronous Service fits in with the overall platform architecture. As you can see it runs somewhat independent from the application server portion of the platform.

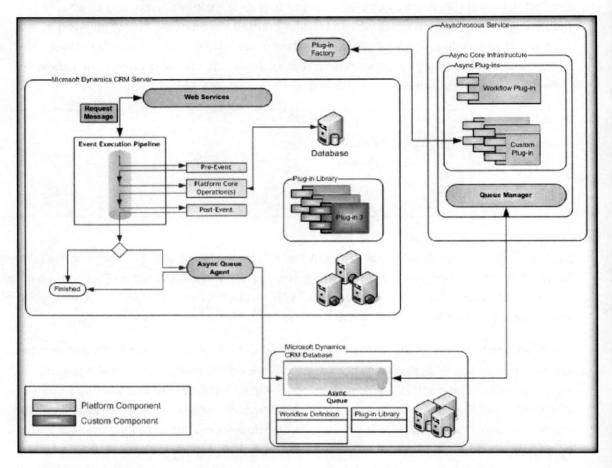

© 2008 Microsoft Corporation

By looking at the above image you can see how the Queue Manager portion of the asynchronous service is responsible for the hookup to the asynchronous queue that provides the work. The Queue Manager creates and manages asynchronous work while it is being executed in the Asynchronous Service. Work gets into the queue as a result of platform operations where either a plug-in or workflow are registered to be triggered on the event.

The workflow plug-in is responsible for the handoff to the workflow runtime by starting an instance of the necessary workflow. This is also where all the necessary context information is setup and passed to the workflow instance.

When registering plug-ins and custom workflow assemblies it is a good idea to stop the Asynchronous Service first.

In addition to just running the workflows, the asynchronous service also registers multiple workflow services with the workflow runtime. Some of these services implement workflow specific services such as for tracking progress. Others are more CRM centric such as the Workflow context service. This service allows you to get CRM specific context information regarding what triggered the workflow to run.

Another key service that CRM registers with the workflow runtime is to support workflow persistence. The persistence capabilities of workflow are what allow workflows to run for months and not cause scalability problems on the server. Imagine if persistence wasn't used thousands of workflows would be attempting to run – we would quickly run out of memory on the server. In addition, it would be difficult to accommodate for failure of a long running workflow. So the workflow runtime will attempt to persist a workflow during shutdown of the runtime or at points in the workflow execution where persistence is possible. A few example of when this can occur during execution is while an activity is waiting for an external event such as a delay or after completion of certain activities like a Create step. You can also explicitly indicate on an activity it should persist by adding the PersistOnClose attribute to the class definition. Not every activity or step as they are referred to in the client interface cause persistence to occur. For example, simple condition checking IfElse activities do not trigger persistence. When the need to persist occurs, the workflow runtime checks to see if a persistence service has been registered. The Asynchronous Service during startup of the workflow runtime registers a custom persistence service with the workflow runtime. When the CRM persistence service is invoked by the runtime the workflow the workflow is persisted to disk inside the CRM organization database. More specifically, the state is stored in the asyncoperationbase table in the WorkflowState column. There's no need to directly use that, as it is managed for you by the platform.

From a developer point of view it's important to understand persistence and the need to serialize the workflow instance. To accomplish persistence, the workflow is serialized using the Binary Formatter. The Binary Formatter performs a deeper serialization than you might be used to. This can cause problems if you build custom activities and they have any data types as properties that are not serializable. If that occurs, your custom workflow activity "may" fail during execution on the CRM Server. I say "may" because it's possible that if the workflow runtime never needs to serialize a workflow with your activity that you might run ok sometimes but then at other times fail. This condition is not a compile time error either, so it's possible to compile fine but encounter errors upon your first execution.

TIP

The Workflow Tester included in the samples provides an option to simulate persistence and the serialization that occurs to try to help you detect any code problems prior to running on the CRM Server.

In addition to using the persistence to help manage the in memory work, it also helps with restart and recovery. The Asynchronous services uses the state on the asyncoperationbase table to indicate that it is currently processing the workflow instance and indicates continued effort by updating the ModifiedOn column. This allows during restart or another server running the Asynchronous service to detect if another server has failed or if a workflow had failed during processing (e.g. the ModifiedOn was not kept current) and pickup processing that workflow on the other node or the newly restarted Asynchronous service. This is a great example of the complexity that is handled by the platform for you.

CRM using the Asynchronous service tightly integrates the workflow runtime engine with the CRM platform. By leveraging a number of the extensibility points of the workflow runtime CRM is able to take care of most of the challenges of hosting a scalable and reliable fashion. This allows users to focus on building workflows with the user interface and developers to focus on creating custom workflow activities.

Supported Workflow Foundation Activities

Windows Workflow Foundation provides a number of activities that ship with the core runtime. CRM allows a subset of these to be used when you are building workflows to run under the CRM hosted workflow runtime engine.

The following are the Windows Workflow Activities that are currently supported.

Technique	Description
CompositeActivity	Inherits from Activity and is the base class for all activities that contain other activities. Basically, a CompositeActivity's only role is to manage the execution of its children activities.
DelayActivity	Allows for causing the workflow to wait for a specified period of time.
EventDrivenActivity	Inherits from SequenceActivity and is used to handle an event - The first child of this activity must implement IEventActivity all subsequent activities can inherit from any type. The first activity will block until the event occurs, then the rest of the activities will occur. For example a DelayActivity might be that first activity then after the delay subsequent activities would execute.
IfElseActivity	Allows for branching based on one or more conditions or rule conditions (more on using rules later in the chapter).
IfElseBranchActivity	Used in conjunction with IfElse.
ListenActivity	ListenActivity inherits from CompositeActivity and manages children activities that inherit from EventDrivenActivity. It requires there to be at least two child activities. ListenActivities can have many branches that are waiting for events to occur before running.
PolicyActvity	Provides for execution of a set of rules as part of a workflow. We will be discussing this activity in more details later in this chapter.
ReplicatorActivity	Think Cloning – this activity works on an array or other type of collection and it will replicate the child activity it contains once for each item in the associated collection.
ParallelActivity	Allows for execution of multiple activities at the same time.
SequenceActivity	Allows for sequencing one or more child activities – it's basically a sequential container.

Technique	Description
ThrowActivity	The throw activity allows you to do declaratively the same thing you would do in code by throwing an exception.
TerminateActivity	Allows for terminating the workflow instance with an abnormal completion.
TransactionScopeActivity	Allows you to declaratively deterine a transaction boundary - when this is encountered a new transaction is started. This activity will force a persist of state to occur upon completion.

One thing to keep in mind is that CRM will do a scan for supported workflow types when you attempt to register a workflow with the platform. In the web.config for the CRM client interface or the web service you will find a list of authorized types. This list is used at workflow compilation time (which happens during the publishing of a workflow) to check if the workflow uses any unauthorized types.

In addition to the above activities, CRM also ships with some CRM platform specific activities. We will also be discussing building custom activities that you can register and use with CRM in Chapter 18.

CRM Workflow Activities

CRM provides several workflow activities out of the box that are used by workflows created using the client interface. Each workflow is stored in the workflowbase table and if you were to browse the table you could see the XAML that defines the workflow steps once a workflow is published. The following are the activities that CRM provides and you will see in the XAML markup to support execution of the workflows users can define in the client interface.

Technique	Description
AssignActivity	This activity allows you to assign a record to another user - it is used when you add an Assign step to a workflow via the client interface. You can accomplish the same thing using by modification to the ownerid on an entity.

Technique	Description
ChildWorkflowActivity	Used to start a child workflow that will run asynchronously to the part that started it. You can accomplish the same thing by using the ExecuteWorkflowRequest message.
CreateActivity	Used to create a new record from a DynamicEntity - you can do the same thing via the API, or also look at Chapter 20 where we provide a utility to generate a custom ModifyActivity for each specific entity you are working with.
RetrieveActivity	Retrieves a dynamic entity for a specify entity type and id. You can also do this directly via the API, or look at the retrieve activities we code generate in Chapter 20.
SendEmailActivity	This activity basically performs the same as the SendEmail message that you can do from the API.
SendEmailFromTemplateActivity	This is the same as the SEndEmailFromTemplate message and just basically sends an email from a known template.
SetStateActivity	Allows for changing of state of an entity.
StageActivity	Inherits from SequenceActivity and basically is a container activity, but you specify a name that is recorded in the asyncoperation when this activity starts execution. This allows tracking of the progress each workflow instance.
StepActivity	A container that inherits from SequenceActivity. All CRM workflow activities are always inside a Step Activity. The Step Activity is also responsible for creation of records in the Workflow log.
StopWorkflowActivity	Stops the workflow instance and allows you to specify a message and status for the workflow instance.
UpdateActivity	Used to update a record from a DynamicEntity - you can do the same thing via the API, or also look at Chapter 20 where we provide a utility to generate a custom ModifyActivity for

	each specific entity you are working with.
WaitForEntityEventActivity	This allows for waiting for an event like an update to occur - it implements the IEventActivity so it qualifies to be used in a ListenActivity as one of the EventDrivenActivity's specified. You will see this used as part of the Wait For steps in workflows.
WaitLoopActivity	Used in conjunction with the WaitFor.

Currently, the above CRM specific activities while used internally by workflows you create in the client interface are not supported for your direct use. You will notice that in the SDK they have a remark that states "Not supported in this release". I believe that is to give the team flexibility to continue to modify them as needed without concern for people already using them in their own code. We have provided them here to help you understand that they exist and that you can do pretty much all the same things either using the web services API or using some of our code generated activities.

Using the PolicyActivity/Rules

One of the built-in workflow activities that we mentioned is worthy of a more complete discussion. The PolicyActivity handles processing and applying the actions of a set of rules. Each rule consists of conditions and resulting actions. For example, a condition would be an evaluation like "If Credit Score is greater than 700" and a action would be the setting of the interest rate to 7% based on that condition being true. In fact, actions can set a field or property on a workflow, call a method on a workflow or object in the workflow, or call a static method. Using a series of these rules and actions can become pretty powerful to implement business rules.

You can place a policy activity in a workflow or in our case as an activity inside of one of our custom activities that we will build in the next chapter. When you configure the policy activity you specify a rule set that will be executed when the policy activity runs. Each rule will indicate a priority that will determine the order that the rules will execute. In the event that rules have the same priority the rules will execute based on the alphabetical order of the rule name.

I didn't provide a sample in the book; however, you could easily use the RuleEngine that the Policy activity uses under the covers to implement your own custom activity that processes rules. In fact, one interesting scenario would be to use that to load the rules from CRM at process time instead of being statically linked with a custom activity. This is an example of another way that you could externalize your business logic.

Handling Faults

Faults can occur in a workflow either due to unexpected exceptions or by intentionally forcing one using the ThrowActivity. You will want to think about how to handle these just as you would if you were writing a non-workflow program. Meaning you will want to put in place a strategy for managing the exceptions. In some cases it will be acceptable to bubble these up so the users see them but in other cases you may want to do your own compensation for the error occurring.

When an unexpected error occurs and is left unhandled it will cause the termination of the workflow instance. When this occurs, CRM will detect it and put the workflow in a wait status. When the user drills into the workflow it won't be obvious that an error has occurred. Ideally, you are better off handling errors and stopping the workflow with a more controlled explanation to the user.

HandleFault Method

Custom activities can implement the HandleFault method as it will get called when an unhandled exception occurs. In this method you should take any steps to cleanup resources used by your activity. This method doesn't allow you to suppress the error and prevent it from being raised to the hosting process. The default processing for the HandleFault method if it is not implemented is to cancel the activity.

Fault Handlers

Composite Activities (activities that contain children activities) have the option of implementing fault handles which are basically specific child activities to run in the event an exception is thrown

Wrapping it up

In this chapter we have looked at how Windows Workflow Foundation is integrated into CRM. By doing this we hope we gave you a little better understanding of how things work so that as your working with workflow you can understand what is going on under the covers.

Additionally, we looked at the various activity types that are available to use with our activities. We also covered the CRM activities that are used when a workflow is built from the client interface. Understanding both of these is important as we start to discuss in the next chapter building our own custom activities.

In reality, we only touched the surface on Windows Workflow Foundation. We tried to focus more on how it is used with CRM because there are a number of books that specifically cover workflow by itself. While CRM has specific ways it uses workflow picking up a book specifically on Windows Workflow Foundation is a great way to supplement the contents of this book.

18

Custom Workflow Activities

One of the most powerful things you can do to leverage the workflow capabilities of the platform is build custom workflow activities. Custom workflow activities allow you to extend the built-in workflow capabilities to include your custom functionality. They can be simple utility activities that do things like build a URL or more complex activities that do complete business processes. These activities are not the same as the standard CRM activities (tasks, emails, etc). Workflow activities may use these, but do not have to.

In the prior chapters we have discussed the basics of how workflow is implemented and that some of the activities ship with CRM and Windows Workflow Foundation. Custom workflow activities allow developers to create their own activities that can be registered with the platform. Once you create the activity and register it, users can include it in workflows they build using the client interface workflow editor. At development time, you will indicate input and output parameters on the workflow activity and these will be visible for users to configure in the workflow editor. The user can then hook these parameters up when creating the workflow in the client interface workflow editor. These custom activities then run as part of the workflows and take advantage of the monitoring and management of workflows that is provided by the platform.

In this chapter we are going to dive into the details of how you use Visual Studio to build custom WF activities. We will then follow this up in the next chapter by discussing ways to build a reusable framework for making building workflow activities easier.

Building a Simple Activity

Workflow activities don't have to be complex. In fact building a simple activity is really pretty straight forward. The following represents what is required for a standard Windows Workflow Foundation activity.

```
public class SimpleActivity : Activity
{
    protected override ActivityExecutionStatus
        Execute(ActivityExecutionContext executionContext)
    {
        //custom logic would go here!
        return ActivityExecutionStatus.Closed;
    }
}
```

Now that is about as simple of an activity that you can create. It isn't CRM specific and doesn't do much but it is a valid basic activity. In Chapter 3 we discussed project types for holding these, but just to recap we recommend a separate project for workflow activities and if you base it on the Workflow Activity Library template you'll get all the correct references except for CRM added for you.

If you were to double click on this class from solution explorer you would now see the following designer a basic activity gets.

Adding CRM Support

Before we get much further, let's add support so the CRM platform would recognize this activity. The first thing you need to do is add references to the CRM assemblies Microsoft.Crm.Sdk and Microsoft .Crm.Sdk.TypeProxy. Next, we need to add a using statement for the CRM namespace.

```
using Microsoft.Crm.Workflow;
```

To allow our activity to be visible in the workflow editor once registered you need to add the CrmWorkflowActivity attribute to the class as you can see in the following example.

```
[CrmWorkflowActivity("Simple Activity", "Activity Group")
public class SimpleActivity : Activity
```

The second parameter on the CrmWorkflowActivity is the friendly group name. This name is used to group together all activities that have the same name when they are shown to the user in the workflow editor step list. The first parameter is the user friendly name that will show to the user.

NOTE

Once a workflow activity is registered with a CRM organization, all users that have access to create/edit workflows will be able to see the custom activity. There is not currently a way to restrict who can see a specific workflow activity. Remember, only that single organization will see it not others unless you register it with each of them also.

Since the names you provide on the CrmWorkflowActivity are visible to users some thought should be given to make sure they are names that will be understood. Additionally, if you are building a product that will go to other companies keep in mind the names you use and consider if they will collide or conflict with other vendors products. You might want to consider using your company name, its initials, or a product name or initials as part of the name of the group to help avoid confusion.

At this point if we were to register our assembly and activity with CRM it would show up in the step list on the workflow editor. We would be able to include it on a workflow and it would run just fine, however, it really wouldn't be doing any work. Yet.

Composite Activities

In our basic activity example above, we inherited from Activity and that is best for a simple activity that performs a single task and doesn't manage other activities. When you want to be able to have your activity manage other child activities you are building a Composite Activity. Using a composite activity, you can drag other activities from the toolbar onto your activity design surface and use the Visual Studio Workflow Designer to modify properties and connect the input properties of activities to the output properties of other activities.

Using composite activities you can build small activities and then combine them together onto a composite activity that is registered with CRM. When building a composite activity you do not need to attribute the children activities with the CrmWorkflowActivity only the outer composite activity itself should have the attribute.

The best way to create a composite activity is to use the Create New Activity by right clicking on the workflow library project. When doing that it will create a class for you that look like the following example.

```
public partial class SimpleCompositeActivity: SequenceActivity
{
       public SimpleCompositeActivity()
       {
             InitializeComponent();
       }
}
```

When you added the activity, Visual Studio generated the above class that inherits from SequenceActivity. The SequenceActivity class comes with Windows Workflow Foundation and is designed to manage child activities and execute them in sequence. You will notice that it uses a partial class, the reason for that is it also generates a <activityname>.designer.cs file. The generate file will contain all the code the Visual Studio Designer creates as you drag other activities onto the design surface and manipulate their settings. If you were to just create your own class by hand without using the Visual Studio new item template the designer file would not be created and Visual Studio would just put the generated code inline in your class file. Using the new item template creates a cleaner implementation.

When you use the activity template, it is not necessary to override the Execute like we did with activity. If you don't, the SequenceActivity will simply execute the child activities that you drag onto the design surface. The following is an example of the default designer surface for a composite activity – notice how it says "Drop Activities Here".

In the following example, I have dragged from the tool bar a few activities onto the design surface of the composite activity. As you can see I have included an ifElse activity like we discussed in the prior chapter along with a code and delay activity.

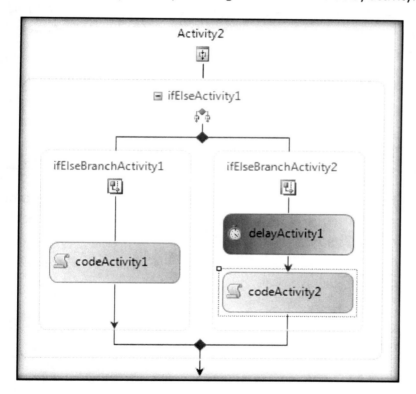

Using this composite approach we can build complex workflows that leverage pre-built workflow activities to build out the complete flow of a process. By attributing our composite activity which is the outer container of the children activities with the CrmWorkflowActivity attribute it can be visible to users in the CRM workflow editor.

You can use a composite activity to build a workflow that is registered with CRM. When you create your work flow in the workflow editor you would end up only having a single activity.

Dependency Properties

Dependency properties are a special type of property that is used by Windows Workflow activities. Dependent properties are standard .NET managed code properties with the added logic of some helper code that comes with Windows Workflow Foundation. They exist to shield a workflow activity developer from the complexities necessary to allow activities to work well with the workflow designers.

To try to understand dependency properties better let's first look at a traditional standard .NET property.

```
public string FirstName { get; set; }
```

The above single line is basically the same as the following code, except the compiler takes care of defining the backing storage for the property. In our example m_FirstName is a string backing variable to hold the value of the property.

```
private string m_FirstName;
 public string FirstName
 {
     get
     {
         return m_FirstName;
     }
     set
     {
         m_FirstName=value;
     }
 }
```

Using this example property on an activity, the activity would depend on someone explicitly setting the property in order for the backing storage to have any value. This works fine where you are writing a lot of code but in a workflow designer this becomes a challenge because it's very inflexible.

Think about our example of the workflow designer before, you are dragging and dropping activities onto the design surface. If you had two activities A and B on the designer, wouldn't it be nice to have B get the first name from a property exposed by A? To accomplish that you would have to write custom code to "glue" together those properties at runtime.

Dependency properties step in to help solve that problem by allowing a traditional property to be more flexible. The following are the scenarios that dependency properties help solve.

- Allow being set to a specific value – just like a traditional property.
- Can be assigned an ActivityBind which basically is a "Redirect" to another item that contains the value.
- Properties that are considered metadata and not changeable at runtime.
- Support for attached properties which are properties that are applied to objects dynamically at runtime.

The most powerful of those scenarios is the ActivityBind which binds the activity property to a property, field, indexer, method, event, or another activity's property. The designer heavily leverages this capability to allow you to "glue" together the activities on the designer surface. The parameters for the ActivityBind are set in the workflow designer in Visual Studio when you click on the property. The designer launches a workflow browser that allows you to bind the property to other activity's properties.

The following is the same FirstName property but created as a dependency property.

```
public string FirstName
{
    get { return (string)GetValue(FirstNameProperty); }
    set { SetValue(FirstNameProperty, value); }
}

// Using a DependencyProperty as the backing store for FirstName.
//        This enables animation, styling, binding, etc...
public static readonly DependencyProperty FirstNameProperty =
    DependencyProperty.Register("FirstName", typeof(string),
    typeof(Activity2), new UIPropertyMetadata(0));
```

If that looks like a bunch of stuff to type there's a snippet that comes with Visual Studio to help you create the property. By right clicking in the editor and following the insert snippet path you can use the snippet to create the property.

Insert Snippet: NetFX30 >

> Define a DependencyProperty
> Define an attached DependencyProperty

Exposing Properties to CRM

Now that you have an understanding of dependency properties let's move on to understand what is necessary for CRM to see your property. In a way similar to how we added attributes to the activity for CRM to be able to see the activity we will expose properties.

The CrmInput and CrmOutput attributes indicate that a property should be visible to the CRM workflow editor. The following is an example of adding these attributes to our FirstName property.

```
[CrmInput("First Name Input")]
[CrmOutput("First Name Output")]
public string FirstName
{
    get { return (string)GetValue(FirstNameProperty); }
    set { SetValue(FirstNameProperty, value); }
}
```

As you can see in the above example it is possible for one property to be both input and output. The parameter to both attributes is the friendly name of the property that the user will see in the workflow editor.

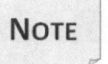

Currently, the friendly name can only be set at compilation time. There is also not support for multiple languages. Maybe in the future the editor will allow dynamic discovery of the name to use.

The CrmInput attribute causes the property to show up in the dynamic value editor inside the workflow editor. This should be used when you want the user to provide a value. The user can specify a hard coded value or they are able to use the Dynamic Value setter to bind a value from the data record being processed or a prior workflow activity to the property. We saw examples in Chapter 16 of how these values are set in the client interface using the workflow editor.

The CrmOutput attribute causes the property to show up in the Dynamic Value editor for any of the steps after the activity exposing the property. This allows users to use the output value in subsequent steps in the workflow.

Supported Property Types

When adding properties to your activity you need to keep in mind there are some restrictions to the data type of the properties. Your custom activity can have properties that are of any type that are serializable and on the authorized types list in the web.config of the CRM web server.

If you want to have your property be visible to the CRM workflow editor, a subset of the possible data types is supported. The following are the currently supported data types for properties that will be marked as CrmInput or CrmOutput : CrmBoolean, CrmDateTime, CrmDecimal, CrmFloat, CrmMoney, CrmNumber, Lookup, Picklist, Status, and String.

When picking your data type keep in mind that the workflow editor will not allow the user to assign values from different data types. For example, you can't assign a string to a CrmNumber property.

Setting a Default Value

You can use the CrmDefault attribute to provide a default value for input and output properties. The workflow editor will then show that as the default value and that value will be used if the user doesn't specify a new value.

The following is an example of adding the CrmDefault attribute to our First Name poperty.

```
[CrmInput("First Name Input")]
[CrmDefault("Dave")]
public string FirstName
{
    get { return (string)GetValue(FirstNameProperty); }
    set { SetValue(FirstNameProperty, value); }
}
```

You can use CrmDefault for any of the valid types and the value you pass as parameter must be valid for the specific type. The following is an example of providing a default number value.

```
[CrmDefault("12345")]
```

Working with Picklist and Status Attributes

When you have properties that use the Picklist or Status data types it is necessary to provide the workflow editor more details on the entity and attribute they are related to. The reason for this is so the editor is able to provide the user of the workflow editor a list of possible values specific to that attribute. The CrmAttributeTarget attribute is used to specify the entity name and attribute name. The following is an example of adding the attribute to a Picklist property.

```
[CrmInput("Building Class")]
[CrmAttributeTarget("ctcre_property","ctcre_buildingclass")]
[CrmDefault("4")]
public Picklist BuildingClass
{
    get { return (Picklist)GetValue(BuildingClassProperty); }
    set { SetValue(BuildingClassProperty, value); }
}
```

Notice in the above example we also used the CrmDefault to specify a default value for the Picklist.

Working with Lookup Attributes

The Lookup data type also requires some special handling so the workflow editor knows what type of entity you want a lookup for. Using the CrmReferenceTarget attribute you can specify the entity name that should be used by the workflow editor. The following is an example of a lookup property using the CrmReferenceTarget.

```
[CrmInput("User")]
[CrmReferenceTarget("systemuser")]
public Lookup User
{
    get { return (Lookup)GetValue(UserProperty); }
    set { SetValue(UserProperty, value); }
}
```

I'd like to see in future releases this attribute become an optional attribute for lookups so you can create generic activities that work for all types of entities. The reason being currently, it's not possible to build some utility workflow activities that don't care what the entity they are working with is ahead of time. If it were to allow skipping specification of that you could determine it at runtime. The real reason it's like that today is to help the workflow editor in the client interface present the user with a nice selection list.

Accessing the Workflow Context

A lot of what we have looked at so far other than the CRM attributes has been related more to standard Windows Workflow Foundation. If you recall from our prior chapter on Workflow Basics we talked about how Windows Workflow provides the ability to register services with the runtime. CRM takes advantage of this and registers a Context Service. The Context service can be located and used to access the current context information for the workflow instance that is currently executing.

The following sample shows how to retrieve the IContextService from the workflow runtime using the activity execution context that is passed into the override method. Once you have retrieved an instance of the IContextService it is then possible to get the actual workflow context using the Context property on the IContextService.

```
protected override ActivityExecutionStatus
        Execute(ActivityExecutionContext executionContext)
{
    IContextService contextSvc =
        executionContext.GetService(typeof(IContextService))
            as IContextService;

    IWorkflowContext wfContext = contextSvc.Context;


    return ActivityExecutionStatus.Closed;
}
```

The IWorkflowContext instance that you get access to is your connection to the Event Pipeline for the platform operation that has taken place. Using this you can get access to a bunch of information about the current request. The IWorkflowContext is very similar to the IPluginContext we discussed in the plug-in chapters. It is important to note that they are not identical. For example, the workflow context does not contain the full organization name, just the organization id.

Using the CRM Web Service

Custom workflow activities are similar to plug-ins in how they make available access to the CRM service from the workflow context. As you can see in the following example you can get a reference to the CRM Web Service by calling the CreateCrmService method.

```
IWorkflowContext wfContext = contextSvc.Context;

    ICrmService crmService = context.CreateCrmService();
```

One thing you might notice that is different than how plug-ins work is CreateCrmService doesn't take a Boolean parameter to use the current user, or a Guid to indicate a specific user. The reason for that is workflows run in the context of the user that owns the workflow unless it was started manually then it runs in the invoker's context.

While possible to use a referenced workflow from the custom workflow activity, I tend to encourage use of the one returned by the CreateCrmService. I do cover in the plug-in some aspects and issues related to using one via a web reference if that is something you're intent on doing. The one returned from the CreateCrmService takes care of handling a lot of the setup you would need to do to properly run.

The one area where you miss out by not using a web referenced CRM service is the typed classes for each entity. You can overcome that by using the generated activities we discuss in Chapter 20. We also talk about typed classes that wrap around the dynamic entities in that chapter if you want to use typed entities with the service returned from CreateCrmService.

Using Metadata Service

Using the metadata service from a workflow activity is very similar to using the CRM service. The following is an example of using the CreateMetadataService to create an instance.

```
IWorkflowContext wfContext = contextSvc.Context;
IMetadataService metaService =
        wfContext.CreateMetadataService();
```

Putting it all Together

In the following example we are going to build a custom activity that will calculate the number of days between a start and end date that will be provided.

Creating our Activity

The first step is to create our activity and to override the Execute method where we will place our code to calculate the TotalDays output property.

```
[CrmWorkflowActivity("Date Diff Days","Date Steps")]
[PersistOnClose()]
public class CalculateDateDayDiffActivity : Activity
{
    protected override ActivityExecutionStatus Execute
            (ActivityExecutionContext executionContext)
    {

        TimeSpan ts =
            this.EndDate.UserTime.Subtract(this.StartDate.UserTime);
        this.TotalDays = new CrmNumber((int)ts.TotalDays);

        return ActivityExecutionStatus.Closed;
    }
//* remaining code omitted for readability - see rest of section */
}
```

Input Properties

Next, we are going to add input properties to the class to allow specification of the start and end dates.

```
[CrmInput("Start Date")]
public CrmDateTime StartDate
{
    get { return (CrmDateTime)GetValue(StartDateProperty); }
    set { SetValue(StartDateProperty, value); }
}

public static readonly DependencyProperty StartDateProperty =
    DependencyProperty.Register("StartDate", typeof(CrmDateTime),
typeof(CalculateDateDayDiffActivity));
```

We will define another property just like this one that will be for EndDate. We have omitted the code since other than name it's identical to StartDate.

Output Property

We need to define an output property that will hold the value of the total days that we calculate. By placing the CrmOutput attribute on our dependent property TotalDays we make it usable in subsequent workflow steps.

```
[CrmOutput("Total Days")]
public CrmNumber TotalDays
{
    get { return (CrmNumber)GetValue(TotalDaysProperty); }
    set { SetValue(TotalDaysProperty, value); }
}


// Using a DependencyProperty as the backing store for TotalDays.  This
enables animation, styling, binding, etc...
public static readonly DependencyProperty TotalDaysProperty =
    DependencyProperty.Register("TotalDays", typeof(CrmNumber),
typeof(CalculateDateDayDiffActivity));
```

You can find the full code to this example in the book sample code
$BookCode/Chapters/Chapter18/ctccrmbook.Ch18WorkflowActivies.sln

Registering the Activity with CRM

Assuming at this point, you now have a project that successfully builds we need to prepare this
to deploy to our CRM server. There are a few different tools or API calls you can use to register a
workflow activity. But to keep it simple we are going to use the tool that you can download
from http://code.msdn.com/crmplugin. This represents an updated version of the registration
tool that is packaged with the SDK. The tool comes with instructions to get it working so we
won't repeat that in the book. Please check the read me on the download for full details. Later
in Chapter 24, we will be discussing deployment in greater detail including how to integrate
deployment of a workflow activity into a setup / provisioning type application.

Once you have started the registration tool and connected to your test CRM server the first thing
we need to do is register the assembly that contains our workflow activity. As you can see in the
following example select Register - Register New Assembly from the tab menu.

Once you select that you will see the following dialog appear. If you click on the button next to the text box it will allow you to locate and select the assembly that contains your workflow activity. Once selected, you will see any workflow activities or plug-in types it found in the display area as you can see in the image below.

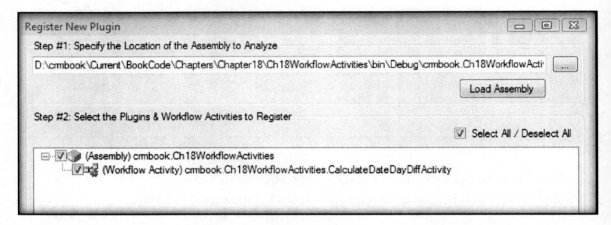

At this point, we are simply registering the assembly with CRM not hooking up when it will be used yet. One other choice we need to make is to identify where CRM should find the assembly. Selecting database will cause the assembly to be stored in the CRM server.

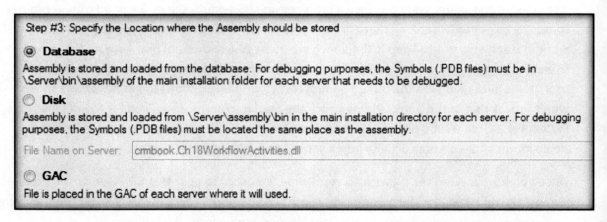

We will be discussing deployment locations in more detail in Chapter 24. For now we will just select Database.

Now after clicking Register Selected Plug-ins make sure that it registers successfully. This tool just registered the plug-in assembly (or workflow in our case) plus it created a plug-in type to identify the workflow activity that we selected above to CRM.

Creating a Test Workflow

Our next step is to create a test workflow to use our activity. Using what we learned in Chapter 16 on how to use the client interface workflow editor we create a workflow that is triggered on demand for Account. What we are going to do is calculate the number of days between when the Account was created and last updated.

Looking at the Add Steps menu - we should now see our Date Steps category show up like you see in the following image.

Selecting our new activity adds it to our new workflow and you should see it appear like below.

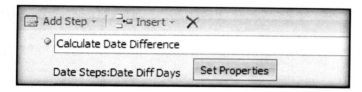

Notice I have given it a title Calculate Date Difference. We will be using that later if we reference our custom activity (now a step) in a subsequent workflow step.

Next, we should configure where the Start and End date will come from. Clicking on set properties will show us the following dialog allowing us to configure the date fields.

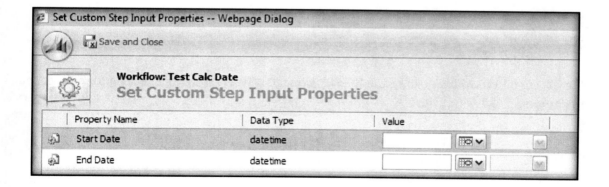

Using the Form Assistant panel on the right we select Created On from the list of properties and click add - followed by OK to add the reference to the Created On to the Start Date

After doing the same thing for Modified date and binding it to the End Date property our values should look like the following image.

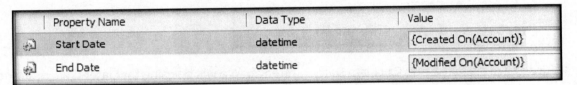

Property Name	Data Type	Value
Start Date	datetime	{Created On(Account)}
End Date	datetime	{Modified On(Account)}

After saving and closing the properties if we could then go back and add a condition check to our workflow that uses the TotalDays output from our custom workflow to do a check to see if it's been greater than 10 days. As you can see on the following image our custom activity shows up in the list of local values using the name we provided on the description.

The full condition would look like the following image which is showing checking for greater than 10 days total.

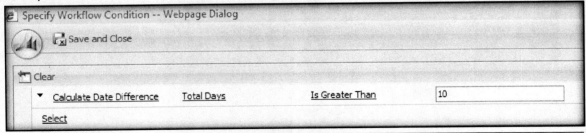

The same calculated value could also be used in an email the same way - here using it in the subject in a notification e-mail.

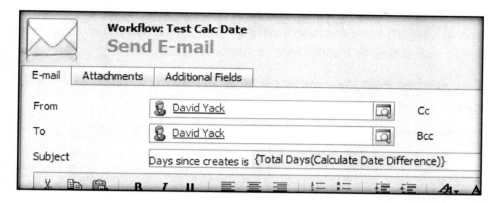

The final step before we can attempt to test our workflow is to publish it.

Testing the Workflow

For our test workflow we connected it to an update of account to trigger it to run. For testing, it's often times good to turn on the "On Demand" option which allows you to just manually run the workflow. Since we decided to do it based on an update, after performing an update on an account if you look at the Workflow list you should see a new workflow in the list like the following image shows.

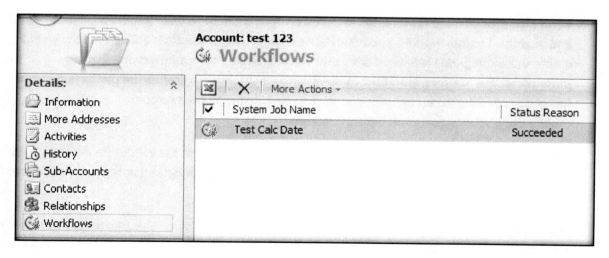

Notice that the status reason indicates success. If we got there soon enough it would say "Waiting for Resources" when the workflow was waiting for the asynchronous service to execute it, then "In Progress" as it performed its work. If there had been an error it would indicate terminate or more likely just sit there and have a state of "Waiting". If that occurs check out Chapter 26 where we discuss how to troubleshoot problems like that.

If you click on the system job, it will allow you to drill down and see the workflow progress as you can see in the following image

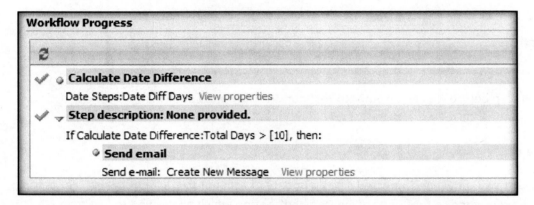

That completes our example workflow and a walkthrough of how to get it registered and tested.

Custom Activity vs. Plug-in

Before we dive into too much detail let's discuss briefly the difference between custom activities and plug-ins. Custom workflow activities are similar to plug-ins in their ability to allow you to create them using .NET managed code and Visual Studio. There is however a few key differences. For starters, workflows always run asynchronous and after the platform operation has occurred. Plug-ins on the other hand can also run during the pre-operation stage and modify the platform operation before it occurs.

Workflow activities offer the ability to allow the user to configure their input parameters using the workflow editor. Plug-ins on the other hand are typically configured at registration time and do not allow the user to interact directly with them.

Workflow activities are designed to be reusable by many workflows. This means you could have ten workflows that include your custom activity all responding to a Create event. Each workflow could be owned by specific users and do slightly different processing. Plug-ins on the other hand, are typically only registered once for an event like Create and execute regardless of the user and their rights to the data.

Both of these capabilities have their place in custom solutions and allow you the opportunity to extend the platform to solve real problems. As you are starting the design work for your solution you should weigh the pros and cons of both approaches and pick the one that best fits what you are trying to accomplish.

Wrapping it up

In this chapter we have looked at how to go about building custom workflow activities. We started out discussing the basics and moved forward to look at the CRM specifics. Building custom workflow activities is an easy way to extend the existing platform capabilities. By allowing them to appear in the client interface workflow editor allows using them as building blocks for putting together larger business process automation flows. In the next chapter, we will continue our exploration of custom workflow activities and look at some of the reusable functionality that is in the book code framework that can help you build custom workflow activities.

19

Workflow Developer Framework

Building on what we learned in Chapter 18 about building custom workflow activities we are going to build some reusable code. Custom workflow activity development can be very simple. They are really just a class that inherits from a base activity class provided by Windows Workflow Foundation and implements a method and uses special CRM attributes. They can also be more complex and depend on similar needs in multiple different custom activities.

So far we have focused on the out of the box capabilities that exist to support custom workflow activity development. In this chapter, we are going to look at some ideas for building a reusable framework to make building workflow activities more consistent and easier to manage.

In this chapter we are going to look at an approach to build some reusable classes that our workflow activities can inherit from and use to improve consistency. In addition, we will look at how to build a test harness that will allow you to test your activities without having to register them on the server or for that matter do your development on a server operating system.

As you look at the implementation of the reusable classes and the test harness you will likely get to know how workflows work at a deeper level. We will start this exploration by looking at the reusable classes and then move on to the test harness and how to use it to test your activities.

Referencing WorkflowCommon

The first thing we should get out of the way is adding a reference to our WorkflowCommon assembly. This assembly and the code is included in the book sample code and contains common code for plug-ins as well as general CRM development.

In order to use this assembly we need to add references to our project to three assemblies from the book framework ctccrm.authhelper, ctccrm.plugincommon and ctccrm.workflowcommon. You can either browse and reference the assemblies or you can include the project in your solution using the add existing project option as we have done in our sample solution for the chapter as you can see below.

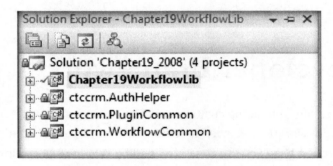

The advantage of using the add existing approach instead of browsing and referencing a pre-built assembly is you can easily navigate to the source code for the framework while getting used to how things work. This can make development and debugging a little easier.

Using a Common Base Class

Similar to how we used a base class for plug-in development we suggest doing the same for building custom workflow activities. The biggest advantage of this approach is it makes it easy to reuse logic across custom activities rather than duplicating logic in each.

We will detail more on the common features later in the chapter. The following are a few of the base class capabilities.

- Incorporates the same tracing we looked at for plug-ins to allow workflow activities to log to our custom trace entities on demand
- Allows for some standard error handling to be wrapped around the Execute method to provide a consistent way to trap and report errors
- Easy access to the SharedVariables properties of the event context

- Easy access to the CRM Service without having to keep coding the logic to retrieve the CRM Service from the workflow execution context as we saw in the prior chapter.
- Easy access to a WebApplicationUrl property to allow a workflow to include links in generated content
- Easy access to the organization name using an OrgName property.
- Easy access to trace simply use this.CTCTrace.Write(...);
- Easy access to a set of utility Retrieve methods that are available by using the this.Retrieve* syntax.
- Ability to easily add more common logic that can be reused across activities.

In the ctccrm.workflowcommon assembly you can find the base class in the Base classes folder in file name BaseSequenceActivity.cs.

Start with a Standard Sequence Activity

I recommend starting with the template for a Sequence Activity (right click on project , New Item then select Activity) provided by Visual Studio. The advantage of this is it creates a designer.cs hidden file that holds any code generated by the Workflow Designer so it's not intermixed in with your code. You could simply create an empty class and have it inherit from BaseSequenceActivity. When you take that approach though it intermixes the designer generated code in with your custom code. While there's nothing wrong with this and it will work fine, it's just not as clean.

The first step once you created the SequenceActivity using the standard Visual Studio template you should add the following using statements at the top of the class. This references both the CRM and the Workflow common name spaces.

```
using ctccrm.WorkflowCommon.BaseClasses;
using Microsoft.Crm.Workflow;
```

Next, you would put the standard CrmWorkflowActivity attribute on the class just like we learned in the prior chapter. Then change the class inherited from to be BaseSequenceActivity instead of SequenceActivity as you can see in the following example.

```
[CrmWorkflowActivity("Add Value", "Math Utilities")]
public  class AddValueActivity: BaseSequenceActivity
{
}
```

Overriding the Execute Method

The next step would normally be to override the Execute method and provide your custom code implementation. This would look like the following example.

```
protected override ActivityExecutionStatus
        Execute(ActivityExecutionContext executionContext)
{
 ///custom activity logic here… ///
}
```

Remember, we want our base class to be able to help provide some common error handling and other services. To accomplish that we need to let the BaseSequenceActivity class control the Execute method and it will provide us with a method to override that it will call. That method is the ProcessRequest method. So instead of overriding the Execute you will override the ProcessRequest method as you can see in the following example.

```
protected override ActivityExecutionStatus
      ProcessRequest(ActivityExecutionContext executionContext)
 {

    //custom code here… //

    this.OutputValue = this.InputValue1 + this.InputValue2;

    return ActivityExecutionStatus.Closed;
 }
```

Other than the difference in name, the ProcessRequest method acts just like the Execute including passing you the ActivityExecutionContext reference.

Public Properties

Using the base classes for the activity doesn't change how we discussed in the prior chapter using properties. You still attribute any properties that you want to show in the CRM workflow designer with the special CRM attributes CrmInput/CrmOutput. Later in the chapter when we start talking about the tester we will see how it looks for those special properties and allows you to provide values during testing.

Using Trace

The base class BaseSequenceActivity exposes a CTCTrace property that you can use to output trace similar to how we saw in the plug-in framework chapter. The output for workflows goes to the same custom entity as it does for the plug-in.

To be able to use the CTCTrace property you must first add a using to your class to the Trace namespace as you can see in the following example.

```
using ctccrm.PluginCommon.Trace;
```

Next, you can use CTCTrace.Write and other Trace functions as we discussed in the plug-in framework chapter – the following is an example of our ProcessRequest method adding in trace statements of the input and output values.

```
protected override ActivityExecutionStatus
    ProcessRequest(ActivityExecutionContext executionContext)
{
    CTCTrace.Write("AddValue", "Input Value 1 = " +
                    this.InputValue1.Value);

    CTCTrace.Write("AddValue", "Input Value 2 = " +
                    this.InputValue2.Value);

    this.OutputValue =
        new CrmNumber( this.InputValue1.Value + this.InputValue2.Value);

    CTCTrace.Write("AddValue", "Output Value = " +
                    this.OutputValue.Value);

    return ActivityExecutionStatus.Closed;
}
```

Trace and Security

One thing that is a little different in how trace works with workflow activities compared to plug-ins is related to security. Plug-ins run in the context of the system and you can choose if you want to impersonate the user when accessing the CRM service. This allows a plug-in to be able to read and update entities that the invoking user does not have access to.

Workflows are different because the workflow runs in the context of the user owning the workflow. That means that from an access point of view to use trace the user owning the workflow must have access to the ctccrm_Traceconfig entity and the ability to append notes to it.

This typically doesn't cause a problem with trace that can't be worked around since it's a short term need. It is good to understand the implications of this because it could impact who you decide to have own workflows in other cases. For trace, typically what you can do is create a CRM security role thats only purpose is to allow correct access to the Trace, since security roles are cumulative, meaning you get the aggregate of all your roles. All you have to do is assign that role to a user during the time you are working on tracing their problem and then remove them from the role once you are done.

Adding trace calls can seem like a pain and many developers object to the idea. Often the real value doesn't show up until you hit production and try to track down a difficult problem without the debugger. Plan ahead and add enough traces to make sure you have the data you need to fix problems!

Using CRM Service

A common thing you will probably do is use the CRM service from a workflow activity to do additional platform operations. As we saw in the prior chapter how you can get a reference to the CRM service from the CRM workflow infrastructure by accessing the IContextService and calling the GetService method. The BaseSequenceActivity wraps up this into a property (CRMServiceInstance) that you can use to access the CRM Service without doing all the work.

The following is an example of making a call to the CRM service.

```
RetrieveMultipleResponse resp =
    this.CRMServiceInstance.Execute(req) as RetrieveMultipleResponse;
```

As you can see from the sample above that's a lot simpler than having to do the calls to lookup the IContextService and then doing the call to get the service. Additionally, the property uses our CTCCRMService wrapper, which allows us to improve error reporting and tracing of calls to the platform service.

The following is the code for the CRMServiceInstance property so you can see how it's implemented.

```
protected ICRMServiceProxy CRMServiceInstance
{
    get
    {
        ICRMServiceProxy m_Service = null;

        if (Context == null)
            return null;

        IContextService contextService =
          (IContextService)m_Context.GetService(typeof(IContextService));

        IWorkflowContext context = contextService.Context;

        ICrmService crmService =
                (ICrmService)context.CreateCrmService();

        if (crmService is ICRMServiceProxy)
            m_Service = crmService as ICRMServiceProxy;
        else
            m_Service = new CTCCRMService(crmService);

        return m_Service;

    }
}
```

Using this property and the IContextService instead of going directly to a Web Service reference allows our tester to help simulate a workflow activity running on the server. It does that by implementing its own IContextService and providing mocked up data during testing. You can see the implementation of the IContextService by looking at TesterCRMContextService in the

Workflow Tester project. You will also want to look at TesterCRMContext which provides a tester version of the CRM Context that would be available on the CRM Server. Both of these are used when the workflow activity is run in the Workflow Tester runtime environment.

Using SharedVariables

In the plug-in chapter we discussed how you can use SharedVariables to be able to hand data from one plug-in to the next. Workflows also have access to the SharedVariables that originate in the plug-ins. If you look back at our discussion about the event pipeline remember that workflows are always post platform operation and branch off and run asynchronous. What that means is variables placed in the SharedVariables during the pre-operation are available post operation but when accessed from workflow could be copies if multiple asynchronous plug-ins or workflows are running. What I mean by that is at the time the workflow is started it gets a copy of the SharedVariables not a reference to a central copy. That means if you have two asynchronous plug-ins or workflows running at the same time they could end up with different values for the same item if they both modify it.

Now that we have that discussion out of the way let's look at what the BaseSequenceActivity does to make it easier to access and use SharedVariables. Similar to the CRM Service, you can access the SharedVariables by going through the Context Service. To make it a little easier to access SharedVariables we have added a few helper methods to the base class.

The following SharedVarExists allows you to pass a name and quickly check to see if it exists in the SharedVariables.

```
bool SharedVarExists(string keyName)
```

Next, you can call SharedVarGetValue to get back an object representation of the item

```
object SharedVarGetValue(string keyName)
```

If you know it's going to be a string you can call the SharedVarGetString to keep from having to cast it after you get it.

```
string SharedVarGetString(string keyName, string defaultValue)
```

Finally, if you want to set a value in SharedVariables you can use SharedVarSetValue.

```
SharedVarSetValue(string keyName, object value)
```

Using these methods you can access items placed in the SharedVariables by plug-ins or add your own data to the SharedVariables so subsequent workflow activities can access them.

In Chapter 21, we will use these methods as part of a SharedVariables custom activity to allow SharedVariables to be accessible from the client workflow editor.

Using the Org Name

For some reason, the Workflow Context currently doesn't have the organization name like the plug-in IPluginContext does. It does have the Organization ID though and with that you can retrieve the Organization Name.

The BaseSequenceActivity exposes a property OrgName that you can use to access this from the workflow code. There's no magic here it simply uses the Organization ID from the workflow context and retrieves the Organization name from the Organization entity.

Using Web Application URL

Another challenge you might encounter when working with Workflows is how to get a URL to the CRM Server if you want to include a link for a user to click on in content generated from a workflow activity. To accommodate for that we added a property to the base class called WebapplicationUrl that can be accessed to provide the caller with a base url for the web application server.

The implementation for this is a little more challenge than you might think at first because there's not a good place to get this value from. You also have to deal with the fact that your workflow activity might run for multiple organizations which in the case of an IFD deployment scenario might each have their own unique web server URL. For now our implantation in the base class uses a registry value that includes the organization name. This allows each organization to have its own registry key and therefore its own server URL. We use our OrgName property we just discussed to retrieve the organization name to use as part of the key

The following is the current implementation of the WebapplicationUrl property.

```
public string WebapplicationUrl
{
    get
    {
        if (m_Context == null)
            return "Software\\CTC\\ctccrm_authhelper\\ not set";

        RegistryKey hklm = Registry.LocalMachine;
        hklm = hklm.OpenSubKey("Software\\CTC\\ctccrm_authhelper\\"
                        + OrgName, false);

        if (hklm == null)
            return "Software\\CTC\\ctccrm_authhelper\\"
                        + OrgName + " not set";

        string url = (string)hklm.GetValue("WebapplicationUrl", "");

        return url;

    }
}
```

Using the Retrieve Methods

Often times convenience is important as it not only increases productivity but increases consistency in the code. Of course we can't forget the simple reason that at times we are lazy and if we can just say this.SomeMethodName it's easier than having to fire up a new instance of a helper class to make some calls. If you read the plug-in chapter you would have seen a similar set of methods that we made available to plug-ins that inherited from the base plug-in class.

The following is an example of using one of these methods – RetrieveFirstBySingleKey which basically calls the Retrieve methods and gives you back the first one with a matching key. In this case we are retrieving the Organization entity.

```
DynamicEntity org = this.RetrieveFirstBySingleKey("organization",
                "organizationid", context.OrganizationId);
```

In this example, you would have written 30-40 lines of code to accomplish the same thing.

The following are the methods supported by the BaseSequenceActivity class.

The first method is RetreiveMultipleBySingleKey. This method basically finds all the records matching the key provided. This is great when you want to find all the child records that have the parent ID on them.

```
List<DynamicEntity> RetrieveMultipleBySingleKey(string entityName,
                string keyAttributeName, Guid keyValue)
```

The RetrieveFirstBySingleKey is a helper method that basically calls the RetrieveMultipleBySingleKey and then returns you back the first record.

```
DynamicEntity RetrieveFirstBySingleKey(string entityName,
                string keyAttributeName, Guid keyValue)
```

The following retrieves the Guid for a lookup value on a record. For example, if you retrieved product you could give the method the defaultuomid and it would give you back the Guid for the defaultuomid property on the product entity matching the keyValue you pass.

```
Guid RetreiveLookupGuid(string entityID,
        string keyAttributeName, Guid keyValue, string lookupAtributeName)
```

Our next helper method is RetrieveMultipleByMultipleKeys. This method lets you pass in an array of key values that you are trying to match to and returns any entity that matches. This can be helpful when you have a set of entity ID's that you want to retrieve all at once.

```
List<DynamicEntity> RetrieveMultipleByMultipleKeys(string entityName,
        string keyAttributeName, object[] keyValues,
        string sortAttributeName, OrderType order)
```

Our final helper method is one to work with queries with multiple entities. It basically allows you to join two entities and the LinkTables object provides details about the related entity.

```
List<DynamicEntity> RetreiveMultipleBySingleKeyJoinTables(
     string entityName, string keyAttributeName, Guid keyValue,
          List<TableLink> linkTables)
```

These methods should get you started thinking about adding some easy to use helper methods. They are located in the BaseSequenceActivity partial class in file BaseSequenceActivityRetrieveHelpers.cs.

Workflow Tester

Code, Build, Deploy, Test, that's the standard pattern when you are building custom activities. The problem is you either need to be running the CRM Server locally on your developer machine or need to use remote debugging to really correctly debug your activity. Even then the steps to deploy and get ready to test are more complex than simply hitting F5 like you would if you were building an ASP.NET web application and wanted to debug it. With that in mind we set out to build a Workflow Activity Tester that would allow you to do some of the testing without being on the CRM server.

One of the projects included in the book sample code in the Framework folder is a Workflow Tester. The idea behind the Workflow Tester is to allow you to test your custom activities and workflows without having to register them with the CRM server. To accomplish this, the tester attempts to create a CRM Server like workflow execution environment and simulates some of the basic CRM functions to allow you to do testing of workflows without deploying them. As we dive deeper in to the features of the tester you will also learn more about how custom workflow activities fit into the overall CRM server architecture.

Setting up to use the Workflow Tester

Before you can start using the Workflow Tester you need to setup a few things. The easiest way to use the tester is to just add a few projects to your existing solution that are required. Then you simply set it as the startup project for debugging and hit F5 to launch it.

You need the following three projects to be added to your solution using the add – existing project option - CTCWorkflowTester, ctccrm.workflowScheduleService and ctccrm.plugincommonsetup.

Connecting to the CRM Server

Launch the workflow tester and then click on the "…" next to the Connect to launch the CRM Server Connection Dialog as you see in the following example.

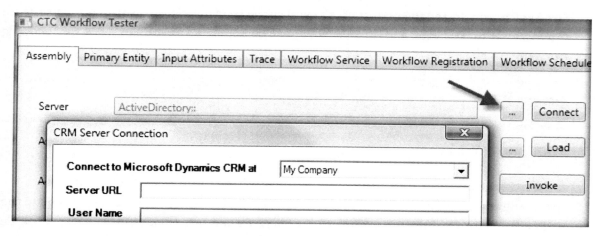

To make it easier you can choose to save your credentials and the connection information so it will be reloaded next time. You still need to click the connect button even if the credentials are saved.

Loading the Assembly

Once you are connected to the CRM server the next step is to load the assembly that contains your custom activity. As you can see in the following image, you click the "…" to launch the standard open dialog and browse to your projects bin\debug folder and select the correct assembly.

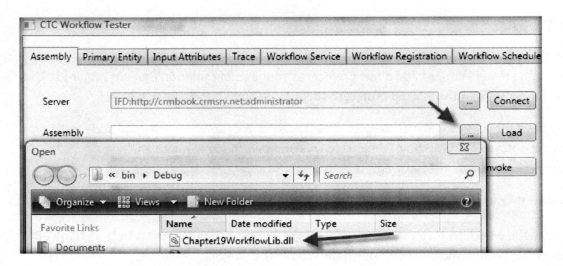

Once you have selected the correct assembly click the Load button. The Load button will cause the assembly to be loaded and list of activities will be populated as you can see in the following example.

Setting Input Values

Once you have chosen a workflow activity from the list the tester will reflect and try to determine any properties that have the CrmInput attribute. For each of these it will add to the grid on the Input Attribute tab as you can see below for our test activity we have two properties with the CrmInput attribute discovered.

CTC Workflow Tester

| Assembly | Primary Entity | Input Attributes | Trace | Workflow Service | Workflow Registration | Workflow |

	PropertyName	Name	Type	Value	EntityName
	InputValue1	Input Value 1	CrmNumber		
	InputValue2	Input Value 2	CrmNumber		

You can simply type in the grid for the Value. In our case since it is a number we could for example put the value of 25 in both items. The EntityName column is used in conjunction with the Value field when the type is CrmLookup.

To make life a little easier and to recognize that during testing you often use the same values. The tester will save the values you input so the next time you choose the same activity those values will be reloaded for you without any extra typing.

Currently validation of the values input is left up to the user! Make sure you provide a value that is appropriate for the data type of the property. E.g. don't provide a string to a number property!

Invoke the Activity

After you set the values for the input parameters you can simply click the Invoke button which will cause the tester to create an instance of the activity in the tester workflow runtime. If there are any problems you might see an error or have the debugger stop on the exception otherwise you will see the following message to indicate your activity (workflow) was launched.

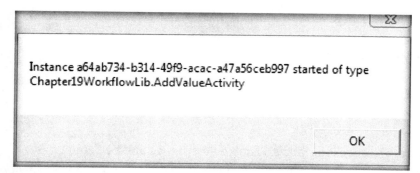

Using the Debugger

One of the nice things about the tester is it allows you to interactively use the debugger to find problems. One of the reasons we suggest adding the tester to your solution is it just makes it easier to set break points in the activity class library project because it's in the solution you are debugging so there's no headache of browsing to find the right code.

If you're going to set a breakpoint it's best to do that before you invoke the workflow otherwise by the time you get to setting it you may find the workflow instance had already finished processing.

In the following example, you can see that we set a breakpoint at the start of our ProcessRequest method.

```
protected override ActivityExecutionStatus
    ProcessRequest(ActivityExecutionContext executionContext)
{
    CTCTrace.Write("AddValue", "Input Value 1 = " + this.InputValue1.Value);
    CTCTrace.Write("AddValue", "Input Value 2 = " + this.InputValue2.Value);

    this.OutputValue =
        new CrmNumber( this.InputValue1.Value + this.InputValue2.Value);

    CTCTrace.Write("AddValue", "Output Value = " + this.OutputValue.Value);

    return ActivityExecutionStatus.Closed;
}
```

All the normal things you can do in the debugger are available. You can set watches, view data properties and even use Set Next Statement to go past problem areas or code that doesn't work well in the tester.

TIP

If you find that you can't set a value or other item before running the tester set a break point and use the Quick Watch capability of the debugger to set the value

Enable Persistence

On the main tab of the tester is a checkbox labeled Enable Persistence and by default it is checked. What this button does is try to help you find any issues where your workflow activity might have persistence issues when run on the server for real.

Persistence or serialization comes into play when a workflow ends or is put to sleep by the workflow runtime. When this occurs, it attempts to serialize and persist the memory version of the workflow instance and all its activities. In doing so if it encounters a non serializable property the serialization will throw an exception. When this occurs on the CRM server your workflow will be put into a "wait" state and if you look at the workflow in the workflow monitor you will see that an error has occurred. It will not be specific what the error is, only that an error has occurred. Turning on the CRM platform trace and reviewing the detail will show if it is related to serialization/persistence.

The Enable Persistence option attempts to save your workflow instance upon completion and if it fails it will indicate to you there's a persistence problem. To demonstrate how this would work the chapter example contains an activity called BadPersistActivity.

If you look at the code for this activity it's really simple first, we define a class called WorkArea that just has a single property. This class will be used to demonstrate a non serializable data type being used. The following is an example of the class.

```
public class WorkArea
{
    public int MyProperty { get; set; }
}
```

In our activity class I created a private variable that will contain an instance of the WorkArea class. It's important to note that this is marked private because often times people think only public properties get serialized. Due to how workflow serialization works, it does a deeper serialization.

```
[CrmWorkflowActivity("Bad Persist Activity", "Breaking CRM")]
public partial class BadPersistActivity: BaseSequenceActivity
{

    private WorkArea m_Work = null;
}
```

If we invoke this activity it will run fine, just as it would on the CRM Server however when it goes to serialize the workflow you will receive the following exception.

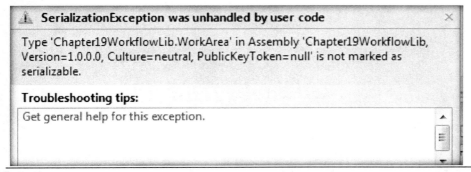

~ 511 ~

As you can see it's nice enough to indicate the type that was unable to be serialized. If we had run this on the CRM server when this type of error occurs you only get this level of detail once you turn on platform tracing.

Wrapping it up

In this chapter, we looked at our base class for building custom activities and a few of the features it adds as reusable capabilities such as tracing and CRMServiceInstance. It also sets the stage for you to add on and build more base class common functionality. By using a base class of concept you can increase the consistency across your workflow activities and also make them easier to debug once you get to production and don't have the Visual Studio debugger.

In the final parts of the chapter, we looked at the Workflow Tester. Using the tester, you can test your custom activities without having to register with CRM. You also do not have to do the debugging on the same server as the CRM server or mess with remote debugging.

20

Workflow Code Generation

In this chapter, we are going to look at a way to combine the power of the platform metadata with the ability to build custom workflow activities. In Chapter 18 we discussed how you can build workflow activities to accomplish tasks ranging from very small things to very large activities that users use and treat as black boxes in terms of not caring what happens inside the activity as long as what they wanted done gets accomplished.

Now we are going to dive down deeper and build some activities that can be used as building blocks to build other workflow activities or complete workflows. These activities are going to be built for us using some simple code generation combined with the platform metadata.

The idea for this came early on during the beta of the CRM 4.0 product as I was doing some work with the declarative workflow activities that come out of the box. These are the activities described in Chapter 18. If you read through Chapter 18 you would see activities like Create, Retrieve and Update. They were generic and exposed and worked with Dynamic Entities. They required you to know the names of the attributes that existed and the activities were not specific to any of the system entities. As I worked with these, I had an idea. Why couldn't we generate similar activities but make them understand the attributes that existed on the entities?

Using the metadata service in this chapter we will build out this concept creating up to two custom workflow activities for each entity we choose in our data model.

Understanding the problem

Using the word problem might be too strong to describe what we are trying to accomplish. There is nothing wrong with the activities that come out of the box with the SDK assembly that provides generic Retrieve, Create and Update.

Some of the challenges when using the built in activities:

- You will find that by using them they require you to know what attributes an entity has in order to retrieve the value or set it.
- You will need to be careful when setting the attributes value to make sure you don't typo the name of the attribute.
- You are also expected to know the data type of that attribute so when you set the value you can create an instance of the correct type of property.
- You just cannot drag (from the toolbox) and go.

Part of the challenge is caused by the goal of these activities; to work in the CRM Online environment or other environments where deploying custom code is not supported. In these environments declarative workflows could be created and these activities were designed to support allowing access to create, update and retrieve entities as part of the flows.

To be clear, our focus in this chapter is not CRM Online or other environments where you can't deploy code. We are going to generate code based custom activities that will need to be deployed to the target server to work.

Concept Goals

Our primary goal is to increase the productivity of the developer building custom workflows or composite activities (they are really the same if you think about it). We want to do that by trying to reduce what they need to know and what they need to be precise about typing to get things to work.

Here are some more specific goals we tried to accomplish when building out this concept.

- Leverage the platform metadata so we can generate activities that are easy to use.
- Allow activities for an entity to be pre-built and able to be dragged and dropped from the toolbox for use by the developer in a workflow or composite activity.
- Recognize there's differences in how a Retrieve and a Modify (Create, Update) activity works, but allow them to work together when placed on a flow. Meaning information from retrieved in the Retrieve activity should be easily updated using the Modify activity.
- The retrieve entity should allow retrieving based on a single key like the entity ID or by passing of a QueryExpression.
- The retrieve activity should expose the retrieved data as properties on the custom Retrieve activity allowing easy development of rules or evaluation by other activities leveraging Intellisense and other tools of the designer to connect the dots.
- The modify activity should expose specific properties for each attribute on the entity. Using Dependency properties you should be able to connect the dots of this property to any other data source inside the workflow using standard workflow design techniques.
- These activities should be capable of running inside the CRM hosted workflow or in standalone workflow that still access the CRM services.
- Tracing and other diagnostics should be baked into the design.
- Inheritance of the generated activities should be used where possible to minimize redundant code.

The list could go on but those should start to give you an idea of what our goals were. Now let's start exploring more about the specific design that we chose. It's important to note this isn't the only way you could accomplish this. Like many things there are numerous approaches that you could take, this is just one of them that we tried to demonstrate the ability to leverage the platform metadata.

50,000 foot view

From a high level perspective our implementation breaks down in to three parts. First, we have two base activities that we created that all our generated activities will inherit from. These base classes reside in the ctccrm.WorkflowCommon project that is included in the samples.

They can be found in the BaseClasses folder:

- **BaseModifyActivity** – This activity is the parent for all modify activities we will generate. The actual Create or Update calls will be handled inside the common code in this activity.

- **BaseRetreiveActivity** – This activity is the parent for all retrieve activities we will generate.

The following class diagram illustrates the relationship of the generated activities to and their inheritance hierarchy.

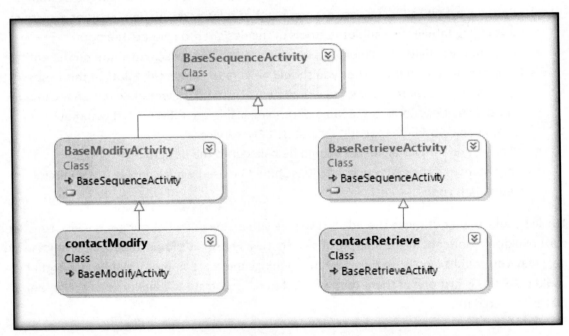

The second part of our solution is a WPF (Windows Presentation Foundation) application that connects to the CRM server and queries the metadata. Using this application, you can select the entities you want to generate retrieve and modify activities for.

We believe that you will not generate for all entities but the ones that you plan to use heavily in your workflows.

The following is a screen shot of the code generation application – you can find the code for this application in the CTCWorkflowEntityGen folder in the samples.

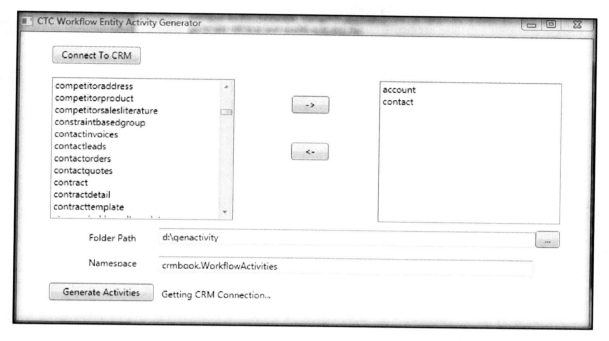

The output from this application is the actual C# code file that you will put into a project and compile. At a minimum, we recommend putting them in their own folder in your workflow activity project. If you plan to have multiple class libraries that will contain your workflows or you plan to register these in the GAC on the server you might want to include them in their own class library.

Once added to your project file these should be treated like any other code. Since they inherit ultimately from the Windows Workflow Activity class, they will automatically show up in the tool box when they are referenced by a workflow project, or if you are editing a workflow or activity in the same project they reside.

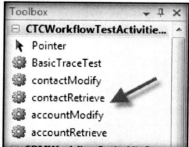

Once you have added them to the project, and created a reference to that project if necessary, you are ready to create a workflow. The following is an example of a simple workflow that uses the contactRetreive and contactModify activities.

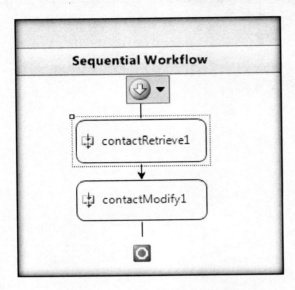

In the above simple workflow we are using a Retrieve to get a contact and then the Modify to update the contact.

To get this to work, on the Retrieve entity we would set the EntityID property to the ID of the contact we are going to retrieve. The EntityID property is a dependent property meaning we hard code it, or simply bind it to another activity property or a local variable to get the value.

Once the activity executes it will expose properties that we can use in subsequent activities. Each Retrieve activity exposes a RecordFound property that can be checked to cause processing to vary.

The following image adds a check of the Record Found and then either executes a modify activity in the Create mode or the Update mode accordingly.

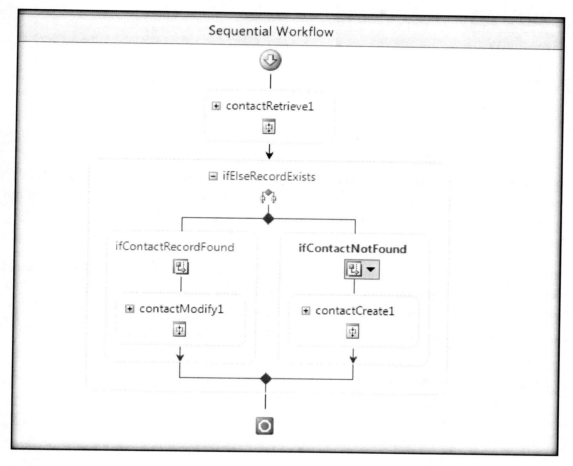

In addition to the RecordFound, the retrieve activity will expose one property for each attribute on the entity. The following shows the property page for the contactRetrieve activity showing a partial list of the properties available for contact.

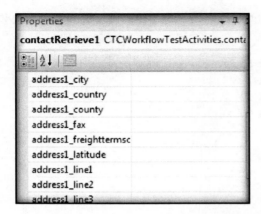

You might notice from the above image that the properties are just normal properties. That's because they are expected to be output properties from the Retrieve Activity. If we look at the contactModify activity, it will expose the same list of properties but they will be workflow dependent properties.

Using the dependent properties on the modify activities we can use the Binding dialog to hook them up to the value that we retrieved or any other activity property or local variable. The following shows the Bind dialog for one of the properties on the modify activity.

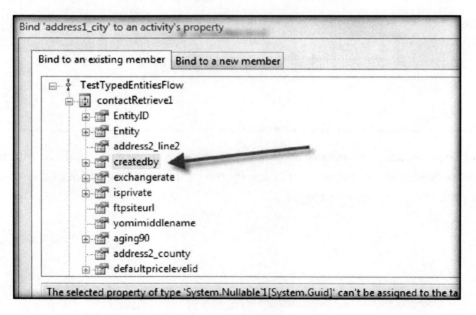

Digging Deeper

If we were to look a little closer at our generated code we would understand what happens. In the retrieve activity it simply takes the EntityID provided and calls a Retrieve. The retrieve is done using a Dynamic Entity because it's part of our generic base class. Each property is implemented as a nullable type.

The following is an example of the property generated for the aging60 attribute on contact.

```
public decimal? aging60
{
    get
    {
        if (this.Entity == null)
            return null;

        if (CTCDEPropHelper.PropertyExists(this.Entity, "aging60"))
            return CTCDEPropHelper.GetMoneyValue(this.Entity, "aging60",0);
        else
            return null;
    }
    set
    {
        if (this.Entity == null)
            return;

        CTCDEPropHelper.AddMoneyProperty(this.Entity, "aging60",
                                         value.Value);
    }
}
```

As you can see from the above example it works with an Entity property that contains the Dynamic Entity that was retrieved. This allows you to work with either the specific properties exposed like aging60 or directly with the Dynamic Entity via the Entity property if desired.

Looking at the same aging60 property on the modify activity we would see the following definition for the property.

```
public decimal? aging60
{
    get { return (decimal?)GetValue(aging60Property); }
    set { SetValue(aging60Property, value); }
}
public static readonly DependencyProperty aging60Property
            = DependencyProperty.Register("aging60",
                    typeof(decimal?), typeof(contactModify));
```

As we have discussed previously this is a dependent property so we can take advantage of the binding capabilities of the workflow designer.

Extending Generated Activities

Each of the activities class files generated are created as partial classes. The reason for this is to allow you if needed to add additional custom logic to each class. This can be done by creating a separate file in the same project that is defined also as a partial class of the same name.

Using this technique for code generation we are able to easily re-generate the workflow activities without affecting your custom code.

It would also be possible to easily modify the code generator to implement some calls to partial methods. Partial methods allow you to define hooks in generated code that only is invoked if the method is provided in another file. This is a new feature of C# 3.0.

Wrapping it up

In this chapter we talked about a concept of leveraging the platform metadata to allow us to generate workflow activities that are specific to the data model. Using this technique we are able to build specific workflow activities for both retrieving and modifying entities.

The idea is these activities, once generated, will show up on your toolbox and allow you to drag and drop them into your workflow. You can then use the workflow designer to work with the typed properties exposed.

Using these activities should reduce the times that you get errors from invalid names or invalid types being added for a specific attribute.

21

Workflow How - To's

In the prior chapters we have covered a lot of ground explaining how workflow works and integrates with the platform. In the custom workflow activity chapter we explored how you can build workflows with Visual Studio that can then be used as part of a workflow defined in the client interface. We also looked at some reusable code as part of the framework library that comes with the book. Now in this chapter we are going to walk through some more examples of workflow how-to's.

This chapter was one of the last chapters I finished and ended up being double the size that I had intended when I originally created the book table of contents. The reason was by the time I got to it, there were so many ideas of things to cover. The key goal for the examples in this chapter was to try to find examples that demonstrated the power of workflow but would be generally useful to the broad audience of the book. Pretty much all of the examples in this chapter can be used as is, or enhanced to meet specific needs that you have. Each has complete source included in the book source code samples or framework folders that you can reference and use.

Our examples will start with some custom workflow activities that perform tasks related to working with dates, math and string manipulation. Building on those, we will look at how to use workflow to grant access to a team. Next, we will detect a changed value and show two approaches to solve the problem. Finally, we will look at the workflow scheduling service that allows automating the scheduling of workflows to run at specific times.

Working with Dates

One of the common tasks that you will encounter with workflow is working with dates. This can be simply including a date in an e-mail you're sending or could be trying to calculate a forward looking date that something will be due. Most of the time you will be manipulating dates using the Form Assistant that is visible on the right side of the "set properties" dialog. Using the form assistant you can do basic date addition or subtraction using offsets of months, days, hours and minutes. The following shows what the Form Assistant looks like when you are working with a date field on the main form area.

Typically you will be working on dates when setting a form for an entity, setting a property on a workflow step (activity) or as part of a condition comparison. In the above image you see that Look For drop down. That determines if you will be getting the date from a property on the primary entity, a property on a related entity or a local value. For either primary or related, once you pick the entity name you will be prompted to pick an attribute from the list of compatible attributes. In other words, you won't see a string show up in the attribute list if you're trying to bind it to a date field. Local values is either a value related to the workflow itself such as in our case Workflow or if you have any prior workflow steps they could show up as eligible for you to select as we will see in subsequent examples. Selecting Workflow on the list of local values will allow us to pick Execution Time since we are working with a date field. Execution time can be used to represent the current date/time.

As you can see in the following image we can simply use it as is to bind to a due date to indicate it's due right now.

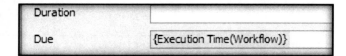

It's also possible using the form assistant to specify a default date as well as increase or decrease the value. By default, if you modify the offset values like days they are subtracted from the date. Changing that to after instead of before will allow you to add to the current date at time of assignment. The following is an example showing adding 3 days to the execution time and storing it in the due date.

As mentioned earlier, you can also do the same thing with attributes on either the primary, related entity or from custom steps that have already executed. The following example shows binding a date one month following the creation of an account.

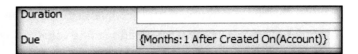

You can do the same type of binding for condition compares to check if a date is before or after the bound date. For example, you could check if the account had been modified in the last 30 days.

Using the built-in capabilities you can actually do a lot of different things with dates. However there are some limitations. In the next section of this chapter we are going to explore some custom activities that allow you to add additional date manipulation to your workflows.

Custom Date Activities

In this section we are going to build four custom activities to do various date related functions. These are pretty simple activities that leverage the ability to develop custom activities and have them be used by users as part of their workflows. The following are the custom date activities that are provided as part of the book framework code and you can find them in the $BookCode/Framework/WorkflowCommon/Activities/Date folder.

Activity	Description
AddToDate	Simple add to either an existing date or get the current date.
CalculateDateDiff	Calculate the difference between two dates.
GetNextDateForDayOfWeek	Calculate a date for the next specific day of the week specified.
GetPeriodDate	Calculate a date for the end of a period such as month or quarter.

Add To Date Activity

Our first custom activity we are going to look at is a simple add to date activity. This custom activity takes optionally an Input Date and then a few options to add to that date. If the Input Date is not provided we will get the current date at the time that the activity executes and then use that.

The output from this activity is the property Output Date that can be used in future steps in a workflow. You might be thinking that you can do similar things with the Form Assistant but the difference is you can only do that in the context of the Form Assistant when binding values. So if you wanted to have a step that just creates a date that you use in a few places that is not possible. This activity is just a simple utility activity that can be used as part of a larger business process.

The following is an example of the input properties that can be set on this activity. Each of these are marked with CrmInput on the custom activity.

Workflow: Test - Add to Date
Set Custom Step Input Properties

Property Name	Data Type	Value
Months to Add	int	
Days to Add	int	{Duration(Task)}
Hours to Add	int	
Input Date	datetime	

The other nice thing about this activity unlike the Form Assistant which uses static values set at design time, this activity can use the value from the data from the primary entity or related entities as part of the calculation. Of course you could still hard code the value at design time if you desire.

Since the activity has a property marked as CrmOutput the step will show in the list of Local Values in the lookup for future steps. It will show using the description you gave on the step when you add it to the workflow in the editor. In the following example you can see us binding the Output Date to the Due Date on the entity.

 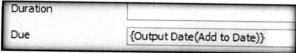

Calculate Date Difference Activity

This is similar to the custom activity that we saw in the prior chapter when we learned about the basics of custom activities. We have included it here for completeness but won't dive into too many details because we already saw it earlier. The following shows the input to this activity which is two dates.

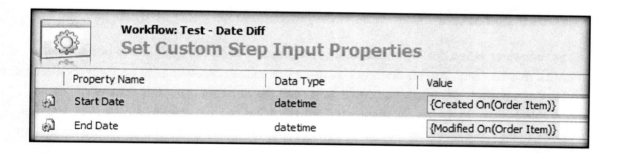

The output from this activity is the Total Days' difference between the two dates. For example, looking at real estate customization you might use this to calculate and store the total days on market.

You can also use this value in condition compares to check that N number of days have occurred or haven't occurred.

Next Day of Week Activity

This next activity is handy where you want to advance a date but also have it land on a specific day of the week. This activity helps where for example you always want to assign calls to Friday or have something expire at the end of a week on Sunday. In the following example we pass in Sunday and then 2 days after the execution date.

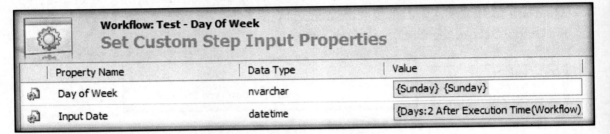

So if today's date was 7/5 (Saturday) and we advance the date 2 days so it would be 7/7 (Monday). But since we have indicated that we want it to be always a Sunday the Output Date property will contain 7/13 which is the next Sunday. In subsequent steps we use the Output Date to get the value calculated by this activity as you can see in the following example.

Get Date Period Activity

A common need when dealing with business processes is to do things at end of periods like months, quarters etc. There's no easy way using the built-in capabilities to easily determine the last day of a period. Obviously you could hard code the date but using this activity you could easily calculate it. To do the calculation the activity takes two parameters a base date and then a period string. The following example shows getting the date for the end of the month that an order was created.

Workflow: Test - Get Date Period		
Set Custom Step Input Properties		
Property Name	Data Type	Value
Period	nvarchar	Month
Base Date	datetime	{Created On(Order)}

In a perfect world we would take the period as a Picklist – but there's no way to create an on the fly Picklist on the activity so we just use a string. The string value we will then parse using an enum in code that ignores case on the string that passed and make it less error prone. The following is an example of the code used to parse the string value and ignore case.

```
enum enumPeriod
{
    Month,
    Quarter,
    HalfYear,
    Year
};


enumPeriod workPeriod = (enumPeriod)
    Enum.Parse(typeof(enumPeriod), this.Period, true);
```

In subsequent steps we can use the Period End Date to bind it to other properties as you can see in the following example.

This type of activity can come in handy for all types of processing like expiring records at the end of a month or quarter.

Wrapping up Date Activities

In this section we have looked at four custom activities that give us new options for working with dates. Several other date related activities could easily be built and added to the collection. While we didn't list code for each of these activities here to save space each is fully implemented and you can find the code in the book code in the framework library.

Custom Math Activities

One area where there really isn't much support is for performing math calculations as part of a workflow. In this section we are going to discuss some custom activities that we built to make it possible to perform basic math. The following are the activities included in the samples.

Activity	Description
Add	Adds two values.
Divide	Divide a value by another value.
Multiply	Multiply a value by a value provided.
Min	Determine the lowest value of two provided.
Max	Determine the highest value of two provided.
Subtract	Subtract one value from another.

You might notice in the above table we talk about value instead of a specific type of value. For our custom activity we want to be able to support CrmNumber, CrmFloat, CrmDecimal and CrmMoney value types. The workflow editor however will not allow us to assign values of different types so we can't just have a property called Input Value 1 and Input Value 2. To work around this we will have a set of properties for each type allowing each activity to be able to perform the operation on each of the types. You can see that in action in the following example where you see a Value 1 and Value 2 for each data type.

Workflow: test math
Set Custom Step Input Properties

Property Name	Data Type	Value
Value 1 Decimal	decimal	
Value 2 Decimal	decimal	
Value 1 Number	int	
Value 2 Number	int	
Value 1 Float	float	
Value 2 Float	float	
Value 1 Money	money	{Est. Revenue(Opportunity)}
Value 2 Money	money	{100.0000}

The values you specify in each of the calculations can be hard coded like you see above for Value 2 or dynamic where they pull from data or subsequent workflow steps like Est. Revenue in the above example. You can chain these math activities together to perform more complex calculations.

Wrapping Up Math Activities

For the book framework we provided a handful of what we thought would be the most common math related activities but you could easily build your own custom ones. In fact, early on when I was doing training on CRM 4.0, I always would talk about using a Credit Score or another custom score type calculation that could be done as a black box and just used by workflows.

Custom String Activities

Using the built-in string capabilities you can perform the basic assignments and compares. For example you can check for exact match, ends with, starts with, contains etc. In this section we are going to expand on those to provide some utility functions that allow you to do even more.

The following are the custom string activities that we are going to be discussing in more detail in the rest of this section.

Activity	Description
String Extract	Extract a portion of a string from another string.
String Concatenate	Combine two strings.
Regular Expression Compare	Allow comparing or checking a string value for match to a regular expression pattern.
Lookup ID to String	Convert an entity ID (Lookup) to a string value.
UrlBuilder	Build out a URL that could be included in a workflow.

String Extract Activity

Our first custom string activity is pretty simple and if you're familiar with the substring function it should look very familiar. The goal is simple, provide start and length and then extract that portion from the original string provided for use by the subsequent activities. As you can see in the following example we take a Start Index, Result Length and the Original String as input.

	Property Name	Data Type	Value
	Original String	nvarchar	{Subject(Task)} {Subject(Task)}
	Starting Index	int	0
	Result Length	int	3

After the activity runs you can access the Result String property as you can see in the following image.

String Concatenate Activity

The string concatenate activity simply takes two strings and combines them together.

The following shows combining a user's name and their manager.

	Property Name	Data Type	Value
	String 1	nvarchar	{Full Name(Owner (User))} -
	String 2	nvarchar	{Manager(Owner (User))}

I should note that it is possible to do some amount of string combining using the Form Assistant by putting more than one item in a field. This activity just can be used at any point in the flow so it gives you a little extra flexibility.

String Regular Expression Compare Activity

The regular expression compare activity is one of my favorites because it allows you to do really simple or really complex compares. If you're not familiar with regular expressions they basically provide a concise (sometimes cryptic) and flexible way to identify strings of text or patterns of characters. The expression is processed by a regular expression processor that determines if the it matches or doesn't match the string provided as input. Using this concept you can implement an amazing number of compares and not be limited to what is provided using the check condition step. The following image shows setting up the properties for testing our regular expression activity. In our example we will be comparing against a SSN (U.S. Social Security Number) pattern.

	Property Name	Data Type	Value
	Original String	nvarchar	123-45-6789
	Expression	nvarchar	^\d{3}-\d{2}-\d{4}$

The above expression will confirm that the SSN follows a NNN-NN-NNN pattern. For example, 123-45-6789 will match, but 12345678 will not. You can also do things like check for correct length and format of digits but that's not shown in this example.

Regular expressions have amazing power but at times can be complicated to understand. The best resource I have seen for understanding using regular expressions with .NET is a community site http://www.regexlib.com. If you want to write an expression from scratch, look at the cheat sheet listed on the site home page. The site also has hundreds if not thousands of prepared regular expressions that you can leverage.

The most common use for the output from this custom activity is to use the Matched output property in a check condition as you can see in the following example.

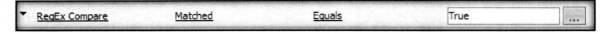

▼ RegEx Compare	Matched	Equals	True	...

Lookup ID to String Activity

The lookup ID activity exists to help work around a challenge with using Lookup properties in the client editor. Before we dive into explaining what it does, let's start by explaining the problem we are trying to solve. If you recall back in the custom workflow activity chapter we talked about what you needed to do to be able to use a Lookup property and have it show up in the client workflow editor. To refresh your memory the following is an example of a Lookup property for Contact.

```
[CrmInput("Contact")]
[CrmReferenceTarget("contact")]
public Lookup ContactLookup
{
    get { return (Lookup)GetValue(ContactLookupProperty); }
    set { SetValue(ContactLookupProperty, value); }
}
```

As you can see we specified a CrmReferenceTarget attribute on the property so that the workflow editor would know what type of lookup property it is. That attribute is required for working with properties that have the CrmInput attribute and you want them to show up in the workflow editor. Doing this isn't a problem until you want to write a utility or general purpose custom workflow activity that takes in any lookup not just ones of a specific type. Later in the chapter we will demonstrate this problem when we try to create a custom workflow activity that will share any record with a team or user. In that example we need to be able to have the entity ID of the record we are going to grant access to.

To work around this limitation we are going to create a custom activity that will act as the bridge and convert a specific Lookup property to a string property. The only negative of this approach is for each specific type of Lookup we are going to work with we need to add a specific Lookup Property to our custom activity for that type. Hopefully, in a future release the requirement to have a CrmReferenceTarget attribute will be removed and you could then have a generic way to get access to the Lookup in a utility type workflow activity.

In another scenario you might want to get access to the ID in a generic way. If you are trying to put the ID for the entity in an e-mail such as in a URL to edit or view a record. We will be covering how to handle that later in this chapter using this custom activity plus a UrlBuilder activity.

So what I decided to do for the book was to place in the book code framework a custom activity that would handle some of the most common entity types. The following image shows the types that are supported.

Property Name	Data Type	Value
Account Lookup	lookup	
Contact Lookup	lookup	
Activity Task Lookup	lookup	{Task(Task)}
Activity Email Lookup	lookup	
Activity Phone Lookup	lookup	
User Lookup	lookup	
Business Unit Lookup	lookup	

In the above list, you will notice that we have separate Lookups for e-mail, task and phone. The reason for that is we tried to use ActivityPointer which they all inherit from, however it wouldn't seem to work correctly so we ended up putting separate Lookups for each type.

You can easily expand this list by either inheriting from our activity or adding more properties for the types you want to support. You could also create your own control with just the types you need for your solution. This approach works for both built-in and custom entities. So if your solution has some custom entities you could still get the ID for them using this approach.

UrlBuilder Activity

One of the things you might want to do is include a link in an email generated from a workflow to a record in CRM. The challenge is there's not an easy way to get the record ID and include it in the workflow. We took care of part of that in our previous section with the Lookup ID to string activity. Using that we can now get the ID. Technically, you could use that and just hard code the rest of the URL in the email. The problem with that is your workflow will have a hard coded server and organization name as part of it and if exported and imported to another server would be incorrect. A common example of that happening would be promoting from development to QA, to production. To accommodate we are going to create a custom workflow activity to help out building the full URL.

Our custom activity will leverage the Lookup ID custom activity that we built previously. The following is an example of a simple workflow that shows getting the ID, building the URL and then using it in an e-mail.

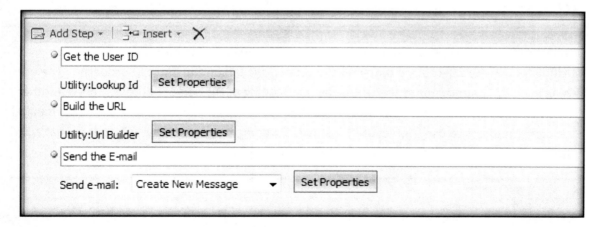

In this example we want to include a link to a user record that was just changed. As you can see in the following image, using the lookup to the User will populate the output property on our lookup with the entity ID for the user.

	Property Name	Data Type	Value
	Account Lookup	lookup	
	Contact Lookup	lookup	
	Activity Task Lookup	lookup	
	Activity Email Lookup	lookup	
	Activity Phone Lookup	lookup	
	User Lookup	lookup	{User(User)}
	Business Unit Lookup	lookup	

Next, our UrlBuilder step will take the ID we extracted to a string and use it as the Input ID. That allows the URL Builder to not be dependent on the entity type it is building the URL for. The other property is the URL template. The template is used to build our output URL.

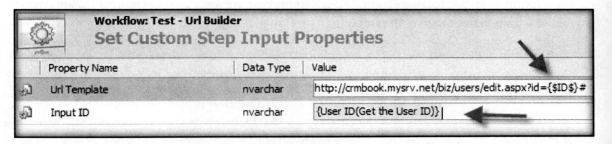

Workflow: Test - Url Builder
Set Custom Step Input Properties

	Property Name	Data Type	Value
	Url Template	nvarchar	http://crmbook.mysrv.net/biz/users/edit.aspx?id={ID}#
	Input ID	nvarchar	{User ID(Get the User ID)}

You probably notice in the above example that ID is included as part of the URL. The UrlBuilder activity will replace that with the value provided on the Input ID property. The one thing you might notice about the URL is the hard coding of the server address. This is another area that the UrlBuilder will help with. In the following image you will notice we have changed the server address to use $ServerURL$ instead. By doing this, UrlBuilder will replace that with the value obtained from the register on the server for that organization.

	Property Name	Data Type	Value
	Url Template	nvarchar	$ServerURL$/biz/users/edit.aspx?id={ID}#
	Input ID	nvarchar	{User ID(Get the User ID)} {User ID(Get the User ID)}

In the UrlBuilder activity as you can see in the following example, we take advantage of the WebapplicationUrl property that is exposed by our base workflow activity from the book code framework.

```
OutputUrl = OutputUrl.Replace("$ServerURL$", this.WebapplicationUrl);
```

You can read about the WebapplicationUrl property in Chapter 19 where we discuss the workflow framework. It basically pulls an organization specific value form the registry.

Our final step is to use the Output URL in our e-mail as you can see in the following image.

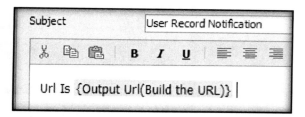

UrlBuilder could easily be enhanced to encapsulate more knowledge of building URLs into the custom activity, but that exercise will be left for the reader.

Sharing with User/Team Activity

Our next custom activity goes to address a need to be able to grant access to either a user or a team on the fly based on conditions that occurred in a workflow. For example, imagine that if once a record reaches a certain stage in the workflow other departments should gain access to it that otherwise would not have had access. Using the built-in capabilities you can re-assign the record to another user but there is no ability to grant access or "share" a record.

To accomplish that we are going to build a custom activity that will allow you to share with a team. On this activity we are going to take the entity name and the ID of the record we are granting access to. To keep this generic, we are going to again use our lookup ID activity we discussed earlier to convert the Lookup to a string version of the Guid.

As you can see in the following image we allow selection of a team and setting of the individual permissions.

	Property Name	Data Type	Value
	Entity Name	nvarchar	{task} {task}
	Entity ID	nvarchar	{Activity Task ID(Lookup Id)} {Activity
	CRM Team	lookup	Team 1
	Append Access	bit	⦿ False ⦿ True
	Append To Access	bit	⦿ False ⦿ True
	Assign Access	bit	⦿ False ⦿ True
	Create Access	bit	⦿ False ⦿ True
	Delete Access	bit	⦿ False ⦿ True
	Read Access	bit	⦿ False ⦿ True
	Share Access	bit	⦿ False ⦿ True
	Write Access	bit	⦿ False ⦿ True

In the workflow activity we are going to use the GrantAccessRequest message to share the record with the team specified. The following is the code from the custom workflow activity.

```
GrantAccessRequest req = new GrantAccessRequest();
req.PrincipalAccess = new PrincipalAccess();
req.PrincipalAccess.Principal = new SecurityPrincipal();
req.PrincipalAccess.Principal.Type = SecurityPrincipalType.Team;
req.PrincipalAccess.Principal.PrincipalId = CRMTeam.Value;

if (AppendAccess != null && AppendAccess.Value)
    req.PrincipalAccess.AccessMask = req.PrincipalAccess.AccessMask |
AccessRights.AppendAccess;

/*checks of other access rights removed for printed copy*/

TargetOwnedDynamic target = new TargetOwnedDynamic();
target.EntityId = new Guid(EntityID);
target.EntityName = EntityName;

req.Target = target;

this.CRMServiceInstance.Execute(req);
```

Workflow Value Change Detection

One of the things you might want to do with CRM Workflow is have a workflow wait for a value to change.

For example, maybe there's a business process you want to happen every time a company changes their name. The most obvious way you might do this is using a wait for as you can see below.

WaitFor Account.name != {account.name}

The problem with this approach might surprise you. If you were to run a workflow instance that had the above wait for condition it would run for ever.

The reason is because each time a workflow wakes up after a Waitfor condition it will pull the current values for the primary and related entities that are used in the workflow. So in our example if Account.Name started out as "Old Name" the workflow would stop and register a wait subscription for a change on the account entity instance in question. When that specific record is updated for any reason (Not just the value in the WaitFor condition) the CRM workflow engine will wake up the workflow instance so it can evaluate its Waitfor condition. The evaluation though is done using current values for Account.Name so Account.Name != {Account.Name} will always be false.

We are going to look at a couple of ways we can address this. One of them we will look at doing without doing any coding, and the other we will use a couple of custom activities.

Custom Entity Approach

To keep this generic, I'm going to use a custom entity called WF Workspace (crmbook_wfworkspaces). Think of it as a scratch pad to use while your workflow is running. We are going to add a few attributes to this custom entity that we will use to store our values. The following are the properties we are going to add:

crmbook_stringvalue , crmbook_intvalue and crmbook_moneyvalue .

Basically one for each data type we want to be able to store in our workspace. The reason the type matters is we want to be able to do this using only the workflow editor and without any custom code (see the custom code method later in the chapter for a more generic approach).

The workflow editor will only allow assignment of values of like data types so that is why it's important to have the various types of attributes.

There's really no reason to add these fields to the form other than it makes it a little easier to set the value later in the workflow editor. The workflow editor puts all fields in an Additional Fields tab if they aren't allocated to the form. Keep that in mind if you're ever trying to set a value of an attribute and can't find it - check the Additional Fields tab!

Now, let's create a new workflow and have it triggered on Create of Account. Our first step in the workflow should be to save the value of Account.Name to the wf workflowstate entity. To do this we are going to add a create step to our workflow and set the values as you can see below.

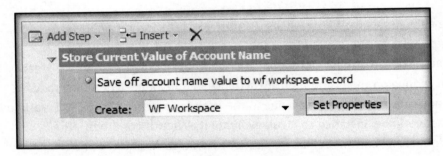

On the set properties page as seen below you need to set the value of stringvalue.

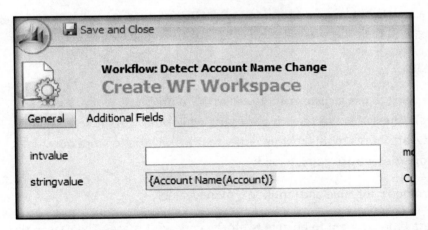

Next, add a Wait Step that we will configure to wait for the account name to change.

After adding the Wait Step, click on the condition link to be able to build the wait for condition. Here we want to compare the account name (which will be the current value) to our saved off value in our workspace.

To get the value from our saved workspace use the Form Assistant Look For list to find our Create Activity. Once you select it from the list you should see our stringvalue property and be able to select it.

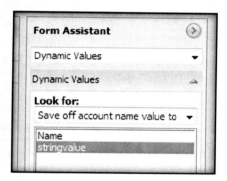

Now, for our example, let's send an e-mail to notify when the account name changes. To do this we add a Send Email step to our workflow.

In the text of the e-mail we can reference the old name (again referencing via our Create Activity string Value) and the new account name (which will just be the Account.Account Name attribute).

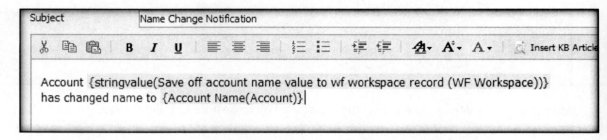

The following is our full workflow. We save the value by creating a workspace record, we wait for the account name change to occur by comparing the current value with our saved name and finally we send an email to notify of the change.

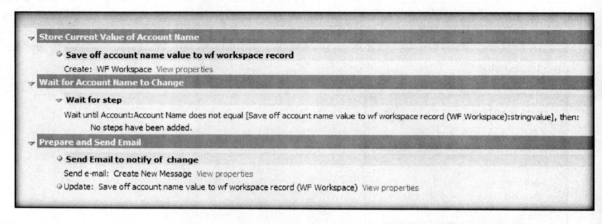

Next, we go create an account and set the account name to "CRM Live" looking at our workflow list we would see that a workflow had started and was waiting for the name change to occur.

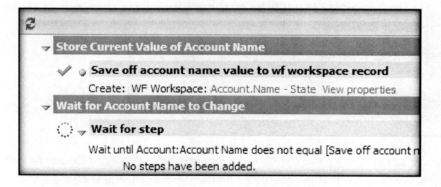

Finally, to finish off the workflow we go modify the account name to "CRM Online". The workflow would detect the change and an e-mail would be created as you can see below

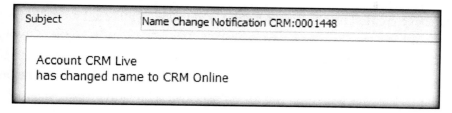

So in this approach we have used a custom entity to save off the value of account name to allow it to be compared. The advantage of this approach is it can be done without any custom code which means it's an approach that can be used in CRM Online. A couple of negatives of this approach are that you have the overhead of creating an instance of the workflow space entity. Additionally, there's no activity that can be used to remove this. So you would have to bulk delete or otherwise get rid of these workflow state records once they are no longer needed.

A possible alternative to this approach is to use a field on the account entity (or whatever entity you are working with) and do an update to the same record. The advantage there is you wouldn't need a custom entity and wouldn't have to clean up old records.

Next, I will look at how you can build a simple custom activity that can be used to accomplish this without the need for a custom entity or extra attributes.

Custom Activity Approach

In this section we are going to attempt to solve the same problem using a different approach. The prior approach is great where you can't deploy custom activities but if you can use a custom activity we can look at using the SharedVariables that exist as part of the workflow context to be able to store the values. So in this implementation we are going to use a SharedVariable's item as a scratch pad to hold our current value so we can use it to compare later.

You probably will recall talking about the SharedVariable property first in the plug-in section. We used the SharedVariables to allow passing down indication that Trace was enabled so that any plug-in in the event pipeline would be able to see the value without having to do the same work. Workflows also see the same SharedVariables and receive a snapshot of it at the time that the workflow is started. I say a snapshot because workflows run asynchronously so it's possible that there are multiple workflows or asynchronous plug-ins running at the same time that each received a copy of the SharedVariables when they started. As our workflow runs we can look at items in the SharedVariables as well as put new items in for use by subsequent steps in our workflow.

To get this to work, we have created two custom activities. One allows you to set items in the SharedVariables and the other allows you to get items from it. We will discuss how these work in more detail but first, let's modify our previous workflow to use our activities instead of using a custom entity. The first thing we do is remove the create of a workflow workspace entity record and replace it with a Shared Variable Set step. The following shows adding that step from the list of available workflow steps.

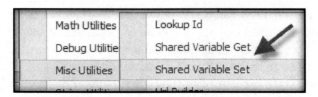

Once the step (workflow activity) is added in replacement of the create activity and we click on the set properties button we see the following dialog.

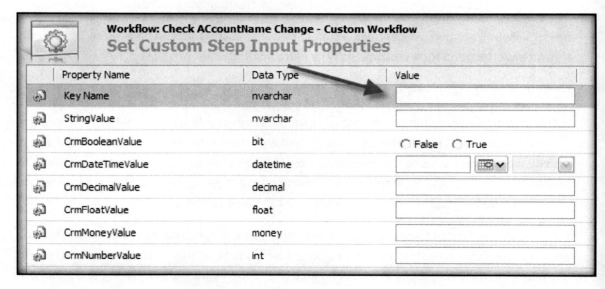

You will notice where the arrow is pointing is the Key Name property. This property indicates the key to use for storing an item in the SharedVariables collection. This must be unique from other items in there or it will overwrite the previous value.

The other properties listed are the majority of the property types supported by workflow. Remember our goal here is to be able to save off a value for use later in a compare or other use where a prior value is needed. This activity could be extended to support other fields like lookups, however since they require special type specific attributes it's not practical to have them on our common general purpose activity.

Using the form assistant on the right, we are going to indicate we want the String Value to be populated with the account name. You can also see in the following image that OriginalName was used as the key name. That's important because we will reference it later to get the value back out using that name.

	Property Name	Data Type	Value
	Key Name	nvarchar	OriginalName
	StringValue	nvarchar	{Account Name(Account)}

You can only use this step to save one value at a time; if you need to save multiple you should use multiple "set" steps. When this step runs, it will save off a copy of the value of Account Name as it is when this step runs.

Next, we will add a get of the value right after the set just to load it up so we can reference the value on the property. As you can see in the following image the only thing we need to specify on the get is the key name.

	Property Name	Data Type	Value
	Key Name	nvarchar	OriginalName

If you are using Stages in your workflow you will need to put the Get step in the same Stage that you plan to use it otherwise it won't show up for use in the form assistant.

Our next step is to modify the wait until condition to compare the Account Name against the Original Name value we retrieved from SharedVariables. In the condition we select the value to compare to using the form assistant and select the StringValue from our "get" step where we retrieved the value. The following shows that you should see the "get" step show up on the Local Values list in form assistant.

After you chose the String Value the condition should look like the following.

▼ Account	Account Name	Does Not Equal	OrigName Value-{String

Our final change to the workflow is to modify the e-mail template to use the prior value from the workflow property instead of the custom entity. The following shows our new e-mail template.

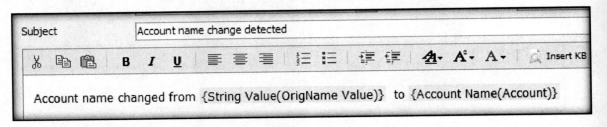

Subject: Account name change detected

Account name changed from {String Value(OrigName Value)} to {Account Name(Account)}

Now our changes are completed and we publish it for testing. If this were to run on a new account named "abc" and we looked at the workflow progress we would see it sitting on the Wait for step.

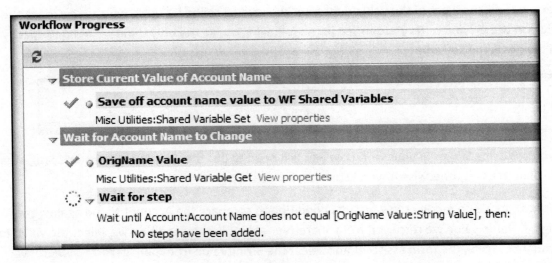

Workflow Progress

Store Current Value of Account Name
✓ ○ **Save off account name value to WF Shared Variables**
Misc Utilities:Shared Variable Set   View properties

Wait for Account Name to Change
✓ ○ **OrigName Value**
Misc Utilities:Shared Variable Get   View properties

○ ▽ **Wait for step**
Wait until Account:Account Name does not equal [OrigName Value:String Value], then:
No steps have been added.

If we then modify the name from "abc" to "XYZZ, LLC" the workflow would detect the update and the fact that the name changed and our e-mail step would trigger.

The following is the e-mail that was created showing the old and new names.

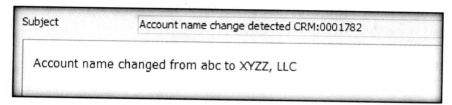

The nice thing about using this approach is there's nothing to clean up later. The data we put in SharedVariables will just go away when the workflow finishes.

One thing you should be aware of related to using the SharedVariables approach is that the SharedVariables are not persisted when things like a wait occur. This means that using the custom activity approach is best used when it's the first wait that occurs otherwise you might encounter inconsistent results.

Using a Router Workflow

Workflows allow you to trigger upon create or update events but they do not allow you evaluate and only launch if certain attribute values are set.

Imagine if you had 10 queues, each having their own new workflow you wanted to run when a new e-mail entered the queue. To accomplish that you would register 10 workflows listening to the E-Mail created event. When a new e-mail arrived it would launch 10 workflows, 9 would simply stop after checking the queue name of the item.

Use a Router Workflow that would do the initial checks to see what workflows to launch and then use Start Child Workflow to launch only the ones that need to run.

Building the Router Workflow

The first step is to create a new workflow that will act as the router.

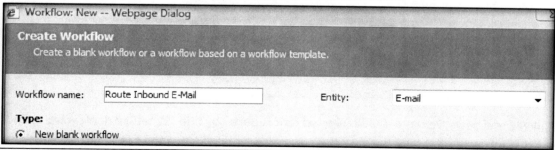

The actual workflow logic for our router will be simple it will consist of one or more Stage(s) and in each stage some check conditions that if true will start a child workflow. That way our child workflows will only start when they need to actually run.

In the following example we are checking if the e-mail was sent to the SouthColorado.NET Queue and if so then we do a Start Child Workflow on the specific workflow to route that message.

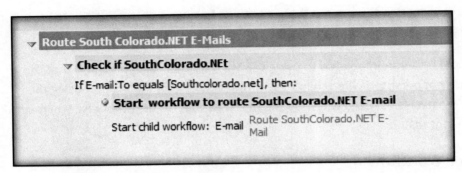

Initially we may just have the one stage, but as we evolve our customizations over time we could add several stages to group various types of sub workflows we want to launch.

Building a Child Workflow

On our Child workflow we will build it similar to our router workflow. However it will do the real work. To allow it to be invoked by our router as a child workflow we must indicate that it is allowed to be run as a child workflow. The following image shows the section to allow it to work as a child workflow.

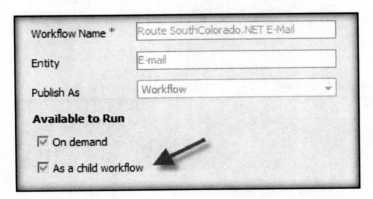

You will notice On Demand is also selected that is perfectly fine. What we don't want to do is check the trigger on Create because the new could be duplicating the run of our workflow.

When to Use This Solution

Using a router type workflow to hand out work to a series of child workflows is a great way to reduce the unnecessary launching of workflows on the create or update of an item. Using this pattern up front provides an easy way to evolve and scale out your workflow without having to re-work your existing process when you decide you have too many workflows firing when a new item is created.

In the example above we demonstrated the concept using e-mail but this pattern could apply to handling creates and routing to different workflow for any number of different entities.

Workflow Scheduler

If I had to pick one key thing that I think is missing from the workflow capabilities of the platform it would be the scheduling of workflows to run at a specific time. Ideally, in addition to being triggered by an event or run on demand, I should be able to configure a workflow to run on a specific schedule. This could be hourly, daily, monthly etc. based on a defined schedule. There are a few common approaches to try to solve this problem using things like the windows scheduler. Another common approach is to have the workflow reschedule itself by doing a start activity. If you use this approach though you end up with a lot of workflow zombies just hanging around just waiting to run again.

So for our example we are going to take a different approach and use a Windows service combined with a custom entity called ctccrm_workflowschedule. The workflow schedule custom entity will contain details about what to run and when. The windows service will be responsible for monitoring the schedules and firing off the workflows as needed or requested by the schedule.

Workflow Schedule Custom Entity

The workflow schedule custom entity will represent the schedule and other information about the workflow schedule to control how it works.

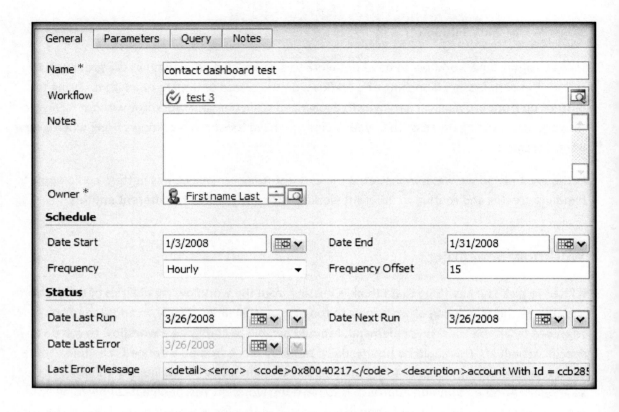

Form Field	Description
Name	This is the name of the schedule. It really isn't used for anything but reference.
Workflow	This is a Lookup for the workflow that is to be run for this schedule. Due to a quirk in the filter for the lookup you must set this before you publish the workflow or the workflow will not show up on the list to select!
Notes	Used for you to remember why you set this up!
Date Start	This is the first date the workflow schedule can run - allows for setting up future schedules.
Date End	Establish a specific date when this workflow should stop running.

Form Field	Description
Frequency	Minutes, Hourly, Daily, Weekly, Monthly, Quarterly, Yearly - used in conjunction with Frequency offset to determine how often to run.
Frequency Offset	Used to set the frequency - e.g Hourly / 15 would cause it to run at 15 minutes past each hour.
Date Last/Next/Error	These maintained by the workflow scheduler to indicate current execution progress.
Last Error Message	This is populated if an error occurs starting a workflow and is designed to save you from having to find the server log!

Parameters Tab

When you schedule a workflow it must be run against a specific entity and record for that entity. In other words, it's not currently possible to just say I want to run workflow X. You have to say I want to run workflow X on entity Account for record XYZ.

When building workflows to work with the scheduler there are three options for indicating how you want the workflow to know which entity / record to use. First, you can specify a hard coded entity name and entity ID on the workflow schedule. You would use this approach when you have a specific custom entity that you want the workflow associated with and in that scenario the workflow will be started and passed that entity ID. The Second option would be to use the Custom Xml Parameter field. When custom xml is provided the workflow to be started must specify that its primary type is the workflow schedule. When the scheduler starts the workflow instance it is passed the entity ID for the workflow schedule record. The workflow can retrieve the custom XML and use it for customization of the processing.

The following is an example of using the custom XML field to store configuration data - the XML can be any well formed XML it doesn't have to follow a specific schema.

| General | Parameters | Query | Notes |

Primary Entity

Primary Entity [   ]   Primary Entity ID [   ]

Custom XML Parameter

```
<config DashboardTemplateID="71AC656D-9BB9-DC11-A372-0003FF23671C" contactid="2C8A02EE-88B5-
DC11-A372-0003FF23671C" imageurl="http://localhost:1576/CTCCRMDashBoardWeb" />
```

Query Tab

The query tab allows you to provide a standard fetch query that will be used to start workflows. This option is perfect where you want to run the query once a week and for any records that match run a workflow. One workflow will be started for each row returned in the fetch results. The Entity ID attribute as you can see in the following image indicates the ID that should be passed to the workflow.

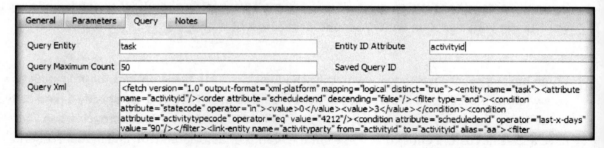

In the above example we run a workflow for each past due task. You could also do this for late accounts, dead opportunities, or even to send a happy birthday wish. In the happy birthday scenario the fetch would look for contacts that had a birthday in the last N days and start a workflow to send them a greeting. That approach is more efficient than have a bunch of workflows just sleeping until the person's birthday occurs.

Wrapping up the Scheduler

The scheduler provides basic support for what I hope in the future is core capabilities of the platform. Until then, use this as a starting point to customize to work with your needs. The workflow custom entity could easily be extended to provide more advanced scheduling if needed. While not mentioned earlier, the workflow service is capable of working with all three deployment options including CRM Online. It is also able to be configured to work with multiple target CRM organizations at once, so you don't need a separate workflow service for each organization or server combination. In that scenario, each organization would have their own set of workflow schedule records and the service would be configured with a list of organizations that it would perform scheduling against.

Wrapping it up

In this chapter we have looked at a number of interesting examples of ways to use workflow. Hopefully, you will find some of them interesting and be able to use them as they are. Each of them is provided in the book code source framework project. Since I had already doubled the length of this chapter already, we didn't include as many code samples in the book pages but you have complete code to all the items discussed in this chapter as part of the book code.

In reality, we just touched on the subject of how-to's with workflows on the CRM platform. The reality is you could probably write a whole book just on that topic. Use the ideas and the samples in this chapter to get you started with your own innovation.

22

Building CRM Online Solutions

Microsoft Dynamics CRM Online is the name of a new service offering from Microsoft that provides a hosted CRM 4.0 platform available on-demand. In this deployment scenario the servers hosting the Microsoft Dynamics CRM solution are located in the Microsoft Datacenter(s) ("in the cloud"). The advantage to a hosted environment is it provides for the opportunity to quickly have a CRM environment up and running without the normal lag time of server setup and software installation. Microsoft Dynamics CRM Online is currently targeted toward organizations that have 5-250 users. As part of the hosted offering, many operational aspects of using the CRM platform are managed by Microsoft. For example, network and data security as well as disaster recovery and support all are part of the service offering. Microsoft charges a simple per user monthly fee for use of their platform in the cloud.

CRM Online runs on the same core code base as the on-premise and partner hosted installs and includes most of the same features and extensibility points. From an application end user point of view, CRM Online offers all of the standard features that the other deployment scenarios offer. There are however a few differences for developers that we will be discussing in more detail in this chapter. Most of these are a result of security and reliability related challenges due to the shared hosting environment. In this chapter we will try to address some of the differences and where possible present some options where you can work around them.

From a solution developer point of view, CRM Online enables the development of rapid solutions. CRM Online offers a familiar application development platform and quick solution deployment for faster business execution. In the rest of this chapter, we will be exploring some of the unique aspects of the CRM Online deployment scenario that you should be aware of when building solutions that target hosted deployment model.

CRM Online Solution Differences

While most of the core features are the same when deploying to a Microsoft Dynamics CRM Online target, there are some differences that a solution developer will need to be aware of. We will highlight them in the following table and then dive into more details in the coming pages.

Area	Description
Authentication	CRM Online uses Windows Live ID.
Server URL	Microsoft assigns the sever URL https://{myorg}.crm.dynamics.com.
Plug-ins	Dependant on custom .NET assemblies being deployed to the server. Custom code deployed to the Microsoft Dynamics CRM Online server is not currently supported.
Custom Workflow Activities	Dependant on custom .NET assemblies deployed to the server. Custom code deployed to the Microsoft Dynamics CRM Online server is not currently supported.
Server Platform Tracing	With the assistance of Microsoft Support because you cannot remote into the server to modify the registry.
Reporting Services/ Filtered Views	Custom reports can be produced with the Report Wizard.
Server Hosted Pages	Server hosted pages are not available on the CRM Online servers but you can host them on your own external servers and reference them from the navigation of your CRM Online environment.

As you can see, the Microsoft hosted model supports nearly all the same scenarios as the other deployment models with only a few differences. In the rest of the chapter we will explore options for enhancing the platform within the supported features.

The above list was completed during the early release period of CRM Online. Keep checking back with Microsoft for the complete list of differences as they will be continuing to look for ways to make all three deployment scenarios as similar as possible.

Connecting to CRM Web Services

CRM Online exposes both the CRM Service and the Metadata Service just like the other deployment scenarios. However, Windows Live ID is used as the authentication mechanism. As we discussed in Chapter 9, authenticating to the platform web services using Windows Live ID is slightly different and has a few extra steps. If you haven't reviewed Chapter 9 yet, I suggest you read the section on authentication where we cover each option in detail.

The easiest way to connect to CRM Online is to use the AuthHelper assembly we provide with the samples for the book. Using this there is very little complications involved as it is mostly hidden from you in the helper assembly. The following is an example of connecting to the CRMService that is hosted on CRM Online.

```
ctccrm.AuthHelper.WinForms.FormCrmConnectInfo formInfo = new
ctccrm.AuthHelper.WinForms.FormCrmConnectInfo();
formInfo.LoadSavedLogin();
if (formInfo.ShowDialog() != DialogResult.OK)
    return;
CrmConnectionInfo connInfo = formInfo.GetConnectionInfo();
formInfo.SaveSavedLogin(connInfo);
connInfo.AllowOfflineUse = true;

try
{
    CrmServiceAuthManager<CrmService, CrmAuthenticationToken> svcMgr =
        new CrmServiceAuthManager<CrmService,
                CrmAuthenticationToken>(connInfo);

    CrmService service = svcMgr.GetService();
    WhoAmIRequest req = new WhoAmIRequest();
    WhoAmIResponse resp =  service.Execute(req) as WhoAmIResponse;
    MessageBox.Show("user id connected is " + resp.UserId.ToString());
}
catch (SoapException ex)
{
    MessageBox.Show(ex.Detail.InnerXml);
}
```

In the above example, we prompt the user with a form for the user/password and deployment type. The deployment type could also be manually set just as easily by building the CrmConnectionInfo object and not prompting the user. The key here is by using the above code and the AuthHelper assembly your code connects without requiring special changes to all three authentication schemes.

Here's an example connecting to the Metadata Service.

```
ctccrm.AuthHelper.WinForms.FormCrmConnectInfo formInfo = new
                    ctccrm.AuthHelper.WinForms.FormCrmConnectInfo();
formInfo.LoadSavedLogin();
if (formInfo.ShowDialog() != DialogResult.OK)
    return;
CrmConnectionInfo connInfo = formInfo.GetConnectionInfo();
formInfo.SaveSavedLogin(connInfo);
connInfo.AllowOfflineUse = true;

try
{
    MetadataAuthManager<MetadataService,
            CrmAuthenticationToken> svcMgr =
            new MetadataAuthManager<MetadataService,
                    CrmAuthenticationToken>(connInfo);

    MetadataService service = svcMgr.GetService();
}
catch (Exception ex)
{
    MessageBox.Show(ex.Message);
}
```

Both the Metadata Service and the CRM Service are pretty full function except for as related to deploying code on the server.

Web Services from Client Script

One of the features that you can rely on heavily to accommodate for the lack of deployed code is the fact that you have access to the full client scripting model we discussed in Chapters 5 and 6. This includes the ability to call the platform web services from events on each of the CRM forms.

To give you a quick refresher, the following is an example of using the CTCCrmService javascript helper class that we provide with the book examples.

The first step is to include the CTCCrmService script as part of your OnLoad event for the form.

```
// CTCCrmWebService 1.2 - 2/12/2008   (c) Colorado Technology
Consultants, Inc.
CTCCrmConditionValue=function(){this.Type='guid'; (Omitted...)
// CTCCrmWebService 1.2 - 2/12/2008
```

Once the script has been added you can then make a web service call from anywhere including OnChange and OnSave events for the form. The following is an example of making a call to retrieve the default unit for the current product.

```
//get the lookup value from the field
lookupItem = crmForm.all.productid.DataValue;

//call WS and get the Product
dynProduct =
          CTCCrmService.RetrieveFirstBySingleKey("product",
                "productid",lookupItem[0].id);

alert(dynProduct.GetStringValue("defaultuomid",""));
```

See Chapter 6 for a complete list of examples using the web services from client script code.

Detecting CRM Online from Script

In a perfect world the feature set and customizations you provide wouldn't vary from deployment model to deployment model. But since we live in reality we do have to deal with the fact that we might be executing client script code that will need to consider the deployment model. CRM does not provide any global variable or other method that you can use to check which environment you are running in.

To help determine which model your script is executing in, we have provided a utility function for you.

The following are the methods that allow you to detect the deployment model.

Method	Description
IsDeployedOnPremise	Indicates you are working with a local user and they are authenticated using Active Directory.
IsDeployedIFD	Indicates you are working with a remote client authenticated with Forms Authentication.
IsDeployedLive	Indicates you are working with a remote client authenticated with Windows Live ID – since only CRM Online supports Live ID this indicates a CRM Online user.

Hide it with Security

One of the challenges you might be faced with is how to take what is traditionally an on-premise solution and deploy it to CRM Online hosted environment as a "Lite" version. In doing so, typically some of the features won't make sense to have in CRM Online. A good example would be some hosted pages – maybe in your Lite version of your product you don't provide these pages. You could simply maintain a separate sitemap that does not contain links to the pages that won't be used in your CRM Online deployments, but that might be messy. Or you could leverage the security model to help you out

CRM Online has the ability to filter the SiteMap presented to the user based on their security access to entities. We can leverage that by creating a dummy entity – let's call it crmbook_onpremise. We don't need to add any special attributes or even make it visible on the site navigation we just need it to exist.

Next, let's look at our SiteMap Sub area

To have it filter by security we must add a privilege element to the sitemap markup as you can see in the following example.

```
<SubArea Id="nav_import" Icon="/_imgs/area/18_import.gif"
```

```
ResourceId="Homepage_Import" Url="/workplace/home_import.aspx"
DescriptionResourceId="Imports_Description">
        <Privilege Entity="crmbook_onpremise" Privilege="Read" />
</SubArea>
```

Now, all we have to do to hide our application CRM Online is just not grant any users read access to our crmbook_onpremise entity. To make the URL visible in our on-premise deployments we could just create an organization level role granting all users access to this entity and magically all of our links would show up in the on-premise installation.

Plugging In, Without Plug-Ins

Depending on your solution needs, not having the ability to deploy custom code to the hosted server can present challenges to getting your solution implemented to CRM Online. While not every scenario can be worked around there are some options that should be considered. Whenever possible see if you can solve the problem using the workflow capabilities that are manageable using the user interface workflow designer. We discuss the workflow designer in detail in Chapter 16.

If you have pre-plug-ins the easiest first step to consider is using Client Script to accomplish what you are doing in your pre-plug-in. Using this approach you would implement your code so it was invoked during the OnSave form event. This event is called prior to posting back to the server where the platform operation would occur. The two most obvious negatives of this approach is the fact that you have to re-write your plug-in as client script, and secondly, this implementation would only be called when the user modifies the data using the built-in forms. This approach would not have any impact on direct calls to the web service API.

If you have post-plug-ins they are more challenging because they depend on running after the platform operation has occurred and there really isn't an easy way to get control back on the form after the save occurs. Your best bet here for now is to see if you can use workflow.

Leverage Workflow

CRM Online has full ability to execute workflows built by using the workflow editor. Often times some of the challenges you will encounter when implementing a solution in CRM Online can be resolved by a workflow or using a workflow to externalize something to another system as we will discuss later in the chapter. So when you get stuck – ask yourself – "Can I use workflow for this?"

Using External Workflow

Another option to consider is if you can leverage workflow with custom code and run it in an external host. Using this approach you would externalize the events from CRM Online and then process them through a workflow that runs in a workflow runtime hosted by your own service running on an external server.

Externalizing Events

Your first challenge is finding a way to externalize the events from CRM Online. There's not currently any built-in capability to post to a URL or call a web service from CRM Online. Polling for changes across all the entities you're interested in to see if something was created, modified or deleted would cause a lot of unnecessary overhead.

Ironically, I stumbled across an idea of how to accomplish this while debugging a completely different workflow related problem. I noticed that when a workflow ran, an entry was recorded in the AsyncOperation entity. The entry has just enough information to know what message was processed (e.g. Create, Update, etc) and which record was affected. The only remaining issue was how to identify which records I wanted to re-publish to my external workflow host. Ideally I wanted to be able to issue one query against the AsyncOperation entity and retrieve all the items I need to republish. To accomplish that I needed to somehow get the record flagged with a common value.

After some additional research I determined that the stage name of the workflow was stored in the workfowstagename attribute on the entity. To leverage that all I would have to do is create a workflow for each entity I want to externalize and have it have a single stage that had a common name. The following is an example workflow that accomplishes publishing the tag CTCEQ as the step name.

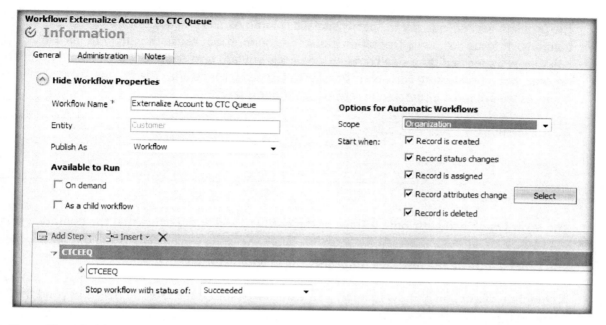

You will probably notice that the workflow is pretty simple and really doesn't do anything. That's the point, low overhead to externalize the event. I have indicated I want this workflow to start for all the different trigger events. That will ensure that all events get sent to my external workflow queue. The only step I have is a StopWorkflow activity that just indicates the workflow ran ok. The key is adding a Stage step to the workflow and setting the description to CTCEQ or some common tag that you consistently use.

The above workflow is created for Account (Customer in this example, since it was renamed using the platform customization capabilities for entities) and you would just replicate this workflow for each entity that you want to externalize events. Using the same tag, they would all put entries into the AsyncOperation entity that you could easily query and externalize.

Query AsyncOperation

The next step is to figure out how to query all the events that have occurred since the last time we checked. To do this we are going to query AsyncOperation and pull any records where the createdon is after the last time we polled and has a workflowstagename equal CTCEQ. Using this approach we only do a single poll regardless of how many entities we are monitoring and externalizing events for.

As it turns out AsyncOperation is a little tricky to query – in fact our first early attempts failed getting back an unknown error. With the help of one of the Microsoft support guys, we realized the problem was we needed to specify specific column names and not just try to retrieve all columns. It turns out, AsyncOperation has some columns that cause the query to fail if all columns are specified (as a side comment, typically you are best to specify the columns needed anyway, but when testing early on it's easier to just say give me all). The following are the columns we are most interested in retrieving for our query.

```
qe.ColumnSet = new ColumnSet(new string[] { "asyncoperationid",
                    "regardingobjectid", "messagename", "createdon",
"workflowstagename" });
```

The regardingobjectid attribute will tell us the entity ID and entity name that the operation was performed on, and the messagename tells us what operation took place. Using this information you could queue up the message for processing in your external host.

A complete discussion on how to build your external host to run the workflows is beyond the scope of this book (Check MSDN.com .NET Developer Center). Using the above information though should arm you with details on how to get enough triggering information out of the target CRM server without increasing overhead too much. Just a side note that this approach could also be used on non CRM Online deployments if you have a similar problem to solve – nothing we used is specific to CRM Online.

External Server Hosted Pages

Microsoft CRM Online currently does not allow you to host pages on their servers however it is possible to write ASP.NET applications that are hosted on external servers. These applications would interact with CRM using the web service API. There are three ways that you can use these pages with CRM Online (same techniques work for on-premise and partner hosted as well!). First, you can host your external page in an IFrame of an existing CRM form Tab / Section. Second, you can have the page show up in the main application area where it takes over the main viewing area. Finally, you can have just a standalone application that is used by non CRM users to provide data or retrieve status from the CRM Online system. Common examples of this type of application are either a lead form to request more information or a custom support form to submit a support request.

IFrame Integration Example

In Chapter 5 we showed an example of integrating an ASP.NET page in an IFrame to show a Virtual Earth map. The following is an example of that application. The image on the left is the first view, and then you can see the Birdseye view once the user selects that option.

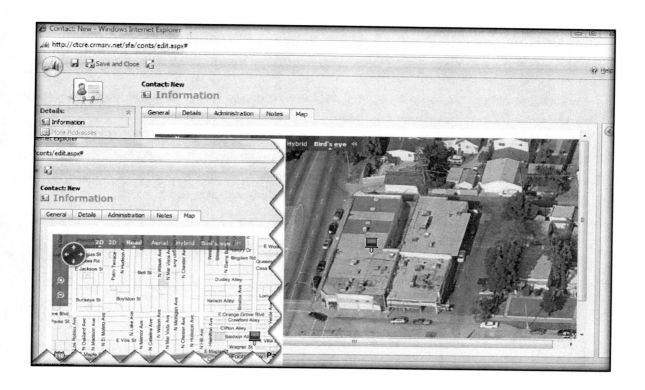

The only tricky part of using this type of application with CRM Online is related to security. First, your application has to be in a separate domain so you will be restricted on what scripting you can do because your page will be loaded from a different domain than your CRM organization. The other problem is around authentication for the externally hosted page to access the CRM Online web service API. When you build an application that is deployed to the CRM server you can use the authentication already done by the browser to that domain. When hosting a page externally you must do your own authentication to the web service API calls. Your choices here are somewhat limited. First, you could prompt the user for their CRM Online credentials. This adds a little more friction to your application as the user would be prompted for credentials again. You would also have to figure out a secure way to store the information which becomes extremely difficult to do safely. The other option is to use a fixed user for all access to the web service API and pull that information from the config file or other secure location on the external server. Using this approach you don't need to prompt the user, however, all access to the CRM Online data would be done using the single user and not the accessing user. This means that the user might see more or less data than they would under their own ID. You need to ensure in this scenario that the user isn't granted access to data they wouldn't normally see logging directly into the CRM Online server.

Web Lead Page Example

Our next example of an externally hosted page is a Web Lead form. This page would typically be part of some publicly facing web site designed to collect interest from a user in the services offered. This same type of scenario could be used for handling Contact Us or Case / Incident submission from users. The following is what our example application looks like. Clearly, this would be styled to fit with your sites style and would have whatever data fields you wanted to collect. However, for our purposes this simple page demonstrates the concept.

Create CRM Lead

Topic

First Name

Last Name

Company

Submit

Let's take a look behind the scenes at what happens when a user presses submit. The first thing I want to point out is the fact that we are inheriting from BaseUIPage in the ctccrm.WebCommon assembly. This class provides some helper methods that we will use to connect to CRM Online or any CRM server web service API.

```
public partial class _Default : ctccrm.WebCommon.BaseClasses.BaseUIPage
{
// Page code goes here //
}
```

The two most important features of the base page are the GetServiceContext method to get access to the API and the Trace support. The base class exposes a CTCTrace property that you can use to write out trace information. Trace can be turned on for a single user of the page and will cause the Trace data to be output to the bottom of the page. This makes tracking down problems a lot easier!

Now let's look at the code that is in the Button click handler for the submit button. The following code connects to CRM, Creates a Dynamic Entity to hold the lead data and then calls the create on the CRM service.

```
using (CrmServiceContext<CTCCRMService> svcContext =
                             this.GetServiceContext())
{
    try
    {
        DynamicEntity de = new DynamicEntity("lead");
        CTCDEPropHelper.AddStringProperty(de, "subject", txtTopic.Text);
        CTCDEPropHelper.AddStringProperty(de,
                  "lastname", txtLastName.Text);
        if (txtFirstName.Text != "")
            CTCDEPropHelper.AddStringProperty(de,
                    "firstname", txtFirstName.Text);
        if (txtCompany.Text != "")
            CTCDEPropHelper.AddStringProperty(de,
                    "companyname", txtCompany.Text);

        svcContext.Service.Create((BusinessEntity)de);

        lbResponse.Text = "Thank you.";
    }
    catch (Exception ex)
    {
        CTCTraceContext.Write(ex);
    }
}
```

As you can see this isn't complicated code and all of the differences to CRM Online have been handled by our GetServiceContext method call and what happens behind the scenes in the AuthHelper assembly code that we discussed in more detail in Chapter 10.

The nice thing is once the lead is created on the server you can then have a workflow trigger and do more automation on the CRM side like assign the lead to a sales person. We use a similar technique to this to handle inquiries on the book web site www.thecrmbook.com when a user submits a Contact Us Request. Behind the scenes on the book site we create an incident in our CRM so that we can get back with the requestor.

One important thing to understand about this type of use is it requires an External Connector license. The good news is when you do this with CRM Online or a partner hosted CRM where you pay monthly the External Connector license is already included. If you were trying to do this for an on-premise install you would need to license the External Connector. As with all licensing questions, I suggest you confirm with your Microsoft licensing contact to ensure you are compliant as we can't give you specific licensing advice.

Using either of these approaches is a great way to add more customization or automation to your CRM Online environment that would probably be too custom for Microsoft to add into the core product.

Wrapping it up

Today, we live in a world where buzz words, acronyms and catchy phrases try to describe a vision for the next generation of computing. Buzz words are sometimes necessary to get the people on board an idea that don't understand the underlying technology but do grasp the concept of the business value the technology brings. We hear things like SaaS (Software as a Service) or S+S (Software plus Services), PaaS (Platform as a Service) and many other variants that can make our heads spin. Rather than attempt to drive toward clarity on what those mean, let's simply look at what we do know about CRM 4.0 and how CRM Online fits into the strategy.

As a developer, I'm able to use similar customization techniques in each of the three deployment scenarios slightly adjusted for the environment of a hosted solution. Where appropriate I could build my solution to run in all three environments or simply target the deployment scenario that best fits how my users or customers will use the solution.

In this chapter we tried to highlight for you some of the differences you might encounter when deploying applications to CRM Online. We also looked at several possible options for handling the differences in the platform when deployed to CRM Online. Like any other emerging technology some of these techniques as well as the feature support for CRM Online will evolve as the product matures so keep your eye on announcements from Microsoft.

23

Multi Currency and Multi Language

Today, our businesses and our customers can easily reach beyond our local area for conducting business. Often times however, when building line of business applications things like handling of multiple currencies or languages are not considered. When they are considered, they are either an afterthought or poorly planned. This is not surprising when you consider that many line of business applications grow out of immediate need to solve a critical opportunity.

The exception here I believe is when you get outside the United States. As I mentioned in the introduction I had the opportunity to travel throughout a lot of Europe doing training for ISVs building their applications on the CRM platform. To them, the need for multiple currency and language support was clear and the number of questions clearly demonstrated the need. In some ways, I think they are ahead in understanding and demonstrating that our boundaries to conduct business across multiple currencies and with varying languages are being taken down. Microsoft CRM 4.0 supports that in providing a framework to help developers build applications that are able to adopt the emerging global business environment that does not have rigid borders.

In this chapter, we will be taking a deeper look at how multiple currencies and multiple languages are supported in the platform. We will be discussing things you need to know and do as part of planning and building your solutions.

Understanding Multi Currency

Simplified, multi currency allows you to define a base currency and then one or more alternate currencies to use for each data record or transaction. The platform then manages tracking and storing the base and transactional currency as part of each data record. Optionally, you can expose on each form a currency selection allowing a choice for each record or allow it to simply default to the users default currency setting.

Establishing a Base Currency

The base currency is established at the organization level and is set during the provisioning of the organization. In a multi tenant deployment where there are multiple organizations, each organization can have its own setting for base currency.

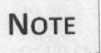

NOTE *After the initial provisioning of an organization there is not currently a supported way to change the base currency to another currency.*

Discovering the Base Currency

If needed you can discover the base currency for an organization by a query to the organization entity. The basecurrencyid property provides you with the base currency ID that can then be used to look up the specific currency entity instance.

The following is an example of retrieving the base currency for an organization

```
public CurrencyInfo GetCurrencyInfoBase()
{
    // Create the Request object
    RetrieveMultipleRequest req = new RetrieveMultipleRequest();
    req.ReturnDynamicEntities = true;

    // Build the Query to get the organization
    QueryExpression qe = new QueryExpression();
    qe.ColumnSet = new ColumnSet(new string[] { "organizationid",
        "basecurrencyid" });
    qe.Distinct = false;
    qe.EntityName = "organization";

    req.Query = qe;

    // Execute the Request
```

```
RetrieveMultipleResponse resp =
    (RetrieveMultipleResponse)this.m_Service.Execute(req);

if (resp.BusinessEntityCollection.BusinessEntities != null &&
    resp.BusinessEntityCollection.BusinessEntities.Count > 0)
{
    DynamicEntity de =
        resp.BusinessEntityCollection.BusinessEntities[0]
        as DynamicEntity;

    // Get ID for base currency
    Guid currencyID = CTCDEPropHelper.GetLookupValue(de,
        "basecurrencyid");

    // Call method to get currency info from ID
    return GetCurrencyInfo(currencyID);
}

return null;
}
```

Adding more Currencies

By default only the base currency will display in the list of available currencies to a user until others are configured. At the time of release of CRM 4.0 there were 142 currencies available that can be configured. The following shows an example of the list of currencies. You will notice that for a given currency there may be multiple entries due to different names or geographic differences.

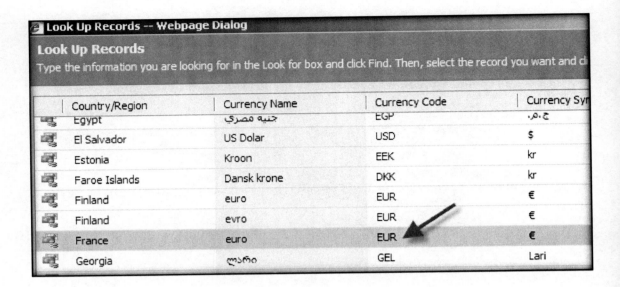

The list above is fixed and you can't add your own additional entries.

Configuration involves setting the currency conversion and optionally altering the name and symbol.

TIP

Currency conversion is fixed and is manually updated. You could also update using the API and implement an automated update on the schedule of your choice.

Digging Deeper

Next, we look at what happens when you add the first money field to either a system entity or a custom entity. The first time a money field is added the platform also adds a relationship between that entity and the Currency entity. This relationship will be used to indicate the transactional currency of each instance of that entity. If you were to look in the relationship list you would see the following.

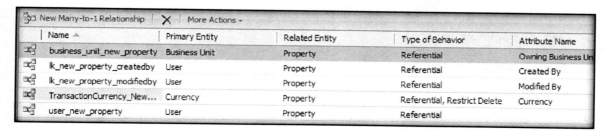

Name ▲	Primary Entity	Related Entity	Type of Behavior	Attribute Name
business_unit_new_property	Business Unit	Property	Referential	Owning Business Un
lk_new_property_createdby	User	Property	Referential	Created By
lk_new_property_modifiedby	User	Property	Referential	Modified By
TransactionCurrency_New...	Currency	Property	Referential, Restrict Delete	Currency
user_new_property	User	Property	Referential	

Now if we visit the attribute list we see the following.

new_currentvalue	Current Value	money	
new_currentvalue_base	Current Value (B...	money	Value of the Current Value in base currency.

You can see from the figure above that two attributes are added to the entity. One will track the base currency amount and the other will store the transactional amount.

Multi-Currency on Forms

When adding fields to a form you have a few choices on how you want to display and allow the user to work with fields of data type Money. For each, you will see a field with the attribute name as well as one with the attribute name plus the word base. The first will represent the transactional amount and the base version will represent the converted base value. The base value will be stored using a calculated value determined by the exchange rate for the selected currency at the time the amount is changed and the record is saved. If you choose to add the base rate to the form, it will show as a read only field and the value is not changeable.

By default, the transactional amount of any money attribute will use the users default currency as set on the Tools-Options dialog by the user. If the user has not selected a specific currency to be their default then all transactions will be conducted using the organizations base currency.

Additionally, you can add the Currency attribute to the form which will create a lookup allowing the user to select a transactional currency for the record when editing the record. The Currency attribute will cause that currency and associated exchange rate to be used for all money fields on that record. It is possible to have multiple currencies available to select, but the user is limited to only one per record.

If you want the user to be able to see the exchange rate that is in use the Exchange Rate attribute can be added to the form. This adds a read only field to the form and will show the exchange rate value based on the transaction currency selected and the base currency for the organization.

Understanding Exchange Rate Updates

When a record is saved and an attribute of data type money is modified the system will calculate the base amount for that money field using the current exchange rate for the records currency. The exchange rate is stored as an attribute on the record saving the exchange rate from the related currency record.

If you update the exchange rate on the system currency record it will not update any of the data in other entities by default. The exchange rate on a data record will only update to match the system currency exchange rate if one of the records money fields are modified. That means you can change any other attribute on the record and it will not affect the exchange rate on that record. When the exchange rate is updated due to one of the money fields being updated, it will also re-calculate all the other base fields for all money fields using the new exchange rate.

NOTE

Exchange rate on a data record is managed by the system and cannot be manually updated either via the client interface or the API. That means if an exchange rate is modified during an update there isn't a supported way to revert it to the original value if needed.

Formatting Data on Reports

Each user has a record in the FilteredUserSettings view in the organization database that indicates format selection for each user. CRM also provides a database function that you can call fn_GetFormatStrings that will give you a single result row with the active users formatting for various types of common fields like dates, numbers and currency. The following is the partial results of calling that user function.

SELECT * FROM dbo.fn_GetFormatStrings()

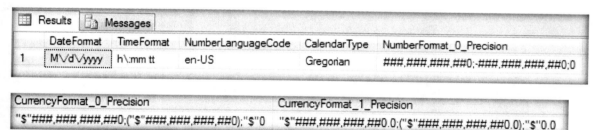

	DateFormat	TimeFormat	NumberLanguageCode	CalendarType	NumberFormat_0_Precision
1	M/d/yyyy	h:mm tt	en-US	Gregorian	###,###,###,##0;-###,###,###,##0;0

CurrencyFormat_0_Precision	CurrencyFormat_1_Precision
"$"###,###,###,##0;("$"###,###,###,##0);"$"0	"$"###,###,###,##0.0;("$"###,###,###,##0.0);"$"0.0

Retrieve Currency Info

If you want to get details about a specific currency you can query the transactioncurrency entity using the entity ID of the currency. The following helper method on the CrmServiceManager class in the framework library can be used.

```
public CurrencyInfo GetCurrencyInfo(Guid ID)
{
    CurrencyInfo currency = new CurrencyInfo();
```

```
// Create the Request object
RetrieveMultipleRequest req = new RetrieveMultipleRequest();
req.ReturnDynamicEntities = true;

// Build the Query
QueryExpression qe = new QueryExpression();
qe.ColumnSet = new ColumnSet(new string[] { "transactioncurrencyid",
"currencyname", "currencysymbol", "exchangerate",
"isocurrencycode" });
qe.Distinct = false;
qe.EntityName = "transactioncurrency";
FilterExpression exp = new FilterExpression();
exp.FilterOperator = LogicalOperator.And;
ConditionExpression cond = new ConditionExpression();
cond.AttributeName = "transactioncurrencyid";
object[] valueList = { ID };
cond.Values = valueList;
cond.Operator = ConditionOperator.Equal;
exp.Conditions.Add(cond);
qe.Criteria = exp;

req.Query = qe;

// Execute the Request
RetrieveMultipleResponse resp =
        (RetrieveMultipleResponse)this.m_Service.Execute(req);

if (resp.BusinessEntityCollection.BusinessEntities != null &&
        resp.BusinessEntityCollection.BusinessEntities.Count > 0)
{
    DynamicEntity de =
 resp.BusinessEntityCollection.BusinessEntities[0] as DynamicEntity;

    currency.ID = CTCDEPropHelper.GetKeyValue(de,
        "transactioncurrencyid");
    currency.Name = CTCDEPropHelper.GetStringValue(de,
        "currencyname", "");
    currency.Symbol = CTCDEPropHelper.GetStringValue(de,
        "currencysymbol", "");
    currency.ISOCode = CTCDEPropHelper.GetStringValue(de,
        "isocurrencycode", "");
    currency.ExchangeRate = CTCDEPropHelper.GetDecimalValue(de,
        "exchangerate", 0);
}

return currency;
}
```

There is also a GetCurrencyInfoallActive method that you can call to get a list of all active currencies.

If you want to update the currency you can do so by updating the exchangerate using the same method you would use to update any other CRM entity.

Using Multiple Languages

The multi-language capabilities of the platform are tightly integrated with the Metadata for each of the entities. For users accessing the system via the built-in client interfaces the system takes care of all the multi language display as long as you have defined translation for the Metadata in the users preferred language. When an available translation is not available the system defaults to the base language string for the item.

The Metadata can be updated using the form editor for the base language. Additionally, a Microsoft Excel file can be exported that contains all the labels allowing a user to modify the labels in Microsoft Excel. Once the modifications are complete, the Excel can be re-imported . Finally, developers can use the Metadata API to alter the Metadata to add display labels. Language strings can only be added for language packs that are installed and active on the organization.

Base Language vs. Language Packs

The base language for all organizations on a deployment is determined by the language of the CRM install. Unlike Multi Currency where you can choose at the time of creation of an organization, language is determined by the installation files and their language choice. When upgrading from a prior version of CRM you must upgrade to a like base language. For example, if you used Dutch in CRM 3.0 then you must upgrade using a Dutch install to get to CRM 4.0.

Once the CRM software install is complete you can install language packs each making an additional language available to be enabled for an organization. The language packs are small installs of 10-15mb each that basically add the necessary Metadata to support that language. Once installed you can go to the Administration -> Language Settings dialog and you would see the following.

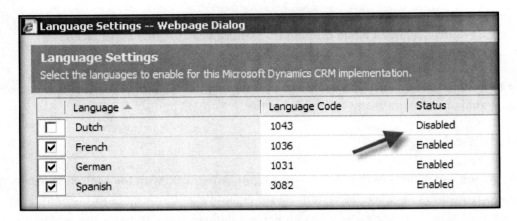

In the above example, I just completed the installation of the Dutch Language pack. As you can see its disabled which is the default status after a new pack is installed. In order for users to be able to select Dutch as their language I would have to check the box and click apply to enable that language. Each organization in a multi-tenant installation can have their own configuration for which languages are enabled from the set of language packs installed on the CRM server.

User Language Selection

Users can select their language at any time from the Tools -> Options page in the client interface. That selection is stored with their CRM user profile and would be in effect anytime that user logged in. The user's culture or local computer setting don't control the CRM language selection. The user can select from the available languages which is any language on the organization that is enabled. The new language selection will take effect immediately as you can see in the following dialog, when I selected Dutch.

Navigation Multi-Language Support

As we saw in Chapter 5 both the SiteMap and the ISVConfig allow us to provide multi-language settings on any of the strings that display to an end user. The following is an example of a multi-language specification of the title for a link.

```
<SubArea Id="nav_dashboard" PassParams="1"

        Url="/dashboard/dashboard.aspx" >
<Titles>
   <Title Title="CRM Dashboard" LCID="1033" />
   <Title Title=" Tableau de bord de CRM" LCID="1053" />
</Titles>
</SubArea>
```

You can also use the PassParams option on links to ensure that parameters are passed to the link that contains the language codes (userlcid and orglcid).

List of Available Languages

If you are building your own interface to CRM and you want to allow the user to choose their language separate from their CRM language you could query for a list of languages. The following helper method on CrmServiceManager returns back a list of all available languages.

```
public List<LanguageInfo> GetLanguagesAvailable()
{
    RetrieveAvailableLanguagesRequest req = new
      RetrieveAvailableLanguagesRequest();

    RetrieveAvailableLanguagesResponse resp =
      (RetrieveAvailableLanguagesResponse)this.m_Service.Execute(req);

    List<LanguageInfo> languages = new List<LanguageInfo>();

    for (int i = 0; i < resp.LocaleIds.Length; i++)
    {
        LanguageInfo lang = new LanguageInfo();
        CultureInfo cultInfo = new CultureInfo(resp.LocaleIds[i]);
```

```
        if (cultInfo != null)
        {
            lang.LanguageCode = cultInfo.LCID;
            lang.ShortDescription = cultInfo.Name;
            lang.Description = cultInfo.EnglishName;

            languages.Add(lang);
        }
    }

    return languages;
}
```

Metadata API

When working with the Metadata API any string value that will be visible to the end user such as display names support storing language specific strings. When you use the API those properties will be of type CrmLabel instead of a simple string data type. The CrmLabel class has two properties that you will work with LocLabels and UserLocLabel. The LocLabels property is just a collection of LocLabel objects which contains the language code and the string value for that language. The User LocLabel class is populated for you based on the user accessing the web service. Using the current user the API is able to determine what the preferred language string is for that value. The system will also automatically downgrade the UserLocLabel to the base language if there's not a language string for the user's specific language. In addition to working with DisplayNames, options on PickList attributes can also specify a value for each language.

In addition to using the Metadata API, if you want to import/export a complete set of language strings you can do that via the CrmService message ImportTranslationslationsWithProgress and the ExportTranslations messages. These methods probably aren't as ideal for installing a language pack for an ISV solution as they deal with all language strings and are not additive. Using the Metadata API calls you can simply add or replace existing values for specific entities, attribute and picklist values. Trying to do the same thing using the Import/Export translations would require extensive manipulation of the exported XML.

Wrapping it up

In this chapter, we took a deeper look at some of the multi language and multi currency support that is new in CRM 4.0. Using the built-in capabilities of these features does not require a lot of effort by the developer. Developers can choose where they need to customize or extend the built-in capabilities. For example, with multi-currency a developer could write an application or a workflow that updates the currency at specific times from an external source. Multi-language works out of the box with the built-in entities and if you add custom entities, you can modify the language strings to pickup translation for your custom entities. Using the user interface import/export you can send that to external translators. Developers can also automate the process of updating the Metadata language strings using the API.

As you read this, you may be saying I do not need these capabilities now our solution is only one currency or language. As I indicated in the opening of the chapter the boundaries for business are becoming broader and often times we cannot anticipate how our solutions will be used when they are built. Having these capabilities as part of your solutions architectural foundation without having to invest precious resources to build them from scratch gives a tremendous amount of future flexibility.

24

Packaging For Deployment

Packaging for deployment can take many forms depending on if you are building an internal solution that will only be installed in one environment or an ISV solution. ISV solutions will need extra steps to ensure that someone who isn't as familiar with the solution is able to install it without breaking anything in the target system. A lot of the things you might want to consider doing can be helpful in both.

One of the most important things to realize is it's very likely your solution will not be the only thing installed on the target system. You could be the first one installed, or you could be installed after other vendors' installation programs have run. What this means is you need to play well in the sandbox and do everything possible to not overwrite or break existing customizations in the target server. It also means because others may install after you, there may be some things you want to do to be able to quickly detect if your customizations have been tampered with so you don't spend time tracking down problems created by others.

CRM does not provide a concept of an install package builder but it does provide you APIs to help you build setup and provisioning tools. Using these APIs, you can automate a good portion of the process.

In this chapter, we are going to look at some of the techniques, APIs and tools for packaging your solution into something that can be installed and provisioned.

Installation vs. Provisioning

Often times we think of install only. Since CRM 4.0 now supports multi tenants, the concept of provisioning is also important. It is possible to look at installation separate from provisioning. For example, my installation might copy the files to the local server file system and then a provisioning utility might be used to make the solution available to each tenant.

For internal type applications, installation and provisioning might occur in the same installation program, as we will see later in the chapter. Another approach would be to have the installation do the provisioning on the first organization and then provide a tool that is separate from the installation that allows it to be provisioned on other tenants.

Understanding Different Types of Customizations

Before we dive deeper looking at specific installation issues let's take a tour of the different type of customizations and some approaches you might use.

Custom Entities and Forms – No Custom Code

The simplest form of customization would be using only the changes you can make from the CRM user interface customization pages. This would include custom entities, new attributes to existing entities, workflows, security roles, some basic scripting on the forms, etc. All of these types of changes don't involve any custom code or pages that need to be deployed to the CRM server. All of these can be handled using export of customizations and import into a target system. This is a very typical scenario for an internal implementation. These types of solutions can be deployed by exporting the customizations and importing them into the target system. The biggest issue is to control where updates are done so that when you deploy you don't overwrite a change that was made in the target system.

Adding New Entities

If you want to automate creating a new entity as part of your install or provisioning you have a couple of choices. Using the new write capabilities of the Metadata API, you could create the new entity on the fly. As it turns out, that may not be the simplest technique because the Metadata API does not allow you to create or make changes to the entity form or views. So using this approach, you would have to handle the form and views separately. If you were to instead embed an XML customization file that was an export of the new entity as part of your install or provisioning tool you could simply use the import customization capabilities to import the new entity in. Import creates not only the new entity and attributes but will import forms and views as well.

Adding or Modifying Existing Entities

When you need to add an attribute or make another change to an existing entity the Metadata API is typically the best for making schema changes. Using the API, you can easily surgically add a single attribute or even a value to an existing picklist. This approach is preferred to importing a customization file because it can just affect a single item. Using the import approach it's possible that if the target entity had any changes they would be overwritten. The only negative of this approach is it still leaves you without a good way to modify the forms or views of that existing entity. Unfortunately, nothing new was added in CRM 4.0 to make that easier. You really have three options at this time on how to handle this problem. First, you could export the XML for the entity and programmatically insert or make your changes. You could go directly to the organizationui entity and do similar types of changes. Both of these approaches require some amount of complexity to navigate the XML to insert or make your changes. I tend to prefer the Export/Import XML approach over the organizationui technique. Finally, when going into an existing entity you could give steps for the end user or consultant to manually make the changes. Forms and View alteration is an area that I suspect we will see more changes to do on the fly form manipulation through the API in future releases. For now you need to find the easiest approach that will work for your particular solution.

Modifications to Site Map

If your solution needs to make changes to sitemap to affect the navigation of the application you can use the Import approach but this would overwrite any changes done directly in CRM. For internal type applications or applications where every deployment should have the same navigation importing can probably be acceptable because the goal is consistency. By exporting the sitemap using the API you can then manipulate it as an XML file to make your changes. Once the changes are complete you can re-import the file.

A big thing to keep in mind with the Site Map is that if a user makes any changes via the Customizations pages to change navigation by checking or unchecking an area to show the entity it will modify the SiteMap. If that occurs and later you import it will overwrite those changes. This can be avoided by making sure your CRM customizers know that you are using the sitemap to handle these navigation updates.

Modifying ISVConfig

The deployment issues here are similar to SiteMap with the exception that there is no way to automatically change this file using the web customization. That means you don't have to worry about a user accidentally modifying the file from the web client customization pages.

MVP Tip: Microsoft CRM MVP Michael Hohne adds there are two options to change the isv configuration: using import/export as for the sitemap or other customizations, or reading and writing to the isv.config entity. It's an entity like any other in the CRM system.

One thing you want to make sure when making changes to the isv configuration is to perform a check if the isv extensions are enabled in the CRM organization. It's a good idea to add it as an option to your installer. At least add appropriate documentation telling the end user or administrator that they have to enable the isv customizations in the system settings in order to user your extensions. You can read Michael's blog at http://www.stunware.com.

Modifying Form Event JavaScript

Client scripts for the CRM forms are stored and will deploy when you import/export entity customizations. If you need to automate installation of the scripts I recommend using some well formed headers and footers to make it really clear where you're scripting starts and ends.

//DYScript-01-01-08-Start

Custom Script goes here...

// DYScript-01-01-08-End

That makes it easier to parse the form xml and identify and find your script that was previously installed.

Another technique that I've recommended is adding a hash code built from the contents of the script to help handle detection that your script was altered since last update. The reason you might want to be able to identify this is simply to keep a user's custom code from being overwritten. Often times end users can edit or intertwine their own customizations inside your script just because they can. By having a hash or CRC type value that you can compare to allows you to detect the alteration and warn the user.

Deploying ASP.NET Applications

ASP.NET applications are a little different than some of the customizations we have discussed so far. To deploy an ASP.NET application to the CRM server you deploy it to the ISV folder inside the CRM web folder. Your application is then able to take advantage of having CRM manage user authentication.   Unlike the other customizations that so far have been deployed to a specific organization in a multi-tenant install the ASP.NET application is by default available to all organizations. If you want to only have it available to certain organizations, you would need to handle that as part of your application on your own.

From an install point of view, this means that your installation program does not really have to deal with provisioning it into each tenant of a multi tenant install. The application would however have to be installed on each node in a multi server deployment where you have more than one server hosting the CRM web application.

We will be discussing more implications of ASP.NET applications later in the chapter.

Deploying Plug-ins

Plug-ins must be registered in the GAC, put in a specific file on each server, or stored in the CRM database. You must then register or hook up to the platform events that you want that plug-in to be invoked to handle. Let's first discuss the location of the assembly by looking at each of the three options and when they work best.

Location	Best Used For
Server File System	<installdir>\Program Files\Microsoft CRM\server\bin\assembly Using this approach is best for Development time where you want to be able to build and run the debugger against the plug-in. This is not ideal for production deployment so we won't cover this technique in the book. This approach typically is only used during development to allow debugging to occur.

Location	Best Used For
CRM Database	Using this option your assembly is copied to the CRM database by making API calls to store it. CRM then manages making sure your assembly is available to each server where plug-ins and workflows can run. Each organization or tenant your plug-in assembly is deployed to must have the assembly registered with the database. The database deployment is the only way to automatically push a plug-in to clients for use when offline. If your plug-in is intended to be used in offline mode as well, the database deployment is required. Using the CRM Database option is best when you have many servers or only a couple organizations using the plug-in. Using this approach you must still register any dependent assemblies of your plug-in assembly in the GAC otherwise they will not be found at runtime. Using this approach each organization gets new binary updates only when applied to that organization. Using this technique it's not necessary to install the plug-in to each server.
GAC	By registering your plug-in assembly with the Windows GAC (Global Assembly Cache) it can be used by all organizations without being stored in the CRM database. You must still register the assembly with each tenant in a multi tenant organization. This solution works best when you want to deploy one copy that is used by all tenants in a multi tenant setup. In that scenario when you update the GAC copy of the assembly all organizations see the update without any update required to the CRM database or registration information. Using this approach you must install the binaries on each server but only need to register the plug-in assembly once with the CRM database.

Regardless of which of the above assembly approaches you take, you need to consider that installation is separate from provisioning or registering the plug-in with the CRM server. One thing we have done before is make the code that calls the registration smart enough to know that if it runs again on another node in a server farm to skip the registration of the plug-in with CRM since it's already registered.

If your plug-in solution consists of multiple assemblies and you want to use the database deployment, you should consider using a tool like ILMerge to merge your assemblies into a single assembly that can then be installed into the database.

Custom Workflow Activities

Deployment issues for Custom Workflow activities are very similar to plug-ins. The only real difference is in the actual API calls to register so we won't re-state the issues we discussed above for plug-ins.

As you can see there are several things to consider based on the type of customization that you are building. In fact, you may find that one install program is not the best approach and it might be better to have one for each specific type such as one for your web applications and one for plug-ins. You may also find the need to have a provisioning utility that administrators run to provision your customizations on each tenant in the multi-tenant deploy. In the rest of the chapter, we will be looking at a few of the different options in more detail as we dive deeper into a couple of examples.

Backup and Logging

I believe two of the most important aspects of a good install or provisioning utility are backup and logging. For backup, obviously if you are using an installer program the system will take care of the basics for you. However, the installer doesn't understand CRM like you do. For example, if you are going to modify any of the metadata I highly recommend doing an export of the target system's customizations before making modifications. The ExportAllCustomizations method can easily do this and we have an example of it in the CrmServiceManager helper class in the framework. The following shows the implementation of that method: you simply pass it a file name when you call it where you want the compressed export file saved.

```
public void ExportAllCustomizationsToFile(string fileName)
{
    ExportCompressedAllXmlRequest req = new
                    ExportCompressedAllXmlRequest();
    req.EmbeddedFileName = "Customizations.xml";

    ExportCompressedAllXmlResponse resp =
```

```
            this.m_Service.Execute(req) as
                ExportCompressedAllXmlResponse;

    FileStream fileStream = new FileStream(fileName, FileMode.Create);
    fileStream.Write(resp.ExportCompressedXml, 0,
                resp.ExportCompressedXml.Length);
    fileStream.Close();

}
```

By taking a backup of customizations before adding new modifications you have a good resource to review in the event that a problem occurs during the installation. It's important to note though that a backup of customizations isn't a replacement for backing up the CRM databases; it's an additional step.

MVP Tip: Microsoft CRM MVP Michael Hohne adds a backup customization file should not be applied automatically when removing your application. There are good chances that you remove customizations that have been added after your solution was installed. You may use it as an option in your uninstaller though. You can read Michael's blog at http://www.stunware.com.

Logging is important because it's almost impossible to anticipate every problem you might encounter when installing a solution. While it's true that adding logging takes extra time up front, it can save many hours of time as well as customer frustration once a problem is encountered in the field. CRM doesn't provide any built-in utilities to help with logging but it can be as simple as writing to a file or you can even leverage some of the free libraries like the logging that comes with the Microsoft Patterns and Practice Enterprise library. In our samples in the book, we leverage the Tracing capabilities and just save it to a formatted html file.

Deploying ASP.NET Applications

Now that we have looked at a high level of the different approaches, let's look specifically at an example of using ASP.NET. Having some ASP.NET pages as part of your solution is a very common approach where you need custom forms or page content. From a deployment perspective, if your ASP.NET application just accesses CRM data such as a Web to Lead form that submits a lead to the CRM server then it's deployed just like any normal ASP.NET application. On the other hand, if you plan to deploy your page to run in a CRM form IFrame there is a little more consideration that needs to take place and we will discuss that some in this chapter.

The first thing to consider is if you plan to make your ASP.NET page(s) accessible by an offline user. Prior to CRM 4.0 that wasn't very feasible because the platform web service wasn't exposed on the offline client. Now the majority of the CRM web service endpoint can be used when the client is offline. To be able to accomplish that you need to deploy your ASP.NET application to each client. CRM does not provide any automation so installation on the client would be your responsibility.

ASP.NET applications should be deployed to the ISV folder using a unique name. The ISV folder is located on the CRM web server typically under Program Files. The same folder can be found on the client in C:\Program Files\Microsoft Dynamics CRM\Client\res\web\ISV. Remember, only clients that have installed the offline capabilities will have that folder and can run your application offline.

Your application will be running as a guest in the CRM web space, so you will need to be on best behavior. Since you will be in a sub folder and not your own application you need to put your applications assemblies either in the CRM bin folder or in the GAC on each machine. Putting the assemblies in the CRM bin folder typically is a little cleaner from what I have seen in practice. You will want to ensure your assemblies have unique names so they won't overwrite or be overwritten by other vendor assemblies. You will notice we use ctccrm.webcommon.dll instead of just "common.dll" which would likely conflict with someone else.

The reason to deploy to the CRM web space is to take advantage of CRM handling authentication for you. This is really only important for applications on the server where IFD is enabled. IFD is Internet Facing Deployment and allows users not associated with the active directory to authenticate to the CRM server. You might be tempted to ignore that support thinking that you aren't planning on using it. But doing so would be short sighted as more and more CRM installations will be enabling that feature now that it's easier to configure. To allow your application to support IFD, you need to use the CrmImpersonator class as shown in the SDK, or our ctccrm.AuthHelper assembly which implements support for CrmImpersonator in a more simple fashion. See Chapter 9 for more details on ctccrm.AuthHelper.

Example Web Deploy Project

Let's walk through a simple web application that we want to deploy to the CRM server in the ISV folder. The web site we are using is part of the Chapter 24 sample code. It simply displays the Guid of the user accessing the page. In this section we are going to add a web setup project to our solution and prepare it for deploying to a CRM Server.

The approach I'm taking in this section is not the only way you could accomplish the deployment, but is pretty streamlined. I'm going to leverage the Web Deployment Project add on that you download and install. It gives you a simple project type template that makes it easy to prepare a website for deployment. More specifically, it takes all the output from your project and compiles it down to a single assembly that is easier to deploy.

The first step is to add a Web Deployment project to our solution by right-clicking on our example website and selecting Add Web Deployment Project as you can see in the following image.

The next thing we need to do is customize the Web Deployment Project (WDP) we just added to have it help us deal with the fact that we need to deploy our binaries to the CRM Bin folder and don't want to have our own Bin folder under our deployed web. The reason for this is the ISV folder is under the CRM application and ASP.NET applications can have only a single bin folder.

To customize a WDP, we right click on the WDP in solution explorer and select open project file as you can see in the following example.

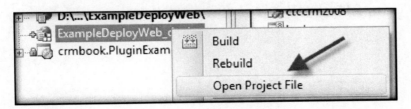

This will open up the XML for the WDP project file to allow us to customize it. Once open, go all the way to the bottom and find the section that is commented out that says "To modify your build process" as you can see in the following example.

```
</ItemGroup>
<Import Project="$(MSB     ldExtension
<!-- To modify your build process,
     Other similar extension points
<Target Name="BeforeBuild">
</Target>
<Target Name="BeforeMerge">
```

We are going to insert at this location our custom AfterBuild target. What we are doing is basically hooking in to the build process of this project. AfterBuild allows us to get control after the output website has been processed but before the project file is done processing. The reason we are hooking in at this point is to copy the assemblies we want to deploy to the CRMweb/Bin folder and copy them to a folder CrmWeb inside our output from the deployment project. To accomplish this, place the following right after the <Import tag.

```
<Target Name="AfterBuild">
        <MakeDir Directories="$(WDTargetDir)crmwebbin"
                Condition="!Exists('$(WDTargetDir)/gac')" />
        <Copy
SourceFiles="$(WDTargetDir)bin\ExampleDeployWeb_deploy.dll"
DestinationFiles="$(WDTargetDir)crmwebbin\ExampleDeployWeb_deploy.dll"
/>
        <Copy SourceFiles="$(WDTargetDir)bin\ctccrm.AuthHelper.dll"
DestinationFiles="$(WDTargetDir)crmwebbin\ctccrm.AuthHelper.dll" />

        <Copy SourceFiles="$(WDTargetDir)bin\ctccrm.webcommon.dll"
DestinationFiles="$(WDTargetDir)crmwebbin\ctccrm.webcommon.dll" />

        <Copy
SourceFiles="$(WDTargetDir)bin\ctccrm.plugincommon.dll"
DestinationFiles="$(WDTargetDir)crmwebbin\ctccrm.plugincommon.dll" />

        <Delete Files="$(WDTargetDir)web.config" />
        <!--<Copy SourceFiles="$(WDTargetDir)SetupWeb.config"
DestinationFiles="$(WDTargetDir)web.config" /> -->
        <RemoveDir Directories="$(WDTargetDir)bin" />
</Target>
```

In the above build actions, we create a directory "crmwebbin" if it doesn't already exist. We copy from the output bin folder of our website the key assemblies that we care about. We then delete the web.config because since we are being deployed under the CRMWeb we don't want to have our own web.config. Finally, we remove the original bin folder that was built for our website.

When you save the WDP project file if it is under source control you might see the following warning dialog. It's ok to select Continue.

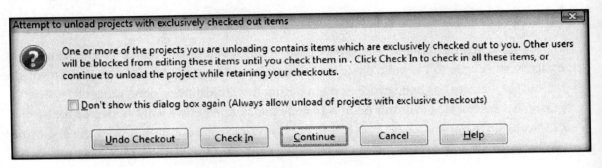

The next thing we are going to do is add a Setup project to our solution. You can find the Setup project under the "Other Templates" category when you do an Add New Project. The following shows the selection of Setup Project. You might notice that we are using just a plane setup. It turns out that handles the type of file copies that we need to do better than a pure web setup project does. If you weren't setting this up under the CRM ISV folder then using a web setup might be a better choice.

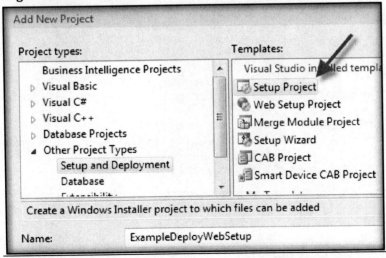

Once you have created the project, right click on the project and select View - > File System.

Right click - properties on the application folder and modify the DefaultLocation attribute to have the following value.

[ProgramFilesFolder]Microsoft Dynamics CRM\CRMWeb\

If this was an installation program to run on the client you would use the following value instead

[ProgramFilesFolder]Microsoft Dynamics CRM\Client\res\web\

For the reason above if you need to deploy to client machines and want to have an installation program you probably will find it easiest to have two, one for the server and one for the client.

The next thing we are going to do is configure the folders we are going to deploy to inside the CRM web.

Right click on the application folder and select "add Folder" and add the following two folders

- bin
- ISV

The following shows how to navigate to the add folder option.

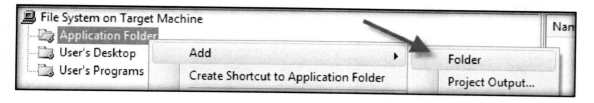

Right click on ISV and add a folder for the name of your application. In our example, we are going to use ExampleDeployWeb

Right click on the ExampleDeployWeb and select "Add Project Output" and you will see the following dialog.

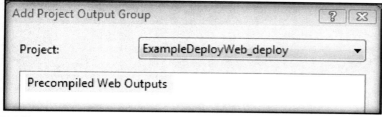

In the project dropdown find and select your web deployment project. This will cause the output from that to be deployed to the ExampleDeployWeb folder.

Next, right click on "bin" and select Add Assembly - you will see a similar dialog as you see in the image below.

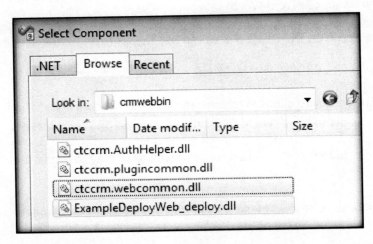

If you have deployed AuthHelper and PluginCommon to the GAC already then just select ExampleDeployWeb and the webcommon assembly. If you aren't using the book code framework at all then just select your assembly for your web application that was built by the web deployment project.

At this point we have completed our setup project and it should build and deploy to the CRM server.

Building a Plug-in/Workflow Activity Installer

In the following section we are going to walk through creating a windows installer that will install and provision plug-in and workflows to a target server. This particular approach where it is combined is targeted more to a single tenant installation than a multi tenant installation. For a multi-tenant installation you would ideally separate the install portion from the provisioning.

Adding the Project

The first thing you need to do is add a setup project to your solution. You can find the setup project template in the Other Project Types category in the Add New Project dialog as you can see in the following image.

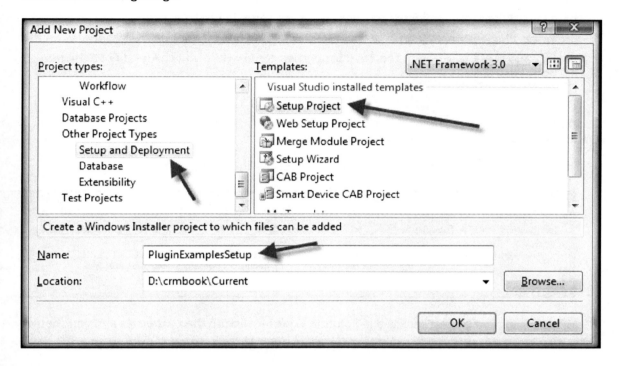

When you're adding the new project, make sure you check the name as well as the location where the project will be located.

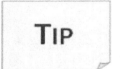

Notice that there are other types of setup project templates that you can use. These are great to keep in mind when you have other projects. For example, the Web Setup would be great for packaging up an ASP.NET customization

Setup the Output File Name

The output from the setup project is an installer file that you would give to anyone that will be installing the application. Depending on the name you choose for your project you might want to modify the name of the setup output to be more fully qualified. For example if our project name was PluginExampleSetup we might want the setup file to be called crmbook_PluginExampleSetup. To accomplish this simply right-click on the properties on the project and it will take you to the build properties panel where you can modify the name.

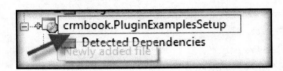

The following is the build panel where you can specify the Output file name.

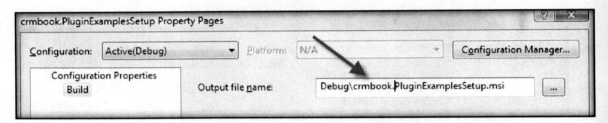

While having the project selected in Solution Explorer click on the properties and you should see a properties panel. On this panel you can control the global settings for the project.

At a minimum, you will want to probably modify the ones with the arrows.

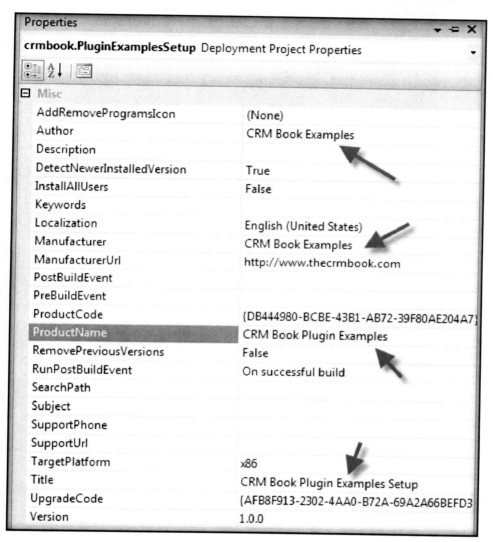

Customize the User Input

The setup program template takes care of a couple of basic things like allowing the user to specify the install directory. You can also add additional dialogs to collect information from the user and make that available to custom actions during the setup process. In our example, we are going to use that capability to collect some CRM server information from the user. This information will be passed along to our registration methods and used to connect to the CRM server to register the plug-in.

To add a dialog the first thing you need to do is right click from the project in Solution Explorer, select View and then User Interface from the menu options.

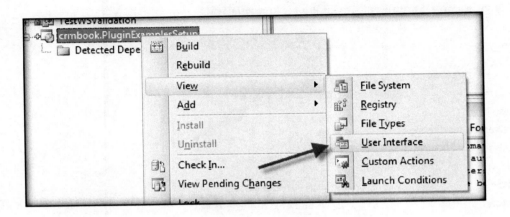

Once you select that you want to View the User Interface you will se e a tree of the current dialog structure of the installer.

From the above tree, you can modify existing items by right clicking and altering the property panel. Additionally, you can right click and select move up and move down to modify the sequence of the dialogs that will be shown to the user.

The next step for our example is to add a dialog to collect information about the CRM server. To add a dialog you select the high level folder in the tree either Start, Progress or End and then right click Add Dialog as you can see in the following example.

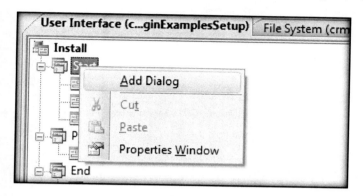

The following shows the possible dialog forms that you can add. Each of the dialogs is pre-configured for specific sets of items. For example, a set of checkboxes or customer information form. For our example we are going to use a simple textbox dialog that has multiple text boxes for input.

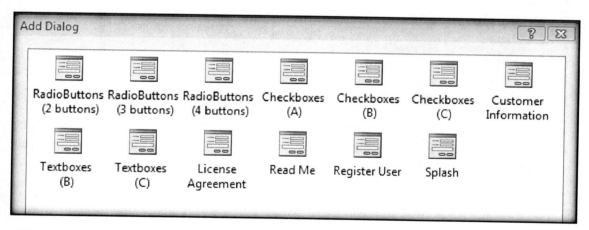

From the list select Textboxes (A) ,once added to your project it will no longer be in the list. This dialog is pre-configured for input of four text boxes.

The dialog is configured using the properties panel as you can see in the following image.

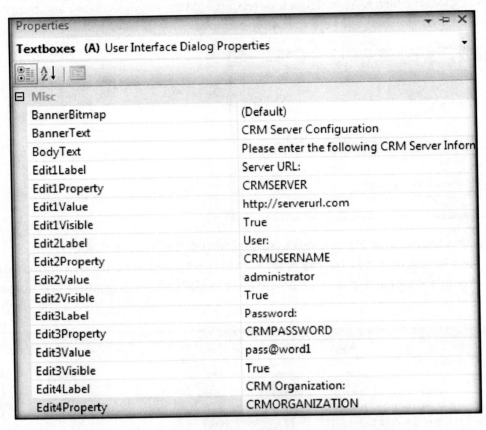

As you can see above we are using the text fields to collect the server url, user, password and organization. These items will collect the information about the CRM server and organization for configuring the plug-in.

Custom Action

We are going to use a setup custom action class to allow us to get control during the commit phase of the setup. At that point our custom action handler class will call out to CRM to do our registration.

In practice, I have found it easiest to have the custom action handler be implemented in a class library that isn't going to be deployed as part of the setup. So for our example we created a new project crmbook_PluginExampleSetupLib that will contain our custom action handler.

We are going to add two files to this project. First, we will add a class file that will implement our custom action handler and second an XML file that describes the plug-in that we want to register.

The following is the skeleton for our custom action handler class.

```
[RunInstaller(true)]
public partial class PluginLogicInstaller : Installer
{
    public override void Commit(IDictionary savedState)
        { /* code will be shown later */}
}
```

You will notice our custom action handler inherits from Installer and is attributed as RunInstaller(true). That makes this class eligible to be a custom action handler. You will also notice in the sample code we override and implement the Commit method.

The following is the important part of the code from the Commit method. Non-key aspects of the code have been removed to keep things simple.

```
PluginRegistrationManager regMgr = new PluginRegistrationManager(svc);
SetRegMgrParms(regMgr);
regMgr.RegisterSolution(regDoc);
```

In the above code we create an instance of our PluginRegistrationManager helper class. We then call SetupRegMgrParms which is responsible for grabbing the data from the user dialog that was passed to us and setting properties on the registration manager class. Finally, we call RegisterSolution passing an XML document that contains information about the plug-in/workflow we are registering.

That XML file looks like the following and describes what plug-in should be registered.

```
<Solution SourceType="0" Assembly="crmbook.PluginExamples.dll">
    <WorkflowTypes>
    </WorkflowTypes>

    <Steps>
```

```
        <Step
        MessageName = "Update"
        Mode = "0"
        PluginTypeFriendlyName = "crmbook.PluginExamples"
        PluginTypeName =
"crmbook.PluginExamples.Plugin101.Plugin101Example"
        PrimaryEntityName = "contact"
        SecondaryEntityName = ""
        Stage = "50"
        SupportedDeployment = "0" >
                <Images>
                    <Image
                                EntityAlias = "PreImage"
                                ImageType="0"
                                MessagePropertyName="Target"
        >
                    </Image>
                </Images>
            </Step>
        </Steps>
</Solution>
```

We need to make sure this XML file is marked as an embedded. You can accomplish that by clicking on properties on the file and selecting Embedded Resource.

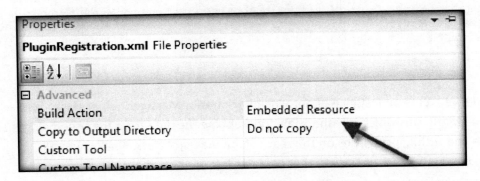

We embed this as a resource so it will be part of the assembly and we don't have to worry about external files.

Custom Action Configuration

The next step is to configure a custom action that will invoke the plug-in registration process after the user input phase is completed. The custom action is configured by specification of an assembly that contains a class that inherits from the Installer class. That class, by overriding a few key methods we will discuss later, gets control during the install process and performs the plug-in registration. By clicking View - > Custom Actions from the setup project as you see in the following dialog we will be presented with the list of existing custom actions.

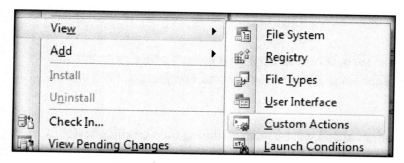

The following shows the custom actions that are configured for each stage in the installation process. Install, commit, Rollback and Uninstall are the stages available.

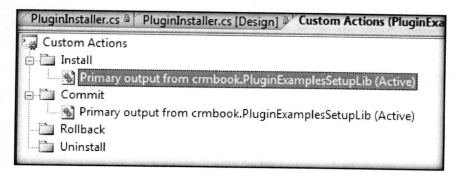

By right clicking on the Commit node and selecting Add Custom action you should see the follow dialog that will allow you to browse to and then select the assembly that contains the custom action.

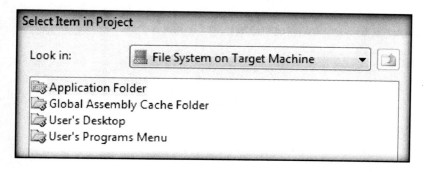

In our example, since the project containing the custom action is part of our solution we can select Application folder by double clicking on it. You will then be presented with a list of primary outputs from each of our projects in the solution. Select the one containing the custom action class which in our example is crmbook.PluginExamplesSetupLib.

It seems to work best to store your custom action in an assembly that is not being deployed by the setup project you are building.

Once that is completed our custom action will be invoked during the Commit phase.

Configuring Custom Action Data

In addition to connecting an assembly as a custom action we also need to configure the custom action data. The custom action data is used to identify the items from our custom dialog form that we want to pass to the custom action. Using the /Name = Value syntax as you can see in the following example we connect the form data to the user action data.

```
/CRMUserName="[CRMUSERNAME]" /CRMPassword="[CRMPASSWORD]"
/CRMServer="[CRMSERVER]" /CRMDomain="[CRMDOMAIN]"
/CRMOrganization="[CRMORGANIZATION]"
```

On the properties for the custom action, you will see the CustomActionData property. Using the above format we paste that into the custom action data property.

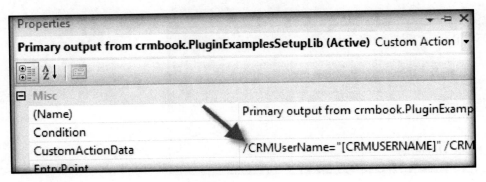

Adding Application Files

The next step we need to do is to indicate that the primary output from our plug-in class library should be added to the application folder. To accomplish this select View –> File System –> Application Folder by right clicking on the setup project in Solution Explorer. From the list, select Add crmbook.pluginexamples primary output.

Adding Files to GAC

One of the challenges we need to overcome is handling that our plug-in references other assemblies. Currently, when you register a plug-in with CRM it only looks in the GAC to pull additional assemblies that your plug-in might be dependent on. Since our common libraries are used by our plug-in we must register them with the GAC. The other option would be to use the ASP.NET Merge utility which has the ability to combine multiple assemblies into a single assembly. If you use the Merge to include the common libraries or any other dependent assemblies then it wouldn't be necessary to use the GAC option for those assemblies.

If you use the GAC option, you can specify the assemblies to be added to the GAC by right clicking View –> File System from the setup project in solution explorer. If these are the first files you are adding to the GAC, then you need to select Add GAC folder from the add special list. For our sample plug-in you need to specify the following dependent assemblies ctccrm.plugincommon, authhelper and workflowcommon to GAC.

MVP Tip: Microsoft CRM MVP Michael Hohne adds the following related to unattended installation on client machines. The above techniques work for server installations. However, you can't use it for client setups if you need to support unattended installations. An alternative is using the information stored in the registry to obtain the CRM web and copying the installed files in the custom installer action. You usually do not have to worry about configuration values at the client, as they can be easily synchronized from the server, e.g. using custom entities holding to store the configuration data. You can read Michael's blog at http://www.stunware.com.

Plug-in Configure Web Example

The next example I want to walk through is a little more complex example of deploying plug-ins and workflows. In the prior example we assumed it was a single organization and everything was going to be deployed at once. In this example, we are going to assume that we want to be able to do incremental provisioning of features that include worklfow and plug-ins.

In our prior example and with the registration tool that comes with the CRM SDK it is assumed that you are registering all steps from an assembly all at once. That's great if you know all at once but what happens if you want to be able to turn on things over time. A great example of that if we wanted to register our data history plug-in we saw in the plug-in case study chapter on a couple of entities. What happens when we want to register a couple more? By default we could just go register a few more steps with the plug-in tool by hand. But if we wanted to automate that as part of the setup we would have to do a little more work. For example, if not the first time, we don't need to register the assembly. The same is true for registering the plug-in type, if it's already created just adding one more step doesn't require any changes to the plug-in type registration.

To be able to keep track of the incremental additions we have created a custom entity called ctccrm_pluginpackage. This entity will be used to track registration of our plug-in packages. A plug-in package for our use here is just the XML file with the Solution XML as we saw in the previous example. The big change to the XML file is we now allow tokens to be provided for the EventName and the EntityName using $$EventName$$ and $$Entityame$$ correspondingly. These tokens are used to know that we need to prompt the user for input

User input is done via a web application that allows the user to navigate around the registered package. From the web application they are able to Register and Unregister packages on the fly. The following is an example of the list screen when you first enter the tool.

Register Packages View Assemblies				
Name	**Description**	**Events**	**Entity**	**Package ID**
DataHistory-Account	Data History For Account	Update	contact	DataHistory-Account ✕
DataHistory-BusinessTrip	Data History For Business Trip	Update	contact	DataHistory-BusinessTrip ✕
DataHistory-Case	Data History For Case	Update	contact	DataHistory-Case ✕
DataHistory-MSDN	Data History For MSDN	Update	contact	DataHistory-MSDN ✕
DataHistory-Project	Data History For Project	Update	contact	DataHistory-Project ✕
DataHistory-Contact	Data History For Contact	Update	contact	DataHistory-Contact ✕

As you can see there are several packages registered for Data History. Each of these is registered using the same XML package file but each time a different entity name is provided.

The following is an example of the Register Package screen.

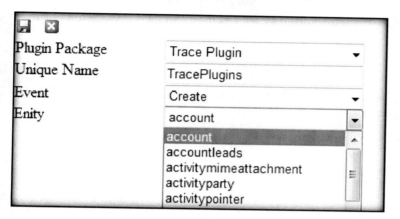

As you can see from the example above, it prompts for the entity that it is to be registered with. Once the entity is selected and the save is clicked the application will register the additional plug-in types with CRM and create a row in the ctccrm_pluginconfig entity.

The real intelligence comes in when you click remove on one of the packages from the list. Using the Package ID and other data from the config entity it will process the remove against the system. The key thing here is not removing all things related to an assembly but only removing the steps that were part of that package and only for the entity that was requested. If nobody else is using the plug-in type after removal of the steps the application will remove the plug-in type as well as the assembly.

This application is intended to be deployed standalone to the CRM server so that it can use active directory authentication to the CRM server. One key thing to mention about registering plug-ins and workflow is it must be done via Active Directory

Hopefully this application will show you a little more about how to register incrementally on the fly. Using this approach you separate your install of the binary files with the use or training of the users of the features. This application is a little rough around the edges but it does work and will hopefully give you ideas on how you could integrate with our own internal processes.

Wrapping it up

In this chapter, we have looked at several aspects of what you need to do when preparing your solution for deployment. If you are building an ISV solution with the intent to get certified you will want to review both the SDK documentation as well as the CRM 4.0 Certification Guidelines published by Microsoft.

Thinking about deployment should start early on in your development process and should not be an afterthought. By planning ahead you can look for issues that might impact your design and accommodate for those earlier in the project.

25

Tracking Down Problems

It would be great if we could simply do unlimited testing of all situations, our code, and customizations. That simply is not the real world, and we need to plan for reality. It is true that the more methodical you are in your testing and if you exercise your solution in the most common ways you will have less production issues.

Problems can start early on during development, so in this chapter we won't just look at production problem resolution but look at how we can help be more productive in each step. During development we can rely heavily on development tools such as a debugger to solve problems. In this chapter we will look at how to use Visual Studio Debug Visualizes to make debugging less painful. Earlier in the book we looked at test harnesses for plug-ins and workflows also aimed at making your life easier.

In addition to development problems, we need to be thinking about testing and production issues. These issues are almost always impacting on users or are on critical path for your project getting rolled out. That means answering managers' questions with "I don't know why it's happening" probably is not a great answer! So in addition to some of what we have talked about so far in the book we will now also dig into some of the system tools such as CRM platform trace and using things like SQL profiler to track down problems. You may also want to look at Chapter 26 on performance tuning because often times performance tools can help with other problems as well because they give you clues to follow up on to track down problems.

Small Bites

Small bites may sounds like advice your Mom would give you to keep you from choking, but the same applies to working with the platform. By small bites I mean make small changes so you know what is different from last time something worked. That's not saying you can't do sweeping changes – but then it becomes more difficult to track down problems.

The same applies when you are doing imports of changes to things like system entities. A great problem solving technique is to divide and conquer. So let's assume you are importing a customization file that contains 20 entities and it fails. More often than not, the error you get won't point to the item that is causing the problem. By cutting the list in half and importing only 10 of the entities and seeing if they work you can start isolating the problem.

Backup Often

Despite all the best intentions, and the most stable applications it's possible we will leave the system in a less than desirable state. It's also likely that at some point a developer will simply delete an entity by accident or make too many changes to know why something isn't working. Good backups of your solution files can help ease the resolution of many problems. It's also absolutely critical if you plan to try to do anything that you think might cause problems. You can't backup too often.

Here are some key items that you should make sure you backup in your development environment.

- The databases used by the CRM platform – see the implementation guide for what should be backed up.
- Export your customizations – consider automating an hourly, daily or weekly program to just export all and save a copy.
- Application configuration files – these are the custom config files if you're using ASP.NET or other server deployed applications.

This is just some ideas to get you going. For your production environment make sure to follow the guidance suggested by Microsoft in the implementation guide. It is a good idea that your disaster recovery plans include your development assets as they too are costly to re-create.

Having good backups gives you several options. The most obvious is restore of data or configurations. While that type of wholesale change can help during big problems, even the small things like being able to look at a customization export file for a single entity can help you solve the mystery of what changed.

People often think that re-importing a set of customizations will restore changes they made – while it's true it will add back things like missing attributes – it won't remove any changes that were made because import of customizations is cumulative.

MVP Tip: Microsoft MVP Ronald Lemmen reminded me to make sure everyone know that backing up their development environments can be just as important as backing up your production system. Often times precious developer changes can be lost due to this oversight. You can read Ronald's blog at http://www.RonaldLemmen.com.

Using Visual Studio Debug Visualizers

Debug Visualizers were a new feature starting in Visual Studio 2005. Their goal is to make it easier to see your data when you are running the debugger and mouse over an item. To accomplish this we have provided a couple of visualizers that are specific to CRM that we will discuss later in the chapter. First, let's take a look at how visualizers can be used in the debugger.

As you can see in the following image, the magnifying glass will let you invoke a visualizer. If you simply clicked on the magnifier you would get the default visualize if one is available. By default, several come out of the box with Visual Studio.

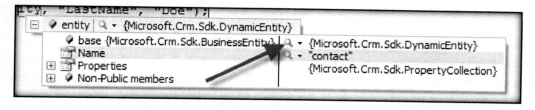

If you were to use the arrow down next to the magnifying glass it would then show you a list of all the visualizers that are available for that particular data type.

In the following example there are three available for you to choose from.

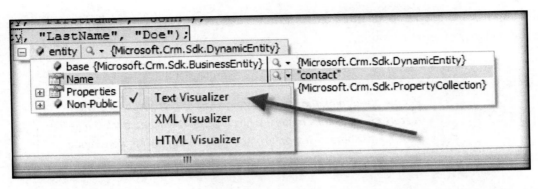

Once you select one typically they will pop up a dialog and show you the data in a format that is more meaningful. The following shows the Text Visualizer on a string.

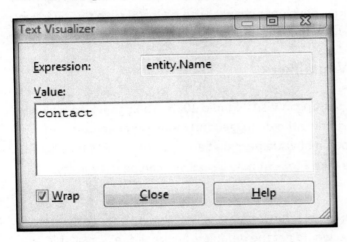

Visualizing Dynamic Entities

Dynamic Entities are very much a general purpose collection that is used for communicating to and from the CRM platform. One of the challenges with them and debugging is if you want to take a look at what properties have been stored. It takes several clicks of the mouse to expand the hierarchy of the collection and can be very tedious to keep the view open while you inspect the data. Looking at multiple properties can be even more of a juggling act.

The following is an example showing what you would see if you mouse over a Dynamic Entity in the debugger and try to drill down to see a property.

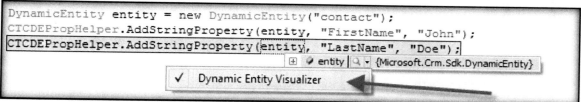

So we have included in our samples for you a debug visualizer that will display all of the properties from the Dynamic Entity in a data grid dialog. Once this visualize is installed, then you run the debugger and mouse over the instance of the Dynamic Entity you will see that you can select the Dynamic Entity Visualizer.

```
DynamicEntity entity = new DynamicEntity("contact");
CTCDEPropHelper.AddStringProperty(entity, "FirstName", "John");
CTCDEPropHelper.AddStringProperty(entity, "LastName", "Doe");
```

If you had just clicked on the magnifying glass it would also auto select that one because there is not any other visualizer available for that class type. Once you select it, the following is the dialog that will show the properties of the Dynamic Entity.

DynamicEntityViewer

Name	Value	ValueEntity	Type
FirstName	John		Microsoft.Crm.Sdk.StringProperty
LastName	Doe		Microsoft.Crm.Sdk.StringProperty
*			

As you can tell this provides a much easier way to view the properties that are currently part of the Dynamic Entity.

Visualizing Web Service Exceptions

It was really hard to decide which to cover first, Soap Exceptions or Dynamic Entity Visualization. Both of these are at the top of the list of things that you will do often during debugging applications using this platform. Soap Exceptions can provide enough data to debug the problem, but you are always required to dig down to the details of the exception to find anything useful. The reason for this is the Message property that you can easily access typically has something like "Unhandled Exception" in it. The reason for this is when a web service call fails it throws a SoapException instead of just a regular Exception instance. When you look at that in the debugger you see the following.

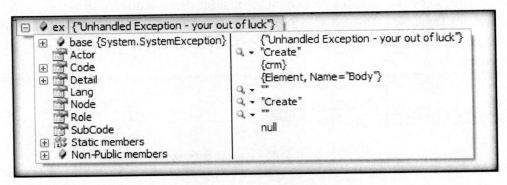

You can clearly tell that something went wrong, but otherwise you really have no additional details. Of course you can drill down and eventually you will find the details but wouldn't it be easier to have a debug visualize helping out?

Turns out this is easier said than done, as the Soap Exception is not a serializable object. This is a problem because in order for the Visual Studio debugger to be able to hand off the data to our visualizer it must serialize it first.

To work around this problem we need to take a little different approach. Our approach is going to be to replace the use of the SoapException with our own class CTCCRMCallException. We are going to do this in our service proxy class where we catch our web service calls and do tracing. Basically when we catch one of the SoapExceptions we are going to turn around and re-throw a CTCCRMCallException that will contain all the data from the call.

Now, when an exception occurs and we invoke the debug visualizer we see the following.

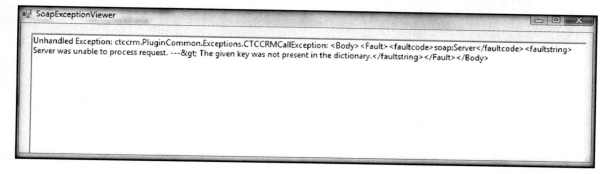

As you can see this provides a much easier to read error message that we can use to determine the error.

Finding errors in JavaScript

One of the most common problems in CRM customization projects are script errors. Either your code doesn't run successfully or it doesn't run at all.

If your OnLoad, OnSave or OnChange code isn't executed at all, make sure that you have enabled the event first. It's always a good idea to check the obvious things first. If you have enabled the event and are not testing the code in the form preview, then ask yourself if you have published the changes.

If your code still isn't executed, place an alert('TEST'); as the first line into your code and try again. If you don't see the alert message, then you have a syntax problem in your code. The most common reason is a missing curly brace somewhere in your code and it may be in any event you have added to the CRM form. It may also be related to an inline comment using the "// my comment" notation. Try using "/* my comment */" instead.

If you see the alert message but your code fails, it's best practice to debug your code. Add "debugger" as the first line in your code and make sure that debugging is enabled in the IE settings:

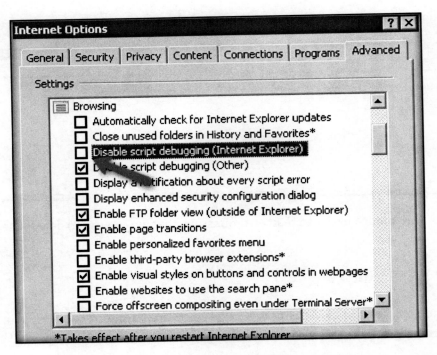

This section was provided by Microsoft CRM MVP Michael Hohne - you can read his blog at http://www.stunware.com

Using Fiddler

Probably one of the most useful tools to use if you are developing any web application or application that makes HTTP or Soap type requests is Fiddler. Fiddler is a free download from www.fiddlertool.com .

You can use Fiddler to monitor and inspect HTTP traffic from a client to a server. You are able to see both the request and the response from the server. For a CRM developer this means you will see all requests for pages from the CRM server which makes a great way to understand more about how CRM works. It also allows you to see URLs for including custom links.

For developers working with the Web Services you can use Fiddler to see what the format of the request and response is. This can be particularly helpful if you are trying to create code that calls the CRM services from the client or a non .NET application where you need to custom format your Soap calls.

The CRM SDK has a Walkthrough on using Fiddler to capture Soap calls so I'm not going to go into further details in this chapter.

Tracing client-side web service calls

When using the CRM web services in a client-side application, you can create your own log files to look at the data being sent and received. It helps optimizing your calls, but only works when using a web service reference. You can find complete details on this at the following location http://www.stunnware.com/crm2/topic.aspx?id=JSWebService.

The following is an example of the output from the tool.

Using Client Diagnostic Wizard

New to the client in CRM 4.0 is the Client Diagnostic Wizard. It's designed to make it easier for an end user to determine and fix some problems. When they can't fix them via the wizard the user can turn on trace and send a package with the trace to a support person. Keep this tool in mind when you get weird requests from the field because it's an easy way for a non technical person to turn on trace and package up the files to send to you.

Turning on DevErrors

In the web.config on both the server and the client you will find a configuration setting named DevErrors. This setting defaults to off and is what causes you to get a generic error page on the client interface when an error occurs. The problem with that is if you are setting up a new custom page or made encountering other errors you don't get a stack trace to help you isolate the problem. By modifying this setting you can allow CRM to output a more useful error page.

Using Platform Tracing

Unfortunately, sometimes the error message you get back from an API call says "Unexpected Exception", or possibly using the client interface, you get the same message. Either way it does not give you enough to tell what is going on. Usually I have found that when I get an error like that there is more information that can be found by looking at a platform trace. Sometimes what you get is just clues. But those clues, as you build your understanding of how the platform works can help you solve your problem.

Just like we can't just spin up the debugger in production neither can Microsoft. Even if you do not use Platform Trace to help you solve problems, if you contact Microsoft Support they will typically ask you to run one. Microsoft CRM is heavily instrumented with trace to allow visibility into what the platform is doing. It's important to understand that when you turn on trace you are turning it on for all organizations that are in the deployment. **Currently, with CRM 4.0 having multiple tenants running on the same server it's not possible to just turn trace on for a single organization**. If you recall in our application tracing for workflow and plug-ins we built it so we could fire it up for a single user. That makes our trace more preferable as the first step before we bring out the big guns of the platform trace. It's important that when you do platform tracing that you do it during times of low activity as it will generate not only extra overhead on the system, but will slow it down and create larger files for you to look at. In fact several times on very active systems I have elected to do the trace real late at night when activity was at its lowest level.

Platform tracing is controlled by registry settings. The following table shows the important settings that you can modify to enable and control tracing.

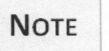

NOTE

Modification to registry settings if done incorrectly can cause system problems. Please ensure you take proper steps when modifying registry settings and if you are not sure what the impact of a change is contact a professional to make the change. Not all registry settings are intended for modification by end users of the platform.

Registry Item	Description
TraceEnabled	(DWORD) Value of 0 to disable, and 1 to enable. This is the master switch to indicate you want trace turned on. After turning on or off use the TraceRefresh item to force the change to be recognized by the system.
TraceRefresh	(DWORD) Valid values are a number between 0 and 99. This item is monitored by the platform for change and when it changes it knows to look at the other Trace related items to pickup new values. So after you change something else modify the value of this item to get the change picked up by the system.
TraceCategories	(String) Indicates the category or feature and how much tracing to output for that given item. The most common values are *:Verbose or Application.*:Verbose. While these produce a lot of output, often they produce results quickly in a quiet system.
TraceCallStack	(DWORD) Valid values are 0 to disable, 1 to enable. I tend to use 1 all the time if I'm using trace – stack can often provide small clues for difficult problems.
TraceFileSizeLimit	(DWORD) This is size in MB and valid range is 0 to 100. Smaller is easier to manage so I recommend 2-4 mb. They open easily in notepad then!
TraceDirectory	The TraceDirectory registry entry specifies the directory for the trace log files. The directory must exist, and the user who starts the Microsoft CRMAppPool must have full control over this directory. When you install Microsoft CRM, the default user is NT AUTHORITY\NETWORK SERVICE.

To modify these settings use regedit. It should look like the following when done with the basic entries required.

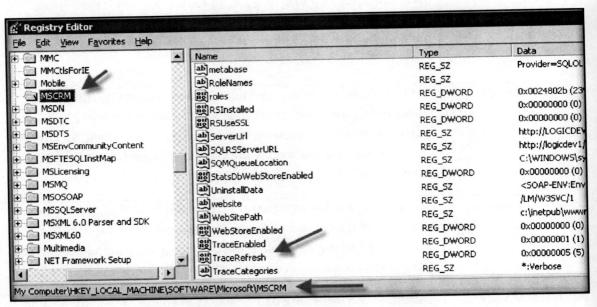

Once enabled, by default you can find the output in a sub folder named trace in the directory you installed CRM.

Make sure you don't leave trace running as it will slow down your system and can easily fill up your servers hard drive. Periods of low use on the CRM server are best for turning on trace because the file is smaller and easier to read.

You can find further details on tracing in the following knowledge base article http://support.microsoft.com/kb/907490/en-us

MVP Tip: Microsoft MVP Michael Hohne adds the following advice on tracing. Often you need to specify the Verbose setting to identify an error. It's a good practice to leave tracing enabled on dev and test machines with the trace level set to Warning. It ensures that you at least have some information in case of an error. The trace files will be pretty small, so it's not a big performance hit. To further investigate an issue, set the trace level to Verbose until you have fixed the error. Don't forget to change it back to Warning afterwards.

It's usually not recommended to enable tracing in production environments. Use it carefully and only for a limited time until the log files are written and disable tracing. An enabled trace in a live environment can easily fill the hard disk drive, leading to an unstable system. You can read Michael's blog at http://www.stunware.com.

Tracking Down Workflow Problems

Status Stuck in Waiting

If you are doing any type of custom activity development, you might encounter where your workflow just hangs with a condition of waiting. The following is an example of what your status list would look like.

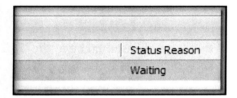

When you drill down into it you see the following message.

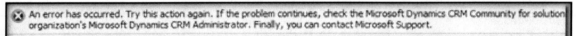

So when you're done scratching your head wondering what to do next, your best bet is probably a quick look at the platform trace if you can, it will likely show you the problem. You will want to look in the file created by the Async service, which typically has a file name that is <ServerName>-CrmAsyncService-bin-<date>-1.log

What you will be looking for is your custom workflow assembly, type name or class in a stack trace due to an exception. The following is an actual example. Where it launched my workflow activity, but encountered an error due to a missing dependent assembly.

at System.Workflow.Runtime.WorkflowRuntime.Load(Guid key, CreationContext context, WorkflowInstance workflowInstance)   at System.Workflow.Runtime.WorkflowRuntime.GetWorkflowExecutor(Guid instanceId, CreationContext context)   at System.Workflow.Runtime.WorkflowRuntime.InternalCreateWorkflow(CreationContext context, Guid instanceId)   at System.Workflow.Runtime.WorkflowRuntime.CreateWorkflow(Type workflowType, Dictionary`2 namedArgumentValues, Guid instanceId)   at

Microsoft.Crm.Workflow.WorkflowHost.StartWorkflowFromType(Guid instanceId, Type workflowType, WorkflowContext context) Inner Exception: System.IO.FileNotFoundException: **Could not load file or assembly 'ctccrm.PluginCommon, Version=1.0.0.0, Culture=neutral, PublicKeyToken=ae5f1456e996f2f0' or one of its dependencies. The system cannot find the file specified. at CTCWorkflowTestActivities.ContactRetrieve**.set_FirstName(String value) at CTCWorkflowTestActivities.TestTypedEntitiesFlow.InitializeComponent() at CTCWorkflowTestActivities.TestTypedEntitiesFlow..ctor() at Compiled.Workflowd0247d5a58bbdc11b8830003ff7bb934.InitializeComponent() at Compiled.Workflowd0247d5a58bbdc11b8830003ff7bb934..ctor()

In the above example the key thing we are looking for is the following line that tells us the problem.

Could not load file or assembly 'ctccrm.PluginCommon

Knowing that is the problem we can go investigate to see if that assembly should be in the GAC.

IIS Logs

The IIS logs can offer you some insight to what's going on with a users interaction with the web server. These can be especially helpful when you are dealing with client authentication related problems.

Using SQL Profiler

Often times SQL profile can also be used to troubleshoot problems that you weren't able to solve by reviewing the platform trace. If nothing else it can give you an idea of where CRM ended up in a transaction or trying to perform an operation. By reviewing the SQL profiler output it might point you to which data is causing the problem..

Wrapping it up

By knowing the tools available to you trouble shooting doesn't have to be a frustrating experience. Often times the challenge is knowing which technique to try first and will provide the greatest value. As you get more comfortable with the platform you will learn some of the common error messages and where to look for more details.

26

Performance Tuning

Performance tuning of the platform is not a onetime event, but an ongoing effort over time to ensure excellent performance. Early on during the initial customization design and then ongoing as you make additional customizations to the platform it's important that you evaluate the impact of the customization prior to implementing it into the live system. On smaller systems this is a trivial task with more focus reacting to specific user issues. In larger implementations this should be a mandatory part of the pre-production deployment check list.

Discussing performance of the platform is different than looking at the performance of a single component such as SQL Server. When you look at a single component, you can focus and typically this can be handled by one person. When you look at performance tuning a platform it's a more involved process that can cross many components that also involve many people in the process. Fortunately, a new toolkit has been published as open source to codeplex.com (Codeplex.com is a repository of open source projects) that can help gather data across the platform. In this chapter we will look at a quick start approach to using the toolkit.

CRM 4.0 offers a number of new performance statistics that can be monitored to understand the performance of the platform. Additionally, some of the sub systems such as SQL Server also offer a wealth of performance monitoring options that can be leveraged. We will explore how these can be used to monitor performance as well as tips for various customization areas and how those can affect performance.

Divide and Conquer

One of the best things you can do when working specific performance problems is to isolate the problem area as much as possible. Using a divide and conquer approach where you eliminate possible problem areas and net down to one or two probable causes is a great approach. Much of what you look for in solving performance problems can also leverage some of the items we discussed in the previous chapter around handling problems. Both can at times seem like you're looking for the needle in a hay stack unless you put a strategy in place and follow it.

Capacity Planning

When dealing with larger systems it's a good idea to do capacity planning before the implementation and ongoing on a regular basis to ensure you have adequate capacity. For new systems it's often times hard to get your hands around how the users will use the system but the key things to look at are number of users, number of concurrent users, amount of data and what type of automated processes will be used. There are a number of other things to look at in large installs but those key metrics will help you highlight some key capacity points.

A good resource for starting to assess capacity is to look at some of the benchmarks that Microsoft has done. You can find these on the CRM page on Microsoft.com and find the one that is closest to your size of deployment.

MVP Tip: Microsoft CRM MVP Matt Parks adds it's important to note that benchmarks are meaningless to many larger deployments. Unless the transaction mix and data load are similar to the specific implementation, the results can be drastically different. The benchmarks can provide some general guidelines, but we have seen many companies get caught because they didn't think about the differences between their implementation and the benchmark. I hate when I get asked, "What hardware do we need to support 1000 users?"

Using the Performance Toolkit

The Performance Toolkit is new with CRM 4.0 and was originally put together by the Microsoft CRM product team. It's now been published to CodePlex.com as an open source project. That means that not only can you use it for free, you can also extend it as necessary if you have additional testing requirements.

The Performance Toolkit is designed to work with Microsoft Visual Studio Team System.

MVP Tip: Microsoft CRM MVP Matt Parks adds that he would encourage people to run performance testing if they have concerns about capacity. The key to using it though is to properly model the data load and transaction mix to be close to what will be expected in the real world. Some of the generic benchmarks use initial data loads that are fairly low when you think about them on a per user basis, which makes the results much better as the SQL server is able to better optimize. Also, if the entities are not loaded up with reflective data, then indexing and other optimization choices aren't accurate.

Performance Counters

To help you to monitor the system a number of new performance counters have been added to help you monitor the performance of both the CRM server and the CRM client. If you set up some basic performance counters that run all the time you will have some good baseline data about your performance. Having history data like that makes troubleshooting a performance problem easier because you can look back to see when the problem started occurring.

The following is an example of some of the client performance counters.

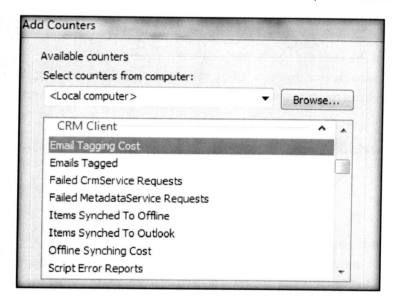

Using SQL Profiler

Often times performance bottlenecks can be traced back to lack of indexes to cover queries that users often perform. One easy way to monitor your CRM data access patterns is to use SQL Profiler against the SQL Server. Using Profiler you can easily have it filter out all the non expensive queries and only show the ones that take excessive resources. Once identified, you can use the published indexing techniques to address problems.

SQL Profiler can also be used to troubleshoot problems that you weren't able to solve by reviewing a platform trace.

Client Script Performance

If you have a lot of client scripting it's easy to quickly add a noticeable amount of delay to user pages. If you utilize some of the techniques in the book for building your scripts and include calls to CTCTrace in the code you can use that to see where your script is taking time since it outputs time since last trace as part of the output.

Web Service APIs

There are a number of places you can get into trouble with the Web Services. When retrieving data make sure you specify columns that you need and don't retrieve all columns unless you really need all the data. Also, keep an eye on your queries especially when they start having a lot of linked entities.

If you're making a lot of calls from the Client to the server web services you might consider exposing a more specific custom web service that your client script can call. Often times you can reduce 10-15 calls back and forth from the client to the server with one call to a custom web service or web page.

Using the platform trace is a good way to see more details on what your web service calls are causing the server to do.

MetaData APIs

One obvious thing you will probably notice around performance is the fact that the new MetaData Service is slower than it used to be in CRM 3.0. There are a few reasons for this. The most significant is because unlike in CRM 3.0 that always pulled from a metadata cache; the API now goes to the database. Another reason is the fact that more data is returned by the API in CRM 4.0 compared to CRM 3.0.

If you are using Metadata in your solution give consideration to caching as much of it as possible for reuse. The more specific you can be about retrieving only the data you need you will see reduced time spent waiting for Metadata. For example, if you just need information on a single attribute don't retrieve the full entity just make a call to retrieve the one attribute.

Plug-in Performance

If you have custom plug-ins that are installed in a CRM system that is another area that can have a hidden performance impact. Plug-ins when configured to run synchronous are part of the response time the user sees when accessing forms. A plug-in that introduces a delay can be tough to track down especially if it's caused by certain data conditions and doesn't happen all the time. Code reviews and other standard development practices can help avoid some of the problems that might be encountered. Using the CTCTrace that is part of the plug-in framework is another way to view more detailed performance of a plug-in at runtime. When using trace you would turn it on for the user having a problem and then review the trace log output to the Trace Config note for that plug-in. The trace outputs time since last trace that can be reviewed to look for hotspots.

Workflow Execution Performance

As you start building workflows or allow users to build workflows it's important to think about and monitor how they impact the system. Since workflows run in the background sometimes it's possible to think of them as a source of problems. If you are experiencing high CPU usage or other delays checking to see what's in your workflow queue to execute should be high on your list of things to check.

As you start designing and training your users, think ahead and use and give productive advice on how to create workflows. In systems with larger amounts of data this can be even more important. In these larger systems a periodic audit of workflow activity would be a good idea to look for things that are using excessive system resources.

For most users, regardless of what they put in the workflow scope, their workflow still will only run for the records that they have access to. The exception of that are the manager type users who can possibly have visibility to all the data. In their case, workflows they create can run more often and cause more load on the system. Providing workflow templates or guidance to this type of users and periodic monitoring can help avoid the workflow performance creep that can happen.

Avoiding Waitfor

One of the powerful abilities of workflow is to wait for an update condition on an entity's attribute. For example, wait for status to change to completed or 30 days. What this does is creates a notification subscription for the workflow instance – the workflow will be put to sleep until an update is performed on the entity. Each time an update is performed regardless of which field has been changed; CRM will wake up the workflow instance so it can retrieve updated data and perform a check to see if it should continue execution. On a small number of records this isn't bad, but it does add overhead that might not be necessary.

Happy Birthday Workflow Zombies

Another pattern I have seen is to use workflow to send Happy Birthday e-mails. Using this pattern a workflow is created that basically will sleep until the person's birthday arrives, then it will send an e-mail and start a new instance of the Happy Birthday workflow. Again, on a small scale this isn't a bad approach as it's quick to create and doesn't require any custom development. Imagine this on a system with 3 million contacts, which would mean 3 million workflows to support Happy Birthday that would just be sitting "waiting" in the system for the magic day to arrive.

I prefer using a daily job type approach when dealing with this scenario. You can still leverage workflow to do the building of the email and any other process you want to do like a follow up call the week after to see how their birthday was. Using a scheduler service, it would daily run a query to determine whose birthday was in the next 24 hours. For each contact found it would launch a Happy Birthday e-mail. In this scenario workflows would only run for a short period of time while they are doing productive work.

The real problem with the wait forever approach is it just creates unnecessary workflows that are active in the system and will increase the database size since they have to be also persisted while they are waiting for the magic day to arrive. So the bottom line is: wherever possible try to minimize workflow zombies that just hang around waiting for some magic day.

Avoiding the Create Traffic Jam

In some situations it's possible you will need or want to create a lot of workflows that are triggered to run when a create occurs. Probably the best example I have seen of this is where you want to do something when an e-mail is created in the system. Since there's no way to say I only want my workflow to run when a record is created and sent to Joe, all registered workflows will always start. In this scenario, typically the workflow will perform the filter check at the start of the workflow and exit if it doesn't need to run. Ideally, the workflow would not start if its run conditions weren't true. The two main areas of impact of this are the overhead of starting, running and tracking unnecessary workflows and the fact that the list of workflows run for the record will be skewed showing all the extra data.

I like to use a "Router" pattern where possible which basically sets up a workflow that will act as a router to the 20 or so other workflows that need to run. Using the Start Child workflow step you can do a simple condition check and only start the other workflows if they need to run. This minimizes the unnecessary starts and only runs workflows when they need to be run. There is an example of using this pattern in Chapter 21.

Test with Real Data

One of the common problems I have seen with many systems, not just CRM, is not making adequate test data available to the development team to do proper testing. Anytime you're building customizations against a system that will be more than just a handful of users doing testing against a full size data set is almost a requirement for success.

Other things to look at

MVP Tip: Microsoft CRM MVP Matt Parks offers the following additional tips of things to consider.

-   HTTP round trips. Adding an IFRAME can result in more HTTP requests from the client to the server when the page loads. This can extend the load time for the page. I've seen this when people want to add things like the Activity grid to the detail page and all the sudden you have extra requests going over a bad network connection.

-   Latency vs. speed – Sometimes improving routing from the client to the server is more beneficial than increasing the connection speed. Especially for distributed users.

-   IFD (Internet Facing Deployment) – The IFD server optimizes a lot of the communication between IE & IIS and can help with remote users, even if they are on the network.

Wrapping it up

Performance testing as we discussed in this chapter should be done both early and ongoing during the operation of a CRM system. Often times a little proactive monitoring can help a lot when faced with specific reports of problems. Knowing what is normal or your baseline performance can help highlight abnormal conditions as well as help you plan for needed increases in capacity as your usage increases.

Since CRM 4.0 has a lot of new capabilities there is a lot we don't know yet about performance tuning. The good news we now have more options for scaling out and adding capacity to an install to handle increased capacity requirements.

INDEX

Lightning Source UK Ltd.
Milton Keynes UK
04 August 2010